Lecture Notes in Computer Science 13752

More information about this series at https://link.springer.com/bookseries/558

Guido Governatori · Anni-Yasmin Turhan (Eds.)

Rules and Reasoning

6th International Joint Conference on Rules and Reasoning, RuleML+RR 2022
Berlin, Germany, September 26–28, 2022
Proceedings

Springer

Editors
Guido Governatori ⓘ
Singapore Management University
Singapore, Singapore

Anni-Yasmin Turhan ⓘ
Dresden University of Technology
Dresden, Germany

ISSN 0302-9743   ISSN 1611-3349 (electronic)
Lecture Notes in Computer Science
ISBN 978-3-031-21540-7   ISBN 978-3-031-21541-4 (eBook)
https://doi.org/10.1007/978-3-031-21541-4

This Springer imprint is published by the registered company Springer Nature Switzerland AG
The registered company address is: Gewerbestrasse 11, 6330 Cham, Switzerland

Preface

In September 2022 the 6th International Joint Conference on Rules and Reasoning (RuleML+RR) took place online. Initially, we had planned to conduct the conference as a physical meeting in Berlin, but the COVID-19 situation prevented it. The RuleML+RR conference was part of the umbrella event DeclarativeAI, which also featured Decision-CAMP and the Reasoning Web Summer School. This year's motto of the event was Rules, Reasoning, Decisions, and Explanations. RuleML+RR itself comprised, besides the conference, the Doctoral Consortium organized by Alexander Steen and Evgeny Kharlamov and the international Rule Challenge organized by Dörthe Arndt, Ahmet Soylu, and Jan Vanthienen. The conference, as expressed in the call for papers, had a focus on explainable algorithmic decision-making involving rule-based representation and reasoning. We appointed well over 75 Program Committee (PC) members, from several scientific sub-communities that work on rule-based reasoning, to ensure a rigorous and robust reviewing process.

There were 52 submissions from 23 countries (and five continents) after a deadline extension of three weeks. Each submitted paper was assigned four PC members to be forearmed against unavailability because of covid-related issues. In the end each paper received at least three reviews. For papers involving one of the chairs or authors from their institutions, the other chair was solely in charge of the review process, and the reviews were anonymised before they were inserted in the submission system. Some of these were provided at short notice by the emergency reviewers Shiqponja Ahmetaj, Sebastian Rudolph, Stefan Schlobach, and Sergio Tessaris. We thank all PC members and additional reviewers for their efforts!

We accepted 19 papers resulting in a 37% acceptance rate for RuleML+RR 2022. From the accepted papers an award committee selected the papers meritorious of the conference awards. The paper plingo: A system for probabilistic reasoning in clingo based on lpmln by Susana Hahn, Tomi Janhunen, Roland Kaminski, Javier Romero, Nicolas Ruehling, and Torsten Schaub won the Harold Boley Best System Description award. The Best Student Paper award went to Faiq Miftakhul Falakh, Sebastian Rudolph, and Kai Sauerwald for the paper Semantic Characterizations of AGM Revision for Arbitrary Tarskian Logics. Finally, the Best Paper award was presented to the paper In the Head of the Beholder: Comparing Different Proof Representations by Christian Alrabbaa, Stefan Borgwardt, Anke Hirsch, Nina Knieriemen, Alisa Kovtunova, Anna Milena Rothermel, and Frederik Wiehr. Congratulations to all of the authors!

Long before we were finalizing the program of the conference, we were lucky to be able to appoint four great keynote speakers. In the evening of the first and the last day we had keynote talks shared with DecisionCamp by Paul Vincent on "The Evolution of Decisioning in IT, and What Happens Next" and by Christian De Saint Marie on "Neuro-Symbolic AI and Decision Rules". The second and the third day of the conference started with keynote talks by Ian Horrocks on "Knowledge Graphs: Theory, Applications and Challenges and by Torsten Schaub on ASP in Industry, Here and There", respectively.

We are grateful to the generous financial contribution of the Artificial Intelligence Journal, Springer, the Fachbereich Künstliche Intelligenz of the Gesellschaft für Informatik, and OASIS LegalRuleML that supported the RuleML+RR 2022 awards, the publication of the proceedings, and the wide participation of students and scholars.

Finally, we deeply acknowledge Adrian Paschke and the Freie Universität Berlin for the kind administrative, technical, and logistic support for the DeclarativeAI event.

September 2022   Guido Governatori
                                                                                Anni-Yasmin Turhan

Organization

General Chair

Adrian Pasckhe — Freie Univerität Berlin and Fraunhofer FOKUS, Germany

Program Committee Chairs

Guido Governatori — Singapore Management University, Singapore
Anni-Yasmin Turhan — Technische Universität Dresden, Germany

Program Committee

Nurulhuda A Manaf	National Defence University of Malaysia, Malaysia
Shqiponja Ahmetaj	TU Wien, Austria
Grigoris Antoniou	University of Huddersfield, UK
Dörthe Arndt	TU Dresden, Germany
Nick Bassiliades	Aristotle University of Thessaloniki, Greece
Roman Bauer	University of Surrey, UK
Leopoldo Bertossi	SKEMA Business School Canada Inc., Canada
Mehul Bhatt	Örebro University, Sweden
Antonis Bikakis	University College London, UK
Andreas Billig	Fraunhofer FOKUS, Germany
Piero Bonatti	University of Naples Federico II, Italy
Richard Booth	Cardiff University, UK
Loris Bozzato	Fondazione Bruno Kessler, Italy
Pedro Cabalar	University of A Coruña, Spain
Diego Calvanese	Free University of Bozen-Bolzano, Italy
Gong Cheng	Nanjing University, China
Horatiu Cirstea	Loria, Université de Lorraine, France
Stefania Costantini	Università degli Studi dell'Aquila, Italy
Matteo Cristani	University of Verona, Italy
Madalina Croitoru	LIRMM, Université Montpellier II, France
Bernardo Cuenca Grau	University of Oxford, UK
Giovanni De Gasperis	Università degli Studi dell'Aquila, Italy
Francesco M. Donini	Università della Tuscia, Italy
Cristina Feier	University of Bremen, Germany

Jan Rauch	Prague University of Economics and Business, Czech Republic
Francesco Ricca	University of Calabria, Italy
Livio Robaldo	University of Swansea, UK
Antonino Rotolo	University of Bologna, Italy
Sebastian Rudolph	TU Dresden, Germany
Emanuel Sallinger	TU Wien, Austria
Francesco Santini	Università di Perugia, Italy
Konstantin Schekotihin	Alpen-Adria Universität Klagenfurt, Austria
Stefan Schlobach	Vrije Universiteit Amsterdam, The Netherlands
Rolf Schwitter	Macquarie University, Australia
Barış Sertkaya	Frankfurt University of Applied Sciences, Germany
Mantas Simkus	TU Vienna, Austria
Tran Cao Son	New Mexico State University, USA
Davide Sottara	Mayo Clinic, USA
Ahmet Soylu	Oslo Metropolitan University, Norway
Giorgos Stamou	National Technical University of Athens, Greece
Alexander Steen	University of Greifswald, Germany
Petros Stefaneas	National Technical University of Athens, Greece
Umberto Straccia	ISTI-CNR, Italy
Theresa Swift	Universidade Nova de Lisboa, Portugal
Alireza Tamaddoni-Nezhad	Imperial College London, UK
Sergio Tessaris	Free University of Bozen-Bolzano, Italy
Kia Teymourian	University of Texas at Austin, USA
Michaël Thomazo	Inria, DIENS, ENS, CNRS, PSL University, France
Dominik Tomaszuk	University of Bialystok, Poland
Hans Tompits	TU Wien, Austria
Ryan Urbanowicz	University of Pennsylvania, USA
William Van Woensel	University of Dalhousie, USA
Jan Vanthienen	Katholieke Universiteit Leuven, Belgium
Serena Villata	CNRS and Université Côte d'Azur, France
Kewen Wang	Griffith University, Australia
Frank Wolter	University of Liverpool, UK
Adam Wyner	Swansea University, UK
Guohui Xiao	University of Bergen, Norway

Additional Reviewers

Artale, Alessandro
Baryannis, George
Bellodi, Elena
Cao, Huiping
Colucci, Simona
Ivliev, Alex
Kain, Tobias
Marte, Cinzia

Mollas, John
Oetsch, Johannes
Rechenberger, Sascha
Ricioppo, Aldo
Rigas, Emmanouil
Scholl, Tobias
Zese, Riccardo

Contents

xii   Contents

Answer Set Programming

Applying Answer Set Optimization to Preventive Maintenance Scheduling for Rotating Machinery

Anssi Yli-Jyrä[✉][ID] and Tomi Janhunen[ID]

Tampere University, Tampere, Finland
{anssi.yli-jyra,tomi.janhunen}@tuni.fi

Abstract. Preventive maintenance (PM) of manufacturing units aims at maintaining the operable condition of the production line while optimizing the maintenance timing and the loss of productivity during maintenance operations. The lesser studied type of preventive maintenance understands a production line as a single machine with multiple components of different maintenance needs. This is relevant when rotating machinery is deployed, e.g., in the paper and steel industries, in the mass production of raw materials consumed by other businesses. A failure in any stage of the production line has the potential of making the entire machine inoperable and enforcing a shutdown and corrective maintenance costs. This work gives an abstract formalization of PM scheduling for multi-component machines as an optimization problem. To provide a lower bound for the complexity of the optimization problem, we prove that the underlying decision problem is NP-complete for varying-size multi-component machines and scheduling timelines. Besides the formalization, the second main contribution of the paper is due to the practical need to solve the problem in industrial applications: the work gives the first encoding of the PM scheduling problem using Answer Set Optimization (ASO). Some preliminary experiments are conducted and reported to set the scene for further algorithm development.

1 Introduction

Preventive maintenance (PM) complements corrective, failure-driven maintenance and plays a key role when it comes to ensuring resource-efficient and timely production as demanded by global manufacturing and resilient industry. While PM brings obvious benefits, the scheduling part of PM is tricky and worth digitalization and optimization. Digitized *PM scheduling* (PMS) is a challenging computational problem. Scheduling for one- or two-component machines has been studied a lot, but research has increasingly shifted to the PMS of multi-component machines with serial or serial-parallel dependencies [9].

Multi-component machines with rotating components are commonly deployed and maintained, e.g., in the dairy, paper and steel industries, for the mass production of raw materials like dairy, newsprint, and rolled steel. Their rotating components, *rotors*, operate in syn-

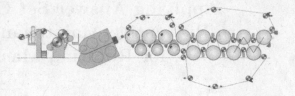

Fig. 1. A paper machine (knowpap.com)

chrony to form a serial, continuous *production line*, the best example of which is perhaps a paper machine (see Fig. 1).

Both preventive and run-to-failure, corrective maintenance policies and respective scheduling are needed for these machines. According to the component-wise failure distribution of paper machines [22], the aging of the components in the first sections of the production line increases their risk of predictable failure. These kinds of components demand time- or condition-based preventive maintenance, while the latter sections of the paper machine demand a corrective maintenance policy and are out of the scope of the current work. Olde Keizer et al. [21] review condition-based maintenance policies for multi-component systems with various dependencies. A particular structural property of serially connected rotating multi-component machines is that their components are *physically dependent* on one another. Not only the independent maintenance of dependent components is restricted, but maintenance of any stage of the machinery often makes the entire production line inoperable [19,20]. For this reason, we concentrate on the maintenance of components that are relevant in this respect.

Selective maintenance is a PM policy whose purpose is to help select a group of components for maintenance operations so as to optimize the PM schedule with respect to chosen optimization criteria such as *system availability, maintenance cost, life cycle cost*, and *reliability*; as analyzed, e.g., in [6,18,23]. Unlike [17], we neither integrate production and maintenance scheduling explicitly nor study concrete machines. Instead, our goal is to investigate options when it comes to the formalization of new kinds of simple optimization criteria. We express a limit for maintenance cost as a limit for maintenance breaks, and we establish new optimization criteria that are somewhat dissimilar to the former criteria. The first criterion, *under-coverage*, measures how often a preventive maintenance action is delayed in the timeline, reducing the reliability of the system. The second criterion, *over-coverage*, measures how often a preventive maintenance action occurs earlier than necessary, increasing the life cycle cost.

According to the survey [17], most approaches to PMS allow no exceptions beyond designated time intervals and flexibility windows around them, but we do not insist on maintenance that is based on such *periodic* recommended maintenance intervals of components. Our target for maintaining a particular component is extremely flexible and opportunistic: We do not only allow delays or advances in timing [1,27], but we allow *arbitrary deviations* from the recommended maintenance interval if this is beneficial to the optimization criteria.

Any maintenance break is an opportunity to maintain components ahead [30] of their due time. Such over-maintenance (over-coverage) can reduce the need for separate scheduled maintenance breaks and help to improve system availability.

Hoai and Luong [18] determine a policy for scheduling one maintenance period. This gives a convex, efficient model for availability and cost. You and Meng [26] present a PM scheduling for small multi-component serial machines and a small timeline. Similarly, our goal is to schedule multiple maintenance breaks and operating periods. This unlocks numerous opportunities to optimize the schedule as a whole. As any future state of the machine has a finite model description, periods longer than individual intervals can ultimately emerge in the optimal schedules. However, due to degradation and random changes in the machine condition, the distant future in the schedule is highly speculative. For this reason, our model is intended to be used inside a modularized predictive maintenance framework with real-time sensory-updated prognostic information of the current machine state and a rescheduling loop [26].

Previous implementations of PMS have deployed a myriad of AI techniques, including *genetic algorithms* (GAs) [8], *mixed-integer programming* (MIP) [7], *dynamic programming* [29], and formulations as *constraint satisfaction problems* (CSPs) [12]. In 1975, Zurn and Quintana [29] classified the PMS search techniques into those that search for (i) a local optimum, (ii) a piece-wise approximation, and (iii) a globally optimal, exact solution. Frost and Dechter [12] showed that a CSP solver can be extended to an iterative framework that solves the PMS as an optimization problem. Since then, the performance of exact solvers, including their extensions for solving optimization problems, has improved drastically. It is already known that *answer set programming* (ASP) is well-suited for solving scheduling problems (see, e.g., [3,10,11]). The ASP paradigm (see [4] for an overview) offers a rule-based language for *encoding* search problems as logic programs such that solutions are captured by *answer sets*. When an objective function is incorporated in the program, the search process turns into answer set optimization (ASO). However, to the best of our knowledge, there is no prior PMS implementation nor up-to-date feasibility studies based on ASO. The current work fills this gap by presenting two PMS models implemented in ASP and their global, iterative optimization supported by modern ASP solvers.

This work claims three major contributions to the area: (1) We present a highly abstracted PMS formalization. While this ignores many previously studied aspects, such as failure models, resource limits, duration of actions, production targets, it is a part of exploratory, non-incremental research and extensible through additional constraints and a modularized framework. (2) By studying the complexity of the formalization, we connect it to other formalizations with a similar complexity (e.g. [12]). (3) By making the ASP encodings publicly available, we facilitate the systematic improvement of encodings for the problem.

The rest of this article is organized as follows. In Sect. 2, we provide the formal definition of a multi-component machine and its maintenance schedule, and investigate some objective functions that are relevant for the optimization of schedules. These definitions are crucial building blocks in Sect. 3 where we formalize PMS for multi-component machines from a number of perspectives. The computational complexity of the resulting decision and function problems is then

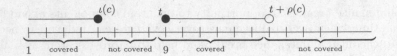

Fig. 2. Illustration of $\iota(c) = 5$ and $\rho(c) = 6$ with a service at time step $t = 9$

roughly characterized in the same section. To move from the theoretical analysis to practice, we present an ASP encoding of the PMS optimization problem in Sect. 4. The performance obtained by this encoding for PMS is preliminarily studied in Sect. 5 using the CLASP solver to implement the actual optimization of schedules. Section 6 concludes the paper.

2   Definitions of Machines and Schedules

In this section, we provide an abstraction of a multi-component machine and a schedule specifying preventive maintenance actions for its components in the scheduling timeline. These definitions pave the way for the definition of the scheduling problem whose variants will be studied further in the next section.

Definition 1. *A multi-component machine is a triple $\mathcal{M} = \langle C, \iota, \rho \rangle$ consisting of a finite set of components C, an initial lifetime function $\iota : C \to \mathbb{N}$, and a recommended maintenance interval function $\rho : C \to \mathbb{N} \backslash \{0\}$.*

Figure 2 illustrates how the values of the functions in Definition 1 are to be interpreted. The *initial lifetime* function ι tells how many time steps are covered by maintenance actions performed prior to the timeline for intended PM scheduling. Quite similarly, the *recommended maintenance interval* (RMI) function ρ indicates how many time steps are covered by each preventive maintenance action. Thus, a preventive maintenance action taking place at a time step t starts an RMI that is over at the time step $t + \rho(c)$. Every time t when a component is maintained it becomes as good as new while all non-maintained components continue aging during the time step t. When multiple components and several preventive maintenance actions are taken into consideration and restricted to a finite timeline, the resulting notion of a schedule is detailed as follows.

Definition 2. *A preventive maintenance schedule (PMS, or schedule for short) for machine $\mathcal{M}$ is represented as a quadruple $S = \langle h, \ell, b, A \rangle$ where*

- *$h \in \mathbb{N} \backslash \{0\}$ marks the horizon of the scheduling timeline,*
- *$\ell \in \{1, \ldots, h\}$ is the limit for the last possible time step of a preventive maintenance action,*
- *$b \in \{0, \ldots, \ell\}$ is the maximum size of a set $B \subseteq \{1, \ldots, \ell\}$ of time steps, also called scheduled maintenance breaks, during which any preventive maintenance action must take place,*

– $A : C \times \{1, \ldots, \ell\} \to \{0, 1\}$, *called the* service selection function, *is a characteristic function indicating, for each component $c \in C$ of the machine $\mathcal{M}$, the set $B_c = \{t \mid A(c, t) = 1\} \subseteq B$ of time steps of preventive maintenance actions used to service component c.*

The limit ℓ controls how far towards the horizon the breaks can be allocated, having a compressing effect on the schedule. If $\ell = h$, any preventive maintenance action performed at the time step h is mainly a wasted investment in the future without a significant effect on the scheduling timeline. The schedule is *empty* if $b = 0$. Four evaluation functions for the quality of component-wise schedules are defined. Their definitions are facilitated by two auxiliary functions: let $\pi(c) = \{(s, t) \in B_c \times B_c \mid s < t$, and $s < u < t$ for no $u \in B_c\}$ be the pairs of consecutive maintenance times of component $c \in C$ and $\delta : \mathbb{Z} \to \mathbb{N}$ a filter function defined in such a way that $\delta(x) = 0$ when $x < 0$ and $\delta(x) = x$ otherwise.

Definition 3. *For each schedule S, we define the component-wise* over-coverage *function* $oc : C \to \mathbb{N}$, *the component-wise* under-coverage *function* $uc : C \to \mathbb{N}$, *the component-wise* miscoverage *function* $mc : C \to \mathbb{N}$, *and the component-wise* action count *function* $ac : C \to \mathbb{N}$ *as follows.*

If B_c is empty, we have $oc(c) = ac(c) = 0$, $uc(c) = mc(c) = h - \iota(c)$. Otherwise, the values of the componentwise functions are given by

$$oc(c) = \delta(\iota(c) - \min B_c + 1) + \sum_{(s,t) \in \pi(c)} \delta(\min(s + \rho(c), h + 1) - t),$$

$$uc(c) = \delta(\min B_c - \iota(c) - 1) + \sum_{(s,t) \in \pi(c) \cup \{(\max B_c, h+1)\}} \delta(t - (s + \rho(c))),$$

$$mc(c) = oc(c) + uc(c), \qquad ac(c) = |B_c|.$$

Intuitively, the value $oc(c)$ indicates the number of time steps during which the implementation of a due preventive maintenance action of component c is advanced earlier from the time suggested by the recommended maintenance interval $\rho(c)$. The value $uc(c)$ indicates, for component c, the number of time steps that are neither covered by the initial lifetime nor a recommended maintenance interval started by a preventive maintenance action. The miscoverage $mc(c)$ simply combines these two quality evaluation functions into a sum, and the action count $ac(c)$ tells the number of preventive maintenance actions of component c.

Lemma 1 links the under-coverage, the over-coverage and the number of preventive maintenance actions to each other. Lemma 2 demonstrates that over-coverage is potentially much larger than under-coverage. Finally, Lemma 3 shows that servicing too often does not help to reduce the under-coverage.

Lemma 1. *Let $c \in C$ and assume that $\ell + \rho(c) \leq h$. Then $uc(c) = h - \iota(c) - ac(c)\rho(c) + oc(c)$.*

Proof. Define first the sequence $B_c^0, B_c^1, \ldots, B_c^{ac(c)}$, in such a way that $B_c^0 = \emptyset$, $B_c^1 = \min B_c$, and $B_c^k = B_c^{k-1} \cup \{t \mid (\max B_c^{k-1}, t) \in \pi(c)\}$. This gives us a growing sequence of service times $t_1 = \max B_c^1, \ldots, t_{ac(c)} = \max B_c^{ac(c)}$.

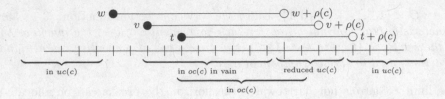

Fig. 3. Servicing too often does not pay off

The lemma is now proven by induction on k, $0 \leq k \leq ac(c)$.

$k = 0$:
$$oc_0(c) = 0,$$
$$uc_0(c) = h - \iota(c) - k\rho(c) + oc_0(c).$$

$k = 1$: (i) $\iota(c) < t_1$:
$$oc_1(c) = 0,$$
$$uc_1(c) = h - \iota(c) - k\rho(c) + oc_1(c).$$

(ii) $\iota(c) \geq t_1$:
$$oc_1(c) = t_1 - \iota(c) + 1,$$
$$uc_1(c) = h - \iota(c) - k\rho(c) + oc_1(c).$$

$k > 1$: (i) $t_{k-1} + \rho(c) \leq t_k$:
$$oc_k(c) = oc_{k-1}(c),$$
$$uc_k(c) = h - \iota(c) - k\rho(c) + oc_k(c).$$

(ii) $t_{k-1} + \rho(c) > t_k$:
$$oc_k(c) = oc_{k-1}(c) + (t_{k-1} + \rho(c) - t_k),$$
$$uc_k(c) = h - \iota(c) - k\rho(c) + oc_k(c).$$

Thus $uc_k(c) = h - \iota(c) - k\rho(c) + oc_k(c)$ for all $k, 1 \leq k \leq ac(c)$.   □

Lemma 2. *Let $c \in C$, and assume that $\ell + \rho(c) - 1 \leq h$ and $\iota(c) = 0$. Then $0 \leq uc(c) \leq h$, and $0 \leq oc(c) \leq (\ell - 1)(\rho(c) - 1)$.*

Proof. Clearly, $uc(c) \geq 0$. On one hand, the value $uc(c)$ reaches 0 when the services of the component c occur at time steps ℓ and $t = \iota(c) + 1 + k\rho(c)$, such that $k \geq 0$ and $t < \ell$. In this way, $uc(c) = h - (\ell + \rho(c) - 1)$. If $\ell = h - \rho(c) + 1$, we reach $uc(c) = h - (h - \rho(c) + 1 + \rho(c) - 1) = 0$. If $\ell > h - \rho(c) + 1$ and $B_c = \{1, \ldots, h\}$, we still have $uc(c) = 0$. On the other hand, the value $uc(c)$ is the greatest when $B_c = \emptyset$. In this case, $uc(c) = h$, and $oc(c) = 0$.

Clearly, $oc(c) \geq 0$. In fact, $oc(c) = 0$ when $B_c = \emptyset$, but the value $oc(c)$ is the greatest when $B_c = \{1, \ldots, \ell\}$. In this case, $oc(c) = (\ell - 1)(\rho(c) - 1)$.   □

Lemma 3. *Let w and t such that $w + 2 \leq t \leq w + \rho(c)$ be two maintenance times of component c, contributing $w + \rho(c) - t$ to $oc(c)$. Adding a maintenance time v, such that $w + 1 \leq v \leq t - 1$, increases $oc(c)$ without decreasing $uc(c)$.* □

Proof. Figure 3 shows a situation described in the lemma. The service at time step v has only an increasing effect on the over-coverage of the schedule.   □

The component-wise evaluation functions are lifted for a machine as follows:

Definition 4. *For every schedule $S = (h, \ell, b, A)$, there are associated measures: the over-coverage $oc(C) = \sum_{c \in C} oc(c)$, the under-coverage $uc(C) = \sum_{c \in C} uc(c)$, the miscoverage $mc(C) = uc(C) + oc(C)$, and action count $ac(C) = \sum_{c \in C} ac(c)$.*

In the rest of the paper, when solving PMS problems, we employ no other measures of quality than under-coverage and miscoverage. The following two lemmas identify corner cases for these measures.

Lemma 4. *Let $\mathcal{M} = \langle C, \iota, \rho \rangle$ be a multi-component machine. For any horizon $h \in \mathbb{N} \setminus \{0\}$, and limit $\ell \in \{1, \ldots, h\}$, there is a schedule $S = \langle h, \ell, b, A \rangle$ such that the over-coverage $oc(C)$ associated with the schedule is 0.*

Proof. The over-coverage $oc(C)$ of the empty schedule is 0.   □

Lemma 5. *Let $\mathcal{M} = \langle C, \iota, \rho \rangle$ be a multi-component machine. For any horizon $h \in \mathbb{N} \setminus \{0\}$, and breakset size $b \geq \lceil h / \min_c \rho(c) \rceil$ there is a schedule $S = \langle h, \ell, b, A \rangle$ such that the under-coverage $uc(C)$ associated with S is 0.*

Proof. Assume without loss of generality that $\iota(C) = \{0\}$. Construct a schedule $\langle h, \ell, b, A \rangle$ such that $B_c = \{1 + i \times (\min_c \rho(c)) \mid i = 0, \ldots, b - 1\}$ for all $c \in C$. These preventive maintenance actions are enough to cover the scheduling timeline, giving under coverage $uc(C) = 0$.   □

3   Basic PMS Problems and Their Complexities

In the following, we define some variants of the PMS problem and study their computational complexities.

Definition 5. *The EXACT MISCOVERAGE PMS problem is a decision problem that assumes, as its input, a multi-component machine $\mathcal{M} = \langle C, \iota, \rho \rangle$ and a quadruple $T = \langle h, \ell, b, m \rangle$ of scheduling parameters, and poses the question of whether the machine has a schedule $S = \langle h, \ell, b, A \rangle$ such that $mc(C) = m$.*

The NP membership of EXACT MISCOVERAGE PMS will be shown under the assumption that all the elements of the scheduling timeline $\{1, \ldots, h\}$ are separate units of the input, i.e., h is essentially encoded in unary. The following lemma gives an upper bound for the computation of the miscoverage.

Lemma 6. *Let $\mathcal{M} = \langle C, \iota, \rho \rangle$ be an arbitrary multi-component machine and $S = \langle h, \ell, b, A \rangle$ be one of its schedules. The miscoverage $mc(C)$ associated with S can be computed in $O(|C|h)$ time and $O(|C|h)$ space.*

Proof. Assume accessing of A takes $O(1)$ time steps. We compute the miscoverage of the schedule S with a loop that runs over C, and with an inner loop over all time steps $\{1, \ldots, h\}$ in $O(|C|h)$ time: For each component c, the inner loop starts from time step 1 and keeps track of the initial lifetime and the RMI that starts at a preventive maintenance action. (i) Every extra RMI covering the time step contributes one over-coverage to $mc(C)$. (ii) Each time step not covered by any RMI contribute one under-coverage to $mc(C)$. In addition, it is safe to say that the space requirement of the computation is $O(|C|h)$.   □

Theorem 1. *The EXACT MISCOVERAGE PMS problem is in NP.*

Proof. Let an EXACT MISCOVERAGE PMS problem instance consist of a multi-component machine $\mathcal{M} = \langle C, \iota, \rho \rangle$ and parameters $T = \langle h, \ell, b, m \rangle$. Since $\iota(c) < \rho(c)$ for all $c \in C$, and $h \geq \ell \geq b$, the input length is $\Omega(|C| \max_c \rho(c) + h + \log m)$. A certificate to the EXACT MISCOVERAGE PMS problem consists of a schedule $S = \langle h, \ell, b, A \rangle$ that requires $O(|C|h)$ space, which is polynomial in the input size. Let S be an arbitrary certificate. To verify it, we only need to check that the miscoverage $mc(C)$ associated with S equals m. By Lemma 6, $mc(C)$ can be computed in a polynomial time and space. $\quad\square$

The SUBSET SUM problem (SSP) is an example of an NP-complete problem [13]. In the sequel, it will be shown to be at most as hard as the EXACT MISCOVERAGE PMS problem by using an appropriate reduction.

Definition 6. *The SSP is a decision problem that assumes as its instance a pair $\langle N, s \rangle$ where $N = \{c_1, c_2, \ldots, c_n\}$ is a multiset of positive integers $c_i \in \mathbb{N} \backslash \{0\}$, $i = 1, \ldots, n$, and $s \in \mathbb{N} \backslash \{0\}$ is the target sum for a subset of these integers. The problem is to decide whether there is a subset $N' \subseteq N$ such that the target s is obtainable as the sum of the elements of N', i.e., $\sum N' = s$.*

Theorem 2. *The EXACT MISCOVERAGE PMS problem is NP-hard.*

Proof. Let $P = \langle N, s \rangle$, $N = \{c_1, c_2, \ldots, c_n\}$ be an arbitrary instance of SSP. Without loss of generality, assume that $c_i \leq c_{i+1}$, for $1 \leq i \leq n - 1$. This SSP instance reduces by a poly-time function to an instance of EXACT MIS-COVERAGE PMS given by machine $\mathcal{M} = \langle C, \iota_0, \rho \rangle$ and scheduling parameters $T = \langle \max N, 1, 1, n \max N - s \rangle$, such that $C = \{1, \ldots, n\}$, and $\iota_0(i) = 0$, $\rho(i) = c_i$ for all $i \in C$. Since all preventive maintenance actions are enforced to occur at time step 1, we have $oc(C) = 0$ for all schedules S. If S is the empty schedule, then $uc(C)$ reaches its maximum value $n \max N$.

Let $N' \subseteq N$ be a multiset subset with sum s, being a solution to the SSP instance $\langle N, s \rangle$. In the reduction, each integer $c_i \in N'$ is encoded by $A(i, 1) = 1$, while $A(i, 1) = 0$ encodes that $c_i \notin N'$. This gives a schedule $\langle \max N, 1, 1, A \rangle$ whose associated under-coverage $uc(C)$ is $n \max N - s$. This schedule is a solution to the EXACT MISCOVERAGE PMS instance $\langle \mathcal{M}, T \rangle$.

Conversely, let $S = \langle \max N, 1, 1, A \rangle$ be a solution to the EXACT MISCOV-ERAGE PMS instance $\langle \mathcal{M}, T \rangle$. The associated under-coverage is $n \max N - s$. The schedule encodes the multiset subset $N' = \{c_i \mid i \in C, A(i, 1) = 1\} \subseteq N$ with sum s. This subset is a solution to the SSP instance $\langle N, s \rangle$. $\quad\square$

Definition 7. *The BOUNDED MISCOVERAGE PMS problem is a decision problem that assumes, as its input, a multi-component machine $\mathcal{M} = \langle C, \iota, \rho \rangle$ and a quadruple $T = \langle h, \ell, b, m \rangle$ of bounds, and poses the question of whether the machine has a schedule $S = \langle h, \ell, b, A \rangle$ such that $mc(C) \leq m$.*

Theorem 3. *The BOUNDED MISCOVERAGE PMS problem is in NP.*

The proof of Theorem 3 is similar to Theorem 1 and thus left to the reader.

Function problems can be defined almost in a similar way as decision problems. The following function problems concern the optimization of schedules with respect to particular measures associated with them.

Listing 1. A PMS problem instance

```
1  comp(1,5,2).     comp(3,7,0).     comp(5,9,0).     comp(7,5,4).
2  comp(2,10,0).    comp(4,4,3).     comp(6,11,2).    comp(8,8,0).
```

Listing 2. PMS encoding: parameters, domains, choices, and service actions

```
1   % Parameters and domains
2   #const h=32.   #const l=32.   #const b=3.
3   time(0..h).
4   comp(C) :- comp(C,_,_).
5
6   % Breaks and the allocation of components for maintenance
7   { break(T): time(T), T>0, T <= l } <= b.
8   1 <= { serv(C,T): comp(C) } :- break(T).
9
10  % End of maintenance interval
11  emi(C,T+R) :- comp(C,R,L), serv(C,T), time(T+R).
12  emi(C,L+1) :- comp(C,R,L), L>0, time(L+1).
```

Definition 8. *The UNDER-COVERAGE PMS and MISCOVERAGE PMS are optimizing function problems whose inputs consists of a multi-component machine $\mathcal{M} = \langle C, \iota, \rho \rangle$ and a triple $\langle h, \ell, b \rangle$ of scheduling parameters. The solution to the UNDER-COVERAGE PMS problem is a schedule $S = \langle h, \ell, b, A \rangle$ such that the under-coverage $uc(C)$ associated with the schedule S is minimized, and the solution to the MISCOVERAGE PMS problem is a schedule $S = \langle h, \ell, b, A \rangle$ such that the miscoverage $mc(C)$ associated with the schedule S is minimized.*

4   An ASO-Based Implementation

In what follows, we present an ASP encoding of the PMS problem. The encoding is presented in the language fragment of the GRINGO grounder as described by Gebser et al. in [16]. Thus existing ASP solvers such as CLASP [14] and WASP [2] can be readily used to implement the search for optimal schedules in practice.

Listing 1 illustrates the representation of an eight-component machine using the domain predicate comp(C,R,L) whose arguments give the identity C, the recommended maintenance interval R, and the initial lifetime L due to a preventive maintenance action before the scheduling timeline. The machine instantiates the PMS problem whose encoding is split into three sections given in Listings 2–4.

In Listing 2 (Line 2), the parameters h, l, and b for the number of time steps, the limit for the last maintenance break, and the number of scheduled

Listing 3. PMS encoding: counting overlap of intervals

```
1   % Component-specific coverage of time steps by RMIs
2   cov1(C,0) :- comp(C,R,L), L>0.
3   cov1(C,T) :- not cov1(C,T-1), not cov2(C,T-1),
4                serv(C,T), not emi(C,T), time(T-1).
5
6   cov1(C,T+1) :- cov1(C,T), not serv(C,T+1), not emi(C,T+1), time(T+1).
7   cov1(C,T+1) :- cov1(C,T), serv(C,T+1), emi(C,T+1), time(T+1).
8   cov2(C,T+1) :- cov1(C,T), serv(C,T+1), not emi(C,T+1), time(T+1).
9
10  cov2(C,T+1) :- cov2(C,T), not serv(C,T+1), not emi(C,T+1), time(T+1).
11  cov2(C,T+1) :- cov2(C,T), serv(C,T+1), emi(C,T+1), time(T+1).
12  cov1(C,T+1) :- cov2(C,T), not serv(C,T+1), emi(C,T+1), time(T+1).
```

Listing 4. PMS encoding: constraints and objective function

```
1   % Deny (excessive) overlaps of RMIs
2   :- cov2(C,T), serv(C,T+1), not emi(C,T+1), time(T+1).
3
4   % Optimization with respect to miscoverage
5   #minimize {1,C,T: not cov1(C,T), not cov2(C,T),
6                     comp(C), time(T), T>0;
7              1,C,T: cov2(C,T), comp(C), time(T)        }.
```

maintenance breaks, respectively, are set to their default values. In Line 3, we define time/1 as a domain predicate for representing time steps. Moreover, the identities of components are extracted as the extension of the comp/1 predicate in Line 4, recall comp/3 from Listing 1. Then we are ready to choose time steps for scheduled maintenance breaks, as formalized by the choice rule in Line 7. At most b scheduled maintenance breaks are picked first and for each of these breaks at least one component is selected for an preventive maintenance action in Line 8. This is represented in terms of the serv/2 predicate that eventually captures solutions to PMS problems. In Line 11, we define when the respective RMI ends using the emi/2 predicate for each such action. For components C with some initial lifetime, the analogous time step is defined in Line 12.

Based on the predicates introduced so far, we may define how time steps are covered by RMIs on a component-by-component basis, see Listing 3. This leads to an encoding ('2-level') with recursive definitions of two predicates cov1(C,T) and cov2(C,T) denoting that a component C is covered by exactly one or two RMIs, respectively, at time T. Naturally, the target is that cov1(C,T) would hold for every C and T, indicating that C is neither under- nor over-serviced over time. The base cases for cov1 are given in Lines 2–4: either C has some initial lifetime L due to recent maintenance, or C is maintained at time T not covered by any earlier maintenance actions at the preceding time step T-1. Based on this, we may infer that cov1(C,T+1) holds for the following time step T+1: either C is not maintained again nor the RMI ends (Line 6), or C is maintained again but the preceding RMI ends at the same time (Line 7). The third possibility is that C is maintained again within the same RMI, a reason for making cov2(C,T+1) true in Line 8. The *inertial* rules for cov2/2 in Lines 10–11 are analogous to the ones of cov1/2 in Lines 6–7. The final possibility is formalized by Line 12: there is an end of a RMI falsifying cov2(C,T+1) but making cov1(C,T+1) true again. Note that according to answer set semantics, any other instances of cov1(C,T) and cov2(C,T) are *false by default* and need not be specified by any rules.

Finally, Listing 4 sets the scene for solving the optimization problem in question. Firstly, in Line 2, more than two overlapping RMIs are banned in the spirit of Lemma 3. This is also why predicates cov1/2 and cov2/2 are sufficient to keep track of overlaps in the first place. Secondly, the objective function penalizes for under servicing (time steps not covered) and over servicing (time steps covered twice) on equal basis in Lines 5 and 7, respectively. For the sake of illustration, we have depicted two globally optimal schedules for the 8-component machine from Listing 1. The one in Fig. 4a is based on the minimization of under-coverage (red cells) only. This leads to a substantial overlap of RMIs and over-coverage indicated in blue. A periodic pattern of 10 time steps seems to be emerging, although the overall applicability of the preventive maintenance actions involved remains open in the future due to finite time horizon. However, if over-coverage is penalized equally, far better schedules result as shown in Fig. 4b. The risks from under service are slightly higher but over servicing resulting from too frequent preventive maintenance actions are decreased substantially. The number of individual preventive maintenance actions is also decreased from 44 to 36. Interestingly, the dimensions of the schedules reflect the space complexity of ground logic

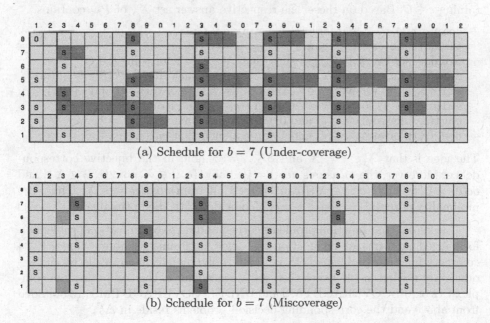

(a) Schedule for $b = 7$ (Under-coverage)

(b) Schedule for $b = 7$ (Miscoverage)

Fig. 4. Globally optimal schedules for the machine of Listing 1: blue lines indicate scheduled maintenance breaks and individual preventive maintenance actions are marked with letter "s"

programs obtained from our encoding (cf. Lemma 6). The effect of the bound b on the size of the ground program is negligible.

Proposition 1. *The size of the ground program resulting from Listings 2–4 is $\mathcal{O}(|C|h)$ for a set of components C and the time horizon h.*

Theorem 4. *Let $\mathcal{M} = \langle C, \iota, \rho \rangle$ be a machine, $\langle h, \ell, b \rangle$ the triple of scheduling parameters, and $P_\mathcal{M}$ their representation as a ground logic program based on Listings 2–4 and a set of facts encoding $\mathcal{M}$.*

1. *If X is an (optimal) answer set of $P_\mathcal{M}$, then there is an (optimal) solution $S_X = \langle h, \ell, b, A_X \rangle$ to the MISCOVERAGE PMS problem $\langle \mathcal{M}, \langle h, \ell, b \rangle \rangle$.*
2. *If a schedule $S = \langle h, \ell, b, A \rangle$ is an (optimal) solution to the MISCOVERAGE PMS problem $\langle \mathcal{M}, \langle h, \ell, b \rangle \rangle$, then there is an (optimal) answer set X_S of $P_\mathcal{M}$.*

Proof (Sketch). Due to space restrictions, we concentrate on describing the one-to-one correspondence between answer sets and schedules as follows. Firstly, given an answer set X of $P_\mathcal{M}$, the respective PMS is $S_X = \langle h, \ell, b, A_X \rangle$ where for a component $c \in C$ and a time step $1 \leq i \leq h$, $A_X(c, i) = 1 \iff \mathtt{serv}(c, i) \in X$.

Secondly, given a PMS $S = \langle h, \ell, b, A \rangle$ for $\mathcal{M}$ subject to scheduling parameters $\langle h, \ell, b \rangle$, we may calculate for each component and a time step $0 \leq i \leq h$,

$$cnt(c, i) = |\{j \in B_c \mid j \leq i < j + \rho(c)\}| + |\{1 \mid \iota(c) > 0, i \leq \iota(c)\}|, \qquad (1)$$

i.e., the number of recommended maintenance intervals covering i while maintaining $c \in C$. Based on these, the respective answer set X_S of $P_\mathcal{M}$ contains

- $\mathtt{comp}(c, \rho(c), \iota(c))$ and $\mathtt{comp}(c)$ for every $c \in C$;
- $\mathtt{time}(i)$ for every $0 \leq i \leq h$;
- $\mathtt{break}(i)$ for every $1 \leq i \leq h$ such that $A(c, i) = 1$ for some $c \in C$;
- $\mathtt{serv}(c, i)$ for every $c \in C$ and $1 \leq i \leq h$ such that $A(c, i) = 1$;
- $\mathtt{emi}(c, i + \rho(c))$ for every $c \in C$ and $1 \leq i \leq h$ with $A(c, i) = 1$ and $i + \rho(c) \leq h$;
- $\mathtt{emi}(c, \iota(c) + 1)$ for every $c \in C$ with $\iota(c) > 0$ and $\iota(c) + 1 \leq h$;
- $\mathtt{cov1}(c, i)$ for every $c \in C$ and $0 \leq i \leq h$ such that $cnt(c, i) = 1$; and
- $\mathtt{cov2}(c, i)$ for every $c \in C$ and $1 \leq i \leq h$ such that $cnt(c, i) = 2$.

The idea is that $X_{(S_X)} = X$ and $S_{(X_S)} = S$ hold in the bijective correspondence. Moreover, the measures $uc(c) = |\{i \mid \mathtt{cov1}(c, i) \notin X, \mathtt{cov2}(c, i) \notin X\}|$ and $oc(c) = |\{i \mid \mathtt{cov2}(c, i) \in X\}|$ can be read off from answer sets X. Thus, the minimality of $mc(C) = uc(C) + oc(C)$ coincides with the optimality of X.   □

It is known that function problems corresponding to optimization problems—formalized in terms of disjunction-free logic programs as above—are $\mathrm{FP}^{\mathrm{NP}}$-complete function problems [24], i.e., only polynomially many calls to an NP-oracle are needed in the worst case. As a consequence, the computational complexities of MISCOVERAGE PMS and UNDER-COVERAGE PMS are bounded from above and the corresponding decision problems reside in Δ_2^P.

Corollary 1. *Given a machine $\mathcal{M} = \langle C, \iota, \rho \rangle$ and the scheduling parameters $\langle h, \ell, b \rangle$, the respective function problems MISCOVERAGE PMS and UNDER-COVERAGE PMS for computing optimal schedules are in $\mathrm{FP}^{\mathrm{NP}}$.*

Hardness results in this respect are left for future work.

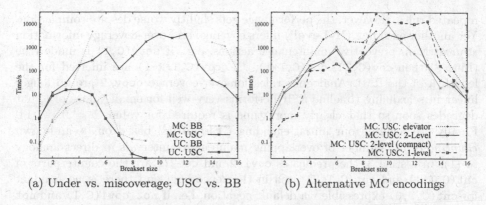

(a) Under vs. miscoverage; USC vs. BB   (b) Alternative MC encodings

Fig. 5. Runtimes in seconds for $b = 1 \ldots 16$ on logarithmic scale

5   Experiments

In this section, we evaluate the performance of the encoding from Listings 2–4. In the experiments, we use GRINGO (v. 5.2.2) as the grounder and CLASP (v. 3.3.6) as the solver. All runs are executed on an Intel(R) Xeon(R) Gold 6248 CPU with a 2.50GHz clock rate under Linux operating system.

Our preliminary screening showed that the 8-component machine from Listing 1 is already sufficient to create great variance with respect to runtimes. Thus, we concentrate on analyzing the performance of CLASP on this particular instance when the number of scheduled maintenance breaks b is increased from 1 to 16 for schedules in a scheduling timeline $h = 32$. The time required for grounding the encoding is negligible and omitted altogether.

The runtime behavior of CLASP as the back-end solver can be inspected from Fig. 5. It turns out that the minimization of under-coverage (UC) is quite easy. The lowest two plots in Fig. 5a concern optimization according to two different strategies based *branch-and-bound* (BB) and *unsatisfiable cores* (USC). For small values of b, the BB strategy is faster but becomes slower than USC when almost fully covered schedules become feasible at $b = 8$. The upper two plots in Fig. 5a relate to the minimization of miscoverage (MC) which seems to be a far more difficult task from the computational point of view. Now the USC strategy performs much better. We think that this is due to the fact that USC approaches optimal solutions from below and since the values of the objective function are relatively small in this example, the optimal value can be reached soon. The BB strategy, however, uses upper bounds and finally, when the optimality of a found schedule is to be proved, a potentially high number of other candidates—not improving the objective value—must be excluded by the solver. Indeed, the last stage of optimization dominates in the BB strategy, and the runtimes for $b = 6 \ldots 13$ are clear outliers that reside beyond the range visible in Fig. 5a.

We have developed several variants of the ASP encoding ('**2-level**') from Sect. 4 and include results for some of them in Fig. 5b. The first alternative encoding ('**2-level (compact)**') expresses predicates cov1(C,T) and cov2(C,T) using a single predicate cov(C,T,N) for N=1..2 and thus amalgamates some repeated rules. However, the performance gets slightly worse despite compaction. Yet another encoding ('**1-Level**') infers coverage and over-coverage information *straight* from preventive maintenance actions, e.g., if `serv(C,T)` is made true (Line 8) then `cov(C,T)`, `cov(C,T+1)`, ..., `cov(C,T+R-1)` are inferred for the length `R` of the RMI. Analogous rules for over-coverage `ocov/2` are no longer linear in scheduling timeline h. It performs very well for small values of b, but degrades soon so that clearly more time is required for values $b = 9, ..., 14$. Finally, we mention our initial encoding ('**Elevator**') based on up-and-down *counting* of the number of overlapping maintenance intervals in direct analogy to (1). In Listing 3, the predicates `cov1/2` and `cov2/2` are the counterparts of `cnt(C,T,1)` and `cnt(C,T,2)` used in that encoding, and there is no pendant for `cnt(C,T,0)` expressible via default negation, i.e., if `not cov1(C,T)` and `not cov2(C,T)` hold simultaneously. The respective plot in Fig. 5b indicates that such a systematic saving in the number of predicates pays off.

To further assess the scalability of the method, we tested the 2-Level encoding of miscoverage and the USC strategy with 8 scheduled maintenance breaks and 10 randomly generated machines per each of the sizes from 1 to 16 components. Figure 6 shows the averages of the running times in this experiment. When optimizing the miscoverage, a majority of the larger machine sizes hit the timeout of 32800 s. This highlights that without approximations and further optimizations, the problem cannot be solved on a large scale.

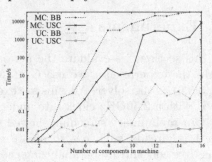

Fig. 6. Effect of machine size

6 Conclusion

This paper studies PMS of continuously operating, rotating multi-component machines and formalizes the PMS problem as a search problem that abstracts away from side-constraints and stochastic aspects of PMS. The focus is on globally optimal maintenance scheduling under discrete-valued optimization criteria.

Although the efficiency of global optimization techniques has been constantly improving, the problem formalization, encoding and optimization techniques can make a major difference in the feasibility of the technological approach. We present an ASP encoding for the EXACT MISCOVERAGE PMS problem and carry out a preliminary feasibility study for it, according to which the quest for performance improvement remains substantial if we extend the breakset size or the machine size. Our problem sizes are on a par with previous research [12,26], but a precise comparison is omitted because prior implementations of PMS are not generally available and they differ substantially in their concepts and parameters. Nevertheless, we show that the EXACT MISCOVERAGE PMS problem is one of the NP-hard (scheduling) problems [13,25]. In addition, by putting our encodings publicly availablewe facilitate their improvement in the future. New kinds of encodings could be devised, e.g., by using recent extensions based on temporal operators [5] or multi-shot solving [15].

It is worth noting that although we compute globally optimal schedules, the same formalization can be approached with local or approximate optimization techniques. It is also within our interests to study extensions of the PMS problem. Hard side-constraints such as availability and resource constraints are easy to incorporate into ASP encodings in an orthogonal way, and the EXACT MIS-COVERAGE PMS problem can be embedded into a modularized framework for condition-based rescheduling. See, e.g., [27,28] where the recommended maintenance intervals depend on the workload or the current condition of the machine.

Acknowledgment. The support from the Academy of Finland within the project AI-ROT (#335718) is gratefully acknowledged.

References

1. Ali, M.B., Sassi, M., Gossa, M., Harrath, Y.: Simultaneous scheduling of production and maintenance tasks in the job shop. Int. J. Prod. Res. **49**, 3891–3918 (2011). https://doi.org/10.1080/00207543.2010.492405
2. Alviano, M., Dodaro, C., Leone, N., Ricca, F.: Advances in WASP. In: LPNMR 2015, pp. 40–54 (2015). https://doi.org/10.1007/978-3-319-23264-5_5
3. Banbara, M., et al.: Teaspoon: solving the curriculum-based course timetabling problems with answer set programming. Ann. Oper. Res. **275**, 3–37 (2019). https://doi.org/10.1007/s10479-018-2757-7
4. Brewka, G., Eiter, T., Truszczynski, M.: Answer set programming at a glance. Commun. ACM **54**(12), 92–103 (2011). https://doi.org/10.1145/2043174.2043195
5. Cabalar, P., Kaminski, R., Morkisch, P., Schaub, T.: Telingo = ASP + time. In: LPNMR 2019, pp. 256–269 (2019). https://doi.org/10.1007/978-3-030-20528-7_19
6. Cassady, C., Murdock, P., Pohl, E.: Selective maintenance for support equipment involving multiple maintenance actions. EJOR **129**(2), 252–258 (2001), a Global View of Industrial Logistics. https://doi.org/10.1016/S0377-2217(00)00222-8
7. Chansombat, S., Pongcharoen, P., Hicks, C.: A mixed-integer linear programming model for integrated production and preventive maintenance scheduling in the capital goods industry. Int. J. Prod. Res. **57**(1), 61–82 (2019). https://doi.org/10.1080/00207543.2018.1459923
8. Chen, X., An, Y., Zhang, Z., Li, Y.: An approximate nondominated sorting genetic algorithm to integrate optimization of production scheduling and accurate maintenance based on reliability intervals. J. Manuf. Syst. **54**, 227–241 (2020). https://doi.org/10.1016/j.jmsy.2019.12.004
9. Do, P., Vu, H.C., Barros, A., Bérenguer, C.: Maintenance grouping for multi-component systems with availability constraints and limited maintenance teams. Reliab. Eng. & Syst. Safety **142**, 56–67 (2015). https://doi.org/10.1016/j.ress.2015.04.022
10. Dodaro, C., Maratea, M.: Nurse scheduling via answer set programming. In: Balduccini, M., Janhunen, T. (eds.) LPNMR 2017. LNCS (LNAI), vol. 10377, pp. 301–307. Springer, Cham (2017). https://doi.org/10.1007/978-3-319-61660-5_27

11. Eiter, T., Geibinger, T., Musliu, N., Oetsch, J., Skocovský, P., Stepanova, D.: Answer-set programming for lexicographical makespan optimisation in parallel machine scheduling. In: KR 2021, pp. 280–290 (2021). http://dx.doi.org/10.24963/kr.2021/27
12. Frost, D., Dechter, R.: Optimizing with constraints: a case study in scheduling maintenance of electric power units. In: Maher, M., Puget, J.-F. (eds.) CP 1998. LNCS, vol. 1520, pp. 469–469. Springer, Heidelberg (1998). https://doi.org/10.1007/3-540-49481-2_40
13. Garey, M.R., Johnson, D.S.: Computers and Intractability: a Guide to the Theory of NP-Completeness. W. H. Freeman & Company (1979)
14. Gebser, M., Kaminski, R., Kaufmann, B., Romero, J., Schaub, T.: Progress in clasp series 3. In: LPNMR 2015, pp. 368–383 (2015). https://doi.org/10.1007/978-3-319-23264-5_31
15. Gebser, M., Kaminski, R., Kaufmann, B., Schaub, T.: Multi-shot ASP solving with clingo. Theor. Pract. Log. Program. **19**(1), 27–82 (2019). https://doi.org/10.1017/S1471068418000054
16. Gebser, M., Kaminski, R., Ostrowski, M., Schaub, T., Thiele, S.: On the input language of ASP grounder *Gringo*. In: Erdem, E., Lin, F., Schaub, T. (eds.) LPNMR 2009. LNCS (LNAI), vol. 5753, pp. 502–508. Springer, Heidelberg (2009). https://doi.org/10.1007/978-3-642-04238-6_49
17. Geurtsen, M., Didden, J.B., Adan, J., Atan, Z., Adan, I.: Production, maintenance and resource scheduling: a review. EJOR (2022). https://doi.org/10.1016/j.ejor.2022.03.045
18. Hoai, M.T., Luong, H.T.: Selective maintenance policy with time-window constraint. In: Proceedings of the 7th Asia Pacific Industrial Engineering and Management Systems Conference 2006. Bangkok, Thailand (2006)
19. Nguyen, K.A., Do, P., Grall, A.: Condition-based maintenance for multi-component systems using importance measure and predictive information. Int. J. Syst. Sci.: Oper. Logist. **1**(4), 228–245 (2014). https://doi.org/10.1080/23302674.2014.983582
20. Nguyen, K.A., Do, P., Grall, A.: Multi-level predictive maintenance for multi-component systems. Reliab. Eng. Syst. Safety **144**, 83–94 (2015). https://doi.org/10.1016/j.ress.2015.07.017
21. Olde Keizer, M., Flapper, S., Teunter, R.: Condition-based maintenance policies for systems with multiple dependent components: a review. EJOR **261**(2), 405–420 (2017). https://doi.org/10.1016/j.ejor.2017.02.044
22. Rajaprasad, S.V.S.: Investigation of reliability, maintainability and availability of a paper machine in an integrated pulp and paper mill. Int. J. Eng. Sci. Technol. **10**(3), 43–56 (2018). https://doi.org/10.4314/ijest.v10i3.5
23. Sachdeva, A., Kumar, D., Kumar, P.: Planning and optimizing the maintenance of paper production systems in a paper plant. Comput. Industr. Eng. **55**, 817–829 (2008). https://doi.org/10.1016/j.cie.2008.03.004
24. Simons, P., Niemelä, I., Soininen, T.: Extending and implementing the stable model semantics. Artif. Intell. **138**(1–2), 181–234 (2002). https://doi.org/10.1016/S0004-3702(02)00187-X
25. Ullman, J.: NP-complete scheduling problems. JCSS **10**(3), 384–393 (1975). https://doi.org/10.1016/S0022-0000(75)80008-0
26. You, M.Y., Meng, G.: A modularized framework for predictive maintenance scheduling. Proc. Instit. Mech. Eng. Part O: J. Risk Reliab. **226**(4), 380–391 (2012). https://doi.org/10.1177/1748006X11431209

27. Youssef, H., Brigitte, C.M., Noureddine, Z.: Lower bounds and multiobjective evolutionary optimisation for combined maintenance and production scheduling in job shop. In: IEEE 2003 Conference on EFTA, vol. 2, pp. 95–100 (2003). https://doi.org/10.1109/ETFA.2003.1248675
28. Zheng, Y., Lian, L., Mesghouni, K.: Comparative study of heuristics algorithms in solving flexible job shop scheduling problem with condition based maintenance. J. Industr. Eng. Manag. **7**(2), 518–531 (2014). http://dx.doi.org/10.3926/jiem.1038
29. Zurn, H., Quintana, V.: Generator maintenance scheduling via successive approximations dynamic programming. IEEE Trans. Power Apparat. Syst. **94**(2), 665–671 (1975). https://doi.org/10.1109/T-PAS.1975.31894
30. Öhman, M., Hiltunen, M., Virtanen, K., Holmström, J.: Frontlog scheduling in aircraft line maintenance: from explorative solution design to theoretical insight into buffer management. J. Oper. Manag. **67**(2), 120–151 (2021). https://doi.org/10.1002/joom.1108

On the Generalization of Learned Constraints for ASP Solving in Temporal Domains

Javier Romero$^{(\boxtimes)}$ ⓘ, Torsten Schaub ⓘ, and Klaus Strauch$^{(\boxtimes)}$ ⓘ

University of Potsdam, Potsdam, Germany
javier@cs.uni-potsdam.de, kstrauch@uni-potsdam.de

Abstract. The representation of a dynamic problem in ASP usually boils down to using copies of variables and constraints, one for each time stamp, no matter whether it is directly encoded or via an action or temporal language. The multiplication of variables and constraints is commonly done during grounding and the solver is completely ignorant about the temporal relationship among the different instances. On the other hand, a key factor in the performance of today's ASP solvers is conflict-driven constraint learning. Our question is now whether a constraint learned for particular time steps can be generalized and reused at other time stamps, and ultimately whether this enhances the overall solver performance on dynamic problems. Knowing full well the domain of time, we study conditions under which learned dynamic constraints can be generalized and propose a simple translation of the original logic program such that, for the translated programs, all learned constraints can be generalized to other time points. Last but not least, we empirically evaluate the impact of adding the generalized constraints to an ASP solver.

Keywords: Answer set programming · Answer set solving · Temporal reasoning

1 Introduction

Although Answer Set Programming (ASP; [12]) experiences an increasing popularity in academia and industry, a closer look reveals that this concerns mostly static domains. There is still quite a chasm between ASP's level of development for addressing static and dynamic domains. This is because its modeling language as well as its solving machinery aim so far primarily at static knowledge, while dynamic knowledge is mostly dealt with indirectly via reductions to the static case. This also applies to dedicated dynamic formalisms like action and temporal languages [1,13]. In fact, their reduction to ASP or SAT usually relies on translations that introduce a copy of each variable for each time step. The actual dynamics of the problem is thus compiled out and a solver treats the result as any other static problem.

ⓒ The Author(s), under exclusive license to Springer Nature Switzerland AG 2022
G. Governatori and A.-Y. Turhan (Eds.): RuleML+RR 2022, LNCS 13752, pp. 20–37, 2022.
https://doi.org/10.1007/978-3-031-21541-4_2

We address this by proposing a way to (partly) break the opaqueness of the actual dynamic problem and equip an ASP solver with means for exploiting its temporal nature. More precisely, we introduce a method to strengthen the conflict-driven constraint learning framework (CDCL) of ASP solvers so that dynamic constraints learned for specific time points can be generalized to other points in time. These additional constraints can in principle reduce the search space and improve the performance of the ASP solvers.

We start by reviewing some background material in Sect. 2. Next, in Sect. 3, we introduce a simple but general language to reason about time in ASP. We then define temporal problems, and characterize their solutions in terms of completion and loop nogoods, paralleling the approach to regular ASP solving [10]. In Sect. 4, using this language, we study conditions under which learned constraints can be generalized to other time steps. With it, in Sect. 5, we propose a simple translation such that, for the translated programs, learned constraints can be generalized to other time points without the need for any proof method. Finally, in Sect. 6 we empirically evaluate the impact of adding the generalized constraints to the ASP solver *clingo*.

Our work can be seen as a continuation of the approach of *ginkgo* [9], which also aimed at generalizing temporal constraints but resorted to an external inductive proof method (in ASP) for warranting correctness. More generally, a lot of work has been conducted over recent years on lazy ASP solving [14,15,17]. Notably, conflict generalization was studied from a general perspective in [4], dealing with several variables over heterogeneous domains. Lazy grounding via propagators was investigated in [5]. Finally, it is worth mentioning that the usage of automata, as done in [3], completely abolishes the use of time points. A detailed formal and empirical comparative study of these approaches is interesting future work.

2   Background

We review the material from [11] about solving normal logic programs, and adapt it for our purposes to cover normal logic programs with choice rules and integrity constraints over some set $\mathcal{P}$ of atoms.

A *rule* r has the form $H \leftarrow B$ where B is a set of literals over $\mathcal{P}$, and H is either an atom $p \in \mathcal{P}$, and we call r a *normal rule*, or $\{p\}$ for some atom $p \in \mathcal{P}$, making r a *choice rule*, or $\bot$, so that r is an *integrity constraint*. We usually drop braces from rule bodies B, and drop the arrow $\leftarrow$ when B is empty. We use the extended choice rule $\{p_1; \ldots; p_n\} \leftarrow B$ as a shorthand for the choice rules $\{p_1\} \leftarrow B, \ldots, \{p_n\} \leftarrow B$. A *program* Π is a set of rules. By Π^n, Π^c, and Π^i we denote its normal rules, choice rules and integrity constraints, respectively. Semantically, a logic program induces a collection of *stable models*, which are distinguished models of the program determined by the stable models semantics (see [10,12] for details).

For a rule r of the form $H \leftarrow B$, let $h(r) = p$ be the *head* of r if H has the form p or $\{p\}$ for some atom $p \in \mathcal{P}$, and let $h(r) = \bot$ otherwise. Let $B(r) = B$

be the *body* of r, $B(r)^+ = \{p \mid p \in \mathcal{P}, p \in B\}$ be the *positive body* of r, and $B(r)^- = \{p \mid p \in \mathcal{P}, \neg p \in B\}$ be the *negative body* of r. The set of atoms occurring in a rule r and in a logic program Π are denoted by $A(r)$ and $A(\Pi)$, respectively. The set of bodies in Π is $B(\Pi) = \{B(r) \mid r \in \Pi\}$. For regrouping rule bodies sharing the same head p, we define $B(p) = \{B(r) \mid r \in \Pi, h(r) = p\}$, and by $B^n(p)$ we denote the restriction of that set to bodies of normal rules, i.e., $\{B(r) \mid r \in \Pi^n, h(r) = p\}$.

A Boolean *assignment* A over a set $\mathcal{A}$, called the domain of A, is a set $\{\sigma_1, \ldots, \sigma_n\}$ of *signed literals* σ_i of the form $\mathbf{T}p$ or $\mathbf{F}p$ for some $p \in \mathcal{A}$ and $1 \leq i \leq n$; $\mathbf{T}p$ expresses that p is *true* and $\mathbf{F}p$ that it is *false*. We omit the attribute *signed* for literals whenever clear from the context. We denote the complement of a literal σ by $\overline{\sigma}$, that is, $\overline{\mathbf{T}p} = \mathbf{F}p$ and $\overline{\mathbf{F}p} = \mathbf{T}p$. Given this, we access true and false propositions in A via $A^{\mathbf{T}} = \{p \in \mathcal{A} \mid \mathbf{T}p \in A\}$ and $A^{\mathbf{F}} = \{p \in \mathcal{A} \mid \mathbf{F}p \in A\}$. We say that a set of atoms X is consistent with an assignment A if $A^{\mathbf{T}} \subseteq X$ and $A^{\mathbf{F}} \cap X = \emptyset$. In our setting, a *nogood* is a set $\{\sigma_1, \ldots, \sigma_n\}$ of signed literals, expressing a constraint violated by any assignment containing $\sigma_1, \ldots, \sigma_n$. Accordingly, the nogood for an integrity constraint r, denoted by $ng(r)$, is $\{\mathbf{T}p \mid p \in B(r)^+\} \cup \{\mathbf{F}p \mid p \in B(r)^-\}$. We say that an assignment A over $\mathcal{A}$ is *total* if $A^{\mathbf{T}} \cup A^{\mathbf{F}} = \mathcal{A}$ and $A^{\mathbf{T}} \cap A^{\mathbf{F}} = \emptyset$. A total assignment A over $\mathcal{A}$ is a *solution* for a set Δ of nogoods, if $\delta \not\subseteq A$ for all $\delta \in \Delta$. A set Δ of nogoods *entails* a nogood δ if $\delta \not\subseteq A$ for all solutions A over $\mathcal{A}$ for Δ, and it entails a set of nogoods ∇ if it entails every nogood $\delta \in \nabla$ in the set.

We say that a nogood δ is a *resolvent* of a set of nogoods Δ if there is a sequence of nogoods $\delta_1, \ldots, \delta_n$ with $n \geq 1$ such that $\delta_n = \delta$, and for all i such that $1 \leq i \leq n$, either $\delta_i \in \Delta$, or there are some δ_j, δ_k with $1 \leq j < k < i$ such that $\delta_i = (\delta_j \setminus \{\sigma\}) \cup (\delta_k \setminus \{\overline{\sigma}\})$ for some signed literal σ. In this case, we say that the sequence $\delta_1, \ldots, \delta_n$ is a proof of δ_n. We say that a signed literal σ is *unit resulting* for a nogood δ and an assignment A if $\delta \setminus A = \{\sigma\}$ and $\overline{\sigma} \notin A$. For a set of nogoods Δ and an assignment A, unit propagation is the process of extending A with unit-resulting literals until no further literal is unit resulting for any nogood in Δ.

Inferences in ASP can be expressed in terms of atoms and rule bodies. We begin with nogoods capturing inferences from the Clark completion. For a body $\beta = \{p_1, \ldots, p_m, \neg p_{m+1}, \ldots, \neg p_n\}$, we have that $\delta(\beta) = \{\mathbf{F}\beta, \mathbf{T}p_1, \ldots, \mathbf{T}p_m, \mathbf{F}p_{m+1}, \ldots, \mathbf{F}p_n\}$ and $\Delta(\beta) = \{\{\mathbf{T}\beta, \mathbf{F}p_1\}, \ldots, \{\mathbf{T}\beta, \mathbf{F}p_m\}, \{\mathbf{T}\beta, \mathbf{T}p_{m+1}\}, \ldots, \{\mathbf{T}\beta, \mathbf{T}p_n\}\}$. For an atom p such that $B^n(p) = \{\beta_1, \ldots, \beta_k\}$, we have that $\Delta(p) = \{\{\mathbf{F}p, \mathbf{T}\beta_1\}, \ldots, \{\mathbf{F}p, \mathbf{T}\beta_k\}\}$, and if $B(p) = \{\beta_1, \ldots, \beta_k\}$ then $\delta(p) = \{\mathbf{T}p, \mathbf{F}\beta_1, \ldots, \mathbf{F}\beta_k\}$. Given this, the *completion nogoods* of a logic program Π are defined as follows:

$$\Delta_\Pi = \{\delta(\beta) \mid \beta \in B(\Pi \setminus \Pi^i)\} \cup \{\delta \in \Delta(\beta) \mid \beta \in B(\Pi \setminus \Pi^i)\}$$
$$\cup \{\delta(p) \mid p \in A(\Pi)\} \cup \{\delta \in \Delta(p) \mid p \in A(\Pi)\}$$
$$\cup \{ng(\beta) \mid \beta \in B(\Pi^i)\}$$

Choice rules of the form $\{p\} \leftarrow \beta$ are considered by not adding the corresponding nogood $\{\mathbf{F}p, \mathbf{T}\beta\}$ to $\Delta(p)$, and integrity constraints from Π^i of the form $\perp \leftarrow \beta$

are considered by adding directly their corresponding nogood $ng(\beta)$. The definition of the *loop nogoods* Λ_Π, capturing the inferences from loop formulas, is the same as in [11]. We do not specify them here since they do not pose any special challenge to our approach, and they are not needed in our (tight) examples.

To simplify the presentation, we slightly deviate from [11] and consider a version of the nogoods of a logic program where the occurrences of the empty body are simplified. Note that $\delta(\emptyset) = \{\mathbf{F}\emptyset\}$ and $\Delta(\emptyset) = \emptyset$. Hence, if $\emptyset \in B(\Pi)$ then any solution to the completion and loop nogoods of Π must contain $\mathbf{T}\emptyset$. Based on this, we can delete from $\Delta_\Pi \cup \Lambda_\Pi$ the nogoods that contain $\mathbf{F}\emptyset$, and eliminate the occurrences of $\mathbf{T}\emptyset$ from the others. Formally, we define the set of (simplified) nogoods for Π as:

$$\Sigma_\Pi = \{\delta \setminus \{\mathbf{T}\emptyset\} \mid \delta \in \Delta_\Pi \cup \Lambda_\Pi, \mathbf{F}\emptyset \notin \delta\}.$$

To accommodate this change, for a program Π, we fix the domain $\mathcal{A}$ of the assignments to the set $A(\Pi) \cup (B(\Pi) \setminus \emptyset)$. Given this, the stable models of a logic program Π can be characterized by the nogoods Σ_Π for that program. This is made precise by the following theorem, which is an adaptation of Theorem 3.4 from [11] to our setting.

Theorem 1. *Let Π be a logic program. Then, $X \subseteq A(\Pi)$ is a stable model of Π iff $X = A^{\mathbf{T}} \cap A(\Pi)$ for a (unique) solution A for Σ_Π.*

To compute the stable models of a logic program Π, we apply the algorithm $CDNL\text{-}ASP(\Pi)$ from [11] implemented in the ASP solver *clingo*. The algorithm searches for a solution A to the set of nogoods Σ_Π, and when it finds one it returns the corresponding set of atoms $A^{\mathbf{T}} \cap A(\Pi)$. *CDNL ASP* maintains a current assignment A and a current set of learned nogoods ∇, both initially empty. The main loop of the algorithm starts by applying unit propagation to $\Sigma_\Pi \cup \nabla$, possibly extending A. Every derived literal is "implied" by some nogood $\delta \in \Sigma_\Pi \cup \nabla$, which is stored in association with the derived literal. This derivation may lead to the violation of another nogood. This situation is called *conflict*. If propagation finishes without conflict, then a (heuristically chosen) literal can be added to A, provided that A is partial, while otherwise A represents a solution and can be directly returned. On the other hand, if there is a conflict, there are two possibilities. Either it is a top-level conflict, independent of heuristically chosen literals, in which case the algorithm returns *unsatisfiable*. Or, if that is not the case, the conflict is analyzed to calculate a conflict nogood δ, that is added to ∇. More in detail, δ is a resolvent of the set of nogoods associated with the literals derived after the last heuristic choice. Hence, every learned nogood δ added to ∇ is a resolvent of $\Sigma_\Pi \cup \nabla$ and, by induction, it is also a resolvent of Σ_Π. After recording δ, the algorithm backjumps to the earliest stage where the complement of some formerly assigned literal is implied by δ, thus triggering propagation and starting the loop again.

This algorithm has been extended for solving under assumptions [7]. In this setting, the procedure $CDNL\text{-}ASP(\Pi, S)$ receives additionally as input a partial assignment S over $A(\Pi)$, the so-called assumptions, and returns some stable model of Π that is consistent with S. To accommodate this extension, the algorithm simply decides first on the literals from S, and returns *unsatisfiable* as soon as any of these literals is undone by backjumping. No more changes are needed. Notably, the learned nogoods are still resolvents of Δ_Π, that are independent of the set of assumptions S.

3 Temporal Programs, Problems and Nogoods

We introduce a simple language of temporal logic programs to represent temporal problems. These programs represent the dynamics of a temporal domain by referring to two time steps: the current step and the previous step. We refer to the former by atoms from a given set $\mathcal{P}$, and to the latter by atoms from the set $\mathcal{P}' = \{p' \mid p \in \mathcal{P}\}$, that we assume to be disjoint from $\mathcal{P}$. Following the common-sense flow of time, normal or choice rules define the atoms of the current step in terms of the atoms of both the current and the previous step. Integrity constraints forbid some current situations, possibly depending on the previous situations. Syntactically, a temporal logic program Π over $\mathcal{P}$ has the form of a (non-temporal) logic program over $\mathcal{P} \cup \mathcal{P}'$ such that for every rule $r \in \Pi$, if $r \in \Pi^n \cup \Pi^c$ then $h(r) \in \mathcal{P}$, and otherwise $(B(r)^+ \cup B(r)^-) \cap \mathcal{P} \neq \emptyset$. Given that temporal logic programs over $\mathcal{P}$ can also be seen as (non-temporal) logic programs over $\mathcal{P} \cup \mathcal{P}'$, in what follows we may apply the notation of the latter to the former. We say that the rules $r \in \Pi$ such that $A(r) \subseteq \mathcal{P}$ are static, and otherwise we say that they are dynamic.

One of the goals of the design of this language was to capture the core of the translations to ASP of action and temporal languages [1,13]. We do not elaborate this further, but from this perspective, temporal programs can be seen as an intermediate language in the workflow of ASP solving for those higher level languages. On the other hand, a variant of this language was used recently to represent the transition function of various types of planning problems [8]. More in detail, this representation consists of choice rules of the form $\{a\} \leftarrow$ to generate the occurrences of actions a, normal rules of the form $f \leftarrow B$ to define the value of the fluents f in terms of the values of other fluents or actions at the current or previous steps, and integrity constraints of the form $\perp \leftarrow B$, where some action a belongs to B, to specify the preconditions of the actions.

Example 1. Our running example is the temporal logic program Π_1 over $\mathcal{P}_1 = \{a, b, c, d\}$ that consists only of choice rules and integrity constraints:

$$
\begin{aligned}
\{a; b; c; d\} &\leftarrow & \perp &\leftarrow a', \neg b \\
\perp &\leftarrow \neg b', b & \perp &\leftarrow \neg c', a \\
\perp &\leftarrow d', b & \perp &\leftarrow c, \neg d \\
\perp &\leftarrow \neg a', \neg c & \perp &\leftarrow \neg a', c', \neg a
\end{aligned}
$$

Temporal logic programs Π can be instantiated to specific time intervals. We introduce some notation for that. Let m and n be integers such that $1 \leq m \leq n$, and $[m, n]$ denote the set of integers $\{i \mid m \leq i \leq n\}$. For $p \in \mathcal{P}$, the symbol $p[m]$

denotes the atom p_m, and for $p' \in \mathcal{P}'$, the symbol $p'[m]$ denotes the atom p_{m-1}. For a set of atoms $X \subseteq \mathcal{P} \cup \mathcal{P}'$, $X[m]$ denotes the set of atoms $\{p[m] \mid p \in X\}$, and $X[m, n]$ denotes the set of atoms $\{p[i] \mid p \in X, i \in [m, n]\}$. For a rule r over $\mathcal{P} \cup \mathcal{P}'$, the symbol $r[m]$ denotes the rule that results from replacing in r every atom $p \in \mathcal{P} \cup \mathcal{P}'$ by $p[m]$, and $r[m, n]$ denotes the set of rules $\{r[i] \mid i \in [m, n]\}$. Finally, for a temporal program Π, $\Pi[m]$ is $\{r[m] \mid r \in \Pi\}$, and $\Pi[m, n]$ is $\{r[i] \mid r \in \Pi, i \in [m, n]\}$.

Example 2. The instantiation of Π_1 at 1, denoted by $\Pi_1[1]$, is:

$$\{a_1; b_1; c_1; d_1\} \leftarrow \qquad\qquad \bot \leftarrow a_0, \neg b_1$$
$$\bot \leftarrow \neg b_0, b_1 \qquad\qquad \bot \leftarrow \neg c_0, a_1$$
$$\bot \leftarrow d_0, b_1 \qquad\qquad \bot \leftarrow c_1, \neg d_1$$
$$\bot \leftarrow \neg a_0, \neg c_1 \qquad\qquad \bot \leftarrow a_0, c_0, \neg a_1$$

The programs $\Pi_1[i]$ for $i \in \{2, 3, 4\}$ are the same, except that the subindex 1 is replaced by i, and the subindex 0 is replaced by $i - 1$. The instantiation of Π_1 at $[1, 4]$, denoted by $\Pi_1[1, 4]$, is $\Pi_1[1] \cup \Pi_1[2] \cup \Pi_1[3] \cup \Pi_1[4]$.

To represent temporal reasoning problems, temporal programs are complemented by assignments I and F that partially or completely describe the initial and the final situation of a problem. Formally, a *temporal logic problem* over some set of atoms $\mathcal{P}$ is a tuple $\langle \Pi, I, F \rangle$ where Π is a temporal logic program over $\mathcal{P}$, and I and F are assignments over $\mathcal{P}$. A solution to such a problem is a sequence of situations that is consistent with the dynamics described by Π and with the information provided by I and F. The possible sequences of situations of length n, for some integer $n \geq 1$, are represented by the *generator program* for Π and n, denoted by $gen(\Pi, n)$, that consists of the rules $\{\{p_0\} \leftarrow \; \mid p \in \mathcal{P}\} \cup \Pi[1, n]$. Then, a *solution* to a temporal problem $\langle \Pi, I, F \rangle$ is defined as a pair (X, n), where n is an integer such that $n \geq 1$, and X is a stable model of $gen(\Pi, n)$ consistent with $I[0] \cup F[n]$.

Temporal problems can be used to formalize planning problems, using a temporal logic program Π of the form described above, a total assignment I that assigns a value to every possible atom (action occurrences are made false initially), and a partial assignment F to fix the goal. The solutions of the temporal problem correspond to the plans of the planning problem.

Example 3. The temporal problem $\langle \Pi_1, \emptyset, \emptyset \rangle$ has three solutions of length 4: $(Y, 4)$, $(Y \cup \{d(2)\}, 4)$, and $(Y \cup \{b(3)\}, 4)$, where Y is the set of atoms $\{a(0), b(0), c(0), a(1), b(1), b(2), c(3), d(3), a(4), c(4), d(4)\}$.

To pave the way to the nogood characterization of temporal logic problems, we define the transition program $trans(\Pi)$ of a temporal logic program Π as the (non-temporal) logic program $\Pi \cup \{\{p'\} \leftarrow \mid p' \in \mathcal{P}'\}$ over $\mathcal{P} \cup \mathcal{P}'$. Each stable model of this program represents a possible transition between a previous and a current step, where the former is selected by the additional choice rules over atoms from $\mathcal{P}'$, and the latter is determined by the rules of Π, interpreted as non-temporal rules.

Example 4. The transition program $trans(\Pi_1)$ is the (non-temporal) program $\Pi_1 \cup \{\{a';b';c';d'\} \leftarrow\}$ over $\mathcal{P}_1 \cup \{p' \mid p \in \mathcal{P}_1\}$. Some stable models of $trans(\Pi_1)$ are $\{a',b',c',a,b\}$ and $\{c',d',a,c,d\}$, that correspond to the transitions to step 1 and step 4 of the solution $(Y,4)$, respectively.

Next, we introduce temporal nogoods and their instantiation. Given a temporal logic program Π over $\mathcal{P}$, a temporal nogood over $\mathcal{P} \cup B(\Pi)$ has the form of a (non-temporal) nogood over $\mathcal{P} \cup \mathcal{P}' \cup B(\Pi)$. For a temporal nogood δ over $\mathcal{P} \cup B(\Pi)$ and an integer $n \geq 1$, the instantiation of δ at n, denoted by $\delta[n]$, is the nogood that results from replacing in δ any signed literal $\mathbf{T}\alpha$ ($\mathbf{F}\alpha$) by $\mathbf{T}\alpha[n]$ (by $\mathbf{F}\alpha[n]$, respectively). We extend this notation to sets of nogoods and to intervals like we did above. For example, $\delta_1 = \{\mathbf{F}b', \mathbf{T}b\}$ is a temporal nogood over $\mathcal{P}_1 \cup B(\Pi_1)$, and $\delta_1[1,2]$ is $\{\{\mathbf{F}b_0, \mathbf{T}b_1\}, \{\mathbf{F}b_1, \mathbf{T}b_2\}\}$.

We are now ready to define the temporal nogoods for a temporal logic program Π over $\mathcal{P}$. Recall that $trans(\Pi)$ is a (non-temporal) logic program over $\mathcal{P} \cup \mathcal{P}'$, whose corresponding nogoods are denoted by $\Sigma_{trans(\Pi)}$. Then, the set of *temporal nogoods* for Π, denoted by Ψ_Π, has the form $\Sigma_{trans(\Pi)}$, interpreted as a set of temporal nogoods over $\mathcal{P} \cup B(\Pi)$, and not as a set of (non-temporal) nogoods over $\mathcal{P} \cup \mathcal{P}' \cup B(\Pi)$.

Example 5.
The set Ψ_{Π_1} of temporal nogoods for Π_1 is $\{\{\mathbf{T}a', \mathbf{F}b\}, \{\mathbf{F}b', \mathbf{T}b\}, \{\mathbf{F}c', \mathbf{T}a\}, \{\mathbf{T}d', \mathbf{T}b\}, \{\mathbf{T}c, \mathbf{F}d\}, \{\mathbf{F}a', \mathbf{F}c\}, \{\mathbf{F}a', \mathbf{T}c', \mathbf{F}a\}\}$.

Temporal nogoods provide an alternative characterization of the nogoods of $gen(\Pi, n)$.

Proposition 1. *Let Π be a temporal logic program, and $n \geq 1$ some integer. Then, $\Sigma_{gen(\Pi,n)} = \Psi_\Pi[1,n]$.*

In words, the nogoods for $gen(\Pi, n)$ are the same as the instantiation of the temporal nogoods for Π, that are nothing else than the nogoods of the logic program $trans(\Pi)$ interpreted as temporal nogoods. Then, by Theorem 1, the temporal nogoods can be used to characterize the solutions of temporal logic problems.

Theorem 2. *Let $\langle \Pi, I, F \rangle$ be a temporal logic problem. The pair (X, n) is a solution to $\langle \Pi, I, F \rangle$ for some integer $n \geq 1$ and $X \subseteq \mathcal{P}[0,n]$ iff $X = A^{\mathbf{T}} \cap \mathcal{P}[0,n]$ for a (unique) solution A for $\Psi_\Pi[1,n]$ such that $I[0] \cup F[n] \subseteq A$.*

4   Generalizing Learned Constraints

A common software architecture to solve a temporal problem $\langle \Pi, I, F \rangle$ combines a scheduler that assigns resources to different values of n, with one or many solvers that look for solutions of the assigned lengths n (see [16], for example). The standard approach for the solvers is to extend the program $gen(\Pi, n)$ with facts and integrity constraints to adequately represent I and F, and call the procedure *CDNL-ASP* with this extended program without assumptions. This method does not work well for our purposes, because it leads to a nogood representation of the initial and the final steps that is different from the nogood representation of the other steps. Hence, the constraints learned using nogoods specific to the initial and final steps may not be generalizable to the other steps. To overcome this issue, in our approach the solvers apply the procedure *CDNL-ASP*$(gen(\Pi, n), I[0] \cup F[n])$ to the generator program for Π and n, using assumptions to fix the assignments about the initial and final situations. Observe that in this case, by Proposition 1, the solver initially contains exactly the nogoods $\Psi_\Pi[1, n]$, and all the nogoods that it learns afterwards are resolvents of $\Psi_\Pi[1, n]$.

Once this is settled, we ask ourselves:

What generalizations of the nogoods learned by the algorithm can be applied to the same or other problems?

We make the question more precise step by step. First, instead of talking about "the nogoods learned by the algorithm", we refer to the resolvents of $\Psi_\Pi[1, n]$ for some temporal problem $\langle \Pi, I, F \rangle$. Or more precisely, we refer to the resolvents of $\Psi_\Pi[i, j]$ for some i and j such that $1 \leq i \leq j \leq n$, since the learned nogoods are always the result of resolving nogoods belonging to some interval $[i, j]$ that may be smaller than $[1, n]$.

To formalize the notion of the "generalizations of nogoods", we introduce some notation for shifting a non-temporal nogood an amount of t time steps. For integers $n \geq 1$ and t, and a non-temporal nogood δ over $(\mathcal{P} \cup \mathcal{P}' \cup B(\Pi))[1, n]$, the symbol $\delta\langle t \rangle$ denotes the nogood that results from replacing in δ any signed literal $\mathbf{T}\alpha_m$ ($\mathbf{F}\alpha_m$) by $\mathbf{T}\alpha_{m+t}$ (by $\mathbf{F}\alpha_{m+t}$, respectively). For example, $\delta\langle 0 \rangle = \delta$, and if $\delta = \{\mathbf{T}a_2, \mathbf{F}b_3\}$, then $\delta\langle 1 \rangle$ is $\{\mathbf{T}a_3, \mathbf{F}b_4\}$, and $\delta\langle -1 \rangle$ is $\{\mathbf{T}a_1, \mathbf{F}b_2\}$. We say that $\delta\langle t \rangle$ is a *shifted version* of the nogood δ, and that a *generalization* of a nogood is a set of some of its shifted versions. For example, $\{\{\mathbf{T}a_2, \mathbf{F}b_3\}\}$ and $\{\{\mathbf{T}a_1, \mathbf{F}b_2\}, \{\mathbf{T}a_2, \mathbf{F}b_3\}, \{\mathbf{T}a_3, \mathbf{F}b_4\}\}$ are generalizations of $\{\mathbf{T}a_2, \mathbf{F}b_3\}$ and of $\{\mathbf{T}a_3, \mathbf{F}b_4\}$.

Next, by the "other problems" mentioned in the question, we refer to variations m of the length of the solution, and to variations $\langle \Pi, I', F' \rangle$ of the original problem where the initial and final situation may change, but the temporal program remains the same. Then, a generalization of a nogood "can be applied" to such problems if it can be added to the set of nogoods used by the algorithm *CDNL-ASP* without changing the solutions to the problem. For any variation $\langle \Pi, I', F' \rangle$, those nogoods are $\Psi_\Pi[1, m]$, and a generalization can be added to them if the generalization is entailed by them. Hence, a generalization of a nogood "can be applied" to "some problem" $\langle \Pi, I', F' \rangle$, searching for a solution of length m, if the generalization is entailed by $\Psi_\Pi[1, m]$. Putting all together, we can rephrase our question as follows:

Given some temporal logic problem $\langle \Pi, I, F \rangle$, what generalizations of a resolvent δ of $\Psi_\Pi[i, j]$ are entailed by $\Psi_\Pi[1, m]$?

Example 6. Consider a call of $CDNL\text{-}ASP(gen(\Pi_1, n), \emptyset)$ to search for a solution of length n to the temporal problem $\langle \Pi_1, \emptyset, \emptyset \rangle$, where n has the value 4. Initially, the solver may choose to make a_3 true by adding $\mathbf{T}a_3$ to the initial assignment. Then, by unit propagation, it could derive the literal $\mathbf{T}c_2$ by $\{\mathbf{F}c', \mathbf{T}a\}[3]$, the literal $\mathbf{T}d_2$ by $\{\mathbf{T}c, \mathbf{F}d\}[2]$, the literal $\mathbf{F}b_3$ by $\{\mathbf{T}d', \mathbf{T}b\}[3]$, and the literal $\mathbf{F}b_4$ by $\{\mathbf{F}b', \mathbf{T}b\}[4]$, leading to a conflict due to the violation of the nogood $\{\mathbf{T}a', \mathbf{F}b\}[4]$. At this stage, the solver would learn the nogood $\delta = \{\mathbf{T}a\}[3]$ by resolving iteratively $\{\mathbf{T}a', \mathbf{F}b\}[4]$ with the nogoods $\{\mathbf{F}b', \mathbf{T}b\}[4]$, $\{\mathbf{T}d', \mathbf{T}b\}[3]$, $\{\mathbf{T}c, \mathbf{F}d\}[2]$, and $\{\mathbf{F}c', \mathbf{T}a\}[3]$ used for propagation. Hence, δ is a resolvent of the set of those nogoods. Moreover, given that those nogoods are instantiations of some temporal nogoods of Ψ_{Π_1} at the interval $[2, 4]$, δ is also a resolvent of $\Psi_{\Pi_1}[2, 4]$ and of $\Psi_{\Pi_1}[1, n]$. Observe that, by shifting the nogoods -1 time points, we obtain that $\delta\langle -1 \rangle = \{\mathbf{T}a\}[2]$ is a resolvent of $\Psi_{\Pi_1}[1, 3]$, and therefore also of $\Psi_{\Pi_1}[1, n]$. Then, by the correctness of resolution, we have that the generalization $\{\{\mathbf{T}a\}[2], \{\mathbf{T}a\}[3]\}$ of δ is entailed by $\Psi_{\Pi_1}[1, n]$. On the other hand, $\delta\langle -2 \rangle = \{\mathbf{T}a\}[1]$ is a resolvent of $\Psi_{\Pi_1}[0, 2]$, but not of $\Psi_{\Pi_1}[1, n]$, (partly) because the instantiations at 0 do not belong to $\Psi_{\Pi_1}[1, n]$. Similarly, $\delta\langle 1 \rangle = \{\mathbf{T}a\}[4]$ is a resolvent of $\Psi_{\Pi_1}[3, 5]$, but not of $\Psi_{\Pi_1}[1, n]$, (partly) because the instantiations at 5 do not belong to $\Psi_{\Pi_1}[1, n]$ (see Fig. 1).

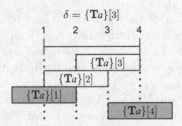

Fig. 1. Representation of different shifted versions of the nogood $\delta = \{\mathbf{T}a\}[3]$. The surrounding rectangles cover the interval of the nogoods needed to prove them. For example, the rectangle of $\{\mathbf{T}a\}[2]$ covers the interval $[1, 3]$ because $\{\mathbf{T}a\}[2]$ is a resolvent of $\Psi_{\Pi_1}[1, 3]$.

This example suggests a sufficient condition for the generalization of a nogood δ learned from $\Psi_\Pi[i, j]$: a shifted version $\delta\langle t \rangle$ of some generalization of δ is entailed by $\Psi_\Pi[1, n]$ if the nogoods that result from shifting $\Psi_\Pi[i, j]$ an amount of t time points belong to $\Psi_\Pi[1, n]$. We answer our previous question by stating this condition precisely in the next theorem.

Theorem 3. *Let $\langle \Pi, I, F \rangle$ be a temporal logic problem, and δ be a resolvent of $\Psi_\Pi[i, j]$ for some i and j such that $1 \leq i \leq j$. Then, for every $n \geq 1$, the generalization consisting of the shifted nogoods $\delta\langle t \rangle$ such that $[i+t, j+t] \subseteq [1, n]$ is entailed by $\Psi_\Pi[1, n]$.*

The proof is based on the fact that the resolution proof that derived δ from $\Psi_\Pi[i, j]$ can be used to derive every $\delta\langle t \rangle$ from $\Psi_\Pi[i + t, j + t]$, simply by shifting the nogoods t time steps. This means that $\delta\langle t \rangle$ is a resolvent of $\Psi_\Pi[i + t, j + t]$. Given that $[i + t, j + t] \subseteq [1, n]$, the nogood $\delta\langle t \rangle$ is also a resolvent of $\Psi_\Pi[1, n]$. Then, the theorem follows from the correctness of resolution.

This result allows us to generalize the learned nogoods to different lengths and different initial and final situations, as long as the specified conditions hold. Following our example, if we were now searching for a solution of length 9 to the temporal problem $\langle \Pi_1, \{\mathbf{T}c\}, \{\mathbf{T}b\} \rangle$, we could add the generalization $\{\{\mathbf{T}a\}[i] \mid i \in [2, 8]\}$ to $CDNL\text{-}ASP(gen(\Pi_1, 9), \{\mathbf{T}c_0, \mathbf{T}b_9\})$.

The theorem can be applied in an online setting, where the generalizations are added while solving, or in an offline setting, where the generalizations are stored to apply them later to other problems. Observe that to benefit the most from the result, we should know what is the specific interval $[i, j]$ of the nogoods used to obtain a learned nogood. We could obtain this information by modifying the solving algorithm, and recording that interval for every learned nogood. We leave that option for future work, and in the next section we follow another approach that does not require to modify the solver.

5   Translations

In this section, we present a translation of the original temporal program such that the nogoods learned using the translated program can be generalized to all time points. We start with a simple translation tr^λ that works for temporal programs where all dynamic rules are integrity constraints. Later, we show that all temporal programs can be translated to this form.

We say that a temporal logic program Π over $\mathcal{P}$ is in *previous normal form* (PNF) if $A(\Pi \setminus \Pi^i) \cap \mathcal{P}' = \emptyset$, and that a temporal logic problem $\langle \Pi, I, F \rangle$ over $\mathcal{P}$ is in PNF if Π is in PNF. Given a temporal logic program Π over $\mathcal{P}$, let Π^{di} denote the set $\{r \mid r \in \Pi^i, A(r) \cap \mathcal{P}' \neq \emptyset\}$ of dynamic integrity constraints of Π. Note that if Π is in PNF, then the dynamic rules of Π belong to Π^{di}. The translation $tr^\lambda(\Pi)$ tags the rules in Π^{di} with a new atom λ, that does not belong to $\mathcal{P}$ or $\mathcal{P}'$, and extends the program with a choice rule for λ. Formally, by $tr^\lambda(\Pi)$ we denote the temporal logic program:

$$\Pi \setminus \Pi^{di} \cup \{\{\lambda\} \leftarrow \} \cup \{\bot \leftarrow B(r) \cup \{\lambda\} \mid r \in \Pi^{di}\}.$$

It is easy to see that when λ is chosen to be true, $tr^\lambda(\Pi)$ generates the same transitions as Π. Then, we can solve temporal programs $\langle \Pi, I, F \rangle$ by solving temporal problems $\langle tr^\lambda(\Pi), I, F \rangle$, if we consider only solutions that make λ true at all steps after the initial one. For convenience, at the initial step we consider only the case where λ is false. To make this precise, we say that a solution (X, n) to a temporal problem is λ-normal if $X \cap (\{\lambda\}[0, n]) = \{\lambda\}[1, n]$. The next proposition states the relation between these λ-normal solutions and the original solutions using Π.

Proposition 2. *Let $T_1 = \langle \Pi, I, F \rangle$ and let $T_2 = \langle tr^\lambda(\Pi), I, F \rangle$ be temporal logic problems. There is a one-to-one correspondence between the solutions to T_1 and the λ-normal solutions to T_2.*

The call $CDNL\text{-}ASP(gen(tr^\lambda(\Pi), n), I[0] \cup F[n] \cup \{\mathbf{F}\lambda_0\} \cup \{\mathbf{T}\lambda\}[1, n])$ computes λ-normal solutions to T_2, enforcing the correct value for λ at every time point using assumptions. The solutions to the original problem T_1 can be extracted from the λ-normal solutions, after deleting the atoms in $\{\lambda\}[1, n]$.

We turn now our attention to the resolvents δ of the set of nogoods $\Psi_{tr^\lambda(\Pi)}[1, n]$ used by the procedure $CDNL\text{-}ASP$. As we will see, just by looking at these resolvents δ, we can approximate the specific interval $[i, j] \subseteq [1, n]$ of the nogoods that were used to prove them.

To this end, we say that the nogoods containing literals of different steps are dynamic nogoods, and they are static nogoods otherwise. All dynamic nogoods in $\Psi_{tr^\lambda(\Pi)}[1, n]$ come from the instantiation of some dynamic integrity constraint $\{\bot \leftarrow B(r) \cup \{\lambda\} \mid r \in \Pi^{di}\}$ at some time step i and, therefore, they contain some literal of the form $\mathbf{T}\lambda_i$. On the other hand, in $\Psi_{tr^\lambda(\Pi)}[1, n]$ there are no literals of the form $\mathbf{F}\lambda_i$. Hence, the literals $\mathbf{T}\lambda_i$ occurring in the dynamic nogoods can never be resolved away. Then, if some dynamic nogood is used to prove a learned nogood δ, the literal $\mathbf{T}\lambda_i$ occurring in that dynamic nogood must belong to δ. This means that the literals $\mathbf{T}\lambda_i$ from a learned nogood δ tell us exactly the steps i of the dynamic nogoods that have been used to prove δ.

Observe now that two nogoods $\delta_1 \in \Psi_{tr^\lambda(\Pi)}[i]$ and $\delta_2 \in \Psi_{tr^\lambda(\Pi)}[i + 1]$ can only be resolved if δ_2 is a dynamic nogood. Otherwise, the nogoods would have no opposite literals to resolve. Applying the same reasoning, if two nogoods $\delta_1 \in \Psi_{tr^\lambda(\Pi)}[i]$ and $\delta_2 \in \Psi_{tr^\lambda(\Pi)}[j]$, such that $i < j$, are part of the same resolution proof of a learned nogood δ, then the proof must also contain some dynamic nogoods from each step in the interval $[i + 1, j]$. Therefore, the learned nogood δ must contain the literals $\{\mathbf{T}\lambda\}[i + 1, j]$.

This implies that, given the literals $\{\mathbf{T}\lambda\}[k, j]$ occurring in a learned nogood δ, we can infer the following about the nogoods from $\Psi_{tr^\lambda(\Pi)}[1, n]$ used to prove δ: dynamic nogoods from all the steps $[k, j]$ were used to prove δ, possibly some static nogoods of the step $k - 1$ were used as well, and no nogoods from other steps were used in the proof. It is possible that some static nogoods at steps $[k, j]$ were also used, but no dynamic nogoods at $k - 1$ could be used, since otherwise δ should contain the literal $\mathbf{T}\lambda_{k-1}$.

We formalize this with the function $step(\delta)$, that approximates the specific interval $[i, j]$ of the nogoods that were used to prove δ: if δ contains some literal of the form $\mathbf{T}\lambda_i$ for $i \in [1, n]$, then $step(\delta)$ is the set of steps $\{j - 1, j \mid \mathbf{T}\lambda_j \in \delta\}$. For example, if δ is $\{\mathbf{T}a_3, \mathbf{T}\lambda_3\}$ then the value of $step(\delta)$ is $\{2, 3\}$. It is clear that δ was derived using some dynamic nogood of step 3, that added the literal $\mathbf{T}\lambda_3$. And it could also happen that some static nogood of step 2 was used, but we are uncertain about it. That is why we say that $step$ is an approximation. To continue, note that it can also be that δ has no literals of the form $\mathbf{T}\lambda_i$. In this case, δ must be the result of resolving some static nogoods of a single time step, and we can extract that time step from the unique time step of the literals occurring in the nogood. Hence, in this case we define $step(\delta)$ as the set of steps $\{i \mid \mathbf{T}p_i \in \delta \text{ or } \mathbf{F}p_i \in \delta\}$. For example, $step(\{\mathbf{T}c_2, \mathbf{T}d_2\}) = \{2\}$. With this, we can generalize a nogood δ to the shifted nogoods $\delta\langle t \rangle$ whose $step$ value fits in the interval $[1, n]$. We state this precisely in part (i) of the next theorem.

Theorem 4. *Let $\langle \Pi, I, F \rangle$ be a temporal logic problem in PNF, and δ be a resolvent of $\Psi_{tr^\lambda(\Pi)}[1, m]$ for some $m \geq 1$. Then, for every $n \geq 1$:*

(i) the generalization $\{\delta\langle t \rangle \mid step(\delta\langle t \rangle) \subseteq [1, n]\}$ is entailed by $\Psi_{tr^\lambda(\Pi)}[1, n]$, and
(ii) the generalization $\{\delta\langle t \rangle \mid step(\delta\langle t \rangle) \subseteq [0, n]\}$ is entailed by $\Psi_{tr^\lambda(\Pi)}[0, n]$.

Observe that part (i) excludes the shifted nogoods $\delta\langle t \rangle$ that contain the literal $\mathbf{T}\lambda_1$, since in that case $step(\delta\langle t \rangle)$ contains the step $0 \notin [1, n]$. This makes sense because to prove $\delta\langle t \rangle$ we could need some static nogoods at step 0, and they do not belong to $\Psi_{tr^\lambda(\Pi)}[1, n]$. However, once we add the nogoods at step 0 in part (ii), those shifted nogoods are entailed. Intuitively, this addition enforces that the initial situation is reachable from some possible previous situation. We note that this restriction holds in most of the temporal problems that we have found. In particular, it holds in all the (classical) planning problems that we tried in our experiments. In fact, in those problems the atoms of the initial step are completely fixed by the given instance, and therefore we can apply part (ii) of the Theorem without having to consider any additional nogoods. In other words, in that case we can add the generalization of part (ii) but keep solving with the nogoods of part (i). Finally, let us mention that, given that the literals $\mathbf{T}\lambda_i$ are only true at steps $i \in [1, n]$, a shifted nogood $\delta\langle t \rangle$ can only be violated if $step(\delta\langle t \rangle) \subseteq [0, n]$. Hence, adding shifted nogoods with $step$ values outside of the interval $[0, n]$ cannot change the solutions computed by the algorithm *CDNL-ASP*. This is why we say that the nogoods learned by the translated program can be generalized to all time points.

Example 7. Consider the call $CDNL\text{-}ASP(gen(tr^\lambda(\Pi_1), 4), \{\})$, similar to the one that we have seen before using the original program Π_1. The nogoods $\Psi_{tr^\lambda(\Pi_1)}[1, n]$ are the same as those in $\Psi_{\Pi_1}[1, n]$, except that every dynamic nogood contains one instantiation of the literal $\mathbf{T}\lambda$. Instead of learning the nogood $\{\mathbf{T}a_3\}$ (written before as $\{\mathbf{T}a\}[3]$) the algorithm would learn the nogood $\delta = \{\mathbf{T}a_3, \mathbf{T}\lambda_3, \mathbf{T}\lambda_4\}$. Then, applying part (i) of Theorem 4 the nogood δ can be generalized to $\delta\langle -1 \rangle = \{\mathbf{T}a_2, \mathbf{T}\lambda_2, \mathbf{T}\lambda_3\}$, but not to $\delta\langle 1 \rangle = \{\mathbf{T}a_4, \mathbf{T}\lambda_4, \mathbf{T}\lambda_5\}$ or to $\delta\langle -2 \rangle = \{\mathbf{T}a_1, \mathbf{T}\lambda_1, \mathbf{T}\lambda_2\}$ (see Fig. 2). On the other hand, with part (ii), the latter is also valid. Observe how in that case we could even add to the algorithm *CDNL-ASP* the nogoods $\delta\langle 1 \rangle$ or $\delta\langle -3 \rangle = \{\mathbf{T}a_0, \mathbf{T}\lambda_0, \mathbf{T}\lambda_1\}$ since their respective literals $\mathbf{T}\lambda_5$ and $\mathbf{T}\lambda_0$ can never be part of any assignment computed by the algorithm.

The next step is to show how temporal programs in general can be translated to PNF form. For this, given a temporal logic program Π over $\mathcal{P}$, let $\mathcal{P}^* = \{p^* \mid p \in \mathcal{P}\}$, and assume that this set is disjoint from $\mathcal{P}$ and $\mathcal{P}'$. The translation $tr^*(\Pi)$ consists of two parts. The first part consists of the result of replacing

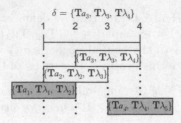

Fig. 2. Representation of different shifted versions of the nogood $\delta = \{\mathbf{T}a_3, \mathbf{T}\lambda_3, \mathbf{T}\lambda_4\}$. The surrounding rectangles cover the interval of their *step* value. For example, the rectangle of $\{\mathbf{T}a_2, \mathbf{T}\lambda_2, \mathbf{T}\lambda_3\}$ covers the interval $[1,3]$ because $step(\{\mathbf{T}a_2, \mathbf{T}\lambda_2, \mathbf{T}\lambda_3\}) = [1,3]$.

in Π every atom $p' \in \mathcal{P}'$ by its corresponding new atom p^*. The second part consists of the union of the rules

$$\{\{p^*\} \leftarrow; \bot \leftarrow p', \neg p^*; \bot \leftarrow \neg p', p^*\}$$

for every $p \in \mathcal{P}$. The idea of the translation is that the atoms $p' \in \mathcal{P}'$ are confined to integrity constraints by replacing them by new atoms $p^* \in \mathcal{P}^*$, whose truth value is completely determined by the corresponding $p' \in \mathcal{P}'$ atoms by means of the last set of rules.

Proposition 3. *For any temporal logic program Π, the program $tr^*(\Pi)$ is in PNF.*

The solutions to temporal problems with Π are the same as the solutions to the same temporal problems with $tr^*(\Pi)$ where the atoms $p^*[i]$ are false at $i = 0$ and have the truth value of $p[i-1]$ at the other time steps i. Just like before, when we use this translation, we have to add to *CDNL-ASP* the correct assumptions to fix the value of the p^* atoms at step 0.

Proposition 4. *Let $\mathcal{T}_1 = \langle \Pi, I, F \rangle$ and let $\mathcal{T}_2 = \langle tr^*(\Pi), I, F \rangle$ be temporal logic problems. There is a one-to-one correspondence between the solutions to $\mathcal{T}_1$ and the solutions to $\mathcal{T}_2$ that do not contain any atom $p^* \in \mathcal{P}^*$ at step 0.*

This proposition allows us to replace any temporal program Π by a temporal program $tr^*(\Pi)$ in PNF. We can then apply the translation tr^λ and benefit from Theorem 4. In fact, we can go one step further, and apply the nogoods learned with the program $tr^\lambda(tr^*(\Pi))$ directly to the original problem with Π. We make this claim precise in the next theorem. For that, we define the simplification of a nogood δ, written $simp(\delta)$, as the nogood $\{\mathbf{V}p_i \mid \mathbf{V}p_i \in \delta, \mathbf{V} \in \{\mathbf{T}, \mathbf{F}\}, p \in \mathcal{P}\} \cup \{\mathbf{V}p_{i-1} \mid \mathbf{V}p_i^* \in \delta, \mathbf{V} \in \{\mathbf{T}, \mathbf{F}\}, p^* \in \mathcal{P}^*\}$ that results from skipping the λ_i literals of δ, and replacing the atoms p_i^* by their corresponding atoms p_{i-1}.

Theorem 5. *Let $\langle \Pi, I, F \rangle$ be a temporal logic problem, and for some $m \geq 1$ let δ be a resolvent of $\Psi_{tr^\lambda(tr^*(\Pi))}[1,m]$. Then, for every $n \geq 1$:*

(i) *the generalization $\{simp(\delta\langle t \rangle) \mid step(\delta\langle t \rangle) \subseteq [1,n]\}$ is entailed by $\Psi_\Pi[1,n]$, and*

(ii) *the generalization $\{simp(\delta\langle t \rangle) \mid step(\delta\langle t \rangle) \subseteq [0,n]\}$ is entailed by $\Psi_\Pi[0,n]$.*

6   Experiments

In this section, we experimentally evaluate the generalization of learned nogoods in ASP planning using the solver *clingo*. The goal of the experiments is to study the performance of *clingo* when the planning encodings are extended by the generalizations of some constraints learned by *clingo* itself. We are interested only in the solving time and not in the grounding time, but in any case we have observed no differences between grounding times among the different configurations compared. We performed experiments in two different settings, single shot and multi shot, that we detail below. Following the approach of [9], in all experiments we disregarded the learned nogoods of size greater than 50 and of degree greater than 10, where the degree of a nogood is defined as the difference between the maximum and minimum step of the literals of the nogood. In all the experiments, the learned nogoods are always sorted either by size or by *literal block distance* (*lbd*, [2]), a measure that is usually associated with the quality of a learned nogood. We tried configurations adding the best 500, 1000, or 1500 nogoods, according to either their nogood size or their *lbd*. The results ordering the nogoods by *lbd* were similar but slightly better than those ordering by size. For reasons of space, from now on we focus on the former. We used two benchmark sets from [6]. The first consists of PDDL benchmarks from planning competitions, translated to ASP using the system *plasp* presented in that paper. This set contains 120 instances of 6 different domains. The second set consists of ASP planning benchmarks from ASP competitions. It contains 136 instances of 9 domains. We adapted the logic programs of these benchmarks to the format of temporal logic programs as follows: we deleted the facts used to specify the initial situation, as well as the integrity constraints used to specify the goal, we added some choice rules to open the initial situation, and we fixed the initial situation and the goal using assumptions. All benchmarks were run using the version 5.5.1 of *clingo* on an Intel Xeon E5-2650v4 under Debian GNU/Linux 10, with a memory limit of 8 GB, and a timeout of 15 min per instance.

The task in the single shot experiment is to find a plan of a fixed length n that is part of the input. For the PDDL benchmarks we consider plan lengths varying from 5 to 75 in steps of 5 units, for a total of 2040 instances. The ASP benchmarks already have a plan length, and we use it. In a preliminary learning step, *clingo* is run with every instance for 10 minutes or until 16000 nogoods are learned, whatever happens first. The actual learning time is disregarded and not taken into account in the tables. Some PDDL instances overcome the memory limit in this phase. We leave them aside and are left with 1663 instances of this type. We compare the performance of *clingo* running normally (baseline), versus the (learning) configurations where we add the best 500, 1000, or 1500 learned nogoods according to their *lbd* value. In this case we apply Theorem 5 and learn the nogoods using a translated encoding, but use the original encoding for the evaluation of all configurations.

Tables 1 and 2 show the results for the PDDL and the ASP benchmarks, respectively. The first columns include the name and number of instances of every domain. The tables show the average solving times and the number of

Table 1. Single shot solving of PDDL benchmarks.

		Baseline	500	1000	1500
Blocks	(300)	0.5 (0)	**0.1** (0)	**0.1** (0)	**0.1** (0)
Depots	(270)	145.9 (30)	138.3 (29)	129.7 (27)	**124.8** (28)
Driverlog	(135)	14.0 (1)	12.6 (1)	**12.5** (1)	12.7 (1)
Elevator	(300)	**3.0** (0)	3.3 (0)	4.1 (0)	7.0 (0)
Grid	(30)	11.3 (0)	5.3 (0)	**3.3** (0)	5.7 (0)
Gripper	(255)	381.1 (96)	372.2 (90)	367.9 (93)	**365.4** (90)
Logistics	(238)	4.2 (1)	**2.3** (0)	2.4 (0)	2.4 (0)
Mystery	(135)	94.4 (8)	79.8 (6)	71.0 (4)	**67.5** (5)
Total	(1663)	92.3 (136)	88.1 (126)	85.4 (125)	**84.5** (124)

Table 2. Single shot solving of ASP benchmarks.

		Baseline	500	1000	1500
HanoiTower	(20)	158.4 (2)	88.4 (0)	86.6 (0)	**79.3** (0)
Labyrinth	(20)	243.8 (3)	243.2 (2)	242.7 (2)	**242.2** (2)
Nomistery	(20)	583.2 (12)	**526.8** (11)	559.8 (11)	566.2 (12)
Ricochet Robots	(20)	463.0 (8)	443.3 (8)	360.7 (6)	**356.5** (4)
Sokoban	(20)	457.0 (9)	**420.2** (8)	424.7 (8)	427.5 (8)
Visit-all	(20)	558.3 (12)	536.2 (11)	**522.3** (10)	553.5 (11)
Total	(120)	410.6 (46)	376.3 (40)	**366.1** (37)	370.9 (37)

timeouts, in parenthesis, for every configuration and domain. We can observe that in general the learning configurations are faster than the baseline and in some domains they solve more instances. The improvement is not huge, but is persistent among the different settings. The only exception is the *elevator* domain in PDDL, where the baseline is a bit faster than the other configurations. We also analyzed the average number of conflicts per domain and configuration, and the results follow the same trend as the solving times.

In the Multi shot solving experiment, the solver first looks for a plan of length 5. If the solver returns that there is no such plan, then it looks for a plan of length 10, and so on until it finds a plan. At each of these solver calls, we collect the best learned nogoods. Then, before the next solver call, we add the generalization of the best 500, 1000, or 1500 of them, depending on the configuration. In this case we rely on Theorem 4 and use the same translated encoding for learning and solving.

The results for PDDL and ASP are shown in Tables 3 and 4, respectively. For PDDL the baseline and the different configurations perform similarly, and we do not observe a clear trend. On the other hand, in the ASP benchmarks

Table 3. Multi shot solving of PDDL benchmarks.

		Baseline	500	1000	1500
Blocks	(20)	2.1 (0)	**2.0** (0)	2.2 (0)	2.3 (0)
Depots	(18)	266.8 (5)	212.7 (3)	248.0 (4)	**207.9** (3)
Driverlog	(9)	106.7 (1)	122.0 (1)	**105.3** (1)	125.7 (1)
Elevator	(20)	280.4 (5)	275.5 (5)	**249.1** (5)	257.7 (5)
Freecell	(16)	900.0 (16)	900.0 (16)	900.0 (16)	900.0 (16)
Grid	(2)	5.7 (0)	**4.0** (0)	4.2 (0)	4.4 (0)
Gripper	(17)	847.9 (16)	847.8 (16)	847.8 (16)	**847.4** (16)
Logistics	(20)	**135.2** (3)	137.5 (3)	137.5 (3)	137.5 (3)
Mystery	(14)	**321.8** (5)	**321.8** (5)	**321.8** (5)	**321.8** (5)
Total	(136)	348.9 (51)	342.3 (49)	342.0 (50)	**339.3** (49)

Table 4. Multi shot solving of ASP benchmarks.

		Baseline	500	1000	1500
HanoiTower	(20)	**536.7** (9)	651.7 (14)	880.4 (19)	827.9 (18)
Labyrinth	(20)	**647.6** (14)	647.8 (14)	647.9 (14)	647.8 (14)
Nomistery	(20)	**427.2** (8)	494.1 (10)	566.7 (11)	586.1 (12)
Ricochet Robots	(20)	527.3 (11)	**521.9** (11)	529.4 (11)	534.5 (11)
Sokoban	(20)	900.0 (20)	900.0 (20)	900.0 (20)	900.0 (20)
Visit-all	(20)	**678.5** (13)	900.0 (20)	900.0 (20)	900.0 (20)
Total	(120)	**619.5** (75)	685.9 (89)	737.4 (95)	732.7 (95)

the learning configurations perform worse than the baseline configuration. The analysis of the average number of conflicts shows similar results.

We expected similar results on the single shot and the multi shot solving experiments. However, this is not what we have observed. The learning configurations perform better than the baseline in the former, but worse in the latter. At the moment, we have found no clear explanation for these results, but we hope to make some progress in this regard in the future.

7   Conclusion

Conflict-driven constraint learning (CDCL) is the key to the success of modern ASP solvers. So far, however, ASP solvers could not exploit the temporal structure of dynamic problems. We addressed this by elaborating upon the generalization of learned constraints in ASP solving for temporal domains. We started with the definition of temporal logic programs and problems. For temporal programs that only refer to previous time steps within integrity constraints, we show that a simple modification of the temporal program is enough to generalize all learned constraints to all time points. This is no real restriction because any temporal program can be translated into this restricted format. Hence, once we apply both translations, we have a representation whose nogoods can always be generalized. Our experiments show mixed results. In some settings, the addition of the learned constraints results in a consistent improvement of performance, while in others the performance clearly deteriorates. We plan to continue this experimental investigation in the future. Another avenue of future work is to continue the approach sketched at the end of Sect. 4, and develop a dedicated implementation within an ASP solver based in Theorem 3.

Acknowledgments. This work was supported by DFG grant SCHA 550/15.

References

1. Aguado, F., Cabalar, P., Diéguez, M., Pérez, G., Vidal, C.: Temporal equilibrium logic: a survey. J. Appl. Non-Classical Logics **23**(1–2), 2–24 (2013). https://doi.org/10.1080/11663081.2013.798985
2. Audemard, G., Simon, L.: Predicting learnt clauses quality in modern SAT solvers. In: Boutilier, C. (ed.) Proceedings of the Twenty-first International Joint Conference on Artificial Intelligence (IJCAI 2009), pp. 399–404. AAAI/MIT Press (2009)
3. Cabalar, P., Diéguez, M., Hahn, S., Schaub, T.: Automata for dynamic answer set solving: preliminary report. In: Proceedings of the Fourteenth Workshop on Answer Set Programming and Other Computing Paradigms (ASPOCP 2021) (2021). http://ceur-ws.org/Vol-2970/aspocpinvited1.pdf
4. Comploi-Taupe, R., Weinzierl, A., Friedrich, G.: Conflict generalisation in asp: learning correct and effective non-ground constraints. Theory Pract. Logic Program. **20**, 799–814 (2020). https://doi.org/10.1017/S1471068420000368
5. Cuteri, B., Dodaro, C., Ricca, F., Schüller, P.: Overcoming the grounding bottleneck due to constraints in ASP solving: constraints become propagators. In: Bessiere, C. (ed.) Proceedings of the Twenty-Ninth International Joint Conference on Artificial Intelligence (IJCAI 2020), pp. 1688–1694. ijcai.org (2020)
6. Dimopoulos, Y., Gebser, M., Lühne, P., Romero, J., Schaub, T.: plasp 3: towards effective ASP planning. Theory Pract. Logic Program. **19**(3), 477–504 (2018)
7. Eén, N., Sörensson, N.: Temporal induction by incremental SAT solving. Electron. Notes Theor. Comput. Sci. **89**(4), 543–560 (2003)
8. Fandinno, J., Laferriere, F., Romero, J., Schaub, T., Son, T.: Planning with incomplete information in quantified answer set programming. Theory Pract. Logic Program. **21**(5), 663–679 (2021). https://doi.org/10.1017/S1471068421000259
9. Gebser, M., Kaminski, R., Kaufmann, B., Lühne, P., Romero, J., Schaub, T.: Answer set solving with generalized learned constraints. In: Carro, M., King, A. (eds.) Technical Communications of the Thirty-Second International Conference on Logic Programming (ICLP 2016). OpenAccess Series in Informatics (OASIcs), vol. 52, pp. 9:1–9:15. Schloss Dagstuhl-Leibniz-Zentrum fuer Informatik (2016)
10. Gebser, M., Kaminski, R., Kaufmann, B., Schaub, T.: Answer Set Solving in Practice. Synthesis Lectures on Artificial Intelligence and Machine Learning. Morgan and Claypool Publishers, San Rafael (2012)
11. Gebser, M., Kaufmann, B., Neumann, A., Schaub, T.: Conflict-driven answer set solving. In: Veloso, M. (ed.) Proceedings of the Twentieth International Joint Conference on Artificial Intelligence (IJCAI 2007), pp. 386–392. AAAI/MIT Press (2007)

12. Gelfond, M., Lifschitz, V.: The stable model semantics for logic programming. In: Kowalski, R., Bowen, K. (eds.) Proceedings of the Fifth International Conference and Symposium of Logic Programming (ICLP 1988), pp. 1070–1080. MIT Press (1988). https://doi.org/10.1201/b10397-6

13. Gelfond, M., Lifschitz, V.: Action languages. Electron. Transac. Artif. Intell. **3**(6), 193–210 (1998). http://www.ep.liu.se/ej/etai/1998/007/

14. Lefèvre, C., Béatrix, C., Stéphan, I., Garcia, L.: ASPeRiX, a first-order forward chaining approach for answer set computing. Theory Pract. Logic Program. **17**(3), 266–310 (2017)

15. Palù, A.D., Dovier, A., Pontelli, E., Rossi, G.: GASP: answer set programming with lazy grounding. Fund. Inform. **96**(3), 297–322 (2009)

16. Rintanen, J., Heljanko, K., Niemelä, I.: Planning as satisfiability: parallel plans and algorithms for plan search. Artif. Intell. **170**(12–13), 1031–1080 (2006)

17. Weinzierl, A., Taupe, R., Friedrich, G.: Advancing lazy-grounding ASP solving techniques – restarts, phase saving, heuristics, and more. Theory Pract. Logic Program. **20**(5), 609–624 (2020). http://arxiv.org/abs/2008.03526

The Stream Reasoning System *I-DLV-sr*: Enhancements and Applications in Smart Cities

Francesco Calimeri[1,2] , Elena Mastria[1(✉)] , Simona Perri[1] ,
and Jessica Zangari[1]

[1] Department of Mathematics and Computer Science,
University of Calabria, Rende, Italy
{francesco.calimeri,elena.mastria,simona.perri,
jessica.zangari}@unical.it
[2] DLVSystem Srl, Rende, Italy
calimeri@dlvsystem.com

Abstract. *I-DLV-sr* is a recently proposed logic-based system for reasoning over data streams, which relies on a framework enabling a tight, fine-tuned interaction between *Apache Flink* and the ASP system $\mathcal{I}^2$-*DLV*. Flink enables distributed stream processing, whereas $\mathcal{I}^2$-*DLV* acts as full-fledged reasoner capable of transparently performing incremental evaluations. In this paper, we present a new and optimized version of *I-DLV-sr* that features an improved management of parallel computations and communications between Flink and $\mathcal{I}^2$-*DLV*, along with new linguistic extensions aiming at allowing its effective application in smart city scenarios.

Keywords: Stream reasoning · Stream processing · Knowledge representation and reasoning · Answer set programming · Smart city · Applications

1 Introduction

A smart city [21,23] is a urban area in which data collected via modern digital technologies are strategically exploited to implement an efficient management of infrastructures, resources and services, with the aim of improving the life quality of residents. First visions of smart cities were basically static and infrastructure-centered (i,e., relying on installation and management of edge devices coupled with analytics over such data), thus leaning towards single-purpose, vertical solutions. Recently, more complex visions have been proposed based on rich

This work has been partially supported by the Italian MIUR Ministry and the Presidency of the Council of Ministers under the project "Declarative Reasoning over Streams" under the "PRIN" 2017 call (CUP *H*24*I*17000080001, project 2017M9C25L_001) and under Italian Ministry of Economic Development (MISE) under the PON project "MAP4ID - Multipurpose Analytics Platform 4 Industrial Data", N. F/190138/01-03/X44.

G. Governatori and A.-Y. Turhan (Eds.): RuleML+RR 2022, LNCS 13752, pp. 38–53, 2022.
https://doi.org/10.1007/978-3-031-21541-4_3

ensembles of physical, human and ICT infrastructures, and on a tight integration of research and technological solutions from different areas [12,15]; across such areas (e.g., Internet of Things, Social Computing, Artificial Intelligence, etc.), a crucial role is played by Stream Reasoning.

Stream Reasoning (SR) [13] consists in the application of inference techniques to highly dynamic and potentially heterogeneous data streams over typically large background knowledge bases. Recently, different SR approaches have been proposed such as those in the contexts of Complex Event Processing (CEP), Semantic Web and Knowledge Representation and Reasoning (KRR) [2,22,26, 27]. Among declarative KRR paradigms, Answer Set Programming (ASP) [7, 20] is acknowledged as a particularly attractive basis for SR [13]. Indeed, some important contributions towards ASP-based SR have been proposed, both for the definition of expressive languages and for the implementation of efficient and reliable systems [3,5,6,14,16,18,25,26,28].

In this respect, *I-DLV-sr* is a recently proposed ASP-based system for reasoning over data streams [10]; thanks to a proper integration with the well-established stream processor *Apache Flink* [11] and the incremental ASP reasoner $\mathcal{I}^2$-*DLV* [24], the system is able to efficiently scale over real-world application domains. It features an input language that inherits the highly declarative nature and ease of use from ASP, while being also extendable with new constructs that are relevant for practical SR scenarios. Since its first prototypical release, *I-DLV-sr* has been significantly improved. In particular, it has been deeply revised with the aim of improving stability, scalability and performance; furthermore, inspired by applications in the smart city domain, the supported language has been further extended with new constructs, that ease the modeling of reasoning tasks and enable new functionalities of practical relevance.

In this paper, we present the system, highlighting updates and novelties, and illustrating applicability in smart city contexts, both from modeling capabilities and performance perspectives. Moreover, we discuss performance improvements with respect to the prototypical version.

2   The *I-DLV-sr* System

I-DLV-sr relies on the tight integration of two well-established solutions in the fields of Stream Processing and ASP: a custom application leveraging on *Apache Flink*, a stream processor for efficiently managing data streams, and $\mathcal{I}^2$-*DLV*, an ASP grounder and a full-fledged deductive database system that enables incremental evaluation via overgrounding [9,24]. The input language inherits the declarative nature and ease of use of ASP; in particular, it consists in normal (i.e., non-disjunctive) stratified ASP programs, enriched with a set of proper constructs for enabling reasoning over streams. More in detail, *I-DLV-sr* programs feature, in the rule bodies, streaming literals. over the operators: *in, always, count, at least,* and *at most*; recursion involving streaming literals is allowed. We recall that, "standard" ASP literals are a special case of streaming literals. For space reasons, we briefly summarize next the main features of *I-DLV-sr*, relying on an example to illustrate its knowledge representation capabilities. Detailed descriptions of the full language and the incremental computational process are reported in the work presenting *I-DLV-sr* [10]; for more details on overgrounding, we refer the reader to the dedicated literature [9,24].

Example 1. [10] Suppose that we need to build an Intelligent Monitoring System (IMS) for a photo-voltaic system (PVS) to promptly detect malfunctions. Without going into technical details, for the sake of simplicity, let us suppose that the PVS is composed by a grid of interconnected panels via solar cables and each panel is provided with a sensor that measures the amount of energy produced and continuously sends data to the IMS. Each panel continuously produces energy to be transferred to a Central Energy Accumulator (CEA), directly or via a path between neighbor panels across the grid. Let us assume that a time point corresponds to a second. A panel is working if it is known to have produced an amount of energy greater than a given threshold within the last 4 s, and, in addition, if it is reachable by the CEA (i.e., there exists a path of working panels linking it to the CEA). If some unreachable working panels have been detected more than 2 times in the last 3 s, an alert must be raised for an identified malfunction. Furthermore, the IMS must request a maintenance intervention if the failure is continuously observed for 5 s. This scenario can be modeled via an *I-DLV-sr* program P_{pvs}, as reported next.

```
r₁ : workingPanel(P) :- energyThreshold(Et),
        energyDelivered(P,W) at least 1 in [4 sec], W>=Et.
r₂ : reachable(cea,P2) :- link(cea,P2), workingPanel(P2).
r₃ : reachable(P1,P3) :- reachable(P1,P2), link(P2,P3),
        workingPanel(P3).
r₄ : unlinked :- workingPanel(P), not reachable(cea,P).
r₅ : regularFunctioning :- unlinked at most 2 in [3 sec].
r₆ : alert :- not regularFunctioning.
r₇ : callMaintenance :- alert always in [5 sec].
```

The predicates `link` and `energyThreshold` represent the PVS configuration and the threshold defining a working panel; these data do not change. The predicate `energyDelivered` represents the amount of energy produced by each panel; at each time point, the current values are sent to the IMS, thus producing a stream. A panel is defined as working by rule r_1 if it has transmitted an amount of energy greater than the threshold at least once in the latest 4 s. r_2 and r_3 recursively define the set of reachable working panels starting from the CEA. r_4 detects if there are unlinked working panels and r_5 defines proper functioning by checking that the atom `unlinked` appeared no more than two times in the last 3 s. Eventually, r_6 raises up an alert if there is not a regular functioning and r_7 asks to call the maintenance if an alert has been raised in all the latest 5 s. □

Hereafter, we provide the reader with a high-level description of the computation workflow performed by *I-DLV-sr* when an input program P has to be evaluated over a data stream Σ. The program P is properly split in subprograms $P_1, \ldots, P_n$ (i.e., set of rules) taking into account dependencies among predicates appearing in streaming literals; such dependencies also induce an evaluation order among subprograms. To grasp the intuition behind predicate dependencies, let us consider again the program P_{pvs} of Example 1. In this case, given that rules are evaluated in a bottom-up way, three subprograms can be individuated: $\{r_1, r_2, r_3, r_4\}$, $\{r_5, r_6\}$, $\{r_7\}$. Intuitively, in order to fulfill the evaluation of r_1 and thus determine the set of working panels (i.e., via the `workingPanel` predicate), the streaming literal `energyDelivered(P,W)` **at least** 1 **in** [4 sec] needs to be evaluated first. Moreover, r_2, r_3 and r_4 are in cascade related to r_1 because their bodies feature the `workingPanel` predicate. It turns out that rules r_1, r_2, r_3 and r_4 require, either directly or indirectly, the evaluation of ener-gyDelivered(P,W) **at least** 1 **in** [4 sec]. Similarly, rules r_5 ad r_6 depends on `unlinked` **at most** 2 **in** [3 sec] and rule r_7 depends on `alert` **always in** [5 sec]; hence, the correct evaluation order is $\{r_1, r_2, r_3, r_4\}$, then $\{r_5, r_6\}$ and finally $\{r_7\}$.

Once subprograms are individuated, they undergo through a rewriting process. In particular, each P_i is rewritten by mapping each streaming literal to a standard ASP literal, thus obtaining a "flattened" version P_i'. At each time point, each $P_i \in P$ is evaluated according to the chosen evaluation order as described next. By making use of properly customised *Flink*-based features, the set L_i of the streaming literals appearing in P_i is evaluated on the basis of both Σ and the results of previous evaluations; this produces the set R_i consisting of ground instances of the standard ASP literals of P_i' that are related to streaming literals of L_i via the aforementioned mapping. Then, the flattened version P_i' is incrementally evaluated by an instance of $\mathcal{I}^2$-*DLV* over the set R_i. Notably, in case of recursion, a subprogram might be evaluated more times. Therefore, for the given time point t, the output of *I-DLV-sr* consists of the composition of the evaluation results of each subprogram P_i at t; continuous evaluations of P, time point by time point, form the output stream.

3   Re-engineering the System and Improving Performance

In this section, we overview how the system has been re-engineered for optimizing the computation; furthermore, we report about some experimental activities aimed at assessing the impact of such changes on performance.

The overall computational process performed by *I-DLV-sr* to evaluate a given input program over a data stream is designed in order to take advantage from both *Flink* parallel and distributed nature and $\mathcal{I}^2$-*DLV* incremental evaluation. According to the program splitting discussed in Sect. 2, *I-DLV-sr* identifies all the activities to be done to properly perform the computation; then, it defines multiple tasks to be executed in parallel, each one incorporating an ordered sequence of activities. Moreover, also the execution of activities in each task is possibly done in parallel via a number of threads. Note that, some activities (and hence, the involved tasks) depend on the results from others, requiring related threads to communicate and synchronize. Consequently, it turns out that a kind of trade-off between the granularity of tasks and the dependencies among them must be found. Indeed, the smaller are the tasks in terms of number of activities, the higher is their number and, consequently, the higher can be the overall level of inter-dependency among tasks. Such dependency level directly influences performance since the synchronization and communication among threads are expensive. In the first *I-DLV-sr* version, much effort was spent on designing strategies to define tasks at a finer granularity, in order to increase parallelism as much as possible. For the herein described re-engineered version, instead, we designed new strategies that induce tasks at a coarser granularity in some points, in order to reduce synchronization and communication duties. One of the main change in this respect regards the *watermark* management strategy, that is the assignment of a timestamp to each event[1].

Furthermore, the interplay between *Flink* and $\mathcal{I}^2$-*DLV* has been significantly improved. In the first *I-DLV-sr* version, different threads interact with a unique $\mathcal{I}^2$-*DLV* instance that represents a shared resource to be accessed in mutual exclusion in order to preserve semantics. The new version of the system uses instead a number of instances of $\mathcal{I}^2$-*DLV* that is greater or equal to the number of subprograms individuated (see Sect. 2). In particular, each thread in charge of executing the task relative to the evaluation of a subprogram has its own $\mathcal{I}^2$-*DLV* instance. Incrementality is still preserved but fruited at subprogram level rather than at program level. Indeed, every $\mathcal{I}^2$-*DLV* instance always considers the same subprogram over different inputs. The goal is again to reduce the synchronization duties among threads, as they can directly communicate with their own reasoner instance without waiting for others to finish.

3.1   Performance Evaluation

In order to assess the effectiveness of the introduced enhancements, we compared the previous version of *I-DLV-sr* with the new one over the *Photo-voltaic System* domain. The measures adopted are (*i*) `total time`, i.e., the total elapsed time for each execution, excepting the time spent for the initial set up; (*ii*) the processing-time latency (`latency` for short), i.e., the time interval between the moment the input relative to a time point is received and the moment when the system actually returns the corresponding output. For the sake of readability, the first version of the system is referred to as *I-DLV-sr-v1*, the second one as *I-DLV-sr-v2*. For this experimental evaluation, we propose the same settings and analyses conducted for evaluating performance of *I-DLV-sr-v1* in [10]. In particular, the encoding showed in Example 1 has been evaluated over problem instances composed by grids of increasing size ranging from 20×20 panels with $11,970$ links up to 30×30 panels with $60,682$ links. For each problem instance, the corresponding input data stream contains data for 60 time points. All experiments have been performed on a NUMA machine equipped with two 2.8 GHz AMD Opteron 6320 CPUs, with 16 cores and 128 GB of RAM.

---

[1] https://nightlies.apache.org/flink/flink-docs-stable/docs/dev/datastream/event-time/generating_watermarks.

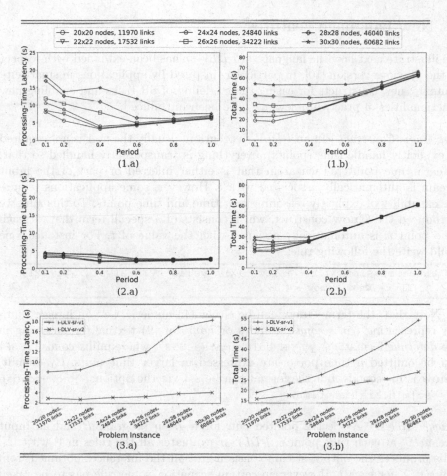

Fig. 1. Top and center plots: results of *I-DLV-sr-v1* and *I-DLV-sr-v2*, resp. Bottom plots: latency (left) and total time (right) for *I-DLV-sr-v1* and *I-DLV-sr-v2*, resp.

Results are reported in Fig. 1: the top plots ((1.a) and (1.b)) report `latency` and `total time` for *I-DLV-sr-v1*, while the center plots ((2.a) and (2.b)) report the same measures for *I-DLV-sr-v2*. Each of these four plots reports results over different fixed periods among consecutive incoming requests; the period ranges from 0.1 s to 1 s. Each line represents a problem instance, while a marker on a line corresponds to the average of the results of three executions for the given fixed period. The plots show that *I-DLV-sr-v2* clearly outperforms *I-DLV-sr-v1*; it enjoys a significant reduction of both `latency` (up to more than 300%) and `total time` (up to 80%). The bottom plots in Fig. 1 ((3.a) and (3.b)) show `latency` and `total time` of both versions when on the x-axis, instance size increases and the period is fixed to *0.1s*; here, it is evident that *I-DLV-sr-v2* scales much better than *I-DLV-sr-v1* thus confirming the positive impact of re-engineering and introduced enhancements.

4   New Language Features

We illustrate next how the language of *I-DLV-sr* has been extended with respect to the previous version [10]. In particular, inspired by applications in smart city contexts, new constructs for easing the modeling of SR tasks and enabling new functionalities of practical relevance have been introduced.

The @now Construct. In an *I-DLV-sr* program, usually the user is not required to explicitly handle time (points); everything is transparently handled so that, at each time point t, each atom that is either inferred or part of the input stream is automatically associated with t. However, some applications require the capability of explicitly reasoning over time and time points. To this aim, we introduced the **@now** construct, which consists of a special term that, at each time point t, is automatically assigned with the value of t. For instance, one could write the following rule:

```
grantPermission(X) :- allowed(X), validityInterval(X,T1,T2),
    T1 <= @now, @now <= T2.
```

Note that, the term **@now** can be either (1) numeric, i.e., an integer number representing t in *seconds*, *minutes* or *hours* or (2) textual, i.e., a string in the *datetime* format: `yyyy-MM-ddTHH:mm:ss.SSS` , where milliseconds (`.SSS`) can be omitted if time points are expressed in larger time units. By default, **@now** is in seconds, but the format can be set via the option: `--now-format = <sec|min|hrs|datetime>`.

Trigger Rules. As Sect. 2 pointed out, for a given program P and an input stream Σ, at each time point t, *I-DLV-sr* evaluates all the rules in P w.r.t. Σ. This produces the output stream consisting of all the inferences obtained from P w.r.t. Σ for each t. However, in certain scenarios, some rule has to be taken into account only with a given time frequency, rather than at each time point; to express this we endowed *I-DLV-sr* with a new form of rule, called *trigger rule*. A trigger rule is of the form:

$$\#\textbf{trigger\_frequency}(f) \ a\text{: -} \ l_1,\dots,l_b.$$

where f indicates the frequency according to which the rule has to be evaluated. The trigger frequency can be expressed in terms of milliseconds, seconds, minutes or hours, by simply indicating `msec`, `sec`, `min` and `hrs` respectively. For instance, the rule r_1 in the program below is a legitimate rule.

```
r₁ : #trigger_frequency(2 min)
        ok :- a(X), b(X) at least 2 in [1 min].
```

Let us assume that time points are expressed in minutes, and that the input stream is always featuring the atoms `b(1)` and `a(1)` at each time point. r_1 is a trigger rule, that will be processed only every 2 min and ignored in all other time points; hence, the trigger frequency impacts on both evaluation and performance, as it allows to explicitly avoid the evaluation in not involved time points. According to the presence of atoms matching with `a(X)` and `b(X)` in the input stream, r_1 allows to infer ok. Indeed, focusing on the first five time points for simplicity, the output stream will contain: $\{0 : \{\}, 1 : \{\}, 2 : \{\text{ok}\}, 3 : \{\}, 4 : \{\text{ok}\}\}$. If instead, **#trigger_frequency**(2 min) is omitted in r_1, then the output stream would be: $\{0 : \{\}, 1 : \{\text{ok}\}, 2 : \{\text{ok}\}, 3 : \{\text{ok}\}, 4 : \{\text{ok}\}\}$.

Variable Counting Terms. In the new version of *I-DLV-sr* herein discussed, some streaming literals have been further generalized. In particular, the counting term of the two operators *at least* and *at most* can now be either a constant or a variable; in the latter case, the variable must be safe. Note that, given a rule r, a variable is safe in r if it appears at least once in the positive body of r excluding the counting terms of other *at least* and *at most* operators. Recursion through predicates appearing in streaming literals with a variable as counting term is currently not allowed.

For instance, it is possible to write rules like the following one.

```
a(X)  :- currentThreshold(X,Y), b(X) at most Y in [10 sec].
```

Here, Y is safe, as it appears in the positive body literal currentThreshold(X,Y).

External Sources of Computation. *I-DLV-sr* now supports *external literals* [8] in rule bodies, that can be used to call external sources of computation via Python3. We recall that a *external atom* e is of the form $\&p(i_0, \ldots, i_n; o_0, \ldots, o_m)$ where $n, m \geq 0$, $\&p$ is a predicate name, $i_0, \ldots, i_n$ are input terms and $o_0, \ldots, o_m$ are output terms; input and output terms can be both constants or variables. An *external literal* is either e or **not** e. The semantics is externally defined via Python and output terms are computed based on input ones by applying such user-defined semantics. This construct is useful in scenarios where the reasoning tasks should also consider the results of domain-specific algorithms. Furthermore, it is worth noting that they allow to use all the Python features, thus paving the way to a number of interesting possibilities, such as the integration of Machine Learning solutions within deductive SR applications.

5   Stream Reasoning via *I-DLV-sr* in Smart City Scenarios

CityBench [1] is a benchmark designed to evaluate the usability of SR systems in real-world smart city scenarios. It has been conceived for RDF-based stream processors but brings a number of requirements and challenges that fit also to other kind of SR systems, such as the ASP-based ones. CityBench collects real-time data streams[2] coming from sensors spread along the city of Aarhus in Denmark. Furthermore, it features 13 continuous queries that require to reason on large background knowledge and dynamic data streams. More in details, the queries are envisioned in the context of the smart city applications described below.

---

[2] http://iot.ee.surrey.ac.uk:8080/datasets.html.

Multi-modal Context-aware Travel Planner: this application aims to find a set of alternative suitable paths based on user's preferences, travel cost and other factors, along with continuously monitored events that change over time (e.g., traffic, weather, etc.), so to provide the best up-to-date option in real time. Five queries are the part of this application and regard the traffic congestion level, the weather conditions, the travel time and the proximity of social events to the users, as they travel along the planned paths.

Parking Space Finder Application: this application aims to help the user finding a parking spot based on parking data streams and availability estimations. Four are the queries proposed in this application to identify what are the current parking conditions on places that are close to the user, its destination or some social event of interest.

Smart City Administration Console: this application aims to ease the identification of both anomalies and trends by the city administrators. Four are the queries proposed in this application to notify to the administrators on critical events related to pollution, weather and traffic congestion level, so that immediate actions can be applied in case of need.

Besides CityBench, another work based on the same Aarhus data streams has been recently proposed [17]: an approach based on Deep Neural Networks allows to perform high-speed query answering at the price of approximating results. It includes 5 queries in smart city scenarios, each focused on identifying the occurrence of special events in temporal windows by analyzing weather, parking, traffic and pollution data streams. As an example, one of the proposed query is: "In the last four timestamps, in which sectors an anomaly has been detected?", where an anomaly occurs in a sector in a given time window, if such sector is a city and it is classified as an industrial sector, together with two of its suburbs.

5.1   Modeling Smart City Applications with *I-DLV-sr*

In the following, we illustrate how some CityBench queries can be expressed via the *I-DLV-sr* language.

Query 5. Let us consider the query: "What is traffic congestion level on the road where a given cultural event X is happening? Notification for congestion level should be generated every minute starting from 10 min before the event X is planned to end, till 10 min after". We can model this query as follows.

```
r₁ : eventsToConsider(E):- eventOfInterest(E),
       eventDuration(E,StartTime,EndTime), CurrentTime=@now,
       CurrentTime>=EndTime-10, CurrentTime<=EndTime+10.
r₂ : closeRoads(RoadID) :- eventsToConsider(E),
       eventLocation(E,X2,Y2), roadLocation(RoadID,X1,Y1),
       &areClose(X1,Y1,X2,Y2;).
r₃ : congestionLevel(RoadID, CL):- closeRoads(RoadID),
       vehicleCount(RoadID,VC), distanceInMeters(RoadID,DM),
       &floatDivision(VC,DM;CL).
```

where `eventDuration`, `eventLocation`, `roadLocation`, `distanceInMeters` represent the background knowledge about cultural events and roads, i.e., the location of an event, the end time of an event, the start location of a road and the length of a road, respectively; `vehicleCount` represents the streaming information on the traffic state of the city roads; `&areClose` is an *external atom* holding if two positions are considered to be close to each other; and, `&floatDivision` is another external atom that performs the division between two integer numbers preserving the decimal part of the result[3]. In this program, r_1 filters the events that must be considered according to the query condition: it uses **@now** to identify the current time and determine if an event ended at most 10 min ago from now, or if it will end in 10 min from now. r_2 selects the roads close to the filtered social events. r_3 computes the congestion level on the selected roads based on the traffic information. Note that this encoding assumes times (i.e., those referred to as `StartTime` and `EndTime`) to be expressed in minutes, hence the `--now-format=min` command-line option is needed. Furthermore, since all the information required to determine if a location is exactly on a road is not available in the provided data set, we suppose an event being on a road if they are close. The semantics of the streaming external atoms used above, i.e., `&areClose` and `&floatDivision`, are defined via two Python functions, as reported below.

```
import haversine as hs
def areClose(Lat1, Lon1, Lat2, Lon2):
    loc1=(Lat1,Lon1)
    loc2=(Lat2,Lon2)
    return hs.haversine(loc1,loc2) <= 1
def floatDivision(VC,DM):
    CL=VC/DM
    return ":.3f".format(CL)
```

The `areClose` function makes use of the `haversine` Python package to determine the geographic distance between two locations, and considers them close if their distance is at most 1 km. The `floatDivision` function computes the division between two integers and returns a string containing the result with a three-digit precision. Notably, returning a string permits to keep the precision while still handling the division result in $\mathcal{I}^2\text{-}DLV$.

Query 10. Let us now consider the query "Notify me every 10 min, about the most polluted area in the city". We can model this problem according to the *European Air Quality Index (EAQI)*. As reported in Table 1, the EAQI is based on concentration values of five pollutants; each of which has six classification levels ranging form *Good* to *Extremely Poor*.

To determine the EAQI level of each pollutant measured in every road, we define a set of rules that straightforwardly encode Table 1, representing as integers the classification levels, from 0 (meaning *Good*) up to 5 (meaning *Extremely*

---

[3] The use of the external atom to compute the division is needed as floating points numbers are not supported yet, and native division among integers would only produce truncated integer results.

Table 1. European Air Quality Index levels as defined by the European Environment Agency: https://www.eea.europa.eu/themes/air/air-quality-index/index – Classification levels are based on pollutant concentrations in $\mu g/m^3$

Pollutant	Good	Fair	Moderate	Poor	Very poor	Extremely poor
Particles $\leq$ 2.5 μm (PM2.5)	0–10	10–20	20–25	25–50	50–75	75–800
Particles $\leq$ 10 μm (PM10)	0–20	20–40	40–50	50–100	100–150	150–1200
Nitrogen dioxide (NO2)	0–40	40–90	90–120	120–230	230–340	340–1000
Ozone (O3)	0–50	50–100	100–130	130–240	240–380	380–800
Sulphur dioxide (SO2)	0–100	100–200	200–350	350–500	500–750	750–1250

Poor). For instance, we encode the *Good* classification of the ozone ("O3") (row 4, column 1) with the rule:

```
roadPollutantLevel(RoadID, "O3", 0):-
    pollutionMeasurement(RoadID,O3,PM10,SO2,NO2), O3<50.
```

where `pollutionMeasurement` represents the streaming information about the air quality indexes of the pollutants measured in each road of the city.

Since pollution level of a road is given by the worst EAQI level measured in that road, r_1 determines the highest pollutant level for each road and r_2 finds the city areas whose pollution level is the maximum.

```
r₁ : #trigger_frequency(10 min) worstAirQualityLevel(Level):-
        #max{L: roadPollutantLevel(RoadID,P,L)}=Level.
r₂ : #trigger_frequency(10 min) mostPollutedArea(RID,P,L):-
        roadPollutantLevel(RID,P,L), worstAirQualityLevel(L).
```

Query 12. Let us consider the query: "Notify me whenever the congestion level on a given road goes beyond a predefined threshold more than 3 times within the last 20 min". We can model this query as follows.

```
r₁ : congestionLevel(RoadID, CL) :- roadOfInterest(RoadID),
        vehicleCount(RoadID,VC), distanceInMeters(RoadID,DM),
        &floatDivision(VC,DM;CL).
r₂ : beyondThreshold :- congestionLevel(_, CL), threshold(T),
        CL>T.
r₃ : warningBeyondThreshold :- minTimesTrigger(X),
        beyondThreshold at least X in [20 min].
```

where `roadOfInterest` specifies the identifier of the road for which notifications on congestion level must be produced; `vehicleCount` represents the streaming information about the number of vehicles currently passing on a road; `distanceInMeters` represents the length of a road; `&floatDivision` is the external atom introduced in Query 5 above; `threshold` contains the threshold that causes a notification to be produced, if the number of times specified via `minTimesTrigger` is exceeded.

In this program, r_1 computes the traffic congestion level on the road of inter-est; r_2 derives the event `beyondThreshold` if it goes beyond the specified thresh-old; r_3 arises a warning if the event `beyondThreshold` has been derived at least X times within the last time window of 20 min. Notice that the `threshold` and `minTimesTrigger` predicates are used to keep the encoding more generic. For instance, supposing that the threshold is 1, and that it must not be exceeded more than 3 times, the following facts can be used to model such information without any need for updates in the rules: `threshold(1)` and `minTimesTrig-ger(4)`.

5.2   Performance Evaluation

We discuss below the result of *I-DLV-sr v2* when tested over the two benchmarks introduced above [1,17], in the following referred to as *SmartCityDomain1* and *SmartCityDomain2*, respectively. All the proposed queries have been properly modeled using the *I-DLV-sr* input language; the encodings, along with the used input streams, are available at: https://demacs-unical.github.io/I-DLV-sr/. The experiments have been performed on a NUMA machine equipped with two 2.8 GHz AMD Opteron 6320 CPUs, with 16 cores and 128 GB of RAM.

Results are reported in Fig. 2. We tested *I-DLV-sr-v2* when receiving input events at each minute; hence, the red line indicates the time limit within which the system has to evaluate one time point before the next one arrives.

In detail, Fig. 2a depicts the results on the 13 queries of CityBench (*SmartC-ityDomain1*) reporting the average `latency` computed over all time points. The nature and the number of input events at each time point depend on the infor-mation related to the query. As an example, for queries $Q1$, $Q2$, $Q3$, $Q5$, $Q12$, and $Q13$, which concern traffic, information on about 100 roads is received: per each road, number of vehicles, average speed, average travel time and median travel time are given; additionally, for $Q2$, also information on weather condi-tions is received. As we can see, *I-DLV-sr-v2* is able to answer in less than 0.8 second in general, much before than events for the next time point arrive (i.e., 1 min)[4]. We also note that $Q11$ and $Q12$ represent the most complex queries as, differently from the others, they require to reason over wide windows of 10 and 20 min, respectively.

Figure 2b reports result on the 5 queries of *SmartCityDomain2*. The plot depicts how the `latency` (y-axis) varies over the time points (x-axis) per each query. The queries in this domain significantly differ from the ones in *SmartC-ityDomain1* as all of them make use of several windows, and these are often joined or temporally dependent. This requires, in general, a more complex rea-soning effort. The input stream features about 2,680 events per time point. We observe that *I-DLV-sr-v2* maintains the `latency` far below the red line for all the queries. For $Q2$ and $Q5$, that make use of less and smaller windows w.r.t.

---

[4] In the original papers [1,17] the minimum arriving frequency of input events for both benchmarks was set to 5 min; we purposely experimented with a higher frequency to test the system in more challenging conditions.

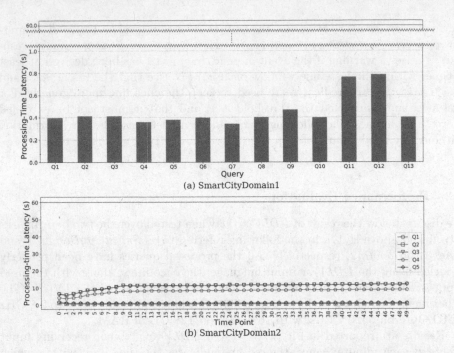

Fig. 2. Results on *SmartCityDomain1* [1] (top) and on *SmartCityDomain2* [17] (bottom).

the others (i.e., 3 and 4 min, respectively), `latency` is always less than 1 s for $Q2$ and 2 s for $Q5$. Higher latency times are registered for $Q1$, $Q3$ and $Q4$, with performance on $Q1$ and $Q3$ basically overlapping: these three queries make use of wider time windows (9 min), thus causing the system to reason on a considerably large amount of events at each time point. For $Q1$ and $Q3$, `latency` ranges from 5.7 to 12.1 s, whereas for $Q4$ from 3.8 to 8.9 s.

6 Related Work

In the latest years, SR gained more and more attention thanks also to real-world application scenarios such as smart city. Diverse proposals have been arising; however, the lack of standards makes the comparison among approaches relying on different formalisms and technologies rather difficult. Even considering proposals more related to *I-DLV-sr*, thus focusing on ASP-based SR solutions, the semantics differ and in turn, the final outcome may not coincide. Indeed, also competitions are still more geared towards "model and solve" rather than performance comparisons [29].

The main well-established ASP-based proposal is *LARS* (Logic for Analytic Reasoning over Streams [5]), a formal framework enriching ASP with temporal modalities and window operators. *LARS* implementations include *Laser* [3], *Ticker* [6], *Distributed-SR* [16] and *BigSR* [28]. All of them support practically relevant *LARS* fragments. *Laser* requires programs to be negation-stratified and stream-stratified, i.e., recursion is not supported if it involves either negation or temporal windows [4]. *Ticker* features two evaluation modes: one is intended for stratified programs admitting a single model and makes use of *clingo* [19] as back-end; the other uses incremental truth maintenance techniques under ASP semantics and, in case of multiple solutions, chooses to maintain just a model. *Distributed-SR* relies on *Ticker* and implements an interval-based semantics of *LARS* to support distributed computation, at the price of disabling the support for recursion through window operators. *BigSR* [28] is a distributed stream reasoner released in two implementations built on top of Spark Streaming and Flink, respectively. The input language features a limited set of window operators and does not include negation. In addition, depending on the stream processor, some limitations are posed. The version relying on Spark Streaming accepts stratified programs that can be recursive but have only global windows. The version built on top of *Flink*, instead, accepts non-recursive stratified programs, but with global windows at rule scope.

I-DLV-sr supports the ASP fragment stratified w.r.t. negation, which is extended with streaming literals over temporal intervals; recursion involving streaming literals is also allowed. Semantics of the supported language, reflected in the computational process, has been conceived to guarantee sound and complete models. The implementation takes advantage of incremental evaluations, thanks to $\mathcal{I}^2$-*DLV*, and parallel/distributed computations, thanks to *Flink*.

7   Conclusions

In this work, we described how the *I-DLV-sr* system has been improved both in performance and linguistic features. First, we described how the implementation has been re-engineered by limiting synchronization to improve benefits stemming from parallel computations. Experiments confirmed that a better scalability has been achieved w.r.t. the first prototypical version released. Second, we presented new constructs, inspired by smart city contexts, that extend the modeling capabilities of *I-DLV-sr*. Eventually, we conducted an experimental analysis on challenging and publicly available benchmarks from the smart city domain, in order to asses *I-DLV-sr* applicability and performance. In the future, we plan to study means to extend the language to deal with disjunction to some extent, and further move towards a more expressive SR reasoner [13].

References

1. Ali, M.I., Gao, F., Mileo, A.: CityBench: a configurable benchmark to evaluate RSP engines using smart city datasets. In: Arenas, M., et al. (eds.) ISWC 2015. LNCS, vol. 9367, pp. 374–389. Springer, Cham (2015). https://doi.org/10.1007/978-3-319-25010-6_25
2. Barbieri, D.F., Braga, D., Ceri, S., Valle, E.D., Grossniklaus, M.: C-SPARQL: a continuous query language for RDF data streams. Int. J. Semantic Comput. 4(1), 3–25 (2010)

3. Bazoobandi, H.R., Beck, H., Urbani, J.: Expressive stream reasoning with laser. In: d'Amato, C., et al. (eds.) ISWC 2017. LNCS, vol. 10587, pp. 87–103. Springer, Cham (2017). https://doi.org/10.1007/978-3-319-68288-4_6

4. Beck, H., Dao-Tran, M., Eiter, T.: Answer update for rule-based stream reasoning. In: IJCAI, pp. 2741–2747. AAAI Press (2015)

5. Beck, H., Dao-Tran, M., Eiter, T.: LARS: a logic-based framework for analytic reasoning over streams. Artif. Intell. **261**, 16–70 (2018)

6. Beck, H., Dao-Tran, M., Eiter, T., Folie, C.: Stream reasoning with LARS. Künstliche Intell. **32**(2–3), 193–195 (2018)

7. Brewka, G., Eiter, T., Truszczynski, M.: Answer set programming at a glance. Commun. ACM **54**(12), 92–103 (2011)

8. Calimeri, F., Fuscà, D., Perri, S., Zangari, J.: External computations and interoperability in the new DLV grounder. In: Esposito, F., Basili, R., Ferilli, S., Lisi, F. (eds.) AI*IA 2017, vol. 10640, pp. 172–185. Springer, Cham (2017). https://doi.org/10.1007/978-3-319-70169-1_13

9. Calimeri, F., Ianni, G., Pacenza, F., Perri, S., Zangari, J.: Incremental answer set programming with overgrounding. TPLP **19**(5–6), 957–973 (2019)

10. Calimeri, F., Manna, M., Mastria, E., Morelli, M.C., Perri, S., Zangari, J.: I-DLV-sr: a stream reasoning system based on I-DLV. TPLP **21**(5), 610–628 (2021)

11. Carbone, P., Katsifodimos, A., Ewen, S., Markl, V., Haridi, S., Tzoumas, K.: Apache flink™: stream and batch processing in a single engine. IEEE Data Eng. Bull. **38**(4), 28–38 (2015)

12. D'Aniello, G., Gaeta, M., Orciuoli, F.: An approach based on semantic stream reasoning to support decision processes in smart cities. Telemat. Inform. **35**(1), 68–81 (2018)

13. Dell'Aglio, D., Valle, E.D., van Harmelen, F., Bernstein, A.: Stream reasoning: a survey and outlook. Data Sci. **1**(1–2), 59–83 (2017)

14. Do, T.M., Loke, S.W., Liu, F.: Answer set programming for stream reasoning. In: Butz, C., Lingras, P. (eds.) AI 2011. LNCS (LNAI), vol. 6657, pp. 104–109. Springer, Heidelberg (2011). https://doi.org/10.1007/978-3-642-21043-3_13

15. Dustdar, S., Nastic, S., Scekic, O.: Smart Cities - The Internet of Things, People and Systems. Springer, Cham (2017). https://doi.org/10.1007/978-3-319-60030-7

16. Eiter, T., Ogris, P., Schekotihin, K.: A distributed approach to LARS stream reasoning (system paper). TPLP **19**(5–6), 974–989 (2019)

17. Ferreira, J., Lavado, D., Gonçalves, R., Knorr, M., Krippahl, L., Leite, J.: Faster than LASER - towards stream reasoning with deep neural networks. In: Marreiros, G., Melo, F.S., Lau, N., Lopes Cardoso, H., Reis, L.P. (eds.) EPIA 2021. LNCS (LNAI), vol. 12981, pp. 363–375. Springer, Cham (2021). https://doi.org/10.1007/978-3-030-86230-5_29

18. Gebser, M., Grote, T., Kaminski, R., Schaub, T.: Reactive answer set programming. In: Delgrande, J.P., Faber, W. (eds.) LPNMR 2011. LNCS (LNAI), vol. 6645, pp. 54–66. Springer, Heidelberg (2011). https://doi.org/10.1007/978-3-642-20895-9_7

19. Gebser, M., Kaminski, R., Kaufmann, B., Schaub, T.: Multi-shot ASP solving with clingo. TPLP **19**(1), 27–82 (2019)

20. Gebser, M., Leone, N., Maratea, M., Perri, S., Ricca, F., Schaub, T.: Evaluation techniques and systems for answer set programming: a survey. In: IJCAI, pp. 5450–5456. ijcai.org (2018)

21. Hall, R.E., Bowerman, B., Braverman, J., Taylor, J., Todosow, H., Von Wimmersperg, U.: The vision of a smart city. Technical report, Brookhaven National Laboratory (BNL), Upton, NY (United States) (2000)

22. Hoeksema, J., Kotoulas, S.: High-performance distributed stream reasoning using S4. In: Ordring Workshop at ISWC (2011)
23. Hollands, R.G.: Will the real smart city please stand up? City **12**(3), 303–320 (2008)
24. Ianni, G., Pacenza, F., Zangari, J.: Incremental maintenance of overgrounded logic programs with tailored simplifications. TPLP **20**(5), 719–734 (2020)
25. Mileo, A., Abdelrahman, A., Policarpio, S., Hauswirth, M.: StreamRule: a non-monotonic stream reasoning system for the semantic web. In: Faber, W., Lembo, D. (eds.) RR 2013. LNCS, vol. 7994, pp. 247–252. Springer, Heidelberg (2013). https://doi.org/10.1007/978-3-642-39666-3_23
26. Pham, T., Ali, M.I., Mileo, A.: C-ASP: continuous asp-based reasoning over RDF streams. In: Balduccini, M., Lierler, Y., Woltran, S. (eds.) LPNMR 2019. LNCS, vol. 11481, pp. 45–50. Springer, Cham (2019). https://doi.org/10.1007/978-3-030-20528-7_4
27. Le-Phuoc, D., Dao-Tran, M., Xavier Parreira, J., Hauswirth, M.: A native and adaptive approach for unified processing of linked streams and linked data. In: Aroyo, L., et al. (eds.) ISWC 2011. LNCS, vol. 7031, pp. 370–388. Springer, Heidelberg (2011). https://doi.org/10.1007/978-3-642-25073-6_24
28. Ren, X., Curé, O., Naacke, H., Xiao, G.: BigSR: real-time expressive RDF stream reasoning on modern big data platforms. In: IEEE BigData, pp. 811–820. IEEE (2018)
29. Schneider, P., Alvarez-Coello, D., Le-Tuan, A., Duc, M.N., Phuoc, D.L.: Stream reasoning playground. In: Groth, P., et al. (eds.) ESWC 2022. LNCS, vol. 13261, pp. 406–424. Springer, Cham (2022). https://doi.org/10.1007/978-3-031-06981-9_24

Plingo: A System for Probabilistic Reasoning in Clingo Based on LP^{MLN}

Susana Hahn[1], Tomi Janhunen[2], Roland Kaminski[1], Javier Romero[1], Nicolas Rühling[1], and Torsten Schaub[1(✉)]

[1] University of Potsdam, Potsdam, Germany
torsten@cs.uni-potsdam.de
[2] University of Tampere, Tampere, Finland

Abstract. We present *plingo*, an extension of the ASP system *clingo* with various probabilistic reasoning modes. *Plingo* is centered upon LP^{MLN}, a probabilistic extension of ASP based on a weight scheme from Markov Logic. This choice is motivated by the fact that the core probabilistic reasoning modes can be mapped onto optimization problems and that LP^{MLN} may serve as a middle-ground formalism connecting to other probabilistic approaches. As a result, *plingo* offers three alternative frontends, for LP^{MLN}, *P-log*, and *ProbLog*. The corresponding input languages and reasoning modes are implemented by means of *clingo*'s multi-shot and theory solving capabilities. The core of *plingo* amounts to a re-implementation of LP^{MLN} in terms of modern ASP technology, extended by an approximation technique based on a new method for answer set enumeration in the order of optimality. We evaluate *plingo*'s performance empirically by comparing it to other probabilistic systems.

Keywords: Answer set programming · Probabilistic reasoning

1 Introduction

Answer Set Programming (ASP; [13]) offers a rich knowledge representation language along with powerful solving technology. In the last years, several probabilisitic extensions of ASP have been proposed, among them LP^{MLN} [10], *ProbLog* [15], and *P-log* [3].

In this work, we present an extension of the ASP system *clingo*, called *plingo*, that features various probabilistic reasoning modes. *Plingo* is centered on LP^{MLN}, a probabilistic extension of ASP based upon a weight scheme from Markov Logic [16]. LP^{MLN} has already proven to be useful in several settings [1,11] and it serves us also as a middle-ground formalism connecting to other probabilistic approaches. We rely on translations from *ProbLog* and *P-log* to LP^{MLN} [10,12], respectively, to capture these approaches as well. In fact, LP^{MLN} has already been implemented in the system *lpmln2asp* [9] by mapping LP^{MLN}-based reasoning into reasoning modes in *clingo* (viz. optimiza-

© The Author(s), under exclusive license to Springer Nature Switzerland AG 2022
G. Governatori and A.-Y. Turhan (Eds.): RuleML+RR 2022, LNCS 13752, pp. 54–62, 2022.
https://doi.org/10.1007/978-3-031-21541-4_4

tion and enumeration of stable models). As such, *plingo* can be seen as a re-implementation of *lpmln2asp* that is well integrated with *clingo* by using its multi-shot and theory reasoning functionalities.

In more detail, the language of *plingo* constitutes a subset of LP^{MLN} restricting the form of weight rules while being extended with ASP's regular weak constraints. This restriction allows us to partition logic programs into two independent parts: A *hard* part generating optimal stable models and a *soft* part determining the probabilities of these optimal stable models. Arguably, this separation yields a simpler semantics that leads in turn to an easier way of modeling probabilistic logic programs. Nonetheless, it turns out that this variant is still general enough to capture full LP^{MLN}. Moreover, *plingo* allows us to capture such probabilistic programs within the input language of *clingo*. The idea is to describe the hard part in terms of normal rules and weak constraints at priority levels different from 0, and the soft part via weak constraints at priority level 0.[1] On top of this, *plingo* offers three alternative frontends, for LP^{MLN}, *P-log*, and *ProbLog*, featuring dedicated language constructs that are in turn translated into the format described above. As regards solving, *plingo* follows the approach of *lpmln2asp* of reducing probabilistic reasoning to *clingo*'s regular optimization and enumeration modes. In addition, *plingo* features an approximation method that calculates probabilities using only the most probable k stable models for an input parameter k. This is accomplished by an improved implementation of answer set enumeration in the order of optimality [14]. We have empirically evaluated *plingo*'s performance by contrasting it to original implementations of LP^{MLN}, *ProbLog* and *P-log*. For reasons of space, we have left the description of the frontends and part of the discussion of the experiments to an extended version of this paper, available at https://arxiv.org/abs/2206.11515.

2 Background

In our setting, a *logic program* is a set of propositional formulas. A *logic program with weak constraints* is a set $\Pi_1 \cup \Pi_2$ where Π_1 is a logic program and Π_2 is a set of weak constraints of the form $:\sim F[w, l]$ where F is a formula, w is a real number, and l is a nonnegative integer. For the definition of the *stable models* of a logic program, possibly with weak constraints, we refer the reader to [4, 6]. We denote by $SM(\Pi)$ the set of stable models of a logic program Π.

We next review the definition of LP^{MLN} from [10], focusing on the *alternative* semantics presented there. An LP^{MLN} program Π is a finite set of weighted formulas $w : F$ where F is a propositional formula and w is either a real number (in which case, the weighted formula is called soft) or α for denoting the infinite weight (in which case, the weighted formula is called hard). If Π is an LP^{MLN} program, by Π^{soft} and Π^{hard} we denote the set of soft and hard formulas of Π, respectively. For any LP^{MLN} program Π and any set X of atoms, $\overline{\Pi}$ denotes the set of (unweighted) formulas obtained from Π by dropping the weights, and

---

[1] This fits well with the semantics of *clingo*, where higher priority levels are more important.

Π_X denotes the set of weighted formulas $w : F$ in Π such that $X \models F$. Given an LP^{MLN} program Π, $SSM(\Pi)$ denotes the set of *soft stable models* $\{X \mid X$ is a (standard) stable model of $\overline{\Pi_X}$ that satisfies $\overline{\Pi^{hard}}\}$, The *total weight* of Π, written $TW(\Pi)$, is defined as $exp(\sum_{w:F \in \Pi} w)$. The *weight* $W_\Pi(X)$ of an interpretation and its *probability* $P_\Pi(X)$ are defined, respectively, as

$$W_\Pi(X) = \begin{cases} TW(\Pi_X^{soft}) & \text{if } X \in SSM(\Pi) \\ 0 & \text{otherwise} \end{cases} \text{ and } P_\Pi(X) = \frac{W_\Pi(X)}{\sum_{Y \in SSM(\Pi)} W_\Pi(Y)}.$$

An interpretation X is called a *probabilistic stable model* of Π if $P_\Pi(X) \neq 0$. Note that the set $SSM(\Pi)$ may be empty if there is no soft stable model that satisfies all hard formulas of Π, in which case $P_\Pi(X)$ is not defined. On the other hand, if $SSM(\Pi)$ is not empty, then the probabilities assigned to each interpretation by this alternative semantics and the standard semantics from [10] coincide (cf. Proposition 2 of that paper).

3 $LP^{MLN\pm}$ and the Language of *Plingo*

$LP^{MLN\pm}$ programs are based on LP^{MLN} programs under the alternative semantics. On the one hand, they are a subset of LP^{MLN} programs where the soft formulas are so-called *soft integrity constraints* of the form $w : \neg F$, for some propositional formula F. This restriction is attractive because it allows us to provide a definition of the semantics that is arguably very simple and intuitive. Interestingly, the translations from *ProbLog* and *P-log* [10,12] fall into this fragment of LP^{MLN}. Recall that in ASP, integrity constraints of the form $\neg F$ do not affect the generation of stable models, but they can only eliminate some of the stable models generated by the rest of the program. In LP^{MLN}, soft integrity constraints parallel that role, since they do not affect the generation of *soft* stable models, but they can only affect the probabilistic weights of the *soft* stable models generated by the rest of the program. More precisely, it holds that the soft models of an LP^{MLN} program Π remain the same if we delete from Π all its soft integrity constraints. This observation leads us to the following proposition.

Proposition 1. *If Π is an LP^{MLN} program such that Π^{soft} contains only soft integrity constraints, then $SSM(\Pi) = SM(\overline{\Pi^{hard}})$.*

This allows us to leave aside the notion of soft stable models and simply replace in $W_\Pi(X)$ and $P_\Pi(X)$ the set $SSM(\Pi)$ by $SM(\overline{\Pi^{hard}})$. From this perspective, an LP^{MLN} program of this restricted form has two separated parts: Π^{hard}, that generates stable models; and Π^{soft}, that determines the weights of the stable models, from which their probabilities can be calculated.

On the other hand, $LP^{MLN\pm}$ extends LP^{MLN} with regular ASP's weak constraints. This is a natural extension that moreover allows us to capture the whole

LP^{MLN} language under both the alternative and the standard semantics (see footnote 2).

With this, we can define the syntax and semantics of $LP^{MLN\pm}$ programs. Formally, an $LP^{MLN\pm}$ program Π is a set of hard rules, soft integrity constraints, and weak constraints, denoted respectively by Π^{hard}, Π^{soft} and Π^{weak}. By $OSM^+(\Pi)$ we denote the optimal stable models of $\overline{\Pi^{hard}} \cup \Pi^{weak}$. Then, the *weight* and the *probability* of an interpretation X, written $W_\Pi^\pm(X)$ and $P_\Pi^\pm(X)$, respectively, are the same as $W_\Pi(X)$ and $P_\Pi(X)$, but replacing the set $SSM(\Pi)$ by $OSM^\pm(\Pi)$:

$$W_\Pi^\pm(X) = \begin{cases} TW(\Pi_X^{soft}) & \text{if } X \in OSM^\pm(\Pi) \\ 0 & \text{otherwise} \end{cases} \text{ and } P_\Pi^\pm(X) = \frac{W_\Pi^\pm(X)}{\sum\limits_{Y \in OSM^\pm(\Pi)} W_\Pi^\pm(Y)}.$$

Note that, as before, $OSM^\pm(\Pi)$ may be empty, in which case $P_\Pi^\pm(X)$ is not defined.

We can capture LP^{MLN} by $LP^{MLN\pm}$ programs using a translation that is based on the translation *lpmln2wc* from [12]. Given an LP^{MLN} program Π under the alternative semantics, by Π^* we denote the $LP^{MLN\pm}$ program that contains the hard formulas $\{\alpha : F \mid w : F \in \Pi, w = \alpha\}$ joined with $\{\alpha : F \vee \neg F \mid w : F \in \Pi, w \neq \alpha\}$, as well as the soft formulas $\{w : \neg\neg F \mid w : F \in \Pi, w \neq \alpha\}$. The hard formulas generate the soft stable models of Π, while the soft rules attach the right weight to each of them, without interfering with their generation.[2]

Proposition 2. *Let Π be an LP^{MLN} program. For every interpretation X, it holds that $P_\Pi(X) = P_{\Pi^*}^\pm(X)$.*

We can move on now to the implementation of $LP^{MLN\pm}$ in *plingo*. The main idea of the system is to keep the input language of *clingo*, and re-interpret weak constraints at priority level 0 as soft integrity constraints. These constraints are not considered to determine the optimal stable models, but instead are used to determine the weights of those models, from which their probabilities are calculated. For propositional formulas, this boils down to interpreting the union of a set Π_1 of propositional formulas with a set Π_2 of weak constraints as the $LP^{MLN\pm}$ program that contains the hard rules $\{\alpha : F \mid F \in \Pi_1\}$, the soft integrity constraints $\{w : \neg\neg F \mid :\sim F[w,0] \in \Pi_2\}$, and the weak constraints $\Pi_2 \setminus \{:\sim F[w,0] \mid :\sim F[w,0] \in \Pi_2\}$. For programs in the input language of *plingo* (or of *clingo*, that is the same) we can in fact provide a general definition that relies on the definitions used for *clingo* [5], and that therefore covers its whole language. We define a *plingo* program Π as a logic program in the language of *clingo*, and we let $OSM^{pl}(\Pi)$ denote the optimal models of Π without considering weak

---

[2] We can capture the *standard* semantics by replacing the two sets of hard formulas by the hard formulas $\{\alpha : F \vee \neg F \mid w : F \in \Pi\}$, and adding the weak constraints $\{:\sim F[-1,1] \mid w : F \in \Pi, w = \alpha\}$. In this case, the hard formulas guess whether or not to satisfy *each* formula occurring in Π, and the weak constraints select the stable models that satisfy most of the hard rules of Π.

constraints at level 0, and $Cost_\Pi(X, 0)$ denote the cost of the interpretation X at priority level 0, according to the definitions of [5]. Then, the *weight* $W_\Pi^{pl}(X)$ of an interpretation X and its *probability* $P_\Pi^{pl}(X)$ are defined as:

$$W_\Pi^{pl}(X) = \begin{cases} exp(Cost_\Pi(X, 0)) & \text{if } X \in OSM^{pl}(\Pi) \\ 0 & \text{otherwise} \end{cases}$$

and

$$P_\Pi^{pl}(X) = \frac{W_\Pi^{pl}(X)}{\displaystyle\sum_{Y \in OSM^{pl}(\Pi)} W_\Pi^{pl}(Y)}.$$

4 The System *Plingo*

The implementation of *plingo* is based on *clingo* and its Python API (v5.5, [8]). The system architecture is described in Fig. 1. The input is a logic program written in some probabilistic language: $LP^{MLN\pm}$, LP^{MLN}, *ProbLog* or *P-log*. For $LP^{MLN\pm}$, the input language (orange element of Fig. 1) is the same as the input language of *clingo*, except for the fact that the weights of the weak constraints can be strings representing real numbers. For the other languages, the system uses the corresponding frontends, that translate the input logic programs (yellow elements of Fig. 1) to the input language of *plingo* using the transformer module, combining the translations from *ProbLog* and *P-log* to LP^{MLN} of [10, 12] with the translation to $LP^{MLN\pm}$ presented in Sect. 3.

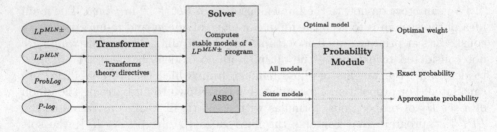

Fig. 1. System architecture of *plingo*. Inputs are yellow for the different frontends provided. Modules of the system are gray boxes. The green flow corresponds to MAP inference, the blue to exact marginal inference, and the purple to approximate marginal inference. (Color figure online)

Plingo can be used to solve two reasoning tasks: maximum a posteriori (MAP) inference and marginal inference. MAP inference is the task of finding a most probable stable model of a probabilistic logic program. Following the approach of [9], this task is reduced in *plingo* to finding one optimal stable model of the input program using *clingo*'s built-in optimization methods. The only changes that have to be made concern handling the strings that may occur as weights of weak constraints, and switching the sign of such weights, since otherwise *clingo* would compute the least probable stable models. Regarding marginal inference, it can be either applied in general, or with respect to a query. In the first case, the task is to find all stable models and their probabilities. In the second case, the task is to find the probability of some query atom, that is defined as the sum of the probabilities of the stable models that contain that atom. The implementation for both cases is the same. First, *plingo* enumerates all optimal stable models of the input program excluding the weak constraints at level 0. Afterwards, those optimal stable models are passed, together with their cost at level 0, to the probability module, that calculates the required probabilities.

In addition to this exact method (represented by the blue arrows in Fig. 1), *plingo* implements an approximation method (purple arrows in Fig. 1) based on the approach presented in [14]. The idea is to simplify the solving process by computing just a subset of the stable models, and using this smaller set to approximate the actual probabilities. Formally, in the definitions of $W_\Pi^{pl}(X)$ and $P_\Pi^{pl}(X)$, this implies replacing the set $OSM^{pl}(\Pi)$ by one of its subsets. In the implementation, the modularity of this change is reflected by the fact that the probability module is agnostic to whether the stable models that it receives as input are all or just some subset of them. For marginal inference in general, this smaller subset consists of k stable models with the highest possible probability, given some positive integer k that is part of the input. To compute this subset, the solver module of *plingo* uses a new implementation for the task of answer set enumeration in the order of optimality (ASEO) presented in [14].[3] Given some positive integer k, the implementation first computes the stable models of the smallest cost, then, among the remaining stable models, computes the ones of the smallest cost, and so on until k stable models (if they exist) have been computed. For marginal inference with respect to a query, the smaller subset consists of k stable models containing the query of the highest possible probability, and another k stable models without the query of the highest possible probability. In this case, the algorithm for ASEO is set to compute $2k$ stable models. But once it has computed k stable models that contain the query, or k stable models that do not contain the query, whichever happens first, it adds a constraint enforcing that the remaining stable models fall into the opposite case.

5   Experiments

In this section, we experimentally evaluate *plingo* and compare it to native implementations of LP^{MLN}, *ProbLog* and *P-log*.[4] For LP^{MLN}, we evaluate the system *lpmln2asp* [9], that is the basis for our implementation of *plingo*. For *ProbLog*, we consider the *problog* system version 2.1 [7], that implements various methods for

---

[3] The implementation of the method for *clingo* in general is available at https://github.com/potassco/clingo/tree/master/examples/clingo/opt-enum.

[4] Available, respectively, at https://github.com/azreasoners/lpmln, https://github.com/ML-KULeuven/problog, and https://github.com/iensen/plog2.0.

probabilistic reasoning. In the experiments, we use one of those methods, that is designed specifically to answer probabilistic queries. It converts the input program to a weighted Boolean formula 'and then applies a knowledge compilation method for weighted model counting. For *P-log*, we evaluate two implementations, that we call *plog-naive* and *plog-dco* [2]. While the former works like *plingo* and *lpmln2asp* by enumerating stable models, the latter implements a different algorithm that builds a computation tree specific to the input query. All benchmarks were run on an Intel Xeon E5-2650v4 under Debian GNU/Linux 10, with 24 GB of memory and a timeout of 1200 seconds per instance.

The goal of our first experiment is to evaluate the performance of the exact and the approximation methods of *plingo* and compare it to the performance of all the other systems on the same domain. In particular, we want to analyze how much faster is the approximation method than the exact one, and how accurate are the probabilities that it returns. To this end, we compare all systems on the task of marginal inference with respect to a query in a probabilistic Grid domain from [17], that appeared in a slightly different form in [7]. We have chosen this domain because it can be easily and similarly represented in all these probabilistic languages, which is required if we want to compare all systems at the same time. In this domain, there is a grid of size $m \times n$, where each node (i, j) passes information to the nodes $(i + 1, j)$ and $(i, j + 1)$ if (i, j) is not faulty, and each node in the grid can be faulty with probability 0.1. The task poses the following question: what is the probability that node (m, n) receives information from node $(1, 1)$? To answer this, we run exact marginal inference with all systems, and approximate marginal inference with *plingo* for different values of k: 10^1, 10^2, ..., and 10^6. The results are shown in Fig. 2. On the left side, there is a cactus plot representing how many instances where solved within a given runtime. The dashed lines represent the runtimes of the approximate marginal inference of *plingo* for $k = 10^5$ and $k = 10^6$. Among the exact implementations, the system *problog* is the clear winner. In this case, its specific algorithm for answering queries is much faster than the other exact systems that either have to enumerate all stable models or, in the case of *plog-dco*, may have to explore its whole solution tree. The runtimes among the rest of the exact systems are comparable, but *plingo* is a bit faster than the others. For the approximation method, on the right side of Fig. 2, for every value of k and every instance, there is a dot whose coordinates represent the probability calculated by the approximation method and the true probability (calculated by *problog*). This is complemented by Table 1, that shows the average absolute error and the maximal absolute error for each value of k in %, where the absolute error for some instance and some k in % is defined as the absolute value of the difference between the calculated probability and the true probability for that instance, multiplied by 100. We can see that, as the value of k increases, the performance of the approximation method deteriorates, while the quality of the approximated probabilities increases. A good compromise is found for $k = 10^5$, where the runtime is better than *problog*, and the average error is below 1%.

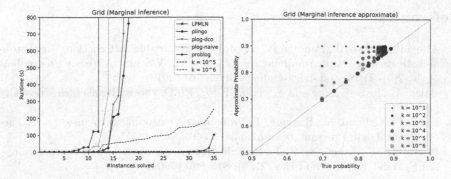

Fig. 2. Runtimes of all systems and quality of the approximation method on the Grid domain.

Table 1. Average and maximal error (in %) of the approximation method on the Grid domain for different values of k.

k	10^1	10^2	10^3	10^4	10^5	10^6
Avg. Error	4.7 ± 4.3	3.3 ± 2.7	2.1 ± 1.5	1.4 ± 1.2	0.9 ± 0.9	0.6 ± 0.8
Max. Error	20.3	12.7	6.5	4.3	2.5	2.3

We carried out another two experiments, where we compared separately *plingo* using the LP^{MLN} frontend with *lpmln2asp*, and *plingo* using the *P-log* frontend with the two native implementations of *P-log*, on domains that are specific to these languages. In general, the results show that the performance of *plingo* is similar to the performance of those systems. For a more detailed description of these experiments, we refer the reader to the longer version of this paper, available at https://arxiv.org/abs/2206.11515.

6   Conclusion

We have presented *plingo*, an extension of the ASP system *clingo* with various probabilistic reasoning modes. Although based on LP^{MLN}, it also supports *P-log* and *ProbLog*. While the basic syntax of *plingo* is the same as the one of *clingo*, its semantics relies on re-interpreting the cost of a stable model at priority level 0 as a measure of its probability. Solving exploits the relation between most probable stable models and optimal stable models [12]; it relies on *clingo*'s optimization and enumeration modes, as well as an approximation method based on answer set enumeration in the order of optimality [14]. Our empirical evaluation has shown that *plingo* is at eye height with other ASP-based probabilistic systems, except for *problog* that relies on well-founded semantics. Notably, the approximation method produced low runtimes and low error rates (below 1%). *Plingo* is freely available at https://github.com/potassco/plingo.

Acknowledgements. This work was supported by DFG grant SCHA 550/15.

References

1. Ahmadi, N., Lee, J., Papotti, P., Saeed, M.: Explainable fact checking with probabilistic answer set programming. In: Liakata, M., Vlachos, A. (eds.) Proceedings of the 2019 Truth and Trust Online Conference (2019)
2. Balaii, E.: Investigating and extending P-log. Ph.D. thesis, Texas Tech University (2017)
3. Baral, C., Gelfond, M., Rushton, J.: Probabilistic reasoning with answer sets. Theory Pract. Logic Program. **9**(1), 57–144 (2009)
4. Buccafurri, F., Leone, N., Rullo, P.: Enhancing disjunctive datalog by constraints. IEEE Trans. Knowl. Data Eng. **12**(5), 845–860 (2000)
5. Calimeri, F., et al.: ASP-Core-2: input language format (2012). https://www.mat.unical.it/aspcomp2013/ASPStandardization
6. Ferraris, P.: Answer sets for propositional theories. In: Baral, C., Greco, G., Leone, N., Terracina, G. (eds.) LPNMR 2005. LNCS (LNAI), vol. 3662, pp. 119–131. Springer, Heidelberg (2005). https://doi.org/10.1007/11546207_10
7. Fierens, D., et al.: Inference and learning in probabilistic logic programs using weighted boolean formulas. Theory Pract. Logic Program. **15**(3), 385–401 (2015)
8. Gebser, M., Kaminski, R., Kaufmann, B., Ostrowski, M., Schaub, T., Wanko, P.: Theory solving made easy with clingo 5. In: Carro, M., King, A. (eds.) Technical Communications of ICLP 2016. OpenAccess Series in Informatics (OASIcs), vol. 52, pp. 2:1–2:15 (2016)
9. Lee, J., Talsania, S., Wang, Y.: Computing LPMLN using ASP and MLN solvers. Theory Pract. Logic Program. **17**(5–6), 942–960 (2017)
10. Lee, J., Wang, Y.: Weighted rules under the stable model semantics. In: Baral, C., Delgrande, J., Wolter, F. (ed.) Proceedings of KR 2016, pp. 145–154. AAAI/MIT Press (2016)
11. Lee, J., Wang, Y.: Weight learning in a probabilistic extension of answer set programs. In: Proceedings of KR 2018, pp. 22–31 (2018)
12. Lee, J., Yang, Z.: LPMLN, weak constraints and P-log. In: Proceedings of the 31st AAAI Conference on Artificial Intelligence, pp. 1170–1177 (2017)
13. Lifschitz, V.: Answer set programming and plan generation. Artif. Intell. **138**(1–2), 39–54 (2002)
14. Pajunen, J., Janhunen, T.: Solution enumeration by optimality in answer set programming. Theory Pract. Logic Program. **21**(1), 750–767 (2021)
15. Raedt, L.D., Kimmig, A., Toivonen, H.: ProbLog: a probabilistic prolog and its applications in link discovery. In: Proceedings of AAAI 2007, pp. 2468–2473. AAAI Press (2007)
16. Richardson, M., Domingos, P.: Markov logic networks. Mach. Learn. **62**(1–2), 107–136 (2006)
17. Zhu, W.: Plog: its algorithms and applications. Ph.D. thesis, Texas Tech University (2012)

Foundations of Nonmonotonic Reasoning

From Defeasible Logic to Counterfactual Reasoning

Matteo Cristani[1], Guido Governatori[2], Francesco Olivieri[3],
and Antonino Rotolo[4(✉)]

[1] University of Verona, Verona 37136, Italy
matteo.cristani@univr.it
[2] Centre for Computational Law, Singapore Management University,
Singapore, Singapore
guido@governatori.net
[3] IIIS, Griffith University, Nathan 4111, Australia
f.oliveri@griffith.edu.au
[4] Alma AI, University of Bologna, Bologna 40121, Italy
antonino.rotolo@unibo.it

Abstract. Counterfactual reasoning has been the subject of extensive study in philosophy, logics, and AI. The connection between counterfactual reasoning and theory revision is well-known since Ramsey's intuition, according to which "to find out whether the counterfactual 'if A were true, then B would be true' is satisfied in a state S, change the state S minimally to include A, and test whether B is satisfied in the resulting state". In this paper we study how to model this idea in Defeasible Logic for devising logics for counterfactual reasoning and suitable selection function models.

Keywords: Defeasible logic · Theory revision · Counterfactual reasoning

1 Introduction

What if everyone got the COVID-19 vaccine, would the pandemics be over? What if JFK had survived the assassination attempt? These modes of reasoning have been the subject of extensive study in philosophy, logics, and AI, among others. As is well-known, the first question exemplifies a case of subjective conditional, while the second is an example of counterfactual, i.e., a subjunctive conditional whose antecedent is assumed to be false.

Subjective conditionals and counterfactuals have been notably modeled through two-place modal operators (see [9,11] for an overview). In this paper we study counterfactuals from another, but related, perspective. We are interested in identifying formal relations between counterfactual logics and Defeasible

© The Author(s), under exclusive license to Springer Nature Switzerland AG 2022
G. Governatori and A.-Y. Turhan (Eds.): RuleML+RR 2022, LNCS 13752, pp. 65–80, 2022.
https://doi.org/10.1007/978-3-031-21541-4_5

Logic (DL), which is an efficient rule-based non-monotonic formalism where the knowledge base consists of a finite set F of facts, a set of rules, and a priority relation to solve conflicts among rules [2]. Despite the wide variety of applications of DL, to the best of our knowledge, no research has been so far developed in this regard.

Suppose that the following rules govern the dynamic spread of COVID-19 infections:

$$R = \{r_1 : positive, quarantine \Rightarrow \neg spread$$
$$r_2 : positive \Rightarrow spread$$
$$r_3 : positive, mask \Rightarrow \neg spread$$
$$r_4 : spread, vax \Rightarrow \neg high\_lethality$$
$$r_5 : spread, old \Rightarrow high\_lethality$$
$$r_6 : high\_lethality \Rightarrow hospital\_collapse\}$$

and assume that r_1 and r_3 are stronger than r_2, while r_4 is stronger than r_5. Also, suppose that the following facts hold:

$$F = \{positive, quarantine, \neg mask, old\}.$$

One can consider different and hypothetical scenarios where

1. quarantine does not work: we could thus change or remove r_1 from R;
2. vax does not prevent high lethality: we could thus make r_4 no longer stronger than r_5;
3. people are not old: we should remove old from F.

In general, this intuition suggests that we can model counterfactual reasoning by changing the knowledge base of Defeasible Logic from three different angles. From the theoretical standpoint, there is nothing radically new in this analysis, which is just an elaboration in Defeasible Logic of the original intuition behind Ramsey's test [13]:

To find out whether the counterfactual "if A were true, then B would be true" is satisfied in a state S, change the state S minimally to include A, and test whether B is satisfied in the resulting state.

However, to the best of our knowledge, no work has proposed minimal change operations over non-monotonic theories that are constructively used to build similarity semantics for counter-factuals.

In this paper we study in Defeasible Logic two mechanisms for changing theories to perform various types of counterfactual reasoning. In particular, we show how to devise semantic structures for counterfactuals that are generated by

1. minimally changing the facts of the knowledge base of Defeasible Logic,
2. contracting or revising the set of defeasible rules of the knowledge base.

In the first case, the resulting sets facts are used to define worlds that are the most similar to the actual one. In the second case, the set of conclusions of the original theory corresponds to the formulas true at the actual world, while the sets of conclusions that follow from the changed sets of rules are used to build an appropriate selection function.

Several issues raise. For example:

- Should the revision of theories be minimal? Would such an idea of minimality be close to the classic concept of similarity between worlds in Lewis' sense [9]?
- What other properties should the facts revision enjoy?

The layout of the paper is as follows. Sections 2 and 3 recall, respectively, the basics of Standard Defeasible Logic and of counterfactual logics (a specific axiomatisation is mentioned simply for the sake of illustration). Section 4 presents a variant of selection function semantics where the function is defined by minimally changing the set of facts of a given Defeasible Theory. Section 5 works instead on contracting or revising the set of rules of a given theory. Some basic results are sketched in Sect. 6. Brief conclusions end the paper.

2   Defeasible Logic

Let us briefly recall the basics of Standard Defeasible Logic (**SDL**) [2]. We start by defining the language L_{SDL}.

Let PROP be the set of propositional atoms, then the set of literals Lit $=$ PROP $\cup \{\neg p \mid p \in$ PROP$\}$. The *complementary* of a literal p is denoted by $\sim p$: if p is a positive literal q then $\sim p$ is $\neg q$, if p is a negative literal $\neg q$ then $\sim p$ is q. Literals are denoted by lower-case Roman letters. Let Lab be a set of labels to represent names of rules, which will be denoted as lower-case Greek letters.

A defeasible theory D is a tuple $(F, R, \prec)$, where F is the set of facts (indisputable statements), R is the rule set, and $\prec$ is a binary relation over R.

R is partitioned into three distinct sets of rules, with different meanings to draw different "types of conclusions". *Strict rules* are rules in the classical fashion: whenever the premises are the case, so is the conclusion. We then have *defeasible rules* which represent the non-monotonic part (along which defeaters) of the logic: if the premises are the case then typically the conclusion holds as well unless we have contrary evidence that opposes and prevents us to draw such a conclusion. Lastly, we have *defeaters*, which are special rules whose purpose is to prevent contrary evidence to be the case. It follows that in DL, through defeasible rules and defeaters, we can represent in a natural way exceptions (and exceptions to exceptions, and so forth).

We finally have the superiority relation $\prec$ a binary relation among couples of rules, that is the mechanism to solve conflicts. Given the two rules α and β, we have $(\alpha, \beta) \in \prec$ (or simply $\alpha \prec \beta$), in the scenario where both rules may fire (can be activated), α's conclusion will be preferred to β's.

A rule $\alpha \in R$ has the form $\alpha: A(\alpha) \rightsquigarrow C(\alpha)$, where: (i) $\alpha \in$ Lab is the unique name of the rule, (ii) $A(\alpha) \subseteq$ Lit is α's (set of) antecedents, (iii) $C(\alpha) = l \in$ Lit is its conclusion, and (iv) $\rightsquigarrow \in \{\rightarrow, \Rightarrow, \rightsquigarrow\}$ defines the type of rule, where: $\rightarrow$ is for strict rules, $\Rightarrow$ is for defeasible rules, and $\rightsquigarrow$ is for defeaters.

Some standard abbreviations. The set of strict rules in R is denoted by R_s, and the set of strict and defeasible rules by Rs; $R[l]$ denotes the set of all rules whose conclusion is l.

A *conclusion* of D is a *tagged literal* with one of the following forms:

$\pm \Delta l$ means that l is *definitely proved* (resp. *strictly refuted/non provable*) in D, i.e., there is a definite proof for l in D (resp. a definite proof does not exist).

$\pm \partial l$ means that l is *defeasibly proved* (resp. *defeasibly refuted*) in D, i.e., there is a defeasible proof for l in D (resp. a definite proof does not exist).

The definition of proof is also the standard in DL. Given a defeasible theory D, a proof P of length n in D is a finite sequence $P(1), P(2), \ldots, P(n)$ of tagged formulas of the type $+\Delta l, -\Delta l, +\partial l, -\partial l$, where the proof conditions defined in the rest of this section hold. $P(1..n)$ denotes the first n steps of P.

All proof tags for literals are standard in DL [2]. We report only the positive ones as the negative proof tags can be straightforwardly obtained by applying the *strong negation principle* to the positive counterparts. The definition of Δ describes forward chaining of strict rules.

Definition 1 $(+\Delta)$.

$+\Delta l$: If $P(n+1) = +\Delta l$ then either
(1) $l \in F$, or
(2) $\exists \alpha \in R_s[l].\forall a \in A(\alpha). + \Delta a \in P(1..n)$.

A literal is strictly proved if it is a(n initial) fact of the theory, or there exists a strict rule that is applicable.

Defeasible derivations are based on the notions of a rule being applicable or discarded. A rule is *applicable* at a given derivation step when every antecedent has been proved at any previous derivation step. Symmetrically, a rule is *discarded* when at least one antecedent has been previously refuted.

Definition 2 (Applicable & Discarded).

Given a defeasible theory D, a literal l, and a prove $P(n)$, we say that

- $\alpha \in R[l]$ is applicable at $P(n+1)$ iff $\forall a \in A(\alpha). + \partial a \in P(1.n)$.
- $\alpha \in R[l]$ is discarded at $P(n+1)$ iff $\exists a \in A(\alpha). - \partial a \in P(1.n)$.

Note that a strict rule can be used to derive defeasible conclusions when is applicable and at least one of its premises is defeasibly but not strictly proved.

Definition 3 $(+\partial)$.

$+\partial l$: If $P(n+1) = +\partial l$ then either
    (1) $+\Delta l \in P(1..n)$, or

(2.1) $-\Delta{\sim}l \in P(1..n)$, *and*
(2.2) $\exists\alpha \in R[l]$ *applicable s.t.*
(2.3) $\forall\beta \in R[{\sim}l]$ *either*
    (2.3.1) β *discarded, or*
    (2.3.2) $\exists\zeta \in R[l]$ *applicable s.t.* $\zeta \prec \beta$.

A literal is defeasibly proved if (1) it has already proved as a strict conclusion, or (2.1) the opposite is not and (2.2) there exists an applicable, defeasible or strict, rule such that any counter-attack is either (2.3.1) discarded or (2.3.2) defeated by an applicable, stronger rule supporting l. Note that, whereas β and ζ may be defeaters, α *may not*, as we need a strict or defeasible, applicable rule to draw a conclusion.

The last notions introduced in this section are those of extension of a defeasible theory and of equivalence of theories. Informally, an extension is everything that is derived and disproved; two theories are *equivalent* iff they have the same extension

Definition 4 (Theory Extension). *Given a defeasible theory D, we define the set of positive and negative conclusions of D as its extension:*

$$E(D) = (\Delta^+(D), \Delta^-(D), \partial^+(D), \partial^-(D)),$$

where $\#^\pm(D) = \{l | l$ *appears in D and $D \vdash \pm\#l\}$, $\# \in \{\Delta, \partial\}$.*

Theorem 1. *[10] Given a defeasible theory D, its extension $E(D)$ can be computed in time polynomial to the size of the theory. (The size of the theory is given by the number of symbols in it.)*

3 Counterfactuals

Let $L_>$ be the language obtained by adding the conditional connective $>$ to propositional language L. The set of (well-formed) formulas of $L_>$ is defined in the usual way. Formulas of $L_>$ are interpreted in terms of Lewis-type semantic structures [6]. While some, like [1], rejected nested conditionals when a probabilistic treatment of them is considered, others admitted this possibility even though it was argued that the intuitive meaning of such formulas is far from clear [7,9,11]. To keep the logical constructions simple, we follow this view and avoid nested counterfactuals.

The following definitions are standard from [6].

Definition 5. *A minimal selection function (MSF) frame is a pair $M = \langle W, f \rangle$ where*

1. *W is a nonempty set (of possible worlds);*
2. *f is a selection function $\mathcal{P}(W) \times W \mapsto \mathcal{P}(\mathcal{P}(W))$.*

Definition 6. *A minimal selection function (MSF) model is a triple $M = \langle W, f, v \rangle$ where*

1. W and f are as in Definition 5;
2. v is a valuation assigning to each u in W and $A \in L$ an element from the set $\{T, F\}$.

In fact, the function f picks out a subset $f(A, u)$ of W for each u in W and $A \in L$.[1] We refer to the set of worlds $f(A, u)$ as the most similar set of worlds with respect to u.

Truth of a formula A at a world u in a model M, $\models_u^M A$, is defined as usual with the counterfactual case given by

$$\models_u^M A > B \text{ iff } \|B\|_M \in f(A, u) \tag{1}$$

where $\|B\|_M$ denotes the set of worlds where B is true in M, i.e., $\|B\|_M = \{w \in W : v(B, w) = T\}$: we omit the subscript M when it is clear from the context the model in which a formula is evaluated. A formula A is valid in a model M ($\models^M$) just when $\models_u^M A$ for all worlds u in M. A formula A is valid ($\models^{SF}$) just when $\models_u^M A$ for all worlds u in all SF models.

Perhaps one of the weakest systems of counterfactuals requires to adopt the following semantics [6,12].

Definition 7. A minimal selection function counterfactual frame *(MSFC)* is an MSF frame $M = \langle W, f, \rangle$ satisfying the following conditions:

1. $X \in f(X, u)$ *(Success)*
2. $\{u\} \in f(X, u)$ if $u \in X$ *(Weak Centering)*

Notice that Success ensures that $f(A, u)$ also contains the set of A-worlds. It is not hard to see that the class of *MSFC* frames fits exactly the conditional logic which contains classical propositional logic, the following axioms

1. $A > A$ **(ID)**
2. $(A > B) \to (A \to B)$ **(> MP)**

and is closed under the usual inference rules

$$\frac{A \equiv B}{(A > C) \equiv (B > C)} \qquad \textbf{(RCEA)}$$

$$\frac{B \equiv C}{(A > B) \equiv (A > C)} \qquad \textbf{(RCEC)}$$

As is well-known, the logic consisting of **RCEA** and **RCEC** is the system **CE** [6]. A standard Henkin-style construction proves the completeness of **CE** $\oplus$ **ID** $\oplus$ **> MP** with respect to the class of *MSFC* frames. Proofs are standard and are omitted. Let us call this system **S** (see [5,6]).

Theorem 2. $\models^{SFC} A$ iff $\vdash_\textbf{S} A$.

---

[1] Notice that $A \notin L_>$ since we do not admit nested conditionals.

4   Counterfactuals in Defeasible Logic: Fact Revision

Consider a counterfactual conditional

$$\phi > \psi \tag{2}$$

As is well-known, on similarity analysis of genuine counterfactuals we hold in possible-world semantics the following:

> $\phi > \psi$ is true in any world w_0 in case all ϕ-worlds most similar worlds to w_0 are ψ-worlds.

In SDL, recall the COVID example from Sect. 1 and assume that we want to block the derivation of *hospital_collapse* without imposing a quarantine, thus by removing *quarantine* from F. We can abuse the notation and see the issue as follows: if $w_0 = F$

$$\neg quarantine > \neg hospital\_collapse \tag{3}$$

Then we can argue that (3) is true in w_0 iff we derive $\neg hospital\_collapse$ (or, alternatively, we block the derivation of *hospital_collapse*) by revising F at least by removing *quarantine* (or replacing *quarantine* with $\neg hospital\_collapse$) in such a way as to minimize the effect of such a revision of F.

The following section formally reconstructs the above intuition in a suitable version of selection function semantics.

4.1   Preliminaries

Definition 8 ([4]). *Let $D = (F, R, \prec)$ be any Defeasible Theory. The non-monotonic consequence relation $\mathrel{|\!\sim}_D$ is defined as follows:*

- *$F \mathrel{|\!\sim}_D l$ iff $D \vdash +\partial l$;*
- *$F \mathrel{|\!\not\sim}_D l$ iff $D \vdash -\partial l$.*

Remark 1. Trivially, given any $D = (F, R, \prec)$ and according to Definition 4 the extension $E(D) = (\Delta^+(D), \Delta^-(D), \partial^+(D), \partial^-(D))$ is such that

- $F \mathrel{|\!\sim}_D l$ iff $l \in \partial^+(D)$
- $F \mathrel{|\!\not\sim}_D l$ iff $l \in \partial^-(D)$.

Definition 9 (Well-formed propositional formulas). *Let* Lit *be the set of literals of $L_{\mathbf{SDL}}$. The set* WFF *of well-formed propositional formulas is defined as follows:*

$$\text{WFF} = \{P | P \in \text{Lit} \cup \{\bigwedge_{i=0}^{n} p | p \in \text{Lit}\}\}.$$

Henceforth, we use the expression "formula" to mean a well-formed propositional formula. A counterfactual is an expression $A > B$ where A, B are well-formed propositional formulas. Thus, as recalled in the previous sections, we do not admit nested conditionals.

Definition 10 (Minimal revision). *Let X be any set of formulas and let $(X)^*_A$ denote the usual AGM-operation of revision. We write $(X)^{*\min}_A$ iff, $\forall Y \supseteq X : A \in Y, (X)^*_A \subseteq Y$.*

Definition 11. *For any set F of literals, let $(F)^-_q$ be the usual AGM operation of contraction in F of q. Let us stipulate that*

$$F^-_{\{q_1 \wedge \cdots \wedge q_n\}} := F^-_{\{q_1,\ldots,q_n\}} := (\ldots(((F)^-_{q_1})^-_{q_2})\ldots)^-_{q_n}$$
$$F^{*\min}_{\{q_1 \wedge \cdots \wedge q_n\}} := F^{*\min}_{\{q_1,\ldots,q_n\}} := (\ldots(((F)^{*\min}_{q_1})^{*\min}_{q_2})\ldots)^{*\min}_{q_n}$$

The above definition is very useful because of the following proposition.

Proposition 1. *Let $X = l_1,\ldots,l_n$ and $Y = \{q_1,\ldots,q_m\}$ be two consistent sets of literals. For any $q_i, q_k \in Y$, the contraction and minimal revision are commutative, i.e.,*

$$(((X)^-_{q_i})^-_{q_k}) = (((X)^-_{q_k})^-_{q_i})$$
$$(((X)^{*\min}_{q_i})^{*\min}_{q_k}) = (((X)^{*\min}_{q_k})^{*\min}_{q_i})$$

Proof. The proof is trivial, since X and Y are consistent sets of literals. Hence, whatever order of contraction and revision we follow, the operations only affect the literal considered.

Definition 12 (D-p-minimality). *Let $D = (F, R, \prec)$ be any Defeasible Theory. For any literal p, the Defeasible Theory $D' = (F', R, \prec)$ is D-m-p-critical iff*

1. *F is consistent;*
2. *$F' \not\vdash_{D'} p$, and*
3. *for some consistent set of literals $\{q_1,\ldots,q_m\}$, either*
   (a) *if $\{q_1,\ldots,q_m\} \not\subseteq F$, then $F' - \{q_1,\ldots,q_m\} \not\vdash_{D'} p$ and $F' = F^{*\min}_{\{q_1,\ldots,q_m\}}$;*
   or
   (b) *if $\{q_1,\ldots,q_m\} \subseteq F$, then and $F \not\vdash_D p$ and $F' = F^-_{\{q_1,\ldots,q_m\}}$.*

The Defeasible Theory D' is D-p-minimal iff there is no Defeasible Theory D'' such that

- *D'' is D-j-p-critical, and*
- *$j < m$.*

We also say that the set F' of facts of D' is D-p-minimal if D' is is D-p-minimal.

Example 1 (Running Example). Let us illustrate Definition 12 by resuming the Covid example from Sect. 1 with some adjustments in the set of facts. The theory

$D = (F, R, \prec)$ is as follows:

$$F = \{positive, vax, \neg mask, old\}$$
$$R = \{r_1 : positive, quarantine \Rightarrow \neg spread,$$
$$r_2 : positive \Rightarrow spread,$$
$$r_3 : positive, mask \Rightarrow \neg spread,$$
$$r_4 : spread, vax \Rightarrow \neg high\_lethality,$$
$$r_5 : spread, old \Rightarrow high\_lethality,$$
$$r_6 : high\_lethality \Rightarrow hospital\_collapse\}$$
$$\prec = \{\langle r_1, r_2 \rangle, \langle r_3, r_2 \rangle, \langle r_4, r_5 \rangle\}.$$

First of all, we trivially observe that F is consistent. The extension $E(D)$ is such that[2]

$$F\!\!\mid\!\sim_D \{positive, vax, \neg mask, old, spread, \neg high\_lethality\}$$

Suppose $F' = F - \{vax\}$. We fall under condition 3.(b) where $\{q_1, \ldots, q_m\} = \{vax\}$ and $p = high\_lethality$: in fact, we note that $F' = F^-_{\{vax\}}$, $F'\!\!\mid\!\sim_{D'} high\_lethality$ while $F \not\!\!\mid\!\sim_D high\_lethality$.

Hence, the theory D is D-1-$high\_lethality$-critical. Also, such a theory is trivially D-$high\_lethality$-minimal because $m = 1$.

We are now ready to use classical AGM contraction and revision to build suitable selection-function structures.[3]

4.2   Mapping SDL into Counterfactuals - Part I

For our purposes, we need to express that each Defeasible Theory D corresponds to a special SFC model where just one word makes the facts of D true: such a world—the actual world w_0—is fixed in the model. Also, we have to capture the idea that, for any formula A, the A-worlds selected by f are the most similar to the world w_0 where a counterfactual formula is evaluated.

Definition 13 (D-1-counterfactual models). *Let* $D = (F, R, \prec)$ *be any Defeasible Theory where* $F = \{f_1, \ldots, f_n\}$. *A selection function D-1-counterfactual model (D-1-SFDC model) is a structure* $M = \langle W, w_0, f, v \rangle$ *where:*

1. *$w_0 \in W$ is the actual world of M such that* $\bigcap_{i=0}^{n} \|f_i\| = \{w_0\}$;
2. *for any set of literals* $\{q_1, \ldots, q_m\}$, *$f(\bigwedge_{i=0}^{m} q_i, w_0)$ is a set X of sets of worlds such that, for each $Y \in X$, there is a set of literals* $F^w_{f(\bigwedge_{i=0}^{m} q_i, w_0)} = \{p_1, \ldots, p_k\}$ *where* $Y = \bigcap_{i=0}^{k} \|p_i\|$ *and, for some set Z of literals, either*

---

[2] We abuse the notation and write $F\!\!\mid\!\sim X$ where X is a set to mean that F non-monotonically imply each element of X.

[3] In Sect. 5 we will go beyond standard AGM operations and exploit specific revision operations devised to handle non-monotonic theories.

$$- F^w_{f(\bigwedge^m_{i=0} q_i, w_0)} = F^{*\min}_Z, \; or$$
$$- F^w_{f(\bigwedge^m_{i=0} q_i, w_0)} = F^-_Z.$$

Definition 14 (Counterfactual 1-evaluation). *Let $D = (F, R, \prec)$ be any Defeasible Theory. The truth of any counterfactual $A > B$ at a world w_0 in an D-1-SFDC model M is defined as follows:*

$$\models^M_{w_0} A > B \tag{4}$$

iff

- $\|B\| \in f(A, w_0);$
- $F^w_{f(A, w_0)}$ *is D-p-minimal.*

The frame conditions of Success and Weak Centering recalled in Definition 7 can be easily adapted for D-1-SFDC models.

The language $L_{D>}$ for the counterfactual logic generated by any Defeasible Theory is clearly a fragment of $L_>$.

Let us illustrate the above definitions with our running example and build a toy model.

Example 2 (Running Example (cont'd)). Resume the theory D from Example 1 and build an appropriate D-1-SFDC model considering the following literals

$$positive, vax, \neg mask, old, spread, \neg high\_lethality, hospital\_collapse, quarantine$$

and only three worlds: w_0, w_1, and w_2. Let proceed as follows:

- Evaluations of propositional formulas are as follows:

$$\|positive\| = \{w_0, w_1\}$$
$$\|vax\| = \{w_0, w_1, w_2\}$$
$$\|\neg mask\| = \{w_0, w_1\}$$
$$\|old\| = \{w_0, w_1\}$$
$$\|spread\| = \{w_1, w_2\}$$
$$\|\neg high\_lethality\| = \{w_1\}$$
$$\|hospital\_collapse\| = \{w_1\}$$
$$\|quarantine\| = \{w_1, w_2\}$$

- Clearly, $\|positive\| \cap \|vax\| \cap \|\neg mask\| \cap \|old\| = \{w_0\};$
- Define, among others,

$$f(\neg vax, w_0) = F^w_{f(\neg vax, w_0)} = \{\{w_1\}\}.$$

where $Z = F - \{vax\} = F^-_{vax}$.

It is easy to check that $F^w_{f(\neg vax, w_0)}$ is D-high_lethality-minimal, thus

$$\models^M_{w_0} \neg vax > high\_lethality.$$

5   Counterfactuals in Defeasible Logic: Theory Revision

[3] reframed AGM operations for SDL, i.e., investigated revision and contraction operators for defeasible theories, and proposed postulates motivated by the form or the intuition of the AGM postulates for classical belief revision. This result is interesting because we can build counterfactual models by exploiting minimality in AGM sense.

5.1   Revising Defeasible Theories

Let us recall the basic definitions and results of [3]. Let $D = (F, R, \prec)$ be a Defeasible Theory and $c = p_1, \ldots p_n$ be the formulas to considered. By convention, for any literal l, by $l \in E(D)$ we mean that $F \hspace{-1pt}\sim_D l$.

Definition 15 (Expansion). *Expansion is defined as follows:*

$$D_c^+ = \begin{cases} D & \text{if } \sim p_i \in \partial^+(D) \text{ or } \sim p_i = p_j \text{ for some } i, j \in \{1, \ldots, n\} \\ (F, R', \prec') & \text{otherwise} \end{cases}$$

where

$$R' = R \cup \{\Rightarrow p_1, \ldots, \Rightarrow p_n\}$$
$$\prec' = (\prec \cup \{\Rightarrow p_i \prec r \mid i \in \{1, \ldots, n\}, r \in R[\sim p_i]\}) -$$
$$\{r \prec \Rightarrow p_i \mid i \in \{1, \ldots, n\}, r \in R[\sim p_i]\}.$$

$$(5)$$

AGM *revision* works in the same way as AGM expansion when the formula to be added does not cause an inconsistency, but revision adds a formula even if its negation is in the belief set. In [3]'s framework the definition of revision is as follows.

Definition 16 (Revision). *Revision is defined as follows:*

$$D_c^* = \begin{cases} D & \text{if } p_1, \ldots, p_n \in E(D) \\ (F, R', \prec') & \text{otherwise} \end{cases}$$

where

$$R' = R \cup \{\Rightarrow p_1, \ldots, \Rightarrow p_n\}$$
$$\prec' = (\prec \cup \{\Rightarrow p_i \prec r \mid i \in \{1, \ldots, n\}, r \in R[\sim p_i]\}) -$$
$$\{r \prec \Rightarrow p_i \mid i \in \{1, \ldots, n\}, r \in R[\sim p_i]\}.$$

$$(6)$$

Definition 17 (Contraction). *Contraction is defined as follows:*

$$D_c^- = \begin{cases} D & \text{if } p_1, \ldots, p_n \notin \partial^+(D) \\ (F, R', \prec') & \text{otherwise} \end{cases}$$

where

$$R' = R \cup \{p_1, \ldots, p_{i-1}, p_{i+1}, \ldots, p_n \leadsto \sim p_i \mid i \in \{1, \ldots, n\}\}$$
$$\prec' = \prec - \{s \prec r \mid r \in R' - R, s \in R\}.$$

$$(7)$$

Theorem 3. *Operations in Definitions 15, 16, and 17 satisfy the reformulation of AGM postulates given in [3].*

As regards minimality in the AGM sense, we have to define belief sets for SDL.

Definition 18. *The belief set $B(D)$ of a Defeasible Theory D is defined as follows:*

$$B(D) = \{P | P \in E(D) \cup \{\bigwedge_{i=0}^{n} p | p \in E(D)\} \ and \ B(D)$$

is closed under sub-formulas\}

Then, it should be noted that the following postulate, among others, holds for any formula c [3]:

$$\text{If } c \notin B(D) \text{ then } B(D)_c^- = B(D). \tag{-3}$$

In general, minimality for modeling counterfactuals is guaranteed by Definitions 16 and 17 since the operations just add the rules only needed, respectively, to prove or to disprove the considered formula. Just notice that SDL is skeptical, so it may happen that revision may lead, e.g., to block other literals that were in the extension, while contraction may contribute to prove new conclusions.

Consider again our running example.

Example 3 (Running Example (cont'd)). In Example 1 we considered how to revise the set of facts by removing *vax* from F. In Example 2, we used this change for building an appropriare semantic structure for counterfactuals. Here operate at a different level, i.e., by considering the defeasible extension of the theory. Suppose we retain F' and aim at applying Definition 17 to contract *spread*:

$$D'' = D_{spread}^-(F', R', \prec')$$

where

$$R' = R \cup \{\rightsquigarrow \sim spread\}$$
$$\prec' = \prec - \{s \prec r \mid r \in R' - R, s \in R\}.$$

It is easy to check that $F' \not\vdash_{D''} \{spread, high\_lethality, hospital\_collapse\}$.

5.2   Mapping SDL into Counterfactuals - Part II

Once minimal contraction and revision for SDL are defined, we can use the extensions of theories and the corresponding belief sets to generate suitable selection function counterfactual models for the logic **S**.

Definition 19 (D-2-counterfactual models). *Let $D = (F, R, \prec)$ be any Defeasible Theory and $E(D) = \{f_1, \ldots, f_n\}$ be its extension. A selection function D-2-counterfactual model (D-2-SFDC model) is a structure $M = \langle W, w_0, f, v \rangle$ where:*

1. $w_0 \in W$ is the actual world of M such that $\bigcap_{i=0}^{n} \|f_i\| = \{w_0\}$;
2. for any set of literals $\{q_1, \ldots, q_m\}$, $f(\bigwedge_{i=0}^{m} q_i, w_0)$ is a set X of worlds such that, for each $w \in X$, there is a set of literals $F_{f(\bigwedge_{i=0}^{m} q_i, w_0)}^{w} = \{p_1, \ldots, p_k\}$ where $w \in \bigcap_{i=0}^{k} \|p_i\|$ and, for some set Z of literals, either
   - $F_{f(\bigwedge_{i=0}^{m} q_i, w_0)}^{w} = B(D_Z^*)$, or
   - $F_{f(\bigwedge_{i=0}^{m} q_i, w_0)}^{w} = B(D_Z^-)$.

Using theory extensions to define the set of worlds allows for keeping standard the notion of evaluation:

Definition 20 (Counterfactual 2-evaluation). *Let $D = (F, R, \prec)$ be any Defeasible Theory. The truth of any counterfactual $A > B$ at a world w_0 in an D-2-SFDC model M is defined as follows:*

$$\models_{w_0}^{M} A > B \text{ iff } \|B\| \in f(A, w_0). \tag{8}$$

Example 4 (Running Example (cont'd)). Let us proceed similarly as we did in Example 2. Consider the usual three worlds: w_0, w_1, and w_2. We modify the scenario as follows:

- Evaluations of propositional formulas:

$$\|positive\| = \{w_0, w_1\}$$
$$\|vax\| = \{w_0, w_1, w_2\}$$
$$\|\neg mask\| = \{w_0, w_1\}$$
$$\|old\| = \{w_0, w_1\}$$
$$\|spread\| = \{w_1, w_2\}$$
$$\|\neg high\_lethality\| = \{w_1\}$$
$$\|hospital\_collapse\| = \{w_1\}$$
$$\|quarantine\| = \{w_1, w_2\}$$

- Clearly, $\|positive\| \cap \|vax\| \cap \|\neg mask\| \cap \|old\| = \{w_0\}$;
- Apply Definition 17 and define, among others (remember that $D'' = D_{spread}^{-}(F', R', \prec')$),

$$f(\neg spread, w_0) = F_{f(\neg spread, w_0)}^{w} = \{\{w_1\}\}.$$

where $Z = B(D'')$.

It is easy to check that the resulting structure M is a D-2-counterfactual model where

$$\models_{w_0}^{M} \neg spread > \neg hospital\_collapse.$$

6   Results

Under the language limitations mentioned above for **S**, completeness is a rather easy result for both versions of the semantics and trivial adjustments from [6] can be settled. Indeed, except for the fact that we fix an actual world, selection function D-1 and D-2-counterfactual models are standard.

Hence, let us consider, for the sake of illustration, canonical frames for selection function D-2-counterfactual semantics [6].

Definition 21 (Canonical structures). *Let W be the set of $L_{D>}$-maximal consistent sets of formulas of $L_{D>}$, and f be a selection function $\mathcal{P}(W) \times W \mapsto \mathcal{P}(\mathcal{P}(W))$ where, for any $w \in W$*

$$A > B \in w_0 \text{ iff } |B|_{L_{D>}} \in f(|A|_{L_{D>}}, w_0).$$

The structure $F = \langle W, w_0, f \rangle$ is a canonical frame for $L_{D>}$.

‐ A second, and perhaps less trivial result is that the models generated from Defeasible Theories are related with the notion of filtration [5,6].

Again, let us focus on the second variant of semantics and define the notion of filtration with a fixed actual world.

Definition 22 (Filtrations). *Let $M = \langle W, w_0, f, v \rangle$ be a D-2-SFDC model, Γ be a finite set of formulas closed under sub-formulas, and $\sim$ be the equivalence relation on the set W of worlds such that*

$$u \sim w \text{ iff, for every } A \in \Gamma, \models_u^M A \text{ iff } \models_w^M A$$

$[w]$ is the $\sim$-equivalence class of worlds in M generated by w and $[X] = \{[w] | w \in X \subseteq W\}$.

A filtration of M through Γ is any model $M^\Gamma = \langle W^\Gamma, w_0^\Gamma, f^\Gamma, v^\Gamma \rangle$ where

- *$W^\Gamma = [W]$;*
- *$w_0^\Gamma = [w_0]$;*
- *f^Γ is a function $\mathcal{P}(W^\Gamma) \times W^\Gamma \mapsto \mathcal{P}(\mathcal{P}(W^\Gamma))$ such that*
  - *$[f(X, w)] = f^\Gamma([X], [w])$;*
  - *$f^\Gamma([X], [w_0]) = [Y]$ where, for every counterfactual $A > B \in \Gamma$ we have that $X = \|A\|_M$, $Y = \|B\|_M$, and $\models_{w_0}^M A > B$.*
- *v^Γ is a valuation assigning to each u^Γ in W^Γ and $A \in \Gamma$ an element from the set $\{T, F\}$.*

All results proved in [5,6] apply as well to this case. We should note however that an additional property holds. Such a property illustrates under what simple conditions a D-2-counterfactual model generated by a theory is a filtration of some other model.

Theorem 4. *Let $D = (F, R, \prec)$ be any Defeasible Theory, $E(D) = \{f_1, \ldots, f_n\}$ be its extension, and M be a selection function D-2-counterfactual model $M = \langle W, w_0, f, v \rangle$ where*

1. w_0 is as in Definition 19;
2. for any set of literals $\{q_1, \ldots, q_m\}$, $f(\bigwedge_{i=0}^{m} q_i, w_0)$ is such that there is no $\{p_1, \ldots, p_n\}$ where $F_{f(\bigwedge_{i=0}^{n} p_i, w_0)}^{w} = F_{f(\bigwedge_{i=0}^{m} q_i, w_0)}^{w}$.

If X_D is the set of literals occurring in D and each $\{q_1, \ldots, q_m\} \subseteq X_D$, then M is a filtration of some model M' through $\bigcup_{j=0}^{s} Y_j$ such that $\{Y_1, \ldots, Y_s\}$ is the codomain of f.

Proof. Since X_D is finite, f is finite as well, so is $\{Y_1, \ldots, Y_s\}$. By construction w_0 is $[\bigwedge_{i=1}^{n} f_i]$ while each set of worlds Y_k in $\{Y_1, \ldots, Y_s\}$ is the set of worlds that make true the elements of the corresponding belief set.

7 Conclusions

In this paper we have investigated in Defeasible Logic two mechanisms for changing theories which can be used to devise semantic structures for counterfactual logics.

We have proposed semantic structures for counterfactuals that are generated by

1. minimally changing the facts of the knowledge base of Defeasible Logic,
2. contracting or revising the set of defeasible rules of the knowledge base.

This paper offers a preliminary but fresh idea: to the best of our knowledge, no work has proposed minimal change operations over non-monotonic theories that are constructively used to build similarity semantics for counter-factuals.

Another work has investigated the relation between Defeasible Logic and possible world semantics [8]. However, that work was meant to address a different research challenge, i.e., to develop neighbourhood semantics for a modal extension of SDL, thus going beyond operational and argumentation semantics for it.

This paper has a rather different goal: interpret Ramsey's test by showing how the change of defeasible theories allows for constructing selection function models for counterfactuals.

One limit of our work is that we exclude nested conditionals from the language. While some, like [1], rejected nested conditionals when a probabilistic treatment is considered, or it was argued that the intuitive meaning of such formulas is not clear [7,9,11], this is still a technical possibility. How to extend our methodology to deal with this case is a matter of future work.

References

1. Adams, E.: The logic of conditionals. Reidel (1975)
2. Antoniou, G., Billington, D., Governatori, G., Maher, M.J.: Representation results for defeasible logic. ACM Trans. Comput. Logic **2**, 255–287 (2001)
3. Billington, D., Antoniou, G., Governatori, G., Maher, M.: Revising nonmonotonic belief sets: the case of defeasible logic. In: Proceedings of the KI-99. Springer (1999)

4. Billington, D.: Defeasible logic is stable. J. Log. Comput. **3**(4), 379–400 (1993). https://doi.org/10.1093/logcom/3.4.379
5. Chellas, B.F.: Modal Logic. Cambridge University Press, An Introduction (1980)
6. Chellas, B.F.: Basic conditional logic. J. Philos. Logic **4**, 133–153 (1975)
7. Delgrande, J.P.: A first-order conditional logic for prototypical properties. Artif. Intell. **33**, 105–130 (1987)
8. Governatori, G., Rotolo, A., Calardo, E.: Possible world semantics for defeasible deontic logic. In: Ågotnes, T., Broersen, J., Elgesem, D. (eds.) DEON 2012. LNCS (LNAI), vol. 7393, pp. 46–60. Springer, Heidelberg (2012). https://doi.org/10.1007/978-3-642-31570-1_4
9. Lewis, D.: Counterfactuals. Harvard University Press, Cambridge, Mass (1973)
10. Maher, M.J.: Propositional defeasible logic has linear complexity. Theor. Pract. Log. Program. **1**(6), 691–711 (2001). https://doi.org/10.1017/S1471068401001168'doi.org/10.1017/S1471068401001168'
11. Nute, D.: Topics in Conditional Logic. Reidel, Dordrecht (1980)
12. Pollock, J.: Subjunctive Reasoning. Reidel, Dordrecht (1976)
13. Ramsey, F.: Truth and probability. In: Braithwaite, R. (ed.) Foundations of Mathematics and other Logical Essays, pp. 156–198. Kegan, Paul, London (1931)

KLM-Style Defeasibility for Restricted First-Order Logic

Giovanni Casini[1,2,3], Thomas Meyer[1,2,3]([⊠]), Guy Paterson-Jones[2,3],
and Ivan Varzinczak[1,3,4,5]

[1] ISTI–CNR, Pisa, Italy
[2] University of Cape Town, Cape Town, South Africa
[3] CAIR, Cape Town, South Africa
tmeyer@cs.uct.ac.za
[4] LIASD, Université Paris 8, Paris, France
[5] Stellenbosch University, Stellenbosch, South Africa

Abstract. In this paper, we extend the KLM approach to defeasible reasoning beyond the propositional setting. We do so by making it applicable to a restricted version of first-order logic. We describe defeasibility for this logic using a set of rationality postulates, provide a suitable and intuitive semantics for it, and present a representation result characterising the semantic description of defeasibility in terms of our postulates. An advantage of our semantics is that it is sufficiently general to be applicable to other restricted versions of first-order logic as well. Based on this theoretical core, we then propose a version of defeasible entailment that is inspired by the well-known notion of Rational Closure as it is defined for defeasible propositional logic and defeasible description logics. We show that this form of defeasible entailment is rational in the sense that it adheres to the full set of rationality postulates.

Keywords: Defeasible reasoning · First-order logic · Rationality

1 Introduction

The past 15 years have seen a flurry of activity to introduce defeasible-reasoning capabilities into languages that are more expressive than that of propositional logic [5,6,9,16,17,27]. Most of the focus has been on defeasibility for description logics (DLs), with much of it devoted to versions of the so-called KLM approach to defeasible reasoning initially advocated for propositional logic by Kraus et al. [22]. In DLs, knowledge is expressed as class inclusions of the form $C \sqsubseteq D$, with the intended meaning that every instance of C is also an instance of D. Defeasible DLs allow, in addition, for defeasible inclusions of the form $C \mathrel{\vcenter{\hbox{$\scriptstyle\sqsubset$}}\mkern-8mu\raise1pt\hbox{$\sim$}} D$ with the intended meaning that instances of C are *usually* instances of D. For example, Student $\mathrel{\vcenter{\hbox{$\scriptstyle\sqsubset$}}\mkern-8mu\raise1pt\hbox{$\sim$}}$ ¬∃pays.Tax (students usually don't pay tax) is a defeasible version of Student $\sqsubseteq$ ¬∃pays.Tax (students don't pay tax).

© The Author(s), under exclusive license to Springer Nature Switzerland AG 2022
G. Governatori and A.-Y. Turhan (Eds.): RuleML+RR 2022, LNCS 13752, pp. 81–94, 2022.
https://doi.org/10.1007/978-3-031-21541-4_6

In this paper, we focus instead on a restricted version of first-order logic (RFOL), for which a semantics in terms of Herbrand interpretations suffices. We provide the theoretical foundations for an extension of RFOL modelling defeasible reasoning (DRFOL). However, the availability of non-unary predicates means that the definition of an appropriate semantics for DRFOL is a non-trivial exercise. This is because the intuition underlying KLM-style defeasibility generally depends on the underlying language. For propositional logics the intuition dictates a notion of typicality over *possible worlds*. The statement "birds usually fly", formalised as bird $\mid\!\sim$ fly, says that in the most typical worlds in which bird is true, fly is also true. In contrast, defeasibility in DLs invokes a form of typicality over *individuals*. Thus Student $\sqsubseteq\!\!\!\sim \neg\exists$pays.Tax states that of all those individuals that are students, the most typical ones don't pay taxes. To see the problem in extending either of these intuitions to the case with non-unary predicates, consider the following version of an example by Delgrande [13].

Example 1. The following DRFOL knowledge base states that humans don't feed wild animals, that elephants are usually wild animals, that keepers are usually human, and that keepers usually feed elephants, but that Fred the keeper usually does not feed elephants (the connective $\rightsquigarrow$ refers to defeasible implication and variables are implicitly quantified).

$$
\mathcal{K} = \left\{
\begin{array}{c}
\mathsf{wild\_animal(x)} \wedge \mathsf{human(y)} \rightarrow \neg\mathsf{feeds(y,x),} \\
\mathsf{elephant(x)} \rightsquigarrow \mathsf{wild\_animal(x),} \\
\mathsf{keeper(x)} \rightsquigarrow \mathsf{human(x),} \\
\mathsf{elephant(x)} \wedge \mathsf{keeper(y)} \rightsquigarrow \mathsf{feeds(y,x),} \\
\mathsf{elephant(x)} \wedge \mathsf{keeper(fred)} \rightsquigarrow \neg\mathsf{feeds(fred,x)}
\end{array}
\right\}
$$

For any appropriate semantics, $\mathcal{K}$ above should be satisfiable (given a suitable notion of satisfiability). Then it soon becomes clear that the propositional approach cannot achieve this. To see why, note that applying the propositional intuition to the example would result in $\mathsf{elephant(x)} \wedge \mathsf{keeper(y)} \rightsquigarrow \mathsf{feeds(y,x)}$, meaning that in the most typical worlds (Herbrand interpretations in this case) all keepers feed all elephants. This is in conflict with $\mathsf{elephant(x)} \wedge \mathsf{keeper(fred)} \rightsquigarrow \neg\mathsf{feeds(fred,x)}$, which states that in the most typical Herbrand interpretations, keeper Fred does not feed any elephants. For any reasonable definition of satisfiability, this would render the knowledge base unsatisfiable.

The DL-based intuition of object typicality is also problematic. Under this intuition, the statement $\mathsf{elephant(x)} \rightsquigarrow \mathsf{wild\_animal(x)}$ would mean that the most typical elephants are wild animals. Similarly, $\mathsf{keeper(x)} \rightsquigarrow \mathsf{human(x)}$ would mean that the most typical keepers are human. Combined with the first statement in $\mathcal{K}$, it would then follow that the most typical keepers (being humans) do not feed the most typical elephants (being wild animals). On the other hand, the fourth statement in $\mathcal{K}$ explicitly states that the most typical keepers feed the most typical elephants, from which we obtain the counter-intuitive conclusion that typical elephants and typical keepers cannot exist simultaneously. Some reflection on this example should be sufficient to indicate that it represents a genuine limitation of the standard propositional and DL approaches to defeasibility when applied to FOL.

In this paper, we resolve this matter with a semantics that is in line with the propositional intuition of a typicality ordering over worlds, but also includes aspects of the DL intuition of typicality of individuals. We achieve the latter by enriching our semantics with *typicality objects*, which are used to represent *typical* individuals. Thus, elephant(x) ∧ keeper(y) ⤳ feeds(y, x) means that in the most typical enriched Herbrand interpretations, all typical keepers feed all typical elephants, with the understanding that there may be exceptional keepers that don't feed some elephants. Note that the term *typical* is used here in two different, but related, ways.

Our central theoretical result is a representation result (Theorems 1 and 2), showing that defeasible implication defined in this way can be characterised w.r.t. a set of KLM-style rationality postulates adapted for DRFOL. Another important consequence of our representation result is that it provides the theoretical foundation for the definition of various forms of defeasible entailment for DRFOL. We present one such form of defeasible entailment and show that it can be viewed as the DRFOL analogue of Rational Closure as originally defined for the propositional case [24].

In the rest of the paper, we start by providing a brief introduction to RFOL and to KLM-style defeasible reasoning (Sect. 2). In Sect. 3, we introduce DRFOL, describe an abstract notion of satisfaction w.r.t. a set of KLM-style postulates, provide a suitable semantics, and prove a representation result, showing that the KLM-style postulates characterise the semantic construction. In Sect. 4, we present a form of defeasible entailment for DRFOL that can be viewed as the DRFOL equivalent of the well-known notion of Rational Closure. Before concluding the paper, we discuss related work in Sect. 5.

2 Background

The language of RFOL builds on three disjoint sets of symbols: a finite set of constants CONST, a countably infinite set of variable symbols VAR, and a finite set of predicate symbols PRED. It has no function symbols. A *term* is an element of CONST ∪ VAR. Each predicate symbol $\alpha \in$ PRED has an *arity*, denoted $\mathsf{ar}(\alpha) \in \mathbb{N}$, representing the number of terms it takes as arguments. We assume the existence of predicate symbols $\top$ and $\bot$, which have arity 0. An *atom* is an expression of the form $\alpha(t_1, \ldots, t_{\mathsf{ar}(\alpha)})$, where $\alpha \in$ PRED and each t_i is a term. Observe that $\top$ and $\bot$ are atoms as well.

A *compound* is a Boolean combination of atoms (i.e., built from atoms and the logical connectives ¬, ∧, and ∨). An *implication* has the form $A(\vec{x}) \to B(\vec{y})$, where $A(\vec{x})$ and $B(\vec{y})$ are compounds, and where the terms occurring in $\vec{x}$ and $\vec{y}$ may overlap. A compound (resp. implication) is *ground* if all the terms contained in it are constants; otherwise it is *open*. Ground atoms are also known as *facts*.

The only formulas we permit are compounds and implications and these are understood to be implicitly universally quantified. We shall also adopt the following conventions. Constant symbols and variables are written in lowercase, with early letters used for constants $(a, b, \ldots)$ and later letters for variables $(x, y, \ldots)$. Compounds are denoted by uppercase letters $(A, B, \ldots)$. Tuples of variables or constants are written with overbars, such as $\vec{x}$ and $\vec{a}$ resp., and $A(\vec{x})$ and $B(\vec{a})$ are used as shorthand for compounds over their respective tuples of terms. We use lowercase early Greek letter $(\alpha, \beta, \ldots)$ to denote RFOL formulas, sometimes with tuples of terms $(\alpha(\vec{x}))$. The set of all formulas (compounds and implications) is denoted by $\mathcal{L}$. A *knowledge base* $\mathcal{K}$ is a finite subset of $\mathcal{L}$.

The Herbrand universe $\mathbb{U}$ is the set CONST. The *Herbrand base* of $\mathbb{U}$, denoted $\mathbb{B}$, is the set of facts defined over $\mathbb{U}$. A *Herbrand interpretation* is a subset $\mathcal{H} \subseteq \mathbb{B}$. The set of Herbrand interpretations is denoted by $\mathscr{H}$. *Substitutions* are defined to be functions $\varphi : \text{VAR} \to \text{VAR} \cup \text{CONST}$ assigning a term to each variable symbol. *Variable substitutions* are substitutions that assign only variables, and *ground substitutions* are substitutions that assign only constants. The application of a substitution φ to a compound $A(\vec{x})$ is denoted $A(\varphi(\vec{x}))$.

RFOL knowledge bases are interpreted by Herbrand interpretations $\mathcal{H}$ as follows: (1) if $A(\vec{a})$ is a ground atom, then $\mathcal{H} \Vdash A(\vec{a})$ iff $A(\vec{a}) \in \mathcal{H}$; (2) if $A(\vec{a})$ and $B(\vec{b})$ are ground compounds (where $\vec{a}$ and $\vec{b}$ may overlap), then $\mathcal{H} \Vdash A(\vec{a})$ and $\mathcal{H} \Vdash A(\vec{a}) \to B(\vec{b})$ as usual for Boolean connectives; (3) if $A(\vec{x})$ is an open compound, then $\mathcal{H} \Vdash A(\vec{x})$ iff $\mathcal{H} \Vdash A(\varphi(\vec{x}))$ for every ground substitution φ; (4) if $A(\vec{x}) \to B(\vec{y})$ is an open implication (where $\vec{x}$ and $\vec{y}$ may overlap), then $\mathcal{H} \Vdash A(\vec{x}) \to B(\vec{y})$ iff $\mathcal{H} \Vdash A(\varphi(\vec{x})) \to B(\varphi(\vec{y}))$ for every ground substitution φ, and (5) if $\mathcal{K}$ is a knowledge base, then $\mathcal{H} \Vdash \mathcal{K}$ iff $\mathcal{H} \Vdash \alpha$ for every $\alpha \in \mathcal{K}$. A Herbrand interpretation satisfying a knowledge base $\mathcal{K}$ is a *Herbrand model* of $\mathcal{K}$.

Kraus et al. [22] originally defined $\mathrel{|\!\sim}$ as a consequence relation over a propositional language, with statements of the form $\alpha \mathrel{|\!\sim} \beta$ to be interpreted as the meta-statement "β is a defeasible consequence of α". Subsequently, Lehmann and Magidor [24] made a subtle shift in considering an object-level language containing statements of the form $\alpha \mathrel{|\!\sim} \beta$, to be interpreted as the object-level statement "α defeasibly implies β", and with $\mathrel{|\!\sim}$ viewed as an object-level connective. This view is captured by a set of *rationality postulates*, which have been widely discussed in the literature. We do not repeat these rationality postulates here, but note that Definition 3, our definition of rationality for DRFOL, the defeasible version of RFOL, relies heavily on versions of the KLM rationality postulates that are lifted to DRFOL (see Sect. 3).

A semantics for defeasible implications is provided by *ranked interpretations* $\mathscr{R}$, with $\mathscr{R}$ a function from U (the set of all valuations) to $\mathbb{N} \cup \{\infty\}$, satisfying the following *convexity property*: for every $i \in \mathbb{N}$, if $\mathscr{R}(u) = i$, then, for every $j < i$, there is a $u' \in U$ for which $\mathscr{R}(u') = j$. $\mathscr{R}(v)$ indicates the degree of *atypicality* of v. The valuations judged most typical are those with rank 0, while those with infinite rank are judged so atypical as to be impossible. A defeasible statement $\alpha \mathrel{|\!\sim} \beta$ is *satisfied in* $\mathscr{R}$ ($\mathscr{R} \Vdash \alpha \mathrel{|\!\sim} \beta$) if the models of α with the smallest *finite* rank in $\mathscr{R}$ are all models of β. A classical statement α is satisfied in $\mathscr{R}$ ($\mathscr{R} \Vdash \alpha$) if every valuation of finite rank satisfies α.

Note that $\mathscr{R} \Vdash \neg\alpha \mathrel{\vert\!\sim} \bot$ iff all the models of $\neg\alpha$ have infinite rank, which is equivalent by definition to $\mathscr{R} \Vdash \alpha$.

3   Defeasible Restricted First-Order Logic

Defeasible Restricted First-Order Logic (DRFOL) extends the logic RFOL presented above with *defeasible implications* of the form $A(\vec{x}) \rightsquigarrow B(\vec{y})$, where $A(\vec{x})$ and $B(\vec{y})$ are compounds, and where $\vec{x}$ and $\vec{y}$ may overlap. The set of defeasible implications is denoted $\mathcal{L}^{\rightsquigarrow}$, and a *DRFOL knowledge base* $\mathcal{K}$ is defined to be a subset of $\mathcal{L} \cup \mathcal{L}^{\rightsquigarrow}$. Note that DRFOL knowledge bases may include (classical) RFOL formulas.

As demonstrated in Example 1, defeasible implications are intended to model properties that *typically* hold, but which may have exceptions. In this example, for instance, elephant(x) $\wedge$ keeper(fred) $\rightsquigarrow$ ¬feeds(fred, x), is an exception to elephant(x) $\wedge$ keeper(y) $\rightsquigarrow$ feeds(y, x). A DRFOL knowledge base containing these statements ought to be satisfiable (for an appropriate notion of satisfaction). The same goes for the DRFOL knowledge base {bird(x) $\rightsquigarrow$ fly(x), bird(tweety), ¬fly(tweety)}. To formalise these intuitions we first describe the intended behaviour of the defeasible connective $\rightsquigarrow$ and its interaction with (classical) RFOL formulas in terms of a set of rationality postulates in the KLM style [22, 24]. These postulates are expressed via an abstract notion of satisfaction:

Definition 1. *A* satisfaction set *is a subset* $\mathcal{S} \subseteq \mathcal{L} \cup \mathcal{L}^{\rightsquigarrow}$.

We denote the classical part of a satisfaction set by $\mathcal{S}_C = \mathcal{S} \cap \mathcal{L}$. The first postulate we consider ensures $\mathcal{S}$ respects the classical notion of satisfaction when restricted to classical formulas, where $\models$ refers to classical entailment:

$$(\text{CLA}) \quad \frac{\mathcal{S}_C \models \alpha}{\alpha \in \mathcal{S}}$$

Next, we consider the interaction between classical and defeasible implications:

$$(\text{SUP}) \quad \frac{A(\vec{x}) \in \mathcal{S}}{\neg A(\vec{x}) \rightsquigarrow \bot \in \mathcal{S}}$$

We now consider the core of the proposal for defining rational satisfaction sets, the KLM rationality postulates, lifted to DRFOL, and expressed in terms of satisfaction sets:

$$(\text{REFL}) \quad A(\vec{x}) \rightsquigarrow A(\vec{x}) \in \mathcal{S}$$

$$(\text{RW}) \quad \frac{A(\vec{x}) \rightsquigarrow B(\vec{y}) \in \mathcal{S}, \ \models B(\vec{y}) \rightarrow C(\vec{z})}{A(\vec{x}) \rightsquigarrow C(\vec{z}) \in \mathcal{S}}$$

$$(\text{LLE}) \quad \frac{A(\vec{x}) \rightsquigarrow C(\vec{z}) \in \mathcal{S}, \ \models A(\vec{x}) \rightarrow B(\vec{y}), \ \models B(\vec{y}) \rightarrow A(\vec{x})}{B(\vec{y}) \rightsquigarrow C(\vec{z}) \in \mathcal{S}}$$

$$(\text{AND}) \quad \frac{A(\vec{x}) \rightsquigarrow B(\vec{y}) \in \mathcal{S}, \ A(\vec{x}) \rightsquigarrow C(\vec{z}) \in \mathcal{S}}{A(\vec{x}) \rightsquigarrow B(\vec{y}) \wedge C(\vec{z}) \in \mathcal{S}}$$

$$(\text{OR}) \quad \frac{A(\vec{x}) \rightsquigarrow C(\vec{z}) \in \mathcal{S}, \ B(\vec{y}) \rightsquigarrow C(\vec{z}) \in \mathcal{S}}{A(\vec{x}) \vee B(\vec{y}) \rightsquigarrow C(\vec{z}) \in \mathcal{S}}$$

$$(\text{RM}) \quad \frac{A(\vec{x}) \rightsquigarrow \neg B(\vec{y}) \notin \mathcal{S}, \ A(\vec{x}) \wedge B(\vec{y}) \rightsquigarrow C(\vec{z}) \notin \mathcal{S}}{A(\vec{x}) \rightsquigarrow C(\vec{z}) \notin \mathcal{S}}$$

Next we consider *instantiations* of implications (applicable to all substitutions of the right type):

$$(\text{DUI}) \quad \frac{A(\vec{x}) \rightsquigarrow B(\vec{y}) \in \mathcal{S}}{A(\varphi(\vec{x})) \rightsquigarrow B(\varphi(\vec{y})) \in \mathcal{S}}$$

To begin with, note that universal instantiation is *not* a desirable property for defeasible implications. To see why, consider a satisfaction set $\mathcal{S}$ containing elephant(x) $\wedge$ keeper(y) $\rightsquigarrow$ feeds(y, x) and elephant(x) $\wedge$ keeper(fred) $\rightsquigarrow$ ¬feeds(fred, x). From (DUI) we have elephant(x) $\wedge$ keeper(fred) $\rightsquigarrow$ feeds(fred, x) $\in \mathcal{S}$, and hence by (AND) and (RW) that elephant(x) $\wedge$ keeper(fred) $\rightsquigarrow \perp \in \mathcal{S}$ as well, which is in conflict with the intuition that exceptional cases (all elephants usually not being fed by keeper Fred) should be permitted to exist alongside the general case (all elephants usually being fed by all keepers).

Weaker forms of instantiation for defeasible implications are more reasonable. Consider keeper(x) $\rightsquigarrow$ feeds(x, y), which states that keepers typically feed everything. While we cannot conclude anything about instances of x, for the reasons discussed above, we should at least be able to conclude things about instances of y, since y only appears in the consequent of the implication. This motivates the following postulate (again, applicable to all substitutions of the right type), where ψ is a variable substitution and $\vec{x} \cap \vec{y} = \emptyset$:

$$(\text{IRR}) \quad \frac{A(\vec{x}) \rightsquigarrow B(\vec{x}, \vec{y}) \in \mathcal{S}}{A(\vec{x}) \rightsquigarrow B(\vec{x}, \varphi(\vec{y})) \in \mathcal{S}}$$

There are some more subtle forms of defeasible instantiation that seem reasonable as well. Consider the following relation defined over $\mathcal{L}$:

Definition 2. $A(\vec{x})$ *is* at least as typical as $B(\vec{y})$ *w.r.t.* $\mathcal{S}$, *denoted* $A(\vec{x}) \preccurlyeq_\mathcal{S} B(\vec{y})$, *iff* $A(\vec{x}) \vee B(\vec{y}) \rightsquigarrow \neg A(\vec{x}) \notin \mathcal{S}$.

Intuitively, $A(\vec{x}) \preccurlyeq_\mathcal{S} B(\vec{y})$ states that typical instances of $A(\vec{x})$ are at least as typical as typical instances of $B(\vec{y})$. Note that for any variable substitution φ, a typical instance of $A(\varphi(\vec{x}))$ is always an instance of $A(\vec{x})$. Thus the following postulate should hold, where φ is any variable substitution:

$$(\text{TYP}) \quad A(\vec{x}) \preccurlyeq_\mathcal{S} A(\varphi(\vec{x}))$$

The last postulate we consider has to do with defeasibly impossible formulas. Suppose $A(\varphi(\vec{x})) \rightsquigarrow \perp \in \mathcal{S}$ for all substitutions $\varphi : \text{VAR} \to \text{VAR} \cup \mathbb{U}$. This states that if *all* specialisations of $A(\vec{x})$ are defeasibly impossible, then we should expect that there are in fact no instances of $A(\vec{x})$ at all:

$$(\text{IMP}) \quad \frac{A(\varphi(\vec{x})) \rightsquigarrow \perp \in \mathcal{S} \text{ for all } \varphi : \text{VAR} \to \text{VAR} \cup \mathbb{U}}{\neg A(\vec{x}) \in \mathcal{S}}$$

This puts us in a position to define the central construction of the paper, namely that of a *rational* satisfaction set.

Definition 3. $\mathcal{S}$ *is* rational *iff it satisfies* (CLA), (SUP), (IRR), (TYP), (IMP) *and* (REFL)-(RM).

Rational satisfaction sets satisfy the following form of label invariance for defeasible implications, where the variable substitution φ is a *permutation*:

$$(\text{PER}) \quad \frac{A(\vec{x}) \leadsto B(\vec{y}) \in \mathcal{S}}{A(\varphi(\vec{x})) \leadsto B(\varphi(\vec{y})) \in \mathcal{S}}$$

Proposition 1. *Let $\mathcal{S}$ be a rational satisfaction set. Then $\mathcal{S}$ satisfies* (PER).

We define a semantics for defeasible implications by enriching the Herbrand universe with a set $\mathcal{T}$ of *typicality objects*. Typicality objects represent individuals that are not explicitly mentioned in a given knowledge base, and are used here to interpret defeasible implications in a ranking of (enriched) Herbrand interpretations.

Definition 4. *Given a set of typicality objects $\mathcal{T}$, the corresponding enriched Herbrand universe is defined to be the set $\mathbb{U}_{\mathcal{T}} = \mathbb{U} \cup \mathcal{T}$. For each possible partition of $\mathbb{U}$ into two sets $\mathbb{U}_t$ and $\mathbb{U}_e$ (both possibly empty), we have a typicality set $Typ = \mathbb{U}_t \cup \mathcal{T}$. An enriched Herbrand interpretation (or EHI) $\mathcal{E}$ is a Herbrand interpretation defined over an enriched Herbrand universe $\mathbb{U}_{\mathcal{T}}$, and associated with $Typ_{\mathcal{E}}$, one of the possible typicality sets in $\mathbb{U}_{\mathcal{T}}$.*

Using the typicality sets in enriched Herbrand interpretations we distinguish between typical and atypical objects. That is, we assume that, given an interpretation $\mathcal{E}$, all the objects in $Typ_{\mathcal{E}}$ are typical objects, while the set $\mathbb{U}_e = \mathbb{U}_{\mathcal{T}} \setminus Typ_{\mathcal{E}}$ represents the exceptional ones.

Every EHI $\mathcal{E}$ restricts to a unique Herbrand interpretation $\mathcal{H}^{\mathcal{E}}$ over $\mathbb{U}$, defined by $\mathcal{H}^{\mathcal{E}} = \mathcal{E} \cap \mathbb{B}$. The set of EHIs over $\mathcal{T}$ is denoted by $\mathscr{H}_{\mathcal{T}}$. To interpret defeasible implications we make use of preference rankings over $\mathscr{H}_{\mathcal{T}}$.

Definition 5. *A ranked interpretation is a function $rk : \mathscr{H}_{\mathcal{T}} \to \Omega \cup \{\infty\}$, for some linear poset Ω, satisfying the following properties, where we define $\mathscr{H}_{\mathcal{T}}^{rk} = \{\mathcal{E} \in \mathscr{H}_{\mathcal{T}} : rk(\mathcal{E}) \neq \infty\}$ to be the set of possible EHIs w.r.t. rk, and $\mathscr{H}_{\mathcal{T}}^{rk}(A(\vec{x})) = \{\mathcal{E} \in \mathscr{H}_{\mathcal{T}}^{rk} : \mathcal{E} \Vdash A(\varphi(\vec{x}))$ for some $\varphi : \text{VAR} \to Typ_{\mathcal{E}}\}$ to be the set of possible EHIs w.r.t. rk satisfying some typical instance of $A(\vec{x}) \in \mathcal{L}$:*

1. *if $rk(\mathcal{E}) = x < \infty$, then for every $y \leq x$ there is some $\mathcal{E}' \in \mathscr{H}_{\mathcal{T}}$ such that $rk(\mathcal{E}') = y$;*
2. *for all $A(\vec{x}) \in \mathcal{L}$, $\mathscr{H}_{\mathcal{T}}^{rk}(A(\vec{x}))$ is either empty or has an element that is an rk-minimal model of $A(\vec{x})$. This is smoothness [22].*

The set of ranked interpretations over $\mathcal{T}$ is denoted $\mathcal{R}_{\mathcal{T}}$.

Definition 6. *Let rk be a ranked interpretation. For all $A(\vec{x}), B(\vec{y}) \in \mathcal{L}$:*

1. *$rk \Vdash A(\vec{x})$ iff $\mathcal{E} \Vdash A(\vec{x})$ for all $\mathcal{E} \in \mathscr{H}_{\mathcal{T}}^{rk}$;*
2. *$rk \Vdash A(\vec{x}) \to B(\vec{y})$ iff $\mathcal{E} \Vdash A(\vec{x}) \to B(\vec{y})$ for all $\mathcal{E} \in \mathscr{H}_{\mathcal{T}}^{rk}$;*
3. *$rk \Vdash A(\vec{x}) \leadsto B(\vec{y})$ iff $\mathcal{E} \Vdash A(\varphi(\vec{x})) \to B(\varphi(\vec{y}))$ for all $\mathcal{E} \in \min_{rk} \mathscr{H}_{\mathcal{T}}^{rk}(A(\vec{x}))$ and all $\varphi : \text{VAR} \to Typ_{\mathcal{E}}$.*

Thus, compounds and classical implications are true in a ranked interpretation rk if they are true in all possible EHIs w.r.t. rk, while a defeasible implication is true in rk if its classical counterparts, with variables substituted by typicality objects, are true in all minimal EHIs (possible w.r.t. rk) in which the antecedent of the defeasible implication is true. A ranked interpretation in which a statement is true is a *ranked model* of the statement.

Example 2. This is a (slightly modified) example proposed by Delgrande [13]. Let CONST = {clyde, fred}, VAR = {x, y}, and PRED = {elephant, keeper, likes}. The following DRFOL knowledge base states that elephants and keepers are disjoint, that elephants usually like keepers, that elephants usually *don't* like keeper Fred, and that elephant Clyde usually *does* like Fred:

$$\mathcal{K} = \left\{ \begin{array}{c} \mathsf{elephant(x)} \rightarrow \neg\mathsf{keeper(x)}, \\ \mathsf{elephant(x)} \wedge \mathsf{keeper(y)} \rightsquigarrow \mathsf{likes(x,y)}, \\ \mathsf{elephant(x)} \wedge \mathsf{keeper(fred)} \rightsquigarrow \neg\mathsf{likes(x,fred)}, \\ \mathsf{elephant(clyde)} \wedge \mathsf{keeper(fred)} \rightsquigarrow \mathsf{likes(clyde,fred)} \end{array} \right\}$$

Let $\mathcal{T} = \{t_1, \ldots\}$ be the set of typicality objects. For readability we abbreviate elephant with e, keeper with k and likes with l.

Consider the EHIs $\mathcal{E}_1 = \{\mathsf{e}(t_1), \mathsf{k}(t_2), \mathsf{l}(t_1, t_2), \mathsf{e}(t_2), \mathsf{e}(\mathsf{clyde}), \mathsf{k}(\mathsf{fred}), \mathsf{l}(\mathsf{clyde}, \mathsf{fred})\}$, $\mathcal{E}_2 = \{\mathsf{e}(t_1), \mathsf{k}(t_2), \mathsf{l}(t_1, t_2), \mathsf{k}(t_3), \mathsf{l}(t_1, t_3), \mathsf{e}(\mathsf{clyde}), \mathsf{k}(\mathsf{fred}), \mathsf{l}(\mathsf{clyde}, \mathsf{fred})\}$, and $\mathcal{E}_3 = \{\mathsf{e}(t_1), \mathsf{k}(t_2), \mathsf{e}(t_2), \mathsf{e}(\mathsf{clyde}), \mathsf{k}(\mathsf{fred}), \mathsf{l}(\mathsf{clyde}, \mathsf{fred})\}$. In all these EHIs let $\mathbb{U}_t = \emptyset$ and consequently $Typ = \mathcal{T}$. That is, in each of them the defeasible implications are evaluated only w.r.t. the typicality objects. Let $rk_1(\mathcal{E}_1) = rk_1(\mathcal{E}_2) = 0$, $rk_1(\mathcal{E}_3) = 1$, and $rk_1(\mathcal{E}) = \infty$ for all other EHIs. Then rk_1 is a ranked model of the knowledge base above. Let $rk_2(\mathcal{E}_1) = rk_2(\mathcal{E}_3) = 0$, $rk_2(\mathcal{E}_2) = 1$, and $rk_2(\mathcal{E}) = \infty$ for all other EHIs. Then rk_2 is not a ranked model of $\mathsf{elephant(x)} \wedge \mathsf{keeper(y)} \rightsquigarrow \mathsf{likes(x,y)}$, but is a ranked model of $\mathsf{elephant(x)} \wedge \mathsf{keeper(fred)} \rightsquigarrow \neg\mathsf{likes(x,fred)}$ and $\mathsf{elephant(clyde)} \wedge \mathsf{keeper(fred)} \rightsquigarrow \mathsf{likes(clyde,fred)}$.

The main important technical result of the paper is a representation result, comprising a *soundness* result (Theorem 1) and a *completeness* result (Theorem 2), showing that ranked interpretations precisely characterise rational satisfaction sets:

Definition 7. *The satisfaction set* $\mathcal{S}^{rk}$ *corresponding to a ranked interpretation rk is:* $\mathcal{S}^{rk} = \{\alpha \in \mathcal{L} \cup \mathcal{L}^{\rightsquigarrow} : rk \Vdash \alpha\}$.

First we show that all ranked interpretations generate rational satisfaction sets as defined above:

Theorem 1. *For every ranked interpretation rk, $\mathcal{S}^{rk}$ is a rational satisfaction set.*

Then we show every rational set $\mathcal{S}$ can be realised as the satisfaction set corresponding to some ranked interpretation:

Theorem 2. *For every rational satisfaction set $\mathcal{S}$ there exists a ranked interpretation rk, over an infinite set of $\mathcal{T}$ of typicality objects, such that $\mathcal{S} = \mathcal{S}^{rk}$.*

4   Defeasible Entailment

A central question that we have postponed until now is *entailment*. That is, given a DRFOL knowledge base $\mathcal{K}$, when are we justified in asserting that a DRFOL formula α follows defeasibly from $\mathcal{K}$? In this section, we provide one answer to this question by defining a semantic version of *Rational Closure* [24] for DRFOL. It is, by now, well-established that systems for defeasible reasoning are amenable to multiple forms of entailment, and the work we present in this section should therefore be viewed as the first step in a larger investigation into defeasible entailment.

In this section we consider the question of defeasible entailment for DRFOL and define a semantic version of *Rational Closure* [24] for DRFOL. Due to the so-called *drowning effect* [4], it is considered inferentially too weak for some application domains. Despite that, it is a semantic construction that can be extended to obtain other interesting entailment relations [10,12,15,23]. It has gained attention in the framework of DLs [6,9,11,17]. An equivalent semantic construction, System Z [26], has been considered for unary first-order logic [2,3,20]. Several equivalent definitions of Rational Closure can be found in the literature. Here we refer to the approach due to Booth and Paris [7] and Giordano et al. [17].

Let a knowledge base $\mathcal{K}$ be a set of propositional defeasible implications $\alpha \mathrel{|\!\sim} \beta$. Booth and Paris provide a construction with the following two immediate consequences: (*i*) Given all the ranked models of $\mathcal{K}$, there is a model $\mathscr{R}^*$ of $\mathcal{K}$, that we can call the *minimal* one, which assigns to every propositional valuation v the *minimal* rank assigned to it by any of the ranked models of $\mathcal{K}$. (*ii*) Propositional Rational Closure can be characterised using $\mathscr{R}^*$. That is, $\alpha \mathrel{|\!\sim} \beta$ is in the (propositional) Rational Closure of $\mathcal{K}$ iff $\mathscr{R}^* \Vdash \alpha \mathrel{|\!\sim} \beta$. The intuition behind the use of the ranked model $\mathscr{R}^*$ for the definition of entailment is that it formalises the *presumption of typicality* [23]: assigning to each valuation the lowest possible rank, we model a reasoning pattern in which we assume that we are in one of the most typical situations that are compatible with our knowledge base.

We can define an analogous construction for DRFOL, but to do so we first need to address a technical restriction regarding typicality objects. More specifically, Theorem 2 requires an infinite set of typicality objects to be true in general. The next result shows that ranked interpretations can be restricted to finite sets of typicality objects, which is exactly what we need for our definition of defeasible entailment.

Proposition 2. *Let $\mathcal{K} \subseteq \mathcal{L} \cup \mathcal{L}^{\frown}$. Then $\mathcal{K}$ has a unique minimal ranked model iff it has a unique minimal ranked model over a finite set $\mathcal{T}'$ of typicality objects, with the size of $\mathcal{T}'$ referred to as the order of $\mathcal{K}$.*

The order of $\mathcal{K}$ depends on the number of formulas in $\mathcal{K}$ and the number of quantifier-bound variables in the formula, and is easy to calculate. The minimal ranked interpretation is defined in two stages, combining the two minimisation approaches used in propositional logic and DLs, respectively: first the rank $rk_{\mathcal{K}}^*$, a minimisation with respect to the rank of the EHIs, in line with the propositional approach [7,17]; then we refine it into the rank $rk_{\mathcal{K}}$, based on the minimisation of the position of the constants inside the EHIs, in line with the DL approach [9,17].

Definition 8. *Let $\mathcal{K} \subseteq \mathcal{L} \cup \mathcal{L}^{\frown}$ be of order n, and take $\mathcal{T}' \subset \mathcal{T}$ to be a finite set of typicality objects of cardinality n. The rank $rk_{\mathcal{K}}^* : \mathcal{H}_{\mathcal{T}'} \to \mathbb{N} \cup \{\infty\}$ is defined as follows:*

$$rk_{\mathcal{K}}^*(\mathcal{E}) = \min\{rk(\mathcal{E}) : rk \in \mathcal{R}_{\mathcal{T}'} \text{ and } rk \Vdash \mathcal{K}\}.$$

The minimal ranked model of $\mathcal{K}$, which we denote by $rk_{\mathcal{K}} : \mathcal{H}_{\mathcal{T}'} \to (\mathbb{N} \times \mathbb{N}) \cup \{\infty\}$, is defined as:

- $rk_{\mathcal{K}}(\mathcal{E}) = \infty$, *if* $rk_{\mathcal{K}}^*(\mathcal{E}) = \infty$;
- $rk_{\mathcal{K}}(\mathcal{E}) = (i, j)$, *if:*

a) $rk_{\mathcal{K}}^*(\mathcal{E}) = i$ *($i \in \mathbb{N}$); and*
b) *for every $k \geq j$, there is no $\mathcal{E}'$ s.t. $Typ'_{\mathcal{E}} \supset Typ_{\mathcal{E}}$ and $rk_{\mathcal{K}}(\mathcal{E}') = (i, k)$; and*
c) *for every $l < j$, there is some $\mathcal{E}'$ s.t. $Typ'_{\mathcal{E}} \supset Typ_{\mathcal{E}}$ and $rk_{\mathcal{K}}(\mathcal{E}') = (i, l)$.*

The order is defined lexicographically: $(i,j) \leq (k,l)$ *iff* $i < j$, *or* $i = j$ *and* $j \leq l$.

Given a consistent $\mathcal{K}$ and fixed a finite set of typicality constants, $rk_{\mathcal{K}}$ exists and is unique.

Proposition 3. *Let $\mathcal{K}$ be a knowledge base with a ranked model rk. Then, for a fixed finite enriched Herbrand universe $\mathbb{U}_{\mathcal{T}}$, $\mathcal{K}$ has exactly one minimal ranked model $rk_{\mathcal{K}}$.*

Note that by convention $\min \emptyset = \infty$, and $rk_{\mathcal{K}}$ is a ranked interpretation over $\mathcal{T}'$, since the lexicographic order defined in Definition 8 can easily be translated into an order defined over $\mathbb{N} \cup \infty$ satisfying the constraints from Definition 5. Hence $rk_{\mathcal{K}} \in \mathcal{R}_{\mathcal{T}'}$. Intuitively, $rk_{\mathcal{K}}$ is the result of first "pushing" every EHI rank as low as possible amongst the models of $\mathcal{K}$, similar to how it's done in the propositional approach, and then giving priority to the EHIs that have a bigger set of objects considered typical. That is, a bigger set Typ, in line with the DL approach. This minimal ranked model can be used to define a defeasible entailment relation for DRFOL:

Definition 9. *Let $\mathcal{K} \subseteq \mathcal{L} \cup \mathcal{L}^{\leadsto}$ and $\alpha \in \mathcal{L} \cup \mathcal{L}^{\leadsto}$. Then α is in the* Rational Closure *of $\mathcal{K}$, denoted $\mathcal{K} \approx_{rc} \alpha$, iff $rk_{\mathcal{K}} \Vdash \alpha$.*

The idea is that we give preference to the EHIs in which the set of typical individuals is maximal. That is, we assume that as many objects as possible behave according to our expectations.

Example 3. Assume $\mathcal{K}$ as in Example 2. The order of $\mathcal{K}$ is 2, so we build our minimal model $rk_{\mathcal{K}}$ using the set of EHIs $\mathscr{H}_{\mathcal{T}'}$, where the set of typical constants is $\mathcal{T}' = \{t_1, t_2\}$. Each EHI $\mathcal{E}$ satisfying $\mathcal{K}$ will be assigned rank $rk_{\mathcal{K}'}^*(\mathcal{E}) = 0$. That is, all the EHIs in which, given two constants $a, b \in Typ_{\mathcal{E}}$, if a is an elephant and b is a keeper, a likes b but, if fred is a keeper, a does not like fred. Also, if fred is a keeper and clyde is an elephant, clyde likes fred. All the other EHIs will be assigned rank 1, apart those in which keepers and elephants are not disjoint, that will have rank ∞. For example, the EHI $\mathcal{E}_1$ from Example 2 would have rank 0, while $\mathcal{E}_3$ would have rank 1, since it does not satisfy the formula elephant(x) $\wedge$ keeper(y) $\leadsto$ likes(x, y) ($\mathcal{E}_2$ is not considered in $rk_{\mathcal{K}}$, since it uses the constant t_3).

Now extend $\mathcal{K}$ into $\mathcal{K}'$ by adding the facts elephant(dustin) and keeper(george). Also, add the unary predicate purple(x) to PRED. The order of $\mathcal{K}'$ is still 2, so we build our minimal model $rk_{\mathcal{K}'}$ using again the set of EHIs $\mathscr{H}_{\mathcal{T}'}$. Again, each EHI $\mathcal{E}$ satisfying $\mathcal{K}'$ will be assigned rank $rk_{\mathcal{K}'}^*(\mathcal{E}) = 0$, while only the EHIs in which elephants and keepers are not disjoint, and either dustin is not an elephant or george is not a keeper, will have rank ∞.

We need to refine $rk_{\mathcal{K}}^*$ into $rk_{\mathcal{K}}$ looking at the relative sizes of the sets Typ associated to each EHI. Among the EHIs $\mathcal{E}$ s.t. $rk_{\mathcal{K}}^*(\mathcal{E}) = 0$, the ones in which $Typ_{\mathcal{E}}$ is bigger are those in which $Typ_{\mathcal{E}} = \mathcal{T} \cup \mathbb{U}$. In order to satisfy $\mathcal{K}'$, in such EHIs it is necessary that fred is not a keeper. Such EHIs will have rank $(0,0)$ in $rk_{\mathcal{K}'}$. Since we have no information forcing the exceptionality of dustin and george, such minimal models must satisfy likes(dustin, george), and we obtain the intuitive conclusion that $\mathcal{K}' \approx_{rc} \top \leadsto$ likes(dustin, george).

Being a ranked interpretation, the desirable form of monotonicity (RM) holds. For example, note that all EHIs $\mathcal{E}$ at rank $(0,0)$ in the minimal model $rk_{\mathcal{K}'}$ would either satisfy purple(a) or not for any $a \in Typ_{\mathcal{E}}$, since it is irrelevant w.r.t. the satisfaction of $\mathcal{K}'$. The outcome would be that, while satisfying elephant(x) $\wedge$ keeper(fred) $\leadsto$ $\neg$likes(x, fred) (which is in $\mathcal{K}'$), $rk_{\mathcal{K}'}$ would not satisfy elephant(x) $\wedge$ keeper(fred) $\leadsto$ $\neg$purple(x), while it would satisfy elephant(x) $\wedge$ purple(x) $\wedge$ keeper(fred) $\leadsto$ $\neg$likes(x, fred).

More generally, Rational Closure, in the propositional and DL cases, satisfies a number of attractive properties:

$$(\textsc{Incl})\quad \alpha \in \mathcal{K} \text{ implies } \mathcal{K} \mathrel{\mathrlap{\sim}{\vdash}}_{rc} \alpha$$

$$(\textsc{Smp})\quad \mathcal{S} = \{\alpha : \mathcal{K} \mathrel{\mathrlap{\sim}{\vdash}}_{rc} \alpha\} \text{ is rational}$$

It is straightforward that these properties carry over to our definition of $\mathrel{\mathrlap{\sim}{\vdash}}_{rc}$.

Theorem 3. $\mathrel{\mathrlap{\sim}{\vdash}}_{rc}$ *satisfies* (\textsc{Incl}) *and* (\textsc{Smp}).

It is worthwhile delving a bit deeper into each of these properties. The first one, (\textsc{Incl}), also known as Inclusion, simply requires that statements in $\mathcal{K}$ also be defeasibly entailed by $\mathcal{K}$. It is a meta-version of the (\textsc{Refl}) rationality postulate for propositional logic (described in Sect. 2) and for DRFOL (described in Sect. 3). While the property itself might seem self-evident, it is instructive to view it in concert with the definition of $rk_{\mathcal{K}}$. From this it follows that $rk_{\mathcal{K}}$, which essentially defines Rational Closure, is the ranked interpretation in which EHIs are assigned a ranking that is truly as low (i.e., as typical) as possible, subject to the constraint that $rk_{\mathcal{K}}$ is a model of $\mathcal{K}$. This aligns with the intuition of propositional Rational Closure which requires of valuations in a ranked interpretation to be as typical as possible.

(\textsc{Smp}) requires the set of statements corresponding to the Rational Closure of $\mathcal{K}$ to be rational (cf. Definition 3). By virtue of Theorem 2, this requires defeasible entailment to be characterised by a *single* ranked interpretation, whence the fact the property is also referred to as Single Model Property.

5   Related Work

Defeasible reasoning is part of a broader research programme on conditional reasoning [1], most of which was developed for propositional logic. This paper falls in the class of approaches aimed at moving beyond propositional expressivity. Besides the many extensions of defeasible reasoning to DLs in the recent literature [5,9,17], there have also been proposals to extend this approach to FOL. Most of these define a preference order on the domain [8,14,28], in line with some of the aforementioned DL proposals, and present rationality postulates, but they do not provide characterisations in terms of rationality postulates. Others [13,21] are formally closer to our work in that they use preference orders over interpretations.

Delgrande [13] proposes a semantics closer to the intuitions behind *circumscription* [25], giving preference to interpretations minimising counter-examples to defeasible conditionals. On the other hand, Kern-Isberner and Thimm [21] propose a technical solution much closer to the work we present here. Like ours, their semantics is based on Herbrand interpretations. They define *ordinal conditional functions* over the set of Herbrand interpretations, obtaining a structure that is very close to our ranked interpretations. They identify some individuals as *representatives* of a conditional. This is done to formalise the same intuition (or, at least, an intuition that is very similar) that underlies our decision to introduce typicality objects. Apart from other formal differences (e.g. the expressivity of their language is slightly different), their work focuses on the definition of a notion of entailment based on a specific semantic construction carried over from the propositional framework known as *c-representations* of a conditional knowledge base [18,19]. In contrast, our focus in this paper is on getting the theoretical foundations of defeasible reasoning for restricted FOL in place. Thus, our work here is centred around a representation result that provides a characterisation of the semantics in terms of structural properties. And while we present some results on defeasible entailment, we have left a more in-depth study of this important topic as future work. Indeed, it is our conjecture that the foundations we have put in place in this paper will allow for the definition of more than one form of defeasible entailment. At the same time, a more in-depth comparison with the proposal of Kern-Isberner and Thimm remains to be done.

Kern-Isberner and Beierle [20] and Beierle et al. [2,3] use the same semantic approach of Kern-Isberner and Thimm [21] to develop an extension of Pearl's System Z [26] for first-order logic, but they restrict their attention to unary predicates. System Z is a form of entailment that is very close to the approach we introduce here.

Brafman [8] suggests preference orders over the domain should result in forms of reasoning quite different from the use of preference orders on interpretations, comparable to the difference between statistical and subjective readings of probabilities. We leave an investigation of the differences between these two modelling solutions as future work.

We conclude this section with some remarks on the differences between DRFOL and the defeasible DL $\mathcal{DALC}$ [9]. When $\mathcal{DALC}$ is stripped of existential and value restrictions and confined to TBox statements, and when DRFOL is restricted to unary predicates and open implications (defeasible and classical), every concept C in $\mathcal{DALC}$ can be mapped to a compound $C(x)$ in DRFOL, and vice versa. It is then possible to obtain a result that is analogous to the propositional case, with one exception: a defeasible implication of the form $C(x) \rightsquigarrow \bot$ has a meaning that is different than $C \sqsubseteq_\sim \bot$, its $\mathcal{DALC}$ counterpart.

This marks an important distinction between DRFOL and both the propositional KLM framework and $\mathcal{DALC}$, in which classical statements are equivalent to certain defeasible implications. In the propositional case, α is equivalent to $\neg\alpha \mathbin{|\!\sim} \bot$ ($\mathscr{R} \Vdash \alpha$ iff $\mathscr{R} \Vdash \neg\alpha \mathbin{|\!\sim} \bot$ for all $\mathscr{R}$) while, for $\mathcal{DALC}$, $C \sqsubseteq \bot$ is equivalent to $C \sqsubseteq_\sim \bot$. But in DRFOL, defeasible implications *cannot* inform us about compounds or classical implications. Formally, rational satisfaction sets do *not* necessarily satisfy the following postulate:

$$(\textsc{Sub}) \quad \frac{A(\vec{x}) \rightsquigarrow \bot \in \mathcal{S}}{A(\vec{x}) \rightarrow \bot \in \mathcal{S}}$$

Note nevertheless that for a ground compound α (including those containing 0-ary predicates) it is indeed the case that $\alpha \rightsquigarrow \bot$ is equivalent to $\alpha \rightarrow \bot$. It is when α is an *open* compound that (Sub) need not hold. As result, DRFOL provides the domain modeler with greater flexibility in that it leaves open the possibility of there being only atypical objects, something that is not possible in the propositional and DL cases.

6   Conclusion and Future Work

In this paper, we have laid the theoretical groundwork for KLM-style defeasible RFOL. Our primary contribution is a set of rationality postulates describing the behaviour of DRFOL, a typicality semantics for interpreting defeasibility, and a representation result, proving that the proposed postulates characterise the semantic behaviour precisely.

With the theoretical core in place, we then proceeded to define a form of defeasible entailment for DRFOL that can be viewed as the DRFOL equivalent of the propositional form of defeasible entailment known as Rational Closure.

With a suitable definition of DRFOL defeasible entailment in place, the next step is to design algorithms for computing DRFOL defeasible entailment. Here we plan to draw inspiration from both the propositional and DL cases, where defeasible entailment can be reduced to a series of classical entailment checks, sometimes in polynomial time and with a polynomial number of classical entailment checks.

The theoretical framework presented in this paper also places us in a position to investigate extensions to other restricted versions of first-order logic.

Acknowledgments. This work was partially supported by the ANR Chaire IA BE4musIA: BElief change FOR better MUlti-Source Information Analysis, and by TAILOR, a project funded by EU Horizon 2020 research and innovation programme under GA No. 952215.

References

1. Arlo-Costa, H.: The logic of conditionals. In: The Stanford Encyclopedia of Philosophy. Summer 2019 edition. Springer Dordrecht (2019). https://doi.org/10.1007/978-94-015-7622-2

2. Beierle, C., Falke, T., Kutsch, S., Kern-Isberner, G.: Minimal tolerance pairs for system Z-like ranking functions for first-order conditional knowledge bases. In: Proceedings of FLAIRS 2016, pp. 626–631. AAAI Press (2016)

3. Beierle, C., Falke, T., Kutsch, S., Kern-Isberner, G.: System Z^{FO}: default reasoning with system Z-like ranking functions for unary first-order conditional knowledge bases. Int. J. Approx. Reason. **90**, 120–143 (2017)

4. Benferhat, S., Cayrol, C., Dubois, D., Lang, J., Prade, H.: Inconsistency management and prioritized syntax-based entailment. In: Proceedings of IJCAI-1993, pp. 640–645. Morgan Kaufmann Publishers Inc. (1993)

5. Bonatti, P.A.: Rational closure for all description logics. Artif. Intell. **274**, 197–223 (2019)

6. Bonatti, P.A., Faella, M., Petrova, I.M., Sauro, L.: A new semantics for overriding in description logics. Artif. Intell. **222**, 1–48 (2015)

7. Booth, R., Paris, J.B.: A note on the rational closure of knowledge bases with both positive and negative knowledge. J. Log. Lang. Inf. **7**(2), 165–190 (1998)

8. Brafman, R.I.: A first-order conditional logic with qualitative statistical semantics. J. Log. Comput. **7**(6), 777–803 (1997)

9. Britz, K., Casini, G., Meyer, T., Moodley, K., Sattler, U., Varzinczak, I.: Principles of KLM-style defeasible description Logics. ACM T. Comput. Log. **22**(1) (2021)

10. Casini, G., Meyer, T., Moodley, K., Nortjé, R.: Relevant closure: a new form of defeasible reasoning for description logics. In: Fermé, E., Leite, J. (eds.) JELIA 2014. LNCS (LNAI), vol. 8761, pp. 92–106. Springer, Cham (2014). https://doi.org/10.1007/978-3-319-11558-0_7

11. Casini, G., Straccia, U.: Rational closure for defeasible description logics. In: Janhunen, T., Niemelä, I. (eds.) JELIA 2010. LNCS (LNAI), vol. 6341, pp. 77–90. Springer, Heidelberg (2010). https://doi.org/10.1007/978-3-642-15675-5_9

12. Casini, G., Straccia, U.: Defeasible inheritance-based description logics. J. Artif. Intell. Res. **48**, 415–473 (2013)

13. Delgrande, J.P.: On first-order conditional logics. Artif. Intell. **105**(1), 105–137 (1998)
14. Delgrande, J.P., Rantsoudis, C.: A Preference-based approach for representing defaults in first-order logic. In: Proceedings of NMR 2020, pp. 120–129 (2020)
15. Giordano, L., Gliozzi, V.: Strengthening the rational closure for description logics: an overview. In: Proceedings of CILC 2019, pp. 68–81. CEUR-WS.org (2019)
16. Giordano, L., Gliozzi, V., Olivetti, N., Pozzato, G.L.: A non-monotonic description Logic for reasoning about typicality. Artif. Intell. **195**, 165–202 (2013)
17. Giordano, L., Gliozzi, V., Olivetti, N., Pozzato, G.L.: Semantic characterization of rational closure: from propositional logic to description logics. Art. Int. **226**, 1–33 (2015)
18. Kern-Isberner, G.: Conditionals in Nonmonotonic Reasoning and Belief Revision - Considering Conditionals as Agents, LNCS, vol. 2087. Springer, Heidelberg (2001). https://doi.org/10.1007/3-540-44600-1
19. Kern-Isberner, G.: A thorough axiomatization of a principle of conditional preservation in belief revision. Ann. Math. Artif. Intell. **40**(1–2), 127–164 (2004)
20. Kern-Isberner, G., Beierle, C.: A system Z-like approach for first-order default reasoning. In: Eiter, T., Strass, H., Truszczyński, M., Woltran, S. (eds.) Advances in Knowledge Representation, Logic Programming, and Abstract Argumentation. LNCS (LNAI), vol. 9060, pp. 81–95. Springer, Cham (2015). https://doi.org/10.1007/978-3-319-14726-0_6
21. Kern-Isberner, G., Thimm, M.: A ranking semantics for first-order conditionals. In: Proceedings of ECAI 2012, pp. 456–461. IOS Press (2012)
22. Kraus, S., Lehmann, D., Magidor, M.: Nonmonotonic reasoning, preferential models and cumulative logics. Artif. Intell. **44**, 167–207 (1990)
23. Lehmann, D.: Another perspective on default reasoning. Ann. Math. Artif. Intell. **15**(1), 61–82 (1995)
24. Lehmann, D., Magidor, M.: What does a conditional knowledge base entail? Art. Intell. **55**, 1–60 (1992)
25. McCarthy, J.: Circumscription, a form of nonmonotonic reasoning. Art. Intell. **13**(1–2), 27–39 (1980)
26. Pearl, J.: System Z: a natural ordering of defaults with tractable applications to nonmonotonic reasoning. In: Proceedings of TARK 1990 (1990)
27. Pensel, M., Turhan, A.Y.: Reasoning in the Defeasible Description Logic $\mathcal{EL}_\perp$ - computing standard inferences under rational and relevant semantics. Int. J. Approx. Reason. **103**, 28–70 (2018)
28. Schlechta, K.: Defaults as generalized quantifiers. J. Log. Comput. **5**(4), 473–494 (1995)

Semantic Characterizations of AGM Revision for Tarskian Logics

Faiq Miftakhul Falakh[1]([⊠]) [iD], Sebastian Rudolph[1] [iD], and Kai Sauerwald[2] [iD]

[1] Technische Universität Dresden, Dresden, Germany
{faiq_miftakhul.falakh,sebastian.rudolph}@tu-dresden.de
[2] FernUniversität in Hagen, Hagen, Germany
kai.sauerwald@fernuni-hagen.de

Abstract. Given the increasingly dynamic nature of knowledge in the era of Web-based information exchange, techniques to revise recorded knowledge – such as knowledge graphs or ontologies – with respect to new findings are more important than ever. For knowledge representation approaches based on formal logics, the AGM belief revision postulates by Alchourrón, Gärdenfors, and Makinson continue to represent a cornerstone in research related to belief change. Katsuno and Mendelzon (K&M) adopted the AGM postulates for changing belief bases and characterized AGM belief base revision in propositional logic over finite signatures. We generalize K&M's approach to (multiple) base revision in arbitrary Tarskian logics, covering all logics with a classical model-theoretic semantics and hence a wide variety of logics used in knowledge representation and beyond. Our generic formulation applies to various notions of "base"; such as belief sets, arbitrary or finite sets of sentences, or single sentences. The core result is a representation theorem showing a two-way correspondence between AGM base revision operators and certain "assignments": functions mapping belief bases to total — yet not transitive — "preference" relations between interpretations. We also provide a characterization of all Tarskian logics for which our result can be strengthened to assignments producing transitive preference relations as in K&M's original work.

Keywords: Belief revision · Tarskian logics · Semantic characterization

1 Introduction

The question of how a rational agent should change her beliefs in the light of new information is crucial to AI systems. It gave rise to the area of *belief change*, which has been massively influenced by the AGM paradigm of Alchourrón, Gärdenfors, and Makinson [2]. The AGM theory assumes that an agent's beliefs are represented by a deductively closed set of sentences (commonly referred to as a *belief set*). A change operator for belief sets is required to satisfy appropriate

G. Governatori and A.-Y. Turhan (Eds.): RuleML+RR 2022, LNCS 13752, pp. 95–110, 2022.
https://doi.org/10.1007/978-3-031-21541-4_7

postulates in order to qualify as a rational change operator. While the contribution of AGM is widely accepted as solid and inspiring foundation, it lacks support for certain relevant aspects: it provides no immediate solution on how to deal with multiple inputs (i.e., several sentences instead of just one), with *bases* (i.e., arbitrary collections of sentences, not necessarily deductively closed), or with the problem of iterated belief changes.

Katsuno and Mendelzon [14] – henceforth abbreviated $K\mathcal{B}M$ – deal with the issues of belief bases and multiple inputs in an elegant way: as in propositional logic, every set of sentences (including an infinite one) is equivalent to one single sentence, belief states and multiple inputs are considered as such single sentences. In this setting, K&M provide the following set of postulates, derived from the AGM revision postulates, where $\varphi, \varphi_1, \varphi_2, \alpha$, and β are propositional sentences, and ∘ is a base change operator:

(KM1) $\varphi \circ \alpha \models \alpha$.
(KM2) If $\varphi \wedge \alpha$ is consistent, then $\varphi \circ \alpha \equiv \varphi \wedge \alpha$.
(KM3) If α is consistent, then $\varphi \circ \alpha$ is consistent.
(KM4) If $\varphi_1 \equiv \varphi_2$ and $\alpha \equiv \beta$, then $\varphi_1 \circ \alpha \equiv \varphi_2 \circ \beta$.
(KM5) $(\varphi \circ \alpha) \wedge \beta \models \varphi \circ (\alpha \wedge \beta)$.
(KM6) If $(\varphi \circ \alpha) \wedge \beta$ is consistent, then $\varphi \circ (\alpha \wedge \beta) \models (\varphi \circ \alpha) \wedge \beta$.

The postulates (KM1)–(KM6) together are equivalent to the AGM revision postulates, thus they also yield minimal change with respect to the initial beliefs. Note that, in this setting, the semantic content of the revision result is fully determined by the semantic contents of the prior base and the new incoming information; syntactic variations are irrelevant. This sets K&M's approach apart from other prominent lines of work, where revision is performed on a syntactic level and thus the syntactic form of the input may have a semantic effect on the result. A prominent example for such syntactic approaches is base change according to Hansson [13].

While the AGM paradigm is axiomatic, much of its success originated from operationalizations via representation theorems. Yet, most existing characterizations of AGM revision impose additional assumptions on the underlying logic such as compactness, closure under standard connectives, deduction, or supraclassicality [22]. Leaving the safe grounds of these assumptions complicates matters; representation theorems do not easily generalize to arbitrary logics. This has sparked investigations into tailored characterizations of AGM belief change for specific logics, such as Horn logic [6], temporal logics [3], action logics [25], first-order logic [28], and description logics [8,12,19]. More general approaches to revision in non-classical logics were given by Ribeiro, Wassermann, and colleagues [20–22], Delgrande, Peppas, and Woltran [7], Pardo, Dellunde, and Godo [17], or Aiguier et al. [1].

In this article, we consider (multiple) base revision in arbitrary Tarskian logics, i.e., logics exhibiting a classically defined model theory. We thereby refine and generalize the popular approach by Katsuno and Mendelzon [14] which was tailored to belief base revision in propositional logic with a finite signature. K&M start out from belief bases, assigning to each a total preorder on the interpretations, which expresses – intuitively speaking – which interpretation is "closer to being a model". The models of the result of any AGM revision then coincide with the preferred (i.e., preorder-minimal) models of the injected information.

We consider base revision in base logics, which provides an abstraction that elegantly captures different notions of bases. Our approach extends the idea of preferences over interpretations from the propositional to the general setting of Tarskian logics. This requires to adjust the nature of the assignments indicating the degree of model-alikeness: We have to explicitly require that minimal models always exist (*min-completeness*) and that they can be described in the logic (*min-expressibility*). Moreover, we show that demanding preference relations to be preorders is infeasible in the general setting; we have to waive transitivity and retain only a weaker property (*min-retractivity*).

The main contributions of this article are the following:

- We introduce the notion of *base logics* to uniformly capture various popular ways of defining belief states by certain sets of sentences over Tarskian logics. Among others, this includes the cases where belief states are *arbitrary sets of sentences* and where belief states are *belief sets*.
- We extend K&M's semantic approach from the setting of singular base revision in propositional logic to multiple base revision in arbitrary base logics.
- For this setting, we provide a representation theorem characterizing AGM belief change operators via appropriate assignments.
- We characterize all those logics for which every AGM operator can even be captured by preorder assignments (i.e., in the classical K&M way). In particular, this condition applies to all logics supporting disjunction and hence all classical logics. For those logics, we provide one representation theorem for the syntax-independent and one for the syntax-dependent setting.

Detailed proofs, illustrative examples and comprehensive discussions on related aspects can be found in the extended online version of the paper [9].

2 Preliminaries

In this section, we introduce the logical and algebraic notions used in the paper.

2.1 Logics with Classical Model-Theoretic Semantics

We consider logics endowed with a classical model-theoretic semantics. The syntax of such a logic $\mathbb{L}$ is given syntactically by a (possibly infinite) set $\mathcal{L}$ of *sentences*, while its model theory is provided by specifying a (potentially infinite) class Ω of *interpretations* (also called *worlds*) and a binary relation $\models$ between Ω and $\mathcal{L}$ where $\omega \models \varphi$ indicates that ω is a model of φ. Hence, a logic $\mathbb{L}$ is identified by the triple $(\mathcal{L}, \Omega, \models)$. We let $[\![\varphi]\!] = \{\omega \in \Omega \mid \omega \models \varphi\}$ denote the set of all models of $\varphi \in \mathcal{L}$. Logical entailment is defined as usual (overloading "$\models$")

via models: for two sentences φ and ψ we say φ *entails* ψ (written $\varphi \models \psi$) if $[\![\varphi]\!] \subseteq [\![\psi]\!]$.

Notions of modelhood and entailment are easily lifted from single sentences to sets. We obtain the models of a set $\mathcal{K} \subseteq \mathcal{L}$ of sentences via $[\![\mathcal{K}]\!] = \bigcap_{\varphi \in \mathcal{K}} [\![\varphi]\!]$. For $\mathcal{K} \subseteq \mathcal{L}$ and $\mathcal{K}' \subseteq \mathcal{L}$ we say $\mathcal{K}$ *entails* $\mathcal{K}'$ (written $\mathcal{K} \models \mathcal{K}'$) if $[\![\mathcal{K}]\!] \subseteq [\![\mathcal{K}']\!]$. We write $\mathcal{K} \equiv \mathcal{K}'$ to express $[\![\mathcal{K}]\!] = [\![\mathcal{K}']\!]$. A (set of) sentence(s) is called *consistent with* another (set of) sentence(s) if the two have models in common. Unlike many other belief revision frameworks, we impose no further requirements on $\mathcal{L}$ (like closure under certain operators or compactness).

The existence of such a classical model-theoretic semantics ensures that the logic is *Tarskian*, meaning that taking all consequences is a closure operator [24,26], which also implies the *monotonicity* condition: if $\mathcal{K}_1 \models \varphi$ and $\mathcal{K}_1 \subseteq \mathcal{K}_2$, then $\mathcal{K}_2 \models \varphi$. Besides many well-known classical logics, the model-theoretic framework assumed by us captures many more (and more expressive) logics, e.g. first-order and second-order predicate logic, modal logics, and description logics. Our considerations do, however, **not** apply to non-monotonic formalisms, such as default logic, circumscription, or logic programming using negation as failure.

2.2   Relations over Interpretations

For describing belief revision on the semantic level, it is purposeful to endow the interpretation space Ω with some structure. In particular, we will employ binary relations $\preceq$ over Ω (formally: $\preceq \subseteq \Omega \times \Omega$), where the intuitive meaning of $\omega_1 \preceq \omega_2$ is that ω_1 is "equally good or better" than ω_2 when it comes to serving as a model. We call $\preceq$ *total* if $\omega_1 \preceq \omega_2$ or $\omega_2 \preceq \omega_1$ for any $\omega_1, \omega_2 \in \Omega$ holds. We write $\omega_1 \prec \omega_2$ as a shorthand, whenever $\omega_1 \preceq \omega_2$ and $\omega_2 \not\preceq \omega_1$ (the intuition being that ω_1 is "strictly better" than ω_2). For a selection $\Omega' \subseteq \Omega$ of interpretations, an $\omega \in \Omega'$ is called $\preceq$-*minimal in* Ω' if $\omega \preceq \omega'$ for all $\omega' \in \Omega'$.[1] We let $\min(\Omega', \preceq)$ denote the set of $\preceq$-minimal interpretations in Ω'. We call $\preceq$ a *preorder* if it is transitive and reflexive.

2.3   Bases

This article addresses the AGM revision of and by *bases*. In the belief revision community, the term of base commonly denotes an arbitrary (possibly infinite) set of sentences [10]. However, in certain scenarios, other assumptions might be more appropriate. Hence, for the sake of generality, we decided to define the notion of a base on an abstract level with minimal requirements (just as we introduced our notion of *logic*), allowing for its instantiation in many ways.

Definition 1. *A base logic is a quintuple* $\mathbb{B} = (\mathcal{L}, \Omega, \models, \mathfrak{B}, \mathbb{U})$, *where*

- $(\mathcal{L}, \Omega, \models)$ *is a logic,*
- $\mathfrak{B} \subseteq \mathcal{P}(\mathcal{L})$ *is a family of sets of sentences, called* bases, *and*

---

[1] If $\preceq$ is total, this definition is equivalent to the *absence* of any $\omega'' \in \Omega'$ with $\omega'' \prec \omega$.

– $\uplus : \mathfrak{B} \times \mathfrak{B} \to \mathfrak{B}$ *is a binary operator over bases, called the* abstract union, *satisfying* $\llbracket \mathcal{B}_1 \uplus \mathcal{B}_2 \rrbracket = \llbracket \mathcal{B}_1 \rrbracket \cap \llbracket \mathcal{B}_2 \rrbracket$.

Next, we will demonstrate how, for some logic $\mathbb{L} = (\mathcal{L}, \Omega, \models)$, a corresponding base logic can be chosen depending on one's preferred notion of *base*.

Arbitrary Sets. If all (finite and infinite) sets of sentences should qualify as bases, one can simply set $\mathfrak{B} = \mathcal{P}(\mathcal{L})$. In that case, $\uplus$ can be instantiated by set union $\cup$, then the claimed behavior follows by definition.

Finite Sets. In some settings, it is more convenient to assume bases to be finite (e.g. when computational properties or implementations are to be investigated). In such cases, one can set $\mathfrak{B} = \mathcal{P}_{\mathsf{fin}}(\mathcal{L})$, i.e., all (and only) the finite sets of sentences are bases. Again, $\uplus$ can be instantiated by set union $\cup$ (as a union of two finite sets will still be finite).

Belief Sets. This setting is closer to the original framework, where the "knowledge states" to be modified were assumed to be deductively closed sets of sentences. We can capture such situations by accordingly letting $\mathfrak{B} = \{\mathcal{B} \subseteq \mathcal{L} \mid \forall \varphi \in \mathcal{L} : \mathcal{B} \models \varphi \Rightarrow \varphi \in \mathcal{B}\}$. In this case, the abstract union operator needs to be defined via $\mathcal{B}_1 \uplus \mathcal{B}_2 = \{\varphi \in \mathcal{L} \mid \mathcal{B}_1 \cup \mathcal{B}_2 \models \varphi\}$.

Single Sentences. In this popular setting, one prefers to operate on single sentences only (rather than on proper collections of those). For this to work properly, an additional assumption needs to be made about the underlying logic $\mathbb{L} = (\mathcal{L}, \Omega, \models)$: it must be possible to express conjunction on a sentence level, either through the explicit presence of the Boolean operator $\wedge$ or by some other means. Formally, we say that $\mathbb{L} = (\mathcal{L}, \Omega, \models)$ *supports conjunction*, if for any two sentences $\varphi, \psi \in \mathcal{L}$ there exists some sentence $\varphi \otimes \psi \in \mathcal{L}$ satisfying $\llbracket \varphi \otimes \psi \rrbracket = \llbracket \varphi \rrbracket \cap \llbracket \psi \rrbracket$ (if $\wedge$ is available within the logic, we would simply have $\varphi \otimes \psi = \varphi \wedge \psi$). For such a logic, we can "implement" the single-sentence setting by letting $\mathfrak{B} = \{\{\varphi\} \mid \varphi \in \mathcal{L}\}$ and defining $\{\varphi\} \uplus \{\psi\} = \{\varphi \otimes \psi\}$.

For any of the four different notions of bases, one can additionally choose to disallow or allow the empty set as a base, while maintaining the required closure under abstract union. In the following, we will always operate on the abstract level of "base logics"; our notions, results and proofs will only make use of the few general properties specified for these. This guarantees that our results are generically applicable to any of the four described (and any other) instantiations, and hence, are independent of the question what the right notion of bases ought to be. The cognitive overload caused by this abstraction should be minimal; e.g., readers only interested in the case of arbitrary sets can safely assume $\mathfrak{B} = \mathcal{P}(\mathcal{L})$ and mentally replace any $\uplus$ by $\cup$.

2.4   Base Change Operators

In this paper, we use base change operators to model multiple revision, which is the process of incorporating multiple new beliefs into the present beliefs held by an agent, in a consistent way (whenever that is possible). We define change operators over a base logic as follows.

Definition 2. *Let* $\mathbb{B} = (\mathcal{L}, \Omega, \models, \mathfrak{B}, \uplus)$ *be a base logic. A function* $\circ : \mathfrak{B} \times \mathfrak{B} \to \mathfrak{B}$ *is called a* multiple base change operator over $\mathbb{B}$.

We will use multiple base change operators in the "standard" way of the belief change community: the first parameter represents the actual beliefs of an agent, the second parameter contains the new beliefs. The operator then yields the agent's revised beliefs. The term "multiple" references the fact that the second input to $\circ$ is not just a single sentence, but a belief base that may consist of several sentences. For convenience, we will henceforth drop the term "multiple" and simply speak of base change operators instead.

So far, the pure notion of base change operator is unconstrained and can be instantiated by an arbitrary binary function over bases. Obviously, this does not reflect the requirements or expectations one might have when speaking of a revision operator. Hence, in line with the traditional approach, we will consider additional constraints (called "postulates") for base change operators, in order to capture the gist of revisions.

2.5   Postulates for Revision

We consider multiple revision, focusing on package semantics for revision, which is that all given sentences have to be incorporated, i.e. given a base $\mathcal{K}$ and new information Γ (also a base here), we demand success of revision, i.e. $\mathcal{K} \circ \Gamma \models \Gamma$.

Besides the success condition, the belief change community has brought up and discussed several further requirements for belief change operators to make them *rational* [10,13]. This has led to the now famous AGM approach of revision [2], originally proposed through a set of rationality postulates, which correspond to the postulates (KM1)–(KM6) by K&M presented in the introduction. In our article, we will make use of the K&M version of the AGM postulates adjusted to our generic notion of a base logic $\mathbb{B} = (\mathcal{L}, \Omega, \models, \mathfrak{B}, \uplus)$:

(G1) $\mathcal{K} \circ \Gamma \models \Gamma$.
(G2) If $[\![\mathcal{K} \uplus \Gamma]\!] \neq \emptyset$ then $\mathcal{K} \circ \Gamma \equiv \mathcal{K} \uplus \Gamma$.
(G3) If $[\![\Gamma]\!] \neq \emptyset$ then $[\![\mathcal{K} \circ \Gamma]\!] \neq \emptyset$.
(G4) If $\mathcal{K}_1 \equiv \mathcal{K}_2$ and $\Gamma_1 \equiv \Gamma_2$ then $\mathcal{K}_1 \circ \Gamma_1 \equiv \mathcal{K}_2 \circ \Gamma_2$.
(G5) $(\mathcal{K} \circ \Gamma_1) \uplus \Gamma_2 \models \mathcal{K} \circ (\Gamma_1 \uplus \Gamma_2)$.
(G6) If $[\![(\mathcal{K} \circ \Gamma_1) \uplus \Gamma_2]\!] \neq \emptyset$ then $\mathcal{K} \circ (\Gamma_1 \uplus \Gamma_2) \models (\mathcal{K} \circ \Gamma_1) \uplus \Gamma_2$.

Together, the postulates implement the paradigm of minimal change, stating that a rational agent should change her beliefs as little as possible in the process of belief revision. We consider the postulates in more detail: (G1) guarantees that the newly added belief must be a logical consequence of the result of the revision. (G2) says that if the expansion of $\mathcal{K}$ by Γ is consistent, then the result of the revision is equivalent to the expansion of $\mathcal{K}$ by Γ. (G3) guarantees the consistency of the revision result if the newly added belief is consistent. (G4) is the principle of the irrelevance of the syntax, stating that the revision operation is independent of the syntactic form of the bases. (G5) and (G6) ensure more careful handling of (abstract) unions of belief bases. In particular, together, they enforce that $\mathcal{K} \circ (\Gamma_1 \uplus \Gamma_2) \equiv (\mathcal{K} \circ \Gamma_1) \uplus \Gamma_2$, unless Γ_2 contradicts $\mathcal{K} \circ \Gamma_1$.

We can see that, item by item, (G1)–(G6) tightly correspond to (KM1)–(KM6) presented in the introduction. Note also that further formulations similar to (G1)–(G6) are given in multiple particular contexts, e.g. in the context of belief base revision specifically for Description Logics [19], for parallel revision [5] and investigations on multiple revision [15,18,27]. An advantage of the specific form of the postulates (G1)–(G6) chosen for our presentation is that it does not require $\mathcal{L}$ to support conjunction (while, of course, conjunction on the sentence level is still implicitly supported via (abstract) union of bases).

3   Base Revision in Propositional Logic

A well-known and by now popular characterization of base revision has been described by Katsuno and Mendelzon [14] for the special case of propositional logic. To be more specific and apply our terminology, K&M's approach applies to the base logic

$$\mathbb{PL}_n = (\mathcal{L}_{\mathrm{PL}_n}, \Omega_{\mathrm{PL}_n}, \models_{\mathrm{PL}_n}, \mathcal{P}_{\mathrm{fin}}(\mathcal{L}_{\mathrm{PL}_n}), \cup)$$

for arbitrary, but fixed n, where $\mathcal{L}_{\mathrm{PL}_n}$ contains all propositional formulae over the atom set $\{p_1, \ldots, p_n\}$ and Ω_{PL_n} consists of all functions mapping $\{p_1, \ldots, p_n\}$ to $\{\mathbf{true}, \mathbf{false}\}$ and $\models_{\mathrm{PL}_n}$ is the usual satisfaction relation of propositional logic. The requirement that the number of propositional atoms must be finite is not overtly explicit in K&M's paper, but it becomes apparent upon investigating their arguments and proofs, and their characterization fails as soon as this assumption is dropped. K&M's approach also hinges on other particularities of this setting: As discussed earlier, any propositional belief base $\mathcal{K}$ can be equivalently written as a single propositional sentence. Consequently, in their approach, belief bases are actually represented by single sentences, without loss of expressivity.

One key contribution of K&M is to provide an alternative characterization of the propositional base revision operators satisfying (KM1)–(KM6) by model-theoretic means, i.e. through comparisons between propositional interpretations. We next present their results in a formulation that facilitates later generalization. One central notion for the characterization is the notion of *faithful assignment*.

Definition 3 (assignment, faithful). *Let* $\mathbb{B} = (\mathcal{L}, \Omega, \models, \mathfrak{B}, \uplus)$ *be a base logic. An* assignment *for* $\mathbb{B}$ *is a function* $\preceq_{(.)}: \mathfrak{B} \to \mathcal{P}(\Omega \times \Omega)$ *that assigns to each belief base* $\mathcal{K} \in \mathfrak{B}$ *a total binary relation* $\preceq_{\mathcal{K}}$ *over* Ω. *An assignment* $\preceq_{(.)}$ *for* $\mathbb{B}$ *is called* faithful *if it satisfies the following conditions for all* $\omega, \omega' \in \Omega$ *and all* $\mathcal{K}, \mathcal{K}' \in \mathfrak{B}$:

(F1) If $\omega, \omega' \models \mathcal{K}$, *then* $\omega \prec_{\mathcal{K}} \omega'$ *does not hold.*
(F2) If $\omega \models \mathcal{K}$ *and* $\omega' \not\models \mathcal{K}$, *then* $\omega \prec_{\mathcal{K}} \omega'$.

(F3) If $\mathcal{K} \equiv \mathcal{K}'$, then $\preceq_{\mathcal{K}} = \preceq_{\mathcal{K}'}$.

An assignment $\preceq_{(.)}$ is called a preorder assignment if $\preceq_{\mathcal{K}}$ is a preorder for every $\mathcal{K} \in \mathfrak{B}$.

Intuitively, faithful assignments provide information about which of the two interpretations is "closer to $\mathcal{K}$-modelhood". Consequently, the actual $\mathcal{K}$-models are $\preceq_{\mathcal{K}}$-minimal. The next definition captures the idea of an assignment adequately representing the behaviour of a revision operator.

Definition 4 (compatible). Let $\mathbb{B} = (\mathcal{L}, \Omega, \models, \mathfrak{B}, \mathbb{U})$ a base logic. A base change operator $\circ$ for $\mathbb{B}$ is called compatible with some assignment $\preceq_{(.)}$ for $\mathbb{B}$ if it satisfies $[\![\mathcal{K} \circ \Gamma]\!] = \min([\![\Gamma]\!], \preceq_{\mathcal{K}})$ for all bases $\mathcal{K}$ and Γ from $\mathfrak{B}$.

With these notions in place, K&M's representation result can be smoothly expressed as follows:

Theorem 1 (Katsuno and Mendelzon [14]). A base change operator $\circ$ for $\mathbb{PL}_n$ satisfies (G1)–(G6) if and only if it is compatible with some faithful preorder assignment for $\mathbb{PL}_n$.

In the next section, we discuss and provide a generalization of this characterization to the setting of arbitrary base logics.

4   Approach for Arbitrary Base Logics

In this section, we prepare our main result by revisiting K&M's concepts for propositional logic and investigating their suitability for our general setting of base logics. The result by Katsuno and Mendelzon established an elegant combination of the notions of preorder assignments, faithfulness, and compatibility in order to semantically characterize AGM base change operators. However, as we mentioned before, K&M's characterization hinges on features of signature-finite propositional logic that do not generally hold for Tarskian logics. Here we go further, by extending the K&M approach by novel notions to the very general setting of base logics.

4.1   First Problem: Non-existence of Minima

The first issue with K&M's original characterization when generalizing to arbitrary base logics is the possible absence of $\preceq_{\mathcal{K}}$-minimal elements in $[\![\Gamma]\!]$: for arbitrary base logics, the minimum from Definition 4, required in Theorem 1, might be empty. To remedy this problem, one needs to impose the requirement that minima exist whenever needed, as specified in the notion of *min-completeness*, defined next.

Definition 5 (min-complete). Let $\mathbb{B} = (\mathcal{L}, \Omega, \models, \mathfrak{B}, \mathbb{U})$ be a base logic. A binary relation $\preceq$ over Ω is called min-complete *(for $\mathbb{B}$)* if $\min([\![\Gamma]\!], \preceq) \neq \emptyset$ holds for every $\Gamma \in \mathfrak{B}$ with $[\![\Gamma]\!] \neq \emptyset$.

In the special case of $\preceq$ being transitive and total, min-completeness trivially holds whenever Ω is finite (as, e.g., in the case of propositional logic over n propositional atoms). In the infinite case, however, it might need to be explicitly imposed, as already noted in earlier works [7] (cf. also the notion of *limit assumption* by Lewis [16]). Note that min-completeness does not entirely disallow infinite descending chains (as well-foundedness would), it only ensures that minima exist inside all model sets of consistent belief bases.

4.2   Second Problem: Transitivity of Preorder

When generalizing from the setting of propositional to arbitrary base logics, the requirement that assignments must produce preorders (and hence transitive relations) turns out to be too restrictive.

In fact, it has been observed before that the incompatibility between transitivity and K&M's approach already arises for propositional Horn logic [6]. As a consequence, we cannot help but waive transitivity (and hence the property of the assignment providing a preorder) if we want our characterization result to hold for all Tarskian logics. However, for our result, we need to retain a new, weaker property (which is implied by transitivity) defined next.

Definition 6 (min-retractive). *Let* $\mathbb{B} = (\mathcal{L}, \Omega, \models, \mathfrak{B}, \mathbb{U})$ *be a base logic. A binary relation* $\preceq$ *over* Ω *is called* min-retractive *(for* $\mathbb{B}$*) if, for every* $\Gamma \in \mathfrak{B}$ *and* $\omega', \omega \in [\![\Gamma]\!]$ *with* $\omega' \preceq \omega$, $\omega \in \min([\![\Gamma]\!], \preceq)$ *implies* $\omega' \in \min([\![\Gamma]\!], \preceq)$.

We conveniently unite the two identified properties into one notion.

Definition 7 (min-friendly). *Let* $\mathbb{B} = (\mathcal{L}, \Omega, \models, \mathfrak{B}, \mathbb{U})$ *be a base logic. A binary relation* $\preceq$ *over* Ω *is called* min-friendly *(for* $\mathbb{B}$*) if it is both min-retractive and min-complete. An assignment* $\preceq_{(\cdot)} : \mathfrak{B} \to \mathcal{P}(\Omega \times \Omega)$ *is called* min-friendly *if* $\preceq_{\mathcal{K}}$ *is min-friendly for all* $\mathcal{K} \in \mathfrak{B}$.

5   One-way Representation Theorem

We are now ready to generalize K&M's representation theorem from propositional to arbitrary Tarskian logics, by employing the notion of compatible min-friendly faithful assignments.

Theorem 2. *Let* $\circ$ *be a base change operator for some base logic* $\mathbb{B}$. *Then,* $\circ$ *satisfies (G1)–(G6) if and only if it is compatible with some min-friendly faithful assignment for* $\mathbb{B}$.

For the "if" direction, we show that the notion of min-friendly compatible assignment is sufficient to enforce that any compatible base revision operator satisfies (G1)–(G6).

For the more involved "only if" direction, we provide a canonical way of obtaining an assignment for a given revision operator and show that our construction indeed yields a compatible min-friendly faithful assignment. To this end, we suggest the following construction, which we consider one of this paper's core contributions. It realizes the idea that one should (strictly) prefer ω_1 over ω_2 only if there is a witness belief base Γ that certifies that $\circ$ prefers ω_1 over ω_2. Should no such witness exist, ω_1 and ω_2 will be deemed equally preferable.

Definition 8. *Let $\mathbb{B} = (\mathcal{L}, \Omega, \models, \mathfrak{B}, \mathbb{U})$ be a base logic, let $\circ$ be a base change operator for $\mathbb{B}$ and let $\mathcal{K} \in \mathfrak{B}$ be a belief base. The relation $\sqsubseteq_{\mathcal{K}}^{\circ}$ over Ω is defined by $\omega_1 \sqsubseteq_{\mathcal{K}}^{\circ} \omega_2$ if $\omega_2 \models \mathcal{K} \circ \Gamma$ implies $\omega_1 \models \mathcal{K} \circ \Gamma$ for all $\Gamma \in \mathfrak{B}$ with $\omega_1, \omega_2 \in [\![\Gamma]\!]$.*

Definition 8 already yields an adequate encoding strategy for many base logics. However, to also properly cope with certain "degenerate" base logics, we have to hard-code that the prior beliefs of an agent are prioritized in all cases, that is, only models of the prior beliefs are minimal. The following relation builds upon the relation $\sqsubseteq_{\mathcal{K}}^{\circ}$ and takes explicit care of handling prior beliefs, which is strong enough for always obtaining a relation that is total and reflexive.

Definition 9. *Let $\mathbb{B} = (\mathcal{L}, \Omega, \models, \mathfrak{B}, \mathbb{U})$ be a base logic, let $\circ$ be a base change operator for $\mathbb{B}$ and let $\mathcal{K} \in \mathfrak{B}$ be a belief base. The relation $\preceq_{\mathcal{K}}^{\circ}$ over Ω is then defined by $\omega_1 \preceq_{\mathcal{K}}^{\circ} \omega_2$ if $\omega_1 \models \mathcal{K}$ or ($\omega_1, \omega_2 \not\models \mathcal{K}$ and $\omega_1 \sqsubseteq_{\mathcal{K}}^{\circ} \omega_2$). Let $\preceq_{(.)}^{\circ}$: $\mathfrak{B} \to \mathcal{P}(\Omega \times \Omega)$ denote the mapping $\mathcal{K} \mapsto \preceq_{\mathcal{K}}^{\circ}$.*

6   Two-way Representation Theorem

Theorem 2 establishes the correspondence between operators and assignments under the assumption that $\circ$ is given and therefore known to exist. What remains unsettled is the question if generally **every** min-friendly faithful assignment is compatible with some base change operator that satisfies (G1)–(G6). As this is not the case, a full, two-way correspondence, requires an additional condition on assignments, capturing operator existence. More specifically, it is essential that any minimal model set of a belief base obtained from an assignment corresponds to some belief base, a property which is formalized by the following notion.

Definition 10 (min-expressible). *Let $\mathbb{B} = (\mathcal{L}, \Omega, \models, \mathfrak{B}, \mathbb{U})$ be a base logic. A binary relation $\preceq$ over Ω is called min-expressible if for each $\Gamma \in \mathfrak{B}$ there exists a belief base $\mathcal{B}_{\Gamma, \preceq} \in \mathfrak{B}$ such that $[\![\mathcal{B}_{\Gamma, \preceq}]\!] = \min([\![\Gamma]\!], \preceq)$. An assignment $\preceq_{(.)}$ will be called min-expressible, if for each $\mathcal{K} \in \mathfrak{B}$, the relation $\preceq_{\mathcal{K}}$ is min-expressible. Given a min-expressible assignment $\preceq_{(.)}$, let $\circ_{\preceq_{(.)}}$ denote the base change operator defined by $\mathcal{K} \circ_{\preceq_{(.)}} \Gamma = \mathcal{B}_{\Gamma, \preceq_{\mathcal{K}}}$.*

It should be noted that min-expressibility is a straightforward generalization of the notion of *regularity* by Delgrande and colleagues [7] to base logics. By virtue of this extra notion, we now find the following bidirectional relationship between assignments and operators, amounting to a full characterization.

Theorem 3. *Let $\mathbb{B}$ be a base logic. Then the following hold:*

– *Every base change operator for $\mathbb{B}$ satisfying (G1)–(G6) is compatible with some min-expressible min-friendly faithful assignment.*

– *Every min-expressible min-friendly faithful assignment for* $\mathbb{B}$ *is compatible with some base change operator satisfying (G1)–(G6).*

As an aside, note that the above theorem also implies that every min-expressible min-friendly faithful assignment is compatible **only** with AGM base change operators. This is because, one the one hand, any such assignment fully determines the corresponding compatible base change operator model-theoretically and, on the other hand, (G1)–(G6) are purely model-theoretic conditions.

7   Total-Preorder-Representability

As we have shown, regrettably, not every AGM belief revision operator in every Tarskian logic can be described by a total preorder assignment. Yet, we also saw that, for some logics (like $\mathbb{PL}_n$), this correspondence does indeed hold. Consequently, this section is dedicated to finding a characterization of precisely those logics wherein every AGM base change operator is representable by a compatible min-complete faithful preorder assignment. The following definition captures the notion of operators that are well-behaved in that sense.

Definition 11 (total-preorder-representable). *A base change operator* $\circ$ *for some base logic is called* total-preorder-representable *if there is a min-complete faithful preorder assignment compatible with* $\circ$.

Recall that transitivity implies min-retractivity, and thus, every min-complete preorder is automatically min-friendly. The following definition describes the occurrence of a certain relationship between several bases. Such an occurrence will turn out to be the one and only reason to prevent total-preorder-representability.

Definition 12 (critical loop). *Let* $\mathbb{B} = (\mathcal{L}, \Omega, \models, \mathfrak{B}, \mathbb{U})$ *be a base logic. Three or more bases* $\Gamma_{0,1}, \Gamma_{1,2}, \ldots, \Gamma_{n,0} \in \mathfrak{B}$ *are said to form a* critical loop *of length* $(n+1)$ *if there are a base* $\mathcal{K} \in \mathfrak{B}$ *and consistent bases* $\Gamma_0, \ldots, \Gamma_n \in \mathfrak{B}$ *such that*

(1) $[\![\mathcal{K} \uplus \Gamma_{i,i\oplus 1}]\!] = \emptyset$ *for every* $i \in \{0, \ldots, n\}$, *where* $\oplus$ *is addition* $\mathrm{mod}\,(n+1)$,
(2) $[\![\Gamma_i]\!] \cup [\![\Gamma_{i\oplus 1}]\!] \subseteq [\![\Gamma_{i,i\oplus 1}]\!]$ *and* $[\![\Gamma_j \uplus \Gamma_i]\!] = \emptyset$ *for each* $i,j \in \{0, \ldots, n\}$ *with* $i \neq j$, *and*
(3) *for each* $\Gamma_\triangledown \in \mathfrak{B}$ *that is consistent with at least three bases from* $\Gamma_0, \ldots, \Gamma_n$, *there is a* $\Gamma'_\triangledown \in \mathfrak{B}$ *such that* $[\![\Gamma'_\triangledown]\!] \neq \emptyset$ *and* $[\![\Gamma'_\triangledown]\!] \subseteq [\![\Gamma_\triangledown]\!] \setminus ([\![\Gamma_{0,1}]\!] \cup \ldots \cup [\![\Gamma_{n,0}]\!])$.

The three conditions in Definition 12, illustrated in Fig. 1, describe the canonic situation brought about by some bases $\Gamma_{0,1}, \ldots, \Gamma_{n,0}$ allowing for the construction of a revision operator that unavoidably gives rise to a circular compatible relation. Note that due to Condition (3), every three of $\Gamma_{0,1}, \Gamma_{1,2}, \ldots, \Gamma_{n,0}$ together are inconsistent, but each two of them which have an index in common are consistent, i.e. $\Gamma_{i,i\oplus 1} \uplus \Gamma_{i\oplus 1,i\oplus 2}$ is consistent for each $i \in \{0, \ldots, n\}$.

The next theorem is the central result of this section, confirming that the notion of critical loop captures exactly those base logics for which some operator exists that is not total-preorder-representable.

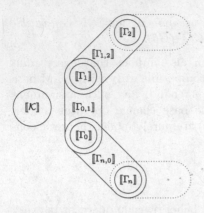
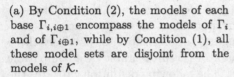
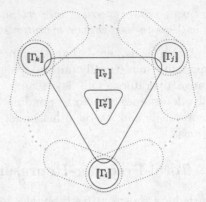

(a) By Condition (2), the models of each base $\Gamma_{i,i\oplus1}$ encompass the models of Γ_i and of $\Gamma_{i\oplus1}$, while by Condition (1), all these model sets are disjoint from the models of $\mathcal{K}$.

(b) By Condition (3), for each $\Gamma_{\triangledown}$ that is consistent with at least three distinct elements $\Gamma_i, \Gamma_j, \Gamma_k \in \{\Gamma_0, \ldots, \Gamma_n\}$, there exists a base $\Gamma_{\triangledown}'$ that is subsumed by $\Gamma_{\triangledown}$ but inconsistent with all $\Gamma_{0,1}, \ldots, \Gamma_{n-1,n}$, $\Gamma_{n,0}$.

Fig. 1. Illustrations of Conditions (1)–(3) of a critical loop from Definition 12.

Theorem 4. *Let $\mathbb{B}$ be a base logic which does not admit a critical loop. Then the following hold:*

– *Every base change operator for $\mathbb{B}$ satisfying (G1)–(G6) is compatible with some min-expressible min-complete faithful preorder assignment.*
– *Every min-expressible min-complete faithful preorder assignment for $\mathbb{B}$ is compatible with some base change operator satisfying (G1)–(G6).*

We close this section with an important implication of Theorem 4. A base logic $\mathbb{B} = (\mathcal{L}, \Omega, \models, \mathfrak{B}, \mathbb{U})$ is called *disjunctive*, if for every two bases $\Gamma_1, \Gamma_2 \in \mathfrak{B}$ there is a base $\Gamma_1 \oslash \Gamma_2 \in \mathfrak{B}$ such that $[\![\Gamma_1 \oslash \Gamma_2]\!] = [\![\Gamma_1]\!] \cup [\![\Gamma_2]\!]$. This includes the case of any (base) logic allowing disjunction to be expressed on the sentence level, i.e., when for every $\gamma, \delta \in \mathcal{L}$ there exists some $\gamma \oslash \delta \in \mathcal{L}$ with $[\![\gamma \oslash \delta]\!] = [\![\gamma]\!] \cup [\![\delta]\!]$, such that $\Gamma_1 \oslash \Gamma_2$ can be obtained as $\{\gamma \oslash \delta \mid \gamma \in \Gamma_1, \delta \in \Gamma_2\}$.

Corollary 1. *In a disjunctive base logic, every belief change operator satisfying (G1)–(G6) is total-preorder-representable.*

As a consequence, for a vast amount of well-known logics, including all classical logics such as first-order and second order predicate logic, one directly obtains total-preorder-representablility of every AGM base change operator by Corollary 1.

8   Related Work

In settings beyond propositional logic, we are aware of three closely related approaches that propose model-based frameworks for revision of belief bases (or sets) without fixing a particular logic or the internal structure of interpretations, and characterize revision operators via minimal models à la K&M with some additional assumptions.

One semantic-based approach related to the one of K&M was proposed by Grove [11] in the setting of Boolean-closed logics. He originally characterized AGM revision operators via *systems of spheres*, collections **S** of sets of interpretations satisfying certain conditions. Delgrande and colleagues [7] then reformulated Grove's representation theorem stating that (expressed in our terminology) any AGM revision operator can be obtained from a compatible min-complete faithful preorder assignment, provided the set of interpretations is Ω-expressible, i.e. for any subset $\Omega' \subseteq \Omega$ there exists a base Γ such that $[\![\Gamma]\!] = \Omega'$. In this formulation, Groves result also holds for logics with infinite Ω. Grove's result constitutes a special case of our representation theorem: from the assumption of Boolean-closedness, it follows that the considered logics are disjunctive and therefore free of critical loops (cf. Theorem 4 and Corollary 1). The assumption of Ω-expressibility immediately implies min-expressibility for all relations.

The representation result of Delgrande et al. [7] confines the considered logics to those where the set Ω of interpretations (or possible worlds) is finite[2] and where any two different interpretations $\omega, \omega' \in \Omega$ can be distinguished by some sentence $\varphi \in \mathcal{L}$, i.e., $\omega \in [\![\varphi]\!]$ and $\omega' \notin [\![\varphi]\!]$. Moreover, they extend the AGM postulates by the following extra one, denoted (Acyc). With these ingredients in place, they [7] establish that, for the logics they consider, there is a two-way correspondence between those AGM revision operators satisfying (Acyc) and min-expressible faithful preorder assignments. Instead of the term "min-expressible", they use the term *regular*. The approach of Delgrande et al. [7] can be seen as complementary to ours. While our proposal is to relinquish the requirement of using preorders, their (Acyc) postulate allows for a preorder characterization even in logics with critical loops by disallowing some "unnatural" AGM revision operators.

The approach of Aiguier et al. [1] considers AGM belief base revision in logics with a possibly infinite set Ω of interpretations. Notably, they propose to consider certain bases, that actually **do** have models, as inconsistent (and thus in need of revision). While, in our view, this is at odds with the foundational assumptions of belief revision (revision should be union/conjunction unless facing unsatisfiability), this appears to be a design choice immaterial to the established results. As far as the postulates are concerned, Aiguier et al. [1] decide to rule out (KM4)/(G4), arguing in favor of syntax-dependence. Like us, they [1] propose to drop the requirement that assignments have to yield preorders. In addition to the standard notion of compatibiliy, their result hinges on an additional correspondence between the assignment and the preorder (third bullet point).

---

[2] Note that this precondition excludes not only more complex logics such as first-order or modal logics and most of their fragments, but also propositional logic with infinite signature. On the positive side, this choice guarantees min-completeness of any preorder.

9   Conclusion

The central objective of our treatise was to provide an exact model-theoretic characterization of AGM belief revision in the most general reasonable sense, i.e., one that uniformly applies to every logic with a classical model theory (i.e., every Tarskian logic), to any notion of bases that allows for taking some kind of "unions" (including the cases of belief sets, sets of sentences, finite sets of sentences, and single sentences), and to all base change operators adhering to the unaltered AGM postulates (without imposing further restrictions through additional postulates).

We found that in the general case considered by us, the original result of K&M for signature-finite propositional logic fails in many ways and needs substantial adaptations. In particular, aside from delivering total relations and being faithful, the assignment now needs to satisfy (i) *min-expressibility*, guaranteeing existence of a describing base for any model set obtained by taking minimal interpretations among some base's models, (ii) *min-completeness*, ensuring that minimal interpretations exist in every base's model set, and (iii) *min-retractivity* instead of transitivity, making sure that minimality is inherited to more preferable elements.

While the first two adjustments have been recognized and described in prior work, the notion of min-retractivity (and the decision to replace transitivity by this weaker notion and thus give up on the requirement that preferences be preorders) seems to be novel. Yet, it turns out to be the missing piece for establishing the desired two-way compatibility-correspondency between AGM revision operators and preference assignments of the described kind (cf. Theorem 3).

Conceding that transitivity is a rather natural choice for preferences and preorder assignments might be held dear by members of the belief revision community, we went on to investigate for which logics our general result holds even if assignments are required to yield preorders. We managed to pinpoint a specific logical phenomenon (called *critical loop*), the absence of which in a logic is necessary and sufficient for *total-preorder-representability*. While the criterion by itself maybe somewhat technical and unwieldy, it can be shown to subsume all logics featuring disjunction and therefore all classical logics.

Next to advancing the general model-theoretic understanding of AGM belief revision for the vast class of Tarskian logics, our research also opens up more concrete opportunities: Among others, it allows for the definition of novel AGM belief revision operators from a model-theoretic perspective, through the design of an appropriate assignment. Another interesting direction may be to study the potential relationship between our notion of min-retractivity and notions of quasi-transitivity and Suzumura-consistency in social choice theory [4] or interval orders in belief set contraction [23].

Acknowledgements. Faiq Miftakhul Falakh was supported by the Indonesia Endowment Fund for Education (LPDP) Scholarship and by the Federal Ministry of Education and Research, Germany (BMBF) in the Center for Scalable Data Analytics and Artificial Intelligence (ScaDS. AI). Sebastian Rudolph is supported by the ERC through his Consolidator Grant 771779 (DeciGUT). Kai Sauerwald is supported by the Deutsche Forschungsgemeinschaft (DFG, German Research Foundation) Grant BE 1700/9-1 and Grant BE 1700/10-1 awarded to Christoph Beierle as part of the priority program "Intentional Forgetting in Organizations" (SPP 1921). We are grateful for the reviews and comments by the three anonymous reviewers.

References

1. Aiguier, M., Atif, J., Bloch, I., Hudelot, C.: Belief revision, minimal change and relaxation: a general framework based on satisfaction systems, and applications to description logics. Artif. Intell. **256**, 160–180 (2018)
2. Alchourrón, C.E., Gärdenfors, P., Makinson, D.: On the logic of theory change: partial meet contraction and revision functions. J. Symb. Log. **50**(22), 510–530 (1985)
3. Bonanno, G.: Axiomatic characterization of the AGM theory of belief revision in a temporal logic. Artif. Intell. **171**(2–3), 144–160 (2007)
4. Bossert, W., Suzumura, K.: Quasi-transitive and suzumura consistent relations. Soc. Choice Welf. **39**(2–3), 323–334 (2012)
5. Delgrande, J., Jin, Y.: Parallel belief revision: revising by sets of formulas. Artif. Intell. **176**(1), 2223–2245 (2012)
6. Delgrande, J.P., Peppas, P.: Belief revision in Horn theories. Artif. Intell. **218**, 1–22 (2015)
7. Delgrande, J.P., Peppas, P., Woltran, S.: General belief revision. J. ACM **65**(5), 29.1–29:34 (2018)
8. Dong, T., Duc, C.L., Lamolle, M.: Tableau-based revision for expressive description logics with individuals. J. Web Semant. **45**, 63–79 (2017)
9. Falakh, F.M., Rudolph, S., Sauerwald, K.: Semantic characterizations of general belief base revision. CoRR abs/2112.13557 (2021)
10. Fermé, E.L., Hansson, S.O.: Belief Change - Introduction and Overview. Springer Briefs in Intelligent Systems, Springer, Cham (2018). https://doi.org/10.1007/978-3-319-60535-7
11. Grove, A.: Two modellings for theory change. J. Philos. Log. **17**(2), 157–170 (1988)
12. Halaschek-Wiener, C., Katz, Y.: Belief base revision for expressive description logics. In: Grau, B.C., Hitzler, P., Shankey, C., Wallace, E. (eds.) Proceedings of the 2nd Workshop on OWL: Experiences and Directions (OWLED 2006). CEUR Workshop Proceedings, vol. 216. CEUR-WS.org (2006)
13. Hansson, S.O.: A Textbook of Belief Dynamics: Theory Change and Database Updating. Springer Dordrecht (1999)
14. Katsuno, H., Mendelzon, A.O.: Propositional knowledge base revision and minimal change. Artif. Intell. **52**(3), 263–294 (1991)
15. Kern-Isberner, G., Huvermann, D.: What kind of independence do we need for multiple iterated belief change? J. Appl. Log. **22**, 91–119 (2017)
16. Lewis, D.K.: Counterfactuals. Harvard University Press, Cambridge (1973)
17. Pardo, P., Dellunde, P., Godo, L.: Base Belief change for finitary monotonic logics. In: Meseguer, P., Mandow, L., Gasca, R.M. (eds.) CAEPIA 2009. LNCS (LNAI), vol. 5988, pp. 81–90. Springer, Heidelberg (2010). https://doi.org/10.1007/978-3-642-14264-2_9
18. Peppas, P.: The limit assumption and multiple revision. J. Log. Comput. **14**(3), 355–371 (2004)

19. Qi, G., Liu, W., Bell, D.A.: Knowledge Base revision in description logics. In: Fisher, M., van der Hoek, W., Konev, B., Lisitsa, A. (eds.) JELIA 2006. LNCS (LNAI), vol. 4160, pp. 386–398. Springer, Heidelberg (2006). https://doi.org/10.1007/11853886_32

20. Ribeiro, M.M.: Belief Revision in Non-Classical Logics. Springer Briefs in Computer Science, Springer, London (2013). https://doi.org/10.1007/978-1-4471-4186-0

21. Ribeiro, M.M., Wassermann, R.: Minimal change in AGM revision for non-classical logics. In: Baral, C., Giacomo, G.D., Eiter, T. (eds.) Proceedings of the 14th International Conference of Principles of Knowledge Representation and Reasoning (KR 2014). AAAI Press (2014)

22. Ribeiro, M.M., Wassermann, R., Flouris, G., Antoniou, G.: Minimal change: relevance and recovery revisited. Artif. Intell. **201**, 59–80 (2013)

23. Rott, H.: Four floors for the theory of theory change: the case of imperfect discrimination. In: Fermé, E., Leite, J. (eds.) JELIA 2014. LNCS (LNAI), vol. 8761, pp. 368–382. Springer, Cham (2014). https://doi.org/10.1007/978-3-319-11558-0_26

24. Sernadas, A., Sernadas, C., Caleiro, C.: Synchronization of logics. Stud. Logica. **59**(1), 217–247 (1997)

25. Shapiro, S., Pagnucco, M., Lespérance, Y., Levesque, H.J.: Iterated belief change in the situation calculus. Artif. Intell. **175**(1), 165–192 (2011)

26. Tarski, A.: Logic Semantics, Metamathematics Papers From 1923 to 1938. Clarendon Press, Translated by J.H. Woodger (1956)

27. Zhang, D.: Belief revision by sets of sentences. J. Comput. Sci. Technol. **11**(2), 108–125 (1996)

28. Zhuang, Z., Wang, Z., Wang, K., Delgrande, J.P.: A generalisation of AGM contraction and revision to fragments of first-order logic. J. Artif. Intell. Res. **64**, 147–179 (2019)

Datalog

iWarded: A Versatile Generator to Benchmark Warded Datalog+/− Reasoning

Paolo Atzeni[1], Teodoro Baldazzi[1(✉)], Luigi Bellomarini[2],
and Emanuel Sallinger[3,4]

[1] Università Roma Tre, Rome, Italy
teodoro.baldazzi@uniroma3.it
[2] Banca d'Italia, Rome, Italy
[3] TU Wien, Vienna, Austria
[4] University of Oxford, Oxford, UK

Abstract. Warded Datalog+/− is a powerful member of the Datalog+/− family, which extends the logic language Datalog with existential quantification and provides full support for recursion. Such expressive power, paired with a promising trade-off with the offered data complexity, was the catalyst for the recent rise of the language as a relevant candidate for knowledge graph traversal and ontological reasoning applications. Despite the growing research and industrial interest towards Warded Datalog+/−, we observe a substantial lack of specific tools able to generate non-trivial settings and benchmark scenarios, essential to evaluate, analyze and compare reasoning systems over such tasks. In this paper, we aim at filling this gap by introducing iWarded, a versatile generator of Warded Datalog+/− benchmarks. Our system is able to efficiently create very large, complex, and realistic reasoning settings while providing extensive control over the theoretical underpinnings of the language. iWarded was developed and employed in the context of the Vadalog system, a state-of-the-art Warded Datalog+/−-based reasoner.

Keywords: Warded Datalog+/− · Vadalog · Ontological reasoning · Benchmark generator

1 Introduction

Recent years have witnessed a rising interest, both in academia and industry, towards querying and exploiting large volumes of data in the form of *knowledge graphs* (KGs). This led to the development of modern intelligent systems with *reasoning* capabilities that allow augmenting extensional data and efficiently derive new intensional knowledge thanks to ontologies encoded in expressive formalisms [23,27]. Among the languages for knowledge representation and ontological reasoning employed by such systems [9], the members (technically,

G. Governatori and A.-Y. Turhan (Eds.): RuleML+RR 2022, LNCS 13752, pp. 113–129, 2022.
https://doi.org/10.1007/978-3-031-21541-4_8

fragments) of the Datalog$^\pm$ family [7,16–19] became broadly adopted over the last decade. Their high expressive power, extending plain Datalog with existential quantification while supporting full recursion and arbitrary joins, and their good trade-off with the computational complexity of the reasoning task, are vital requirements for KG navigation and complex real-world applications [10,12].

The growing importance of developing efficient reasoning methodologies and systems determined a consequential and pressing demand for benchmarks. As Patterson [37] states, "When a field has good benchmarks, we settle debates and the field makes rapid progress". For instance, numerous benchmarking solutions have been proposed in the database and the theorem proving communities over the years: among them, the TPC family [33,35,38,39], the standard option to evaluate database systems, SMTLIB [8] and TPTP [41], for theorem proving ones, as well as advanced research tools like IBENCH [2], a schema mapping generator for the analysis of data integration and data exchange scenarios.

An essential aspect in reasoning evaluation, especially Datalog+/−based, involves analyzing how the theoretical underpinnings of the employed language affect performance. Indeed, the combinations of existentials, recursion, joins (and aggregations to some extent) allowed by the syntax of the fragments determine their complexity. Moreover, specifically chosen interactions between these features have crucial impact on the reasoning runtime [11,42]: this is also confirmed by the adoption of rewriting and optimization techniques, such as *Harmful Join Elimination* [6], to improve reasoning performance under certain syntactic conditions. Yet, developing tools that enable such a fine-grained impact analysis is by no means trivial, and hardly any benchmarks covering this aspect exist to this day. Currently, experimental evaluation and comparison of reasoning methodologies and systems are mostly represented by CHASEBENCH [13], a set of query answering benchmarks focused on *chase*-based techniques [20]. However, such benchmarks only allow for generic testing of a very limited subset of the above features, considering them individually and not with a combined approach.

With this work, we tackle such limitations, aiming to contribute to benchmarking Datalog$^\pm$-based reasoners. To achieve this, we propose a generator of Datalog$^\pm$ programs that leverages the theoretical bases of the language to create heterogeneous reasoning benchmarks with different characteristics. Specifically, our tool is based on Warded Datalog $^\pm$ [24], a broad and powerful fragment that features relevant correlations with multiple Datalog$^\pm$ members of interest for the community, such as *Shy* [5,30] and *Guarded* [16]. Also, it keeps the reasoning task PTIME in data complexity, while capturing SPARQL queries under OWL 2 QL entailment regime and set semantics [10]. It is implemented in the VADALOG system [9], a state-of-the-art reasoner for complex and real-world scenarios.

Contributions. The generator we propose fulfills a number of different requirements, as we shall see. First, it supports *versatility*, efficiently creating benchmark scenarios to be employed in the evaluation and the comparison of chase techniques, reasoning strategies, and systems [9], with respect to specific combinations of features in the Warded fragment. Also, it enables *adaptability* of such scenarios in benchmarks with different purposes, to sustain a comprehensive and effective analysis of the language. Moreover, it provides full *support* for Warded Datalog$^{\pm}$, thus allowing users to generate benchmarks that include all the language features while building a foundation for novel reasoning systems to effectively employ the fragment. Finally, it sustains straightforward *extensibility* and *usability*, to integrate and test new features with minimal effort.

Specifically, our contributions in this work can be summarized as follows.

- We present IWARDED, the first, to the best of our knowledge, generator of Warded Datalog$^{\pm}$ programs for reasoning benchmarks, designed according to the fundamental requirements listed above.
- We provide an *open-source implementation* [3] of IWARDED that encapsulates the Warded fragment, and we illustrate how it is operated in practice.
- We discuss an *experimental evaluation*, comparing VADALOG with the top reasoning systems over IWARDED benchmarks, with the twofold aim of confirming the usefulness of the benchmark, thus providing a baseline for future analysis, and giving us some insight into the VADALOG system itself.

Overview. The remainder of this paper is organized as follows. In Sect. 2 we provide an overview of Warded Datalog$^{\pm}$. In Sect. 3 we present features and operating principles of our generator. Section 4 is dedicated to experiments. In Sect. 5 we discuss the related work. We draw our conclusions in Sect. 6.

2 Syntax and Semantics of Warded Datalog$^{\perp}$

In this section, we briefly recall the syntax and the semantics of Warded Datalog$^{\pm}$, focusing on the main concepts that are relevant to guide our discussion.

Background Notions. A (*relational*) *schema* **S** is a finite set of relation symbols (or *predicates*) with associated arity. A *term* is a either a constant or a variable. An *atom* over **S** is an expression of the form $R(\bar{v})$, where $R \in$ **S** is of arity $n > 0$ and $\bar{v}$ is an n-tuple of terms. A *database* (*instance*) over **S** associates with each relation symbol in **S** a relation of the respective arity over the domain of constants and nulls. The members of the relations are called *tuples* or *facts* [11].

Rules and Existentials. Datalog$^{\pm}$ languages extend standard Datalog by introducing existential quantifiers and other features to make it suitable for ontological reasoning, while employing restrictions to the syntax for scalability and decidability [18]. A Datalog$^{\pm}$ program consists of a set of facts and *existential rules*, or *tuple-generating dependencies* (TGDs), of the form $\forall \bar{x} \forall \bar{y}(\varphi(\bar{x}, \bar{y}) \rightarrow \exists \bar{z} \ \psi(\bar{x}, \bar{z}))$, where φ (the *body*) and ψ (the *head*) are conjunctions of atoms over the respective predicates and the arguments are vectors of variables and constants. An alternate syntax is $\psi(\bar{x}, \bar{z})$:- $\varphi(\bar{x}, \bar{y})$, adopting right-to-left implication, ":-" for "←", and omitting quantifiers. A predicate is *intensional* (idb) if it occurs in at least one head, otherwise it is *extensional* (edb).

Chase and Reasoning. Given a database D and a set Σ of TGDs, the satisfaction of Σ over D is enforced by means of *chase*-based procedures [34]. Intuitively, the chase expands D into a new instance $chase(D, \Sigma)$ with additional facts derived from the application of the rules in Σ. Such facts may contain freshly generated symbols (technically, *labelled nulls*) that act as placeholders for the existentially quantified variables. A TGD $\sigma : \varphi(\bar{x}, \bar{y}) \rightarrow \exists \bar{z} \; \psi(\bar{x}, \bar{z}) \in \Sigma$ is *applicable* to D if there exists a homomorphism θ that maps the atoms of $\varphi(\bar{x}, \bar{y})$ to facts in D (i.e., $\theta(\varphi(\bar{x}, \bar{y})) \subseteq D$). In such case, a *chase step* occurs and the fact $\theta'(\psi(\bar{x}, \bar{z}))$ is added to D (if not present), where $\theta' \supseteq \theta$ extends θ by mapping the variables in $\bar{z}$ to new labelled nulls in lexicographic order. Given a pair $Q = (\Sigma, Ans)$, where Ans is an n-ary predicate, the evaluation of a *query* Q over D is the set of tuples $Q(D) = \{\bar{t} \in dom(D)^n \mid Ans(\bar{t}) \in chase(D, \Sigma)\}$, where $\bar{t}$ is a tuple of constants. An *ontological reasoning task* consists in finding an instance J s.t.: (i) $Ans(\bar{t}) \in J$ iff $\bar{t} \in Q(D)$; and (ii) for every other J' s.t. $Ans(\bar{t}) \in J'$ iff $\bar{t} \in Q(D)$, there is a homomorphism from J to J' [9]. An application of the chase is provided below.

Example 1 (Chase Procedure). Let $D = \{$Person(a),Person(b),Parent(a,b)$\}$ be a database instance, Σ be a set of Datalog$^\pm$ rules with existential quantification

$$\text{Person}(x) \rightarrow \exists y \, \text{Ancestor}(y, x). \qquad (\alpha)$$

$$\text{Parent}(x, z), \text{Ancestor}(y, x) \rightarrow \text{Ancestor}(y, z). \qquad (\beta)$$

and let $Q = (\Sigma, Ans)$, $Ans = $ Ancestor be the reasoning task of finding all the Ancestor facts. First, the extensional facts Person(a), Person(b) trigger the existential rule α, the chase starts and the intensional facts Ancestor(ν_1, a), Ancestor(ν_2, b) are added to D, where ν_1, ν_2 are labelled nulls. Then, via the join in rule β between Ancestor(ν_1, a) and the extensional Parent(a, b) on a, Ancestor(ν_1, b) is created. Thus, the instance $J = D \cup \{$Ancestor(ν_1, a), Ancestor(ν_1, b), Ancestor$(\nu_2, b)\}$ is the solution to the reasoning task.

Affectedness and Wardedness. Warded Datalog$^\pm$ introduces a syntactic restriction whose goal is to constrain the propagation of labelled nulls in the chase. Let Σ be a set of rules and $p[i]$ a position (i.e., the i-th term of a predicate p with arity k, where $i \leq k$). We inductively define $p[i]$ as *affected* if: (i) p appears in the head of a rule in Σ with an existentially quantified variable ($\exists$-*variable*) in position $p[i]$; (ii) there is a rule in Σ such that a universally quantified variable ($\forall$-*variable*) is in $p[i]$ in the head and only in affected positions in the body. A $\forall$-variable x is *harmful*, with respect to a rule ρ in Σ, if x appears only in affected positions in ρ, otherwise it is *harmless*: a rule that contains a harmful variable is a *harmful* rule, otherwise it is a *harmless* rule. If the harmful variable also appears in the head of ρ, it is *dangerous*: rules containing dangerous variables are called *dangerous* rules. We define a set Σ as *warded* if, for each rule $\sigma \in \Sigma$, the following conditions hold: (1) all the dangerous variables only appear in a single body atom, called *ward*; and, (2) the ward only shares harmless variables with other atoms. Such restrictions, collectively known as *wardedness*, isolate the dangerous variables of a rule, taming the propagation of labelled nulls possibly binding to them in the chase, to guarantee reasoning decidability and data tractability [11]. In Example 1 Ancestor[1] is affected due to the existential in rule α and the variable y in rule β is dangerous: the rules belong to Warded Datalog$^\pm$, as Person(x) and Ancestor(y, x) are wards for α and β, respectively.

3   iWarded System

We are now ready to discuss IWARDED. In Sect. 3.1, we provide an overview of the generator and its features. In Sect. 3.2, we illustrate its operating principles and the generation procedure of reasoning benchmarks.

3.1   Overview of the Generator

The goal of IWARDED is to provide tailored benchmarks for ontological reasoning, in the form of Warded Datalog$^\pm$ programs and data sources that enable the evaluation of how specific features affect performance over distinct chase techniques, reasoning strategies and systems [9]. Program generation is based on the concept of *dependency graph*, which is a directed graph such that there is a node for each predicate x and an edge from x to a predicate y if there is a rule where x appears in a body atom and y appears in the head atom. Intuitively, IWARDED builds such a graph as a set of unique paths, from the extensional predicates linked to input data sources (namely, *input predicates*, labelling *input nodes*) to the intensional ones that form the output of the reasoning tasks (namely, *output predicates*, labelling *output nodes*). Before illustrating this procedure in detail, we discuss the features that the generated programs may include.

Types of Rules. IWARDED programs are comprised of sets of existential rules and, in particular, harmless, harmful and dangerous rules, both *linear* (i.e., single body atom) and *join*. To sustain readability, rules are generated at most with two body atoms and only with joins on single variables. This design choice does not affect generality or finiteness of the chase [11]. In this setting, joins can be *harmless-harmless*, *harmless-harmful* and *harmful-harmful*, depending on the nature of the variables involved. To preserve wardedness, the generated harmful-harmful joins must not contain dangerous variables. Harmless-harmless joins can in turn be created *with ward* (one of the body atoms is a ward containing the dangerous variables), and *without ward* (with no dangerous variables). These types of rules model different forms of propagation of and interplay between affected positions. Indeed, they (harmful and dangerous rules, in particular) are an essential aspect to integrate in benchmarks with the goal of evaluating the impact of existential quantification on reasoning performance.

Types of Recursion. Generated programs may feature different kinds of *recursion*. Intuitively, a rule is involved in a recursion if it contains at least one *recursive atom*, that is, an atom whose predicate is a node in a cycle of the dependency graph. The *length* of the recursion is the number of edges that form the corresponding cycle in the graph. Specifically, IWARDED can build *direct* recursions, consisting of only a body atom that also appears in the head of the same rule (i.e., with length = 1), and *indirect* ones (i.e., with length $\geq$ 2): distinct recursions may be linked to form strongly connected components in the dependency graph. With the goal of varying the structure of such components, according to the nature of the generated rule that closes each cycle (namely, *recursion-closing rule*), *left join*, *right join*, *left-right join* and *linear* recursions are possible, if the recursive join atom is the left one, the right one or both, or the rule is linear, respectively: for instance, rule β in Example 1 models a direct, right join recursion, with Ancestor as recursive atom.

Language Extensions. IWARDED supports the generation of real-world like benchmarks expressed in an extension of the standard Warded Datalog$^{\pm}$. For instance, it integrates into the programs *equality-generating dependencies* (EGDs), first-order implications of the form $\forall \bar{x} \forall \bar{y}(\varphi(\bar{x}, \bar{y}) \rightarrow x_i = x_j)$, where φ is a conjunction of atoms over the respective predicates and $x_i, x_j \in \bar{x}$, that allow to fully exploit the power of existential quantification [19]. Similarly, it enables the creation of warded programs that also belong to other relevant Datalog$^{\pm}$ fragments, such as *Shy* [5,30] (i.e., with rules not containing harmful join variables or dangerous variables affected by the same existential) and *Guarded* [16] (i.e., all the $\forall$-variables in a rule are comprised within a single *guard* atom of the body). Additional features, such as expressions enriched with *selection conditions* $(=, >, <, \dots)$ and *monotonic aggregations* (*sum*, *min*, *max*, $\dots$) [40] are also supported.

Benchmark Parameters. To sustain versatility and adaptability, IWARDED is enriched with an ergonomic design that allows generating combinations of the above features by manually tuning the following set of structural parameters.

- *Predicate-level* parameters: they control the dimension of the benchmark, setting the number of input and output predicates in the program, while determining predicate arity from mean and variance.
- *Rule-level* parameters: they control the heterogeneity of the benchmark, determining the number of linear and join rules (of the different types) in the program, as well as how many of those are harmless, harmful, dangerous and existential. Regarding the latter, they also regulate the number of existential variables in the head atom of each rule, based on mean and variance.
- *Program-level* parameters: they control the complexity of the benchmark. They set number and length of recursions (of the different types), affecting the strongly connected components in the dependency graph. They also regulate number and length of the paths from input to output nodes.
- *Benchmark-level* parameters: they extend the benchmark with additional features, setting the number of linear and join EGDs, monotonic aggregations and conditions in the rules of the program, as well as their average selectivity (i.e., the number of facts filtered in by the condition). They also determine whether the warded program is required to belong to other fragments, such as Shy or Guarded. Finally, they regulate the number of records in the input data sources, taking into account the selectivity of possible conditions.

Indeed, such a variety of parameters and features allows for an accurate and fine-grained control over the properties of the generated program, an essential and yet, to the best of our knowledge, not currently covered requirement for Datalog$^\pm$ benchmarks. However, it also poses multiple technical challenges, such as managing the generation in the face of possibly incompatible user requirements, as well as ensuring the wardedness of the program in an efficient fashion, overseeing and limiting the complexity of rules and recursions, generating data sources that take into account selectivity to produce realistic results in the reasoning tasks, etc. These topics will be covered in the upcoming section.

3.2 Benchmark Generation Procedure

The generation procedure of Warded Datalog$^\pm$ programs and data sources in IWARDED is structured in the following five main phases.

1. *Graph Definition*: the first step involves tuning the properties of the benchmark, with respect to user requirements, and beginning the creation of the dependency graph with input and output nodes.
2. *Main Rule Path Generation*: the main set of rules in the program is created, building paths in the corresponding dependency graph from input to output nodes, with respect to the properties of the benchmark.
3. *Recursion Generation with Wardedness*: recursions are then added, grouping the nodes into strongly connected components of the graph, while adopting specific precautions to uphold the wardedness of the program.
4. *Secondary Rule Path Generation*: secondary input-output paths and single rules are now built in the graph, to satisfy remaining user requirements.
5. *Data Generation*: finally, the input data sources are generated, taking into account the characteristics of the program to produce realistic results.

In the following paragraphs, we discuss each phase of the generation more in detail, with a specific focus on its main technical challenges and the adopted solutions. Algorithm 1 provides the pseudo-code for the overall procedure.

1. Graph Definition. First, IWARDED performs the tuning of the benchmark properties, according to user requirements provided via configuration files that list the input parameters as key-value pairs: for instance, it determines the length of each recursion and each path from input to output nodes, based on the corresponding average length. However, this heterogeneous collection of parameters could hamper the usability of the generator. Indeed, such a fine-grained control over the generation could not be required by the user, and it could also lead to combinations of incompatible requirements: for example, an erroneous assignment of mean and variance could cause the number of expected ∃-variables in a rule to be greater than the arity of the head atom. To address this issue and provide a baseline for practical usage, IWARDED is enriched with a set of default configuration settings and pre-built scenarios [3]. Moreover, to sustain extensibility, it features a component responsible for adjusting conflicting parameters, modifying them according to a pre-defined priority (line 2). If some values are not provided by the user, the corresponding parameters are set to their default. Then, the graph is initialized with the set of nodes corresponding to input and output predicates, whose arity is selected via Gaussian distribution from mean and variance parameters. Note that such predicates are identified via *input* and *output annotations* [9]: specifically, output ones designate the *Ans* predicates, each corresponding to a distinct query for a reasoning task (line 4).

2. **Main Rule Path Generation.** The main foundation of IWARDED consists in abstracting any set of rules as a network of *input-output sequences*, each corresponding to a path in the dependency graph from input to output nodes. A sequence is a chain of rules $\rho_1, \ldots, \rho_n$, where the head of ρ_i appears as a body atom of ρ_{i+1}, from *input atoms* to *output atoms* (atoms over an input or output predicate, resp.) and with possible *intensional atoms* in between. This approach allows creating sets of rules following a common design, easy to inspect, debug, adapt and reuse in different settings. Specifically, this phase involves generating one *main* sequence for each output predicate (line 8). The warded rules are created taking into account the benchmark properties, choosing if they are linear or join rules (of the different types), if they introduce affected positions via existential quantification and how they propagate them (that is, whether they are harmless, harmful or dangerous), as well as if they are required to also satisfy syntactic restrictions for other Datalog$^\pm$ fragments and if they feature aggregations and selection conditions. The number of rules in each main sequence derives from the input-output length, set in Phase 1: intuitively, this dimension identifies the depth of the chase, that is, the number of chase steps (not involving recursions) triggered at most to generate facts for an output predicate (line 10).

3. **Recursion Generation with Wardedness.** In this phase, IWARDED enriches the program with direct and indirect *recursions* that group the nodes of the dependency graph into strongly connected components (line 14). Each component includes edges from the main input-output sequences generated in Phase 2, as well as additional ones responsible for completing the corresponding strongly connected component and satisfying the recursion length assigned in Phase 1: similarly to the input-output length, such dimension corresponds to the number of chase steps triggered by the rules involved in a recursion and is an indicator of the complexity of the component and of the overall program, due to multiple recursions possibly linked to one another. Each recursive-closing rule, which closes the corresponding cycle by linking it to the input-output sequences, is built according to whether the recursion is linear, left, right or left-right (line 16).

In general, when reasoning with Warded Datalog$^\pm$, verifying the wardedness of a program is by no means trivial: this is due to its syntactic properties, which require monitoring the interplay between recursion and existential quantification and determining how it impacts the propagation of affected positions [11]. This is an essential aspect to consider in our generation procedure, as IWARDED is tasked to enforce the wardedness on the rules it creates. Indeed, the naïve brute-force approach would first require creating the full program; then, by backtracking along each affected position up to the ∃-variable introducing it, it would amend the rules that are found not to be warded. Yet, this would computation-ally be very costly, with possible exponential blowup in the number of rules. Instead, IWARDED's network structure allows to proceed inductively, incremen-tally building rules in such a way that each addition does not hamper warded-ness. Such *memory-free generation* approach is based on the design principle that the affected positions in a predicate only depend on the ones propagated from the parent nodes in the input-output sequences of the dependency graph. As a consequence, recursions cannot introduce new affected positions, as they might otherwise undermine the wardedness of the rules in the input-output sequence they belong to; conversely, they can feature existential quantification in positions that are already known to be affected due to the main input-output sequences. This approach offers multiple benefits, such as avoiding complex memory struc-tures to keep track of how affected positions are propagated: wardedness is easy to enforce and verify even when inspecting elaborate sequences, and, once a rule has been classified as warded, it becomes an invariant throughout the generation.

4. Secondary Rule Path Generation. This phase covers the creation of additional rules and features to satisfy remaining input requirements, such as the expected number of sequences for a certain output predicate (line 18). Impli-cations with EGDs are generated as well. IWARDED either builds single rules (such as in the case of EGDs) or full *secondary* input-output sequences, whose length was set in Phase 1. To achieve this, note that additional adjustments to the benchmark properties may be performed in this phase.

5. Data Generation. The last phase of the generation involves creating the data sources to be employed as input facts of the extensional predicates in the chase. Such facts are produced as records in CSV files that are linked to the corresponding predicates via *bind* and *mapping* annotations [9], which bind input and output predicates to data sources (line 20). Indeed, input data is an essential part of the benchmarks and its generation is non-trivial, as it is required to populate the chase in a way that balances the impact of the output predicates over the reasoning task. To achieve this, IWARDED's rule sequence network comes into play, allowing us to employ a *forward-propagating* approach: the tuples in the CSV files are defined according to the joins in the generated rules, such that each join rule is guaranteed to activate an average number of times, whereas linear rules simply propagate the values from body to head. Additionally, the selectivity of the condition is taken into account, managing the average number of the facts that will be filtered in when the corresponding rule activates. Finally, we enrich the discussion by illustrating the generation of a simple bench-mark with IWARDED, based on the following configuration scenario:

- input predicates, 2; output predicates, 1; mean arity, 1; variance arity, 1.
- linear rules, 4; harmless-harmful join rules, 1; harmful-harmful join rules, 1; existen-tial rules, 2; harmless rules, 3; harmful rules, 2; dangerous rules, 2; mean existentials per rule, 1; variance existentials per rule, 1;
- direct recursions, 1; indirect recursions, 1; average recursion length, 2; linear recur-sions, 1; left-right join recursions, 1; number of input-output sequences, 2; average input-output sequence length, 2;

Algorithm 1. Benchmark Generation in IWARDED.

Input: Set Σ of benchmark parameters
Output: Pair $\langle$program Π,data sources $\Delta\rangle$
```
 1: function IWARDEDBENCHMARKGENERATION(Σ)
 2:     Σ ← tuneAndAdaptProperties(Σ)                              ▷ phase 1 generation
 3:     G ← empty dependency graph
 4:     G ← G ∪ generateInputOutputPredicates(Σ)
 5:     for outPred in G.getOutputPredicates() do                 ▷ phase 2 generation
 6:         nChaseSteps ← 0
 7:         while nChaseSteps ≤ outPred.getInputOutputLength(Σ, G) do
 8:             G ← G ∪ generateRuleMainSequence(Σ, G)
 9:             nChaseSteps ← nChaseSteps + 1
10:         G ← G ∪ generateOutputRuleMainSequence(Σ, G, outPred)
11:     for rec in getRecursions(Σ) do                            ▷ phase 3 generation
12:         recLength ← 0
13:         while recLength ≤ rec.getRecursionLength(Σ, G) do
14:             G ← G ∪ generateRecursion(Σ, G)
15:             recLength ← recLength + 1
16:         G ← G ∪ generateRecursionClosingRule(Σ, G, rec)
17:     while hasRemainingRequirements(Σ, G) = true do            ▷ phase 4 generation
18:         G ← G ∪ generateRuleSecondarySequence(Σ, G)
19:     Π ← extractProgramFromGraph(G)                            ▷ phase 5 generation
20:     Δ ← generateDataSources(Π)
        return ⟨Π,Δ⟩
```

– conditions, 1; mean selectivity, 50%; input facts per EDB, 100;

Figure 1 shows the generated program and its dependency graph. A description of the figure and of the underlying generation procedure is provided below.

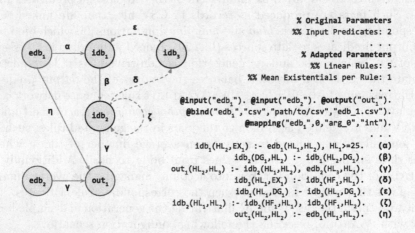

```
% Original Parameters
%% Input Predicates: 2
            . . .
% Adapted Parameters
%% Linear Rules: 5
%% Mean Existentials per Rule: 1
            . . .
@input("edb₁"). @input("edb₂"). @output("out₁").
@bind("edb₁","csv","path/to/csv","edb_1.csv").
    @mapping("edb₁",0,"arg_0","int").

    idb₁(HL₂,EX₁) :- edb₁(HL₁,HL₂), HL₂>=25.        (α)
    idb₂(DG₁,HL₂) :- idb₁(HL₂,DG₁).                  (β)
out₁(HL₂,HL₃) :- idb₁(HL₁,HL₂), edb₂(HL₃,HL₁).      (γ)
    idb₃(HL₁,EX₁) :- idb₂(HF₁,HL₁).                  (δ)
    idb₁(HL₁,DG₁) :- idb₃(HL₁,DG₁).                  (ε)
idb₂(HL₁,HL₂) :- idb₂(HF₁,HL₁), idb₂(HF₁,HL₂).      (ζ)
    out₁(HL₂,HL₂) :- edb₁(HL₁,HL₂).                  (η)
```

Fig. 1. Dependency graph and program generated by IWARDED

Phase 1 first checks the compatibility of the input parameters, adjusting the number of existentials in a rule to 1, according to mean and variance of predicate arity. Then, it performs the tuning of the benchmark properties, setting, for instance, the length of the input-output sequences for the output predicate out_1

(3 and 1) and the length for the recursions rec_1, rec_2 (3 and 1, respectively). Finally, it creates input (blue) and output (red) nodes, labelled by edb_1, edb_2 and out_1, respectively, whose arity derives from provided mean and variance. **Phase** 2 creates the main input-output sequence (plain arrows) for out_1, of length 3. The names of the variables reflect their type, thus existential, harmless, harmful and dangerous ones are named EX_i, HL_i, HF_i and DG_i, respectively. Here, harmless linear rule α introduces an existential EX_1 in position $idb_1[2]$, which is then propagated to $idb_2[1]$ via dangerous linear rule β. Finally, harmless rule γ contains a harmless-harmful join with edb_2: as the number of chase steps is 3, out_1 is the head of rule γ and the corresponding output node is thus reached. Moreover, rule α is integrated with a selection condition in the body over HL_1. **Phase** 3 covers the generation of the recursive sequences (dotted arrows) rec_1, of length 3, and rec_2, of length 1. The former is a linear indirect recursion, involving β, the harmless linear rule δ, which contains an existential, and the dangerous linear rule ϵ, which completes the cycle. By memory-free generation approach, rule ϵ propagates the new affected position from $idb_3[2]$ to $idb_1[2]$, which is already affected due to rule α. The latter is a left-right join direct recursion on idb_2 via harmful rule ζ, involving a harmful-harmful join. **Phase** 4 builds the secondary input-output sequence for out_1. As the current number of harmless rules is 2, the sequence consists in the harmless linear rule η: to achieve this, the total number of linear rules in the program is increased to 5. **Phase** 5 completes the benchmark generation by creating and mapping the data sources to edb_1 and edb_2. The input facts for edb_1 are integers, defined taking into account the selectivity of the condition in rule α such that only 50% of them is filtered in: according to it, only half of them is equal to or greater than 25. All the requirements are now satisfied and the program is warded. The program and its data sources are the output of the generation procedure.

4   Experimental Evaluation

Let us first remark that the goal of this work is to propose and present our benchmark generator, its operating principles and features, rather than employing it to develop a benchmarking suite for reasoners. In this section, however, we enrich the discussion with a set of experiments for known systems over relevant IWARDED benchmarks, to provide a baseline for future evaluations and analysis with it. With this goal in mind, we illustrate 3 sets of experiments, each corresponding to a distinct use case for our generator. We ran each experiment 10 times, averaging the elapsed times. Specifically, Fig. 2(a_2),(b),(c) report the average execution times, i.e., the sum of chase times and query answering times.

Hardware Configuration. Experiments were performed on a local installation of the compared systems, using a machine with an M1 Pro CPU and 32 GB of RAM. The benchmarks were made public in the online version of IWARDED [3].

(a) **Structural Scenarios.** The first set of experiments consists in evaluating the VADALOG system over synthetic benchmarks featuring distinct combinations of relevant syntactic properties. This system, available upon request, performs reasoning via a *streaming* approach, building a *reasoning query graph* as a processing pipeline, where nodes correspond to algebra operators that execute transformations over the data pulled from their predecessors, and edges are dependency connections between the rules [9]. We tested it over 8 benchmarks generated with IWARDED, each comprising 100 rules and $10k$ input facts, based on the scenarios provided in Fig. 3. Specifically, *SynthA* and *SynthB* feature a prevalence of linear and join rules (equally distributed among harmless-harmful and harmless-harmless), respectively. *SynthC* and *SynthD* include distinct proportions of the various types of join. Similarly, *SynthE* and *SynthF* are built to determine how recursions affect reasoning in the presence of existentials. Finally, *SynthG* and *SynthH* allow to assess the effect of (linear and join, respectively) EGDs. Each scenario features an average of 30 input-output sequences. Regarding program generation (Fig. $2(a_1)$), IWARDED requires less than 3 second to create each benchmark, even in cases with a high number of complex recursions such as *SynthE* and *SynthF*, thanks to the memory-free generation approach. Regarding reasoning execution (Fig. $2(a_2)$), the results show the significant impact of complex recursive sequences, especially linear ones from *SynthE* and in the presence of multiple existential quantifications. Such behaviour can be motivated by the injection of many labelled nulls in the linear rules, which, combined with the presence of harmful joins activating on them, cause a longer time for the chase procedure to complete. This is also confirmed by the time of *SynthD*, featuring fewer recursions but more harmful join rules. Similarly, *SynthH* indicates that a high number of join EGDs heavily affects reasoning performance.

(b) Scalability Scenarios. The goal of this benchmark is to assess how relevant properties of the programs affect the behaviour of distinct reasoning systems. Specifically, we evaluate the impact of the length for input-output sequences (i.e., number of chase steps) and recursions, both key indicators for measuring the complexity of a program. The comparison involves the VADALOG system and DLV$^\exists$ [30], an extension of the answer set programming system DLV [31] for query answering in the Shy fragment. This system, available online [29], employs a *materialization* approach, producing and storing all the facts for each predicate via *semi-naive* evaluation [1], where rules are evaluated according to a bottom-up strategy from the database. We tested them over shy IWARDED programs, with 10 input-output sequences and recursions of increasing length, and data sources with $10k$ records as input facts: regarding the other benchmark parameters, the same values, selected arbitrarily, are employed. As the syntax of the programs did not comply with the one required by DLV$^\exists$, we employed a script to rewrite them in a form that enables the evaluation.

We observe that DLV$^\exists$ outperforms the VADALOG system over input-output sequences of increasing complexity, thanks to its powerful optimization and chase techniques that limit the loading of redundant data and the space to materialize the query results [30]. On the other hand, the efficient recursion control provided by the latter prevents the exploration of redundant areas of the reasoning space and allows for better performance in increasingly complex recursive settings [9].

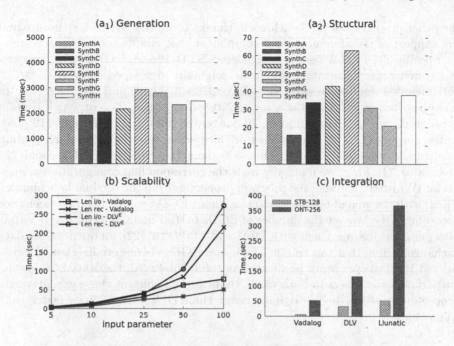

Fig. 2. Reasoning statistics for the experimental evaluation.

	Σ rules	Π rules	L recursions	H recursions	∃ rules	hrml ⋈ hrmf	hrml ⋈ hrml with ward	hrml ⋈ hrml w/o ward	hrml ⋈ hrmf	L EGDs	H EGDs
SynthA	90	10	27	3	20	5	4	1	0	0	0
SynthB	10	90	3	27	20	45	40	5	0	0	0
SynthC	30	70	9	27	40	25	20	5	20	0	0
SynthD	30	70	10	9	22	10	9	1	50	0	0
SynthE	70	30	40	10	50	10	9	1	10	0	0
SynthF	30	70	10	40	50	40	29	1	0	0	0
SynthG	50	20	21	9	30	0	10	10	0	20	10
SynthH	20	50	9	21	30	0	25	25	0	10	20

Fig. 3. Configuration settings of the structural scenarios.

(c) Integration Scenarios. The last set of tests provides insight into a distinct use case of IWARDED to contribute to benchmarking Warded Datalog$^{\pm}$ reasoning. A typical and straightforward approach to compare systems and methodologies involves evaluating them over well-known real-world benchmarks that provide interesting combinations of features to be tested. Indeed, a related goal would consist in testing novel variants of such benchmarks, to determine how specific changes to one or more properties affect reasoning. However, attempting to manually modify some of their characteristics while preserving the others is by no means trivial and it could lead to subtle issues, such as an erroneous propagation of affected positions that undermines the wardedness of the program. In this context, IWARDED solves such issues and enables the creation and the evaluation of workable variants for real-world benchmark scenarios. Indeed, once the configuration file corresponding to the original program has been provided, our generator allows modifying individual parameters while preserving the other properties of the benchmark, thanks to its rule network structure and the support of the aforementioned component that adapts conflicting settings.

Specifically, in this test we considered STB-128 and ONT-256, two relevant first-order integration scenarios originally developed with IBENCH [2] and included, for instance, in the CHASEBENCH benchmarking suite [13]. In IWARDED terms, STB-128 is a set of 250 warded rules, 25% of which contain existentials, with 15 harmful joins, 30 dangerous rules, 193 EGDs and 112 predicates; conversely, ONT-256 is a set of 789 warded rules, 35% of which contain existentials, with 295 harmful joins, 300 dangerous rules, 921 EGDs and 220 predicates [11]. First, we manually built the corresponding configuration scenarios for IWARDED, deriving the program properties from the original benchmarks. Then, with the goal of testing variants without EGDs, we modified the scenarios accordingly (i.e., we set the number of EGDs to 0). Finally, we compared VADALOG performance over them with DLV and LLUNATIC [22], an open-source data exchange system that can handle TGDs and EGDs via materialization. We considered $10k$ facts per input predicate. As can be observed, the VADALOG system outperforms the others in both cases, thanks to its efficient chase execution via processing pipeline, being 3 times faster than DLV and 7 times faster than LLUNATIC.

5　Related Work

Benchmarking is a crucial aspect in the development of efficient systems and methodologies in every field [37]. Great effort in empiric evaluation has been spent by both the database systems community (e.g., with TCP [33,35,38,39]) and the theorem proving one (e.g., with SMTLib [8] and TPTP [41]). On the other hand, the literature about extending data management tools with reasoning capabilities does not feature equivalent richness. Benchmarks for ontology-based data access and query rewriting systems have been proposed and employed [25,28] and the evaluation of many systems has been carried out [15,21,26]. Yet, to this day the two main pillars for benchmarking are IBENCH [2] and CHASEBENCH [13]. IBENCH is a popular metadata and schema mapping generator for data integration settings that provides the user with high customization capabilities; yet, there is no coverage for reasoning settings and only standard TGD-based schema mappings are supported. On the other hand, CHASEBENCH offers a comprehensive benchmarking suite for chase-based systems and techniques; yet, it does not focus on Datalog$^\pm$ nor on analyzing how combinations of the properties of the employed language affect performance, as it only allows to control chase depth and overall TGD and EGD complexity. To the best of our knowledge, IWARDED is the first attempt to provide the logic-based reasoning community with a tool to generate tailored Datalog$^\pm$ benchmarks. The goal of our work has been to fully develop the user control idea of IBENCH into the specificities of the Datalog$^\pm$ fragments, taking into account the countless aspects deriving from the interplay between existential quantification and recursion and making them tunable by the user. Many reasoning systems can be considered IWARDED target. Besides Vadalog [11], specifically motivating the research, systems able to operate data integration and data exchange settings can benefit from IWARDED scenarios: among them, LLUNATIC [22] and DLV [32], as shown in our experiment section, as well as GRAAL [4], RDFOX [36] and PDQ [14].

6 Conclusion

In this paper, we presented IWARDED, a new generator of Warded Datalog$^{\pm}$-based reasoning benchmarks. An essential aspect in reasoning evaluation, and yet showing a very limited coverage in current benchmarks, involves analyzing the impact of the language underpinnings over performance. Our generator enables such analysis, providing accurate and extensible control over the benchmark properties and features to be tested. We hope that IWARDED will contribute to benchmarking Datalog$^{\pm}$-based reasoning, providing a solid foundation to evaluate, compare and improve reasoning systems and methodologies.

Acknowledgements. The work on this paper was partially supported by the Vienna Science and Technology Fund (WWTF) grant VRG18-013.

References

1. Abiteboul, S., Hull, R., Vianu, V.: Foundations of Databases, vol. 8. Addison-Wesley Reading, Reading (1995)
2. Arocena, P.C., Glavic, B., Ciucanu, R., Miller, R.J.: The iBench integration metadata generator. VLDB Endow. **9**(3), 108–119 (2015)
3. Atzeni, P., Baldazzi, T., Bellomarini, L., Sallinger, E.: iWarded. https://github.com/joint-kg-labs/iWarded (2022) . Accessed 23 June 2022
4. Baget, J.-F., Leclère, M., Mugnier, M.-L., Rocher, S., Sipieter, C.: Graal: a toolkit for query answering with existential rules. In: Bassiliades, N., Gottlob, G., Sadri, F., Paschke, A., Roman, D. (eds.) RuleML 2015. LNCS, vol. 9202, pp. 328–344. Springer, Cham (2015). https://doi.org/10.1007/978-3-319-21542-6_21
5. Baldazzi, T., Bellomarini, L., Favorito, M., Sallinger, E.: On the relationship between shy and warded datalog+/-. arXiv preprint arXiv:2202.06285 (2022)
6. Baldazzi, T., Bellomarini, L., Sallinger, E., Atzeni, P.: Eliminating harmful joins in warded datalog+/−. In: Moschoyiannis, S., Peñaloza, R., Vanthienen, J., Soylu, A., Roman, D. (eds.) RuleML+RR 2021. LNCS, vol. 12851, pp. 267–275. Springer, Cham (2021). https://doi.org/10.1007/978-3-030-91167-6_18
7. Barceló, P., Pichler, R. (eds.): Datalog in academia and Industry. In: Second International Workshop, Datalog 2.0, Vienna, Austria, 11–13 September 2012. Proceedings, LNCS, vol. 7494. Springer (2012). https://doi.org/10.1007/978-3-642-32925-8
8. Barrett, C., et al.: The SMT-LIB standard: Version 2.0. In: Proceedings of the 8th International Workshop on Satisfiability Modulo Theories (Edinburgh, England). vol. 13, p. 14 (2010)
9. Bellomarini, L., Benedetto, D., Gottlob, G., Sallinger, E.: Vadalog: a modern architecture for automated reasoning with large knowledge graphs. Inf. Syst. **IS** (2020)

10. Bellomarini, L., Gottlob, G., Pieris, A., Sallinger, E.: Swift logic for big data and knowledge graphs. In: Tjoa, A.M., Bellatreche, L., Biffl, S., van Leeuwen, J., Wiedermann, J. (eds.) SOFSEM 2018. LNCS, vol. 10706, pp. 3–16. Springer, Cham (2018). https://doi.org/10.1007/978-3-319-73117-9_1
11. Bellomarini, L., Sallinger, E., Gottlob, G.: The Vadalog system: datalog-based reasoning for knowledge graphs. VLDB Endow. **11**(9) (2018)
12. Bellomarini, L., Sallinger, E., Vahdati, S.: Chapter 6 reasoning in knowledge graphs: an embeddings spotlight. In: Janev, V., Graux, D., Jabeen, H., Sallinger, E. (eds.) Knowledge Graphs and Big Data Processing. LNCS, vol. 12072, pp. 87–101. Springer, Cham (2020). https://doi.org/10.1007/978-3-030-53199-7_6
13. Benedikt, M., et al.: Benchmarking the chase. In: PODS, pp. 37–52 (2017)
14. Benedikt, M., Leblay, J., Tsamoura, E.: PDQ: proof-driven query answering over web-based data. VLDB Endow. **7**(13), 1553–1556 (2014)
15. Bonifati, A., Ileana, I., Linardi, M.: Functional dependencies unleashed for scalable data exchange. CoRR abs/1602.00563 (2016)
16. Calì, A., Gottlob, G., Kifer, M.: Taming the infinite chase: query answering under expressive relational constraints. J. Artif. Intell. Res. **48**, 115–174 (2013)
17. Calì, A., Gottlob, G., Lukasiewicz, T.: A general datalog-based framework for tractable query answering over ontologies. J. Web Seman. **14**, 57–83 (2012)
18. Calì, A., Gottlob, G., Lukasiewicz, T., Marnette, B., Pieris, A.: Datalog+/-: A family of logical knowledge representation and query languages for new applications. In: 2010 25th Annual IEEE Symposium on Logic in Computer Science (2010)
19. Calì, A., Gottlob, G., Pieris, A.: Towards more expressive ontology languages: the query answering problem. Artif. Intell. **193**, 87–128 (2012)
20. Fagin, R., Kolaitis, P.G., Miller, R.J., Popa, L.: Data exchange: semantics and query answering. In: ICDT (2003)
21. Geerts, F., Mecca, G., Papotti, P., Santoro, D.: Mapping and cleaning. In: ICDE, pp. 232–243. IEEE Computer Society (2014)
22. Geerts, F., Mecca, G., Papotti, P., Santoro, D.: That's all folks! llunatic goes open source. VLDB Endow. **7**(13), 1565–1568 (2014)
23. Gottlob, G., Pieris, A.: Beyond SPARQL under OWL 2 QL entailment regime: Rules to the rescue. In: IJCAI (2015)
24. Gottlob, G., Pieris, A., Sallinger, E.: Vadalog: recent advances and applications. In: Calimeri, F., Leone, N., Manna, M. (eds.) JELIA 2019. LNCS (LNAI), vol. 11468, pp. 21–37. Springer, Cham (2019). https://doi.org/10.1007/978-3-030-19570-0_2
25. Imprialou, M., Stoilos, G., Grau, B.C.: Benchmarking ontology-based query rewriting systems. In: Twenty-Sixth AAAI Conference on Artificial Intelligence (2012)
26. Konstantinidis, G., Ambite, J.L.: Optimizing the chase: scalable data integration under constraints. VLDB Endow. **7**(14), 1869–1880 (2014)
27. Krötzsch, M., Thost, V.: Ontologies for knowledge graphs: breaking the rules. In: Groth, P., et al. (eds.) ISWC 2016. LNCS, vol. 9981, pp. 376–392. Springer, Cham (2016). https://doi.org/10.1007/978-3-319-46523-4_23
28. Lanti, D., Rezk, M.I., Xiao, G., Calvanese, D.: The NPD benchmark: reality check for OBDA systems. In: Advances in database technology-EDBT 2015: 18th International Conference on Extending Database Technology. Brussels, Belgium, 23–27 March 2015, Proceedings, pp. 617–628. University of Konstanz, University Library (2015)
29. Leone, N., Manna, M., Terracina, G., Veltri, P.: Dlv^E system. https://www.mat.unical.it/dlve/ (2017). Accessed 23 June 2022
30. Leone, N., Manna, M., Terracina, G., Veltri, P.: Fast query answering over existential rules. ToCL **20**(2), 1–48 (2019)

31. Leone, N., et al.: The dlv system for knowledge representation and reasoning. ACM Trans. Comput. Logic (TOCL) **7**(3), 499–562 (2006)
32. Leone, N., et al.: The DLV system for knowledge representation and reasoning. ACM Trans. Comput. Log. **7**(3), 499–562 (2006)
33. Leutenegger, S.T., Dias, D.: A modeling study of the TPC-C benchmark. ACM SIGMOD Rec. **22**(2), 22–31 (1993)
34. Maier, D., Mendelzon, A.O., Sagiv, Y.: Testing implications of data dependencies. ACM Trans. Database Syst. **4**(4), 455–469 (1979)
35. Menascé, D.A.: TPC-W: a benchmark for e-commerce. IEEE Internet Comput. **6**(3), 83–87 (2002)
36. Motik, B., Nenov, Y., Piro, R., Horrocks, I., Olteanu, D.: Parallel materialisation of datalog programs in centralised, main-memory RDF systems. In: AAAI (2014)
37. Patterson, D.: Technical perspective for better or worse, benchmarks shape a field. Commun. ACM **55**(7) (2012)
38. Poess, M., Floyd, C.: New TPC benchmarks for decision support and web commerce. ACM SIGMOD Rec. **29**(4), 64–71 (2000)
39. Poess, M., Rabl, T., Jacobsen, H.A., Caufield, B.: TPC-DI: the first industry benchmark for data integration. PVLDB **7**(13), 1367–1378 (2014)
40. Shkapsky, A., Yang, M., Zaniolo, C.: Optimizing recursive queries with monotonic aggregates in deals. In: 2015 IEEE 31st International Conference on Data Engineering, pp. 867–878. IEEE (2015)
41. Sutcliffe, G.: The TPTP problem library and associated infrastructure. J. Autom. Reason. **43**(4), 337–362 (2009)
42. Zaniolo, C., Yang, M., Das, A., Shkapsky, A., Condie, T., Interlandi, M.: Fixpoint semantics and optimization of recursive datalog programs with aggregates. Theory Pract. Logic Program. **17**(5–6), 1048–1065 (2017)

The Temporal Vadalog System

Luigi Bellomarini[1], Livia Blasi[1,2(✉)], Markus Nissl[2], and Emanuel Sallinger[2,3]

[1] Bank of Italy, Rome, Italy
livia.blasi@bancaditalia.it
[2] TU Wien, Vienna, Austria
[3] University of Oxford, Oxford, UK

Abstract. The need for reasoning over temporal data has recently emerged. DatalogMTL is a highly suitable language to handle many real-world applications. In spite of the deep theoretical contribution and the first experimental implementations of DatalogMTL, practical temporal reasoning applications call for a fully engineered system, able to reason with DatalogMTL while supporting a number of features of fundamental utility such as recursion, aggregation, and negation.

We introduce Temporal Vadalog, a new reasoning system for DatalogMTL that is capable of handling, among other elements, stratified negation and a form of aggregation. We evaluate the system in real-world and synthetic scenarios, comparatively showing its performance.

Keywords: Temporal reasoning · DatalogMTL · Vadalog

1 Introduction

Since recent years, Datalog [16] has been experiencing an unabated resurgence in both theory and practice. On the research side, the Datalog$^\pm$ family [15] is proving to be a key ingredient in the *Knowledge Representation and Reasoning* (KRR) context, with special regards to *Knowledge Graph* (KG) applications [5,10,11,19,23], where the appreciation for deductive solutions has been reignited by the favorable balance between computational complexity and expressive power of recent fragments such as Warded [21] and Shy [26]. On the practical side, aided by the efficiency of modern systems [9,25], Datalog is experiencing success in production domains, such as the economic and financial fields. In such practical endeavors, the need to support temporal reasoning clearly emerges, e.g., to analyze stock market data [34], to capture time-dependent interactions among IoT objects [31], to gain insights from log data [13].

Meanwhile, the rule-based AI community has been furthering a new extension of Datalog with the support for temporal reasoning, namely *DatalogMTL* [13], which promises to respond well to the uprising practical challenges. DatalogMTL

Supplementary Information The online version contains supplementary material available at https://doi.org/10.1007/978-3-031-21541-4_9.

G. Governatori and A.-Y. Turhan (Eds.): RuleML+RR 2022, LNCS 13752, pp. 130–145, 2022.
https://doi.org/10.1007/978-3-031-21541-4_9

inherits from Datalog the support for full recursion, of paramount importance in KG applications, that require graph traversals and pattern matching, together with forms of time awareness.

Let us start with a case from the economic domain encoded in DatalogMTL, in Example 1. Albeit simplified, this setting is derived from a family of financial applications in which we have experience and highlights some of the core features a production system for temporal reasoning with DatalogMTL should support.

Example 1. A governmental institution is supervising the changes in the corporate structure of some companies that operate in economic sectors of national strategic relevance. Not only does it wish to keep watch over such companies, but also their shareholders' actions, especially those who are buying into the companies later in the game. Consider the set of rules Π:

$$\Diamond_{[0,1]}\, significantShare(X,Y),$$
$$\neg\Diamond_{[0,1]}\, significantShare(X,Y) \rightarrow significantOwner(X,Y) \quad (1)$$
$$watchCompany(Y),\, significantOwner(X,Y),$$
$$connected(X,Z) \rightarrow watchCompany(Z) \quad (2)$$

The atom $watchCompany(Y)$ denotes that some company Y is in a watchlist and $significantShare(X,Y)$ models that X owns a relevant amount of shares of Y. DatalogMTL is ideal for capturing the dynamics of new shareholders buying in or increasing their shares, with the *diamond* operator: if at a certain interval in the past (expressed by $\Diamond_{[0,1]}$), X does not hold a significant amount of shares of Y, while that is the case at some point in a future interval (denoted by $\Diamond_{[0,1]}$), then we consider X as a $significantOwner(X,Y)$. Now, for every new $significantOwner(X,Y)$, we add to the watchlist all companies Z that are *connected*—for instance, according to the definition of connection given by other rules, omitted here—to the new owner X.

Functional Desiderata. The required characteristics of DatalogMTL reasoners can be laid out along the lines of the desiderata of *Graph Knowledge Management Systems* [5]. They should support simple, modular, highly expressive and low-complexity fragments of DatalogMTL; they should have the ability to perform basic operations over numeric values, as well as aggregations and negation. The recent DatalogMTL fragments, such as DatalogMTL^{FP} [31] and its core and linear eponymous DatalogMTL $\overset{\Diamond}{_{core}}$ and DatalogMTL $\overset{\Diamond}{_{lin}}$ [33], or Integer DatalogMTL [32] bode well in this direction, offering simple structure, recursion, and good complexity characteristics.

Yet, the development of temporal reasoners based on DatalogMTL is still in its infancy: the two implementations currently available are experimental in nature and do not satisfy these needs altogether. For example, the system proposed by Brandt et al. [12] does not support recursion and is not yet engineered for production use, as far as we are aware of. The second system, MeTeoR [35], does support recursive queries, using a combination of materialisation for non-recursive and automata-based reasoning for checking fact entailment for recursive settings. However, despite showing efficient reasoning capabilities, MeTeoR lacks support for aggregation and basic numeric operations.

Architectural Desiderata. The semantics of DatalogMTL is enforced by existing systems by inference algorithms based on time-aware variants of the well-known CHASE procedure [27]. The native adoption of the chase presents a number of limitations in the development of production architectures. For example, it requires the entirety of the database and the generated data to be available at every possible chase step. Also, it does not offer simple extension points, for instance to plug in different termination control policies. This is essential when infinite temporal patterns can be generated to toggle between different memory management policies, and, with specific respect to temporal reasoning, to choose among multiple time interval merging strategies, needed to handle temporal operators.

In this work, we make the first step towards a production-ready temporal reasoner and present the first system that, to the best of our knowledge, captures the functional and architectural limitations we have laid out.

Contribution. The Temporal Vadalog System is built around the core of Vadalog [9], a state-of-the-art reasoner for the Datalog$^\pm$ family [15]. It offers:

- a fully engineered *pipes-and-filter architecture* that enables:
  - the application of *rewriting-based optimization*, for instance, to deal with more complex temporal operators;
  - configurable *termination strategies*, activated by the system thanks to a form of *fragment awareness*, that is, the ability to single out the specific fragment of DatalogMTL used in the input programs, to guarantee termination of the reasoning process with pluggable algorithms that exploit the specific theoretical underpinnings of the fragments;
  - a clear *interface* between temporal and non-temporal reasoning;
- *high expressive power*, implementing:
  - the DatalogMTL *box* and *diamond* operators natively, as well as
  - recursion and stratified negation, and
  - *aggregate functions and numeric operations* over time.

The paper discusses the system architecture, delving into our optimization techniques, including specific termination strategies to detect *infinite models* as well as *query rewriting* methods. We contribute an experimental evaluation of the system on a variety of scenarios on real-world and synthetic data, compared to the other available temporal reasoner and a number of temporal benchmarks.

Overview. In Sect. 2, we provide a short introduction to DatalogMTL. Section 3 illustrates the system. Section 4 covers a comparative evaluation of performance. We discuss related work in Sect. 5 and conclude the paper in Sect. 6. More experimental details and algorithms are in the on-line Appendix [1].

2 DatalogMTL

DatalogMTL extends Datalog with metric temporal logic. In this section we summarize DatalogMTL with stratified negation under continuous semantics.

The timeline of DatalogMTL is defined over an ordered set of rational numbers $\mathbb{Q}$, where each time point t is an element of the timeline. An *interval* $\varrho = \langle \varrho^-, \varrho^+ \rangle$ is a subset of $\mathbb{Q}$, such that the endpoints $\varrho^-, \varrho^+ \in \mathbb{Q} \cup \{-\infty, \infty\}$, and for each $t \in \mathbb{Q}$ where $\varrho^- < t < \varrho^+$ we have $t \in \varrho$, and where brackets denote whether the endpoints are included ([]) or not (()).

An interval is *punctual* if it is of the form $[t, t]$, *positive* if $\varrho^- \geq 0$, and *bounded* if $\varrho^-, \varrho^+ \in \mathbb{Q}$.

The syntax of DatalogMTL extends Datalog with negation [30] with temporal operators: we consider a function-free first-order vocabulary consisting of disjoint sets of constants, variables and predicates equipped with a non-negative arity. A *term* is either a constant or a variable. An *atom* is of the form $P(\tau)$, where P is a predicate and τ is a n-ary tuple of terms matching the arity of P. An atom is *ground* if it contains no variables. A *fact* is an expression $P(\tau)@\varrho$, where ϱ is a non-empty interval and $P(\tau)$ a ground atom. A *dataset* is a set of facts. A *literal* is an expression of the form $A := \top \mid \bot \mid P(\tau) \mid \boxminus_\varrho A \mid \boxplus_\varrho A \mid \diamondsuit_\varrho A \mid \diamondsuit_\varrho A \mid A \, \mathcal{S}_\varrho A \mid A \, \mathcal{U}_\varrho A$, where ϱ is a positive interval. A *rule* is an expression of form: $A_1 \wedge \cdots \wedge A_i \wedge \text{not} A_{i+1} \wedge \cdots \wedge \text{not} A_{i+j} \rightarrow B$, where $i, j \geq 0$, each A_k is a literal and B is an atom. The atom B is the head of the rule and the conjunction is the body of the rule, where the literals $A_1 \wedge \cdots \wedge A_i$ denote the positive body atoms and $A_{i+1} \wedge \cdots \wedge A_{i+j}$ are the negated body atoms. A rule is *safe* if each variable occurs in at least one positive body atom, *positive* if $j = 0$ and *ground* if it contains no variables. A program Π is a set of safe rules. A program Π is *stratifiable* if there exists a stratification of a program Π. A stratification of Π is given as a function σ that maps each predicate P in Π to positive integers s.t. for each rule it holds $\sigma(P^+) \leq \sigma(P)$ and $\sigma(P^-) < \sigma(P)$ for P^+ mentioned in a positive body literal, P^- in a negated body literal and P in the rule head.

The semantics is given by an interpretation $\mathfrak{M}$ that specifies for each time point $t \in \mathbb{Q}$ and each ground atom $P(\tau)$, whether $P(\tau)$ is satisfied at t, in which case we write $\mathfrak{M}, t \models P(\tau)$. An interpretation $\mathfrak{M}$ is a model of a fact $P(\tau)@\varrho$, if $\mathfrak{M}, t \models P(\tau)$ for all $t \in \varrho$ and a model of a set of facts D if it is a model of each fact in D. The notion of satisfiability of an interpretation $\mathfrak{M}$ is extended to ground literals as follows:

$\mathfrak{M}, t \models \top$ for each t

$\mathfrak{M}, t \models \bot$ for no t

$\mathfrak{M}, t \models \boxminus_\varrho A$ iff $\mathfrak{M}, s \models A$ for all s with $t - s \in \varrho$

$\mathfrak{M}, t \models \boxplus_\varrho A$ iff $\mathfrak{M}, s \models A$ for all s with $s - t \in \varrho$

$\mathfrak{M}, t \models A \, \mathcal{S}_\varrho \, A'$ iff $\mathfrak{M}, s \models A'$ for some s with $t - s \in \varrho \wedge \mathfrak{M}, r \models A$ for all $r \in (s, t)$

$\mathfrak{M}, t \models A \, \mathcal{U}_\varrho \, A'$ iff $\mathfrak{M}, s \models A'$ for some s with $s - t \in \varrho \wedge \mathfrak{M}, r \models A$ for all $r \in (t, s)$

$\mathfrak{M}, t \models \diamondminus_\varrho A$ iff $\mathfrak{M}, s \models A$ for some s with $t - s \in \varrho$

$\mathfrak{M}, t \models \diamondplus_\varrho A$ iff $\mathfrak{M}, s \models A$ for some s with $s - t \in \varrho$

An interpretation $\mathfrak{M}$ satisfies not A ($\mathfrak{M}, t \models$ not A), if $\mathfrak{M}, t \not\models A$ and a ground rule r, if $\mathfrak{M}, t \models A_k$ for $0 \leq k \leq i$ and $\mathfrak{M}, t \models$ not A_k for $i + 1 \leq k \leq i + j$ for every t. An interpretation $\mathfrak{M}$ is a model of a rule when it satisfies every possible grounding of the rule, and of a program, if it satisfies every rule in the program and the program has a stratification. A program Π and a dataset D entail a fact $P(\tau)@\varrho$ (($\Pi, D) \models P(\tau)@\varrho$) if $\mathfrak{M} \models P(\tau)@\varrho$ for each model of both Π and D. Each dataset D has a unique least model $\mathfrak{M}_D$ and the canonical interpretation $\mathfrak{C}_{\Pi,D}$ is the least model of Π and D.

3   The Temporal Vadalog System

We take inspiration from the vast amount of available experience in building database and knowledge graph management systems [9] and propose a novel reasoning architecture based on the *volcano iterator model* [22] implemented in the form of a *time-aware execution pipeline*. Shunning an exhaustive taxonomy of all the architectural components, we opt for a thematic walk-through in the system, where our interest is in addressing the temporal reasoning challenges. To get started, let us see our time-aware execution pipeline in the next section.

3.1   A Time-Aware Execution Pipeline

Along the lines of the *pipe and filters* architectural style [14], a DatalogMTL program Π is compiled into an execution pipeline that reads the data from the input sources, applies the needed transformations, be they relational algebra operators (e.g., projection, selection) or time-based ones, and finally produces the desired output as a result.

Construction of the Pipeline. The pipeline is built in four steps: (i) A *logic optimizer* performs a set of rewriting tasks, with the aim of reducing programs to a canonical form, where only combined (and not chains of) individual operators are allowed. (ii) A *logic compiler* then transforms the DatalogMTL rules into in-memory placeholder objects, each with the "responsibility of knowing" which transformation needs to be performed. (iii) A *heuristic optimizer* intervenes at this point, introducing perturbations and producing variants of the generated

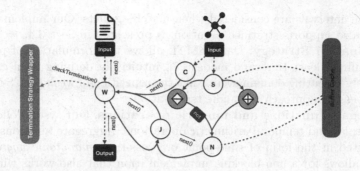

Fig. 1. The reasoning pipeline for Example 1. The atom *significantShare* is denoted by the filter S, *significantOwner* by N, *watchCompany* by W, *connected* by C, and J is an artificial filter to decompose, for simplicity, the ternary join of Rule 2 into binary joins.

pipeline to target higher performance, with ad-hoc simplifications. (iv) A *query compiler* finally translates this logical graph structure into a *reasoning query plan*, where a *filter*, with the "responsibility of doing" the transformations, is generated out of each placeholder, and a pipe is induced by each read-write dependency between the rules. The pipeline for our running Example 1 is shown in Fig. 1.

Runtime Model. The reasoning process then consists of a *pull-based* approach, where some rule heads are marked as *sinks* and iteratively pull data by issuing next() and get() messages to their preceding filters, which in turn propagate such messages to their predecessors and eventually to a set of *source* filters that directly read from initial data source, thanks to dedicated *record managers*, i.e., data adapters. Each filter applies specific transformations, depending on the form of the associated rules (e.g., linear, joins, temporal operators, aggregations, etc.). Clearly, the next() primitive succeeds as long as facts are available in the cascade of invoked filters. For instance, in Fig. 1, the facts for our output filter W are generated directly from the input data, but also recursively from J, since in fact *watchCompany* is recursive in Rule 2.

Temporal Challenges. Implementing and optimizing the different relational algebra operators is certainly interesting, but not of central relevance in this work. Conversely, many time-related challenges arise, for which the Temporal Vadalog System provides support. We give an overview next.

- **Applying Temporal Operators.** How the temporal operators are encoded in the pipeline (e.g., the ⬦ operator in Fig. 1) is dealt with in Sect. 3.2.
- **Merging strategies**. In order to correctly apply the semantics of the ⊟ operator, we must merge adjacent and overlapping time intervals. The adoption of different merging strategies is discussed in Sect. 3.3.
- **Temporal Joins and Stratified Negation**. Temporal reasoning needs a time-aware version of the usual join (e.g., filter W in the figure), where the

different intervals are considered when matching facts. Our implementation, which also supports stratified negation, is presented in Sect. 3.4.

- **Termination Strategy**. DatalogMTL allows the formulation of programs with infinite least Herbrand models [7], intuitively deriving from capturing infinitely repeating domain events, like the repetition of weekdays. Section 3.5 describes our approach to handle termination.
- **Aggregate functions and numeric operations**. Our system offers standard scalar and temporal arithmetic operations. Aggregate functions are also supported in the form of time-point or cross-time *monotonic aggregations*, which allows for a non-blocking implementation that also works with recursion. To the best of our knowledge, the Temporal Vadalog System is the only DatalogMTL reasoner that implements aggregations; their syntax and semantics is explained in our recent work [6].
- **Temporal and non-Temporal Reasoning**. The Temporal Vadalog systems combines temporal and non-temporal reasoning, as detailed in Sect. 3.6.

3.2 Temporal Operators in the Execution Pipeline

DatalogMTL provides six temporal operators, which are pairwise symmetric; we can therefore concentrate only on the forward propagating ones: $\Diamond$, $\mathcal{S}$, and $\boxminus$. The main idea of the reasoning pipeline is to introduce a filter node for each occurrence of an operator in a rule, and feed it with the output of the operand atom. Then, the output of the operator filter is provided as an intermediate result. This process is straightforward for the $\Diamond$ operator, which is converted into a single filter that applies a transformation of the interval according to its semantics. Conversely, the $\boxminus$ operator may require an additional pipeline filter, to preliminarily merge adjacent and overlapping intervals, as we discuss in Sect. 3.3.

3.3 Merging Strategies

The evaluation of the box operator, that is, deciding whether $\mathfrak{M}, t \models \boxminus_\varrho A$, requires to check that for all s such that $t - s \in \varrho$, it holds that $\mathfrak{M}, s \models A$. Consider, for instance, Example 2, assuming the time unit is years.

Example 2. The variable X in the rule is a *longTimeInvestor* of Y if X has continuously held a *significantShare* of Y for at least 2 years.

$$\boxminus_{[0,2]} significantShare(X, Y) \rightarrow longTimeInvestor(X, Y) \quad (1)$$
$$D = \{significantShare(A, B)@[1.6, 1.9], significantShare(A, B)@(1.8, 3.7],$$
$$significantShare(A, B)@(2.9, 4.0]\}$$

Observe that the *significantShare* facts in D do not individually cover a 2-years interval, while when considered together, their combined intervals result

Algorithm 1 Blocking Strategy

1: mergeStructure ← *createMergeStructure*()
2: counter ← 0
3: **function** NEXT
4:     changed ← *false*;
5:     **if** counter ≥ mergeStructure.*length* **then**
6:         **while** *super*.*next*() **do**
7:             (changed, mergedEntry) ← mergeStructure.*add*(*getCurrentEntry*())
8:     **if** changed **then**
9:         counter ← 0
10:     **else**
11:         counter ← counter + 1
12:     **return** counter < mergeStructure.*length*

in the fact $significantShare(A, B)@[1.6, 4.0]$ and hence the rule derives the final fact $longTimeInvestor(A, B)@[3.6, 4.0]$.

Intuitively, a software component implementing the box operator in a reasoning pipeline will accumulate enough evidence of ground atoms of A in ϱ, until the entire interval ϱ is covered. One typical tradeoff in data pipelines is between streaming processing, responsiveness, limited memory footprint, in-memory computation vs. blocking processing, overall performance optimization, large memory occupation, materialization of intermediate results. In relational systems such a balance depends on both the semantics of the individual relational algebra operators and the optimization choices. Some operators are inherently streaming-oriented, or stateless (e.g., selection or projection), whereas others are partially or fully blocking, or stateful (e.g., join or sort) [29]. Moreover, the optimizer may interleave intermediate materialization filters into the pipeline to pre-compute and store parts of it and maximize the reuse of intermediate results.

When it comes to the architecture of a modern temporal reasoning system, we recognize similar challenges, and merging interval plays the same role as data materialization in relational systems. Like the join, the box operator is partially blocking: when invoked via a **next**() call, it is able to answer positively only once it has accumulated enough evidence to cover ϱ. Yet, unlike the sort operator, once it starts to produce output, not necessarily is it finished with consuming its input facts and therefore issues **next**() calls, in turn.

The Temporal Vadalog System offers two orthogonal options: two implementations of the box operators and three interleaving strategies.

Streaming and Blocking Box. The *streaming box* generates facts as soon as it has merged enough input facts. The *blocking box* pulls and merges intervals until **next**() returns false; then, for each **next**() call, it forwards a single stored fact without calling the parent streams. The streaming box supports reactivity as merging is done on-the-fly and the intermediate merging results are forwarded without waiting for all the incoming data to be processed, while the blocking box reduces the amount of facts and intervals in the system.

Algorithm 2 Streaming Strategy

1: mergeStructure ← *createMergeStructure*()
2: **function** NEXT
3:     next ← *super.next*()
4:     **if** next **then**
5:         (changed, mergedEntry) ← mergeStructure.*add*(*getCurrentEntry*())
6:         *setCurrentEntry*(mergedEntry)
7:     **return** next

Algorithms 1 and 2 present the logic for the blocking and the streaming strategy, respectively. Both inherit the logic of the linear filter of Vadalog to retrieve the next entry, which is visualized by a call to *super.next*(). The next() function returns a Boolean value denoting whether a new fact has been derived. The access to the terms is handled in successive calls to getter functions returning the value of a term's position only if required by the next pipeline step. The call *createMergeStructure* creates a data structure for merging[1], and the call of *getCurrentEntry* retrieves the current entry retrieved with the *super.next*() call and *setCurrentEntry* updates the entry with the merged intervals. To exemplify the difference between strategies, let us look at a variation on Example 2.

Example 3. Consider Example 2 again. The *Streaming* strategy would read the first two entries, which is sufficient to apply the $\boxminus_{[0,2]}$ operator to derive the intermediate result *longTimeInvestor(A,B)@[3.6,3.7]*, before the final *longTimeInvestor(A,B)@[3.6,4.0]* is derived; a *Blocking* strategy would wait for all *significantShare* facts to be read first, and applies the box operator only then.

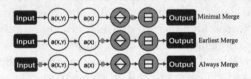

Fig. 2. Overview of interleaving strategies; merging positions are marked in red. (Color figure online)

Interleaving Strategies. The planner is equipped with multiple options to decide how to interleave explicit interval merge operations in the pipeline so as to achieve different performance goals or even just to guarantee correctness. We support the following options.

---

[1] Our data structure is built around a hashmap, whose key is the fact and whose values are a collection of intervals. Currently, we use a tree-like structure as a collection that auto-merges adjacent intervals on insert.

- *Minimal Merge.* The planner inserts a merge operation only before each box operator. In addition, one can provide to the planner hints regarding merging s.t. it inserts an additional merge transformation prior to a linear transformation. Typically, such hints are useful after unions of different rules, after a diamond operator that could produce many overlapping intervals that should be combined, after the input or before the output to eliminate duplicates before showing the results.
- *Always Merge.* The planner inserts merge operations whenever the intervals are not merged. The application of temporal operators on a set of intervals will always result in a merged set, as the coalescing is applied directly on the set.
- *Earliest Merge.* If no merge operation is required (i.e., there is no box operator) the planner avoids merging; otherwise it inserts the merge in the earliest position so that each fact contains all intervals when the box operator is reached; previous operations benefit from the reduced number of facts.

3.4   Temporal Joins and Stratified Negation

In Temporal Vadalog, we extend the slot machine join algorithm of Vadalog [4]. This algorithm is based on an index nested loop join [20], enhanced with dynamic in-memory indexing. In comparison to an index-nested loop join, there is no persistent pre-calculated index, but the index is built in-memory during the first full scan of each predicate A_k with $0 \leq k < n$ to be joined. That is, for each A_k, we first check whether a matching fact can be found in the index matching the known terms from the previous A_j with $0 \leq j < k$, and if not, we continue with the full scan until a fact matches in case the index is not yet fully built.

The index is unaware of intervals: when a fact matches, we either intersect (join) or subtract (in case of stratified negation) the interval from the current partially computed interval (i.e., the computed interval up to A_j), both operations ignoring non-overlapping intervals. In addition, for stratified negation we consider all matching tuples of A_k. The full algorithm is in the Appendix.

3.5   Termination Strategy for the Infinite Chase of Intervals

We discussed in a previous work that fragments of DatalogMTL can produce infinite models [7], which however admit a finite representation in DatalogMTL^{FP} (and symmetrically in DatalogMTL^{BP}). In detail, three cases are possible for a DatalogMTL^{FP} (resp. BP) program Π: (i) it is *harmless*, a sufficient condition to admit a finite model; (ii) it is *DatalogMTL$_\Diamond$ temporal linear* or *DatalogMTL$_\boxminus$ union free*, a sufficient condition to admit an eventually constant model under certain conditions; (iii) it is not in the previous sets but in DatalogMTL^{FP}, a sufficient condition to admit an eventually periodic model.

The Temporal Vadalog System guarantees termination of the reasoning process, with a two-phases *compile time* and *runtime* technique. At **compile time**, the planner determines the fragment of Π, according to the following procedure.

- Using [7, Algorithm 1], that checks if the program has "harmful" temporal cycles, it determines if Π is *harmless*. If so, we fix *modelKind = Finite*.
- Else, it determines whether Π is *temporal linear*, checking that for each rule there is at most one body predicate that is mutually temporal recursive with the head in the dependency graph of Π; if it is the case and temporal linear operators $\diamondsuit_{[t_1,t_2]}$ are such that $t_1 \neq t_2$, then we fix *modelKind = Constant*.
- Else, it determines whether Π is *union free*, checking that there are no rules of Π sharing the same head predicate; if it is the case and the box operators $\boxminus_{[t_1,t_2]}$ are such that $t_1 \neq t_2$, then we fix *modelKind = Constant*.
- Else, we are in DatalogMTL^{FP} and fix *modelKind = Periodic*.

In all the non-finite cases, according to [7, Lemma 2], and [7, Theorem 4], the system determines the repetition pattern length *pLength*, based on the combination of the pattern lengths of the different Strongly Connected Components (SCC) of Π. This will result in the production, at runtime, of facts of the form $P(\tau)@\varrho$ and $\{P(\tau)@\langle o_1, o_2\rangle, n\}$, where the intervals are given by $\langle o_1 + x * pLength, o_2 + x * pLength\rangle$ for all $x \in \mathbb{N}$, where $x \geq n$, in the periodic case, or $\langle o_1 + x * pLength, \infty\rangle$, in the constant case. All the pipeline filters are wrapped by functional components named *termination strategies*, whose goal is inhibiting the runtime generation of specific facts that may cause non-termination. All termination strategies are instructed with *modelKind* and, where applicable, *pLength*.

At **runtime**, the system behaves in a fragment-aware fashion, depending on *modelKind*. If it is *finite*, the only causes of non-termination may be the usual Datalog recursion, which is easily checked by the termination strategies with an embedded hash index. The reasoning process will produce facts of the form $P(\tau)@\varrho$. If *modelKind* is *eventually constant* or *eventually periodic*, then the termination strategies intercept the facts generated by the "non-finite" filters and detect when they match a repeating pattern. If the model is eventually constant, the reference interval of ground atoms is immediately converted by the termination strategies into $\langle o_1 + x * pLength, \infty\rangle$, therefore preventing the generation of redundant facts in sub-intervals; else, if eventually periodic, the termination strategies associated to non-finite filters, generalize the numeric intervals, with their pattern-based symbolic equivalent, so that redundant sub-intervals are not generated in this case either.

Example 4.

$$\diamondsuit_{[7,7]} StockMarketOpeningDays \rightarrow StockMarketOpeningDays \quad (1)$$

$$\diamondsuit_{[0,2]} Anniversary(X) \rightarrow Celebration(X) \quad (2)$$

$$StockMarketOpeningDays, Celebration(X)$$
$$\rightarrow CelebrationDuringStockMarketDays(X) \quad (3)$$

$$D = \{StockMarketOpeningDays@[0,4], Anniversary(A)@[125,125], ...\}$$

Example 4 shows one of such cases. The stock market opening days are from Monday to Friday (Rule 1). When there is an anniversary for a company X of our multinational holding, the celebration lasts for two days (Rule 2). We want to intercept all the cases in which a celebration coincides with the stock market opening days for our company A, to study the impact on its business. In other terms, we want to compute whether $CelebrationDuringStockMarketDays(A)$ holds.

At compile time, the planner determines that $modelKind = Periodic$ and from Rule 2, we have that $pLength = 4$. At runtime, after the generation of the fact $StockMarketOpeningDays@[7, 11]$, the termination strategy for $Celebration$, infers that $n = 0$, and so all facts generated by Rule 2 have the form $StockMarketOpeningDays@[x \times 7, x \times 7 + 4]$, for $x \geq 0$, and their generation is blocked. It remains to apply the join of Rule 3 between $Celebration(A)@[125, 127]$ produced by Rule 2 and the pattern generated by Rule 1, that is, computing $x \in \mathbb{N}$ such that $[x \times 7, x \times 7 + 4] \cap [125, 127]$ is not the empty interval, which holds for $x = 18$. Thus we can conclude $CelebrationDuringStockMarketDays(A)@[126, 127]$.

3.6   Combining Temporal and Non-Temporal Reasoning

Current studies have not considered the combination of existentials (e.g., Warded Datalog) and DatalogMTL, together. Hence, for the current implementation, we consider the two fragments orthogonal—in Datalog with existentials [4] we forbid temporal operators and in DatalogMTL we forbid existentials—to avoid undecidability of the program. In order to support both modes within one program we added support for temporal wrapping and unwrapping of rules which are of form:

$$P_1(\tau)@temporalAtom(\mathrm{LB}, \varrho^-, \varrho^+, \mathrm{RB}) \rightarrow P_0(\tau, \mathrm{LB}, \varrho^-, \varrho^+, \mathrm{RB})$$

$$P_0(\tau, \mathrm{LB}, \varrho^-, \varrho^+, \mathrm{RB}) \rightarrow P_1(\tau)@temporalAtom(\mathrm{LB}, \varrho^-, \varrho^+, \mathrm{RB})$$

where LB (RB) denotes if the left (right) bracket is closed and $temporalAtom$ is an atom annotation to denote wrapping/unwrapping of intervals. Note that not all terms in the tuple are required in the non-temporal atom and constants can be used.

Example 5. Consider the conversion of a temporal fact $P_1(a)@[0, 4)$ and a non-temporal fact $P_0(b, false, 0, 3, true)$ according to rules. Such rules will map the temporal fact to $P_0(a, true, 0, 4, false)$ and the non-temporal fact to $P_1(b)@(0, 3]$.

4   Experiments

We evaluated our system in a variety of scenarios with temporal operators, recursion, negation, numerical computation and aggregate functions, on real-world, realistic, and synthetic datasets. The performance has been compared with MeTeoR, when applicable, and against several benchmarks.

Setup. The execution environment for the experiment is a memory-optimized virtual machine with 16 cores and 256 GB RAM on an Intel Xeon architecture.

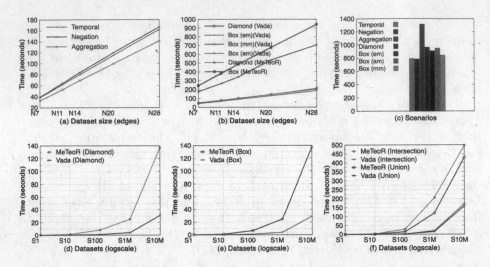

Fig. 3. (a) *Temporal, Negation,* and *Aggregation* on N7-N28 over time; (b) *Box* and *Diamond* in Temporal Vadalog and MeTeoR; (c) RW dataset in all scenarios; (d) iTemporal Diamond; (e) iTemporal Box; (f) iTemporal Union and Intersection.

Datasets. We used *real-world, realistic,* and *synthetic* datasets. The *real-world dataset* (RW) comes from the KG of the Italian companies [3] and represents the proprietary chains from the second half of 2019 to the end of 2021, taken at 6-months snapshots with a monthly granularity, for a total of 5 timepoints and around 31M edges evolving through time. The *realistic datasets* (N7, N11, N14, N20, N28) represent the ownerships in a synthetic graph, generated as variations on RW. These graphs evolve through time, e.g., with changes in shares, new shareholders, exit of shareholders, and so on, over 5 timepoints, and have from 700K to 2.8M nodes and from 2.7M to 10.8M edges. The *synthetic datasets* (S1-S10M) are randomly distributed over a given domain and comprise from 1K to 10M facts. More details are in the Appendix.

4.1   Experiments with Realistic and Real-World Data

Scenarios. We ran the experiments on realistic and real-world data on 5 scenarios: 1) *Temporal*: temporal operator, recursion, and constraints on variables; 2) *Negation*: stratified negation and recursion; 3) *Aggregation*: aggregation; 4) *Diamond*: diamond operator and recursion; 5) *Box*: box operator and recursion. We ran each scenario against the datasets N7-N28 and RW in the Temporal Vadalog System and, for *Box* and *Diamond*, also in MeTeoR—scenarios not including features not supported by MeTeoR. For *Temporal, Negation,* and *Aggregation* we performed 3 runs each and averaged the elapsed time; the merging strategy was *always merge*. For the *Box* scenario, we tested *minimal, earliest* and *always merge*. We used an one-hour timeout to abort long-running experiments.

Discussion of the Results. Figure 3a shows the performance of our system on the scenarios *Temporal*, *Negation*, and *Aggregation* over the realistic datasets N7-N28. We have good scalability, with a linear increase in the elapsed time. The more expensive *Negation* runs at just over 166 s for the biggest dataset, N28, while *Aggregation* performs best at 32–141 s, given the non-recursive setting.

Figure 3b shows the *Diamond* and *Box* scenarios comparatively with MeTeoR. Temporal Vadalog is 80% faster than MeTeoR in the *Diamond* scenario. For *Box*, Temporal Vadalog is 80% faster with *earliest merge* (*em*) and *always merge* (*am*). This test also highlights the importance of the merging strategy choice. In fact, in the case of *earliest merge* the performance is better, ranging from 43 to 186 s, while the *minimal merge* requires 4x of it, as more data is sent through the pipeline until the merging operation is applied. In the case of *earliest merge*, the merging operations are concentrated, and the same happens for *always merge*.

Finally, Fig. 3c shows the performance of the 5 scenarios (plus 3 merging strategy variations for *Box*) on our *real-world* dataset. While MeTeoR exceeds the established timeout in all applicable scenarios, our system always terminates within one hour, with the *Temporal* and the *Negation* scenarios being the best, having an elapsed time of 780–790 s (~13 min). In the case of *Temporal*, this depends on the presence of one variable constraint in the scenario, which allows to skip many edges. In fact, we can spot this behavior comparatively looking at the *Diamond* scenario, which shares the same rules except for the constraint: it shows a worse performance, with an elapsed of 904 s (~16 min). The *Box* scenario shows differences of around 2 min between the strategies, favoring minimal merge due to less overlapping intervals in the graph.

4.2   Temporal Foundation Benchmark

Observing a substantial speedup of the Temporal Vadalog System with respect to MeTeoR in the realistic scenarios, we generated specific temporal benchmarks to confirm this aspect. In particular, we compared the systems as of their main temporal operations, that is, temporal operators, joins and unions. To generate our benchmarks, we used *iTemporal* [8], a generator for DatalogMTL with different data sizes per input atom. Figures 3d-f present the results. For all operations, we see that our system outperforms MeTeoR with a factor of 3 to 4 (depending on the benchmark) for $10M$ facts.

5   Related Work

The first proposals for a temporal version of Datalog include $Datalog_{1S}$ [17] (using successor functions) and Datalog extensions with temporal logic operators from Linear Temporal Logic (LTL) [28] and Computation Tree Logic (CTL) [18]. More recently, Metric Temporal Logic [2,24] has been considered as a formalism that can provide an expressive temporal extension for Datalog. The first results have been presented by Brandt et al. [12,13], who introduced

DatalogMTL and presented a practical, although non-recursive, implementation through SQL rewriting.

Theory for continuous semantics DatalogMTL [30–34] has been studied extensively in recent years. Most recently Wałęga et al. introduced MeTeoR [35], a reasoner that employs a combination of materialisation and automata-based reasoning, referred to in our comparative experiments.

6   Conclusion

In this paper, we presented a novel architecture and system for reasoning with DatalogMTL. We emphasized its performance and scalability with various benchmarks and outperformed state-of-the-art reasoners in this language. In future work, we want to improve the reasoner, as well as work on additional fragments that allow tractable reasoning in DatalogMTL.

Acknowledgements. This work was supported by the Vienna Science and Technology Fund (WWTF) grant VRG18-013, and the "rAIson data" Royal Society grant of Prof. Georg Gottlob.

References

1. The Temporal Vadalog System: Appendix. http://shorturl.at/biGR8
2. Alur, R., Henzinger, T.A.: Real-time logics: complexity and expressiveness. Inf. Comput. **104**(1), 35–77 (1993)
3. Bellomarini, L., et al.: Reasoning on company takeovers during the COVID-19 crisis with knowledge graphs. In: RuleML+RR (Supplement), vol. 2644, pp. 145–156 (2020)
4. Bellomarini, L., Benedetto, D., Gottlob, G., Sallinger, E.: Vadalog: A modern architecture for automated reasoning with large knowledge graphs. Inf. Syst. 101528 (2020)
5. Bellomarini, L., Gottlob, G., Pieris, A., Sallinger, E.: Swift logic for big data and knowledge graphs. In: IJCAI (2017)
6. Bellomarini, L., Nissl, M., Sallinger, E.: Monotonic aggregation for temporal datalog. In: Proceedings of the 15th International Rule Challenge, vol. 2956 (2021)
7. Bellomarini, L., Nissl, M., Sallinger, E.: Query evaluation in DatalogMTL - taming infinite query results. CoRR abs/2109.10691 (2021)
8. Bellomarini, L., Nissl, M., Sallinger, E.: iTemporal: an extensible generator of temporal benchmarks. In: ICDE, pp. 2021–2033. IEEE (2022)
9. Bellomarini, L., Sallinger, E., Gottlob, G.: The Vadalog system: datalog-based reasoning for knowledge graphs. PVLDB **11**(9), 975–987 (2018)
10. Bellomarini, L., Sallinger, E., Vahdati, S.: Knowledge graphs: the layered perspective. In: Janev, V., Graux, D., Jabeen, H., Sallinger, E. (eds.) Knowledge Graphs and Big Data Processing. LNCS, vol. 12072, pp. 20–34. Springer, Cham (2020). https://doi.org/10.1007/978-3-030-53199-7_2
11. Bellomarini, L., Sallinger, E., Vahdati, S.: Reasoning in knowledge graphs: an embeddings spotlight. In: Janev, V., Graux, D., Jabeen, H., Sallinger, E. (eds.) Knowledge Graphs and Big Data Processing. LNCS, vol. 12072, pp. 87–101. Springer, Cham (2020). https://doi.org/10.1007/978-3-030-53199-7_6

12. Brandt, S., Kalayci, E.G., Kontchakov, R., Ryzhikov, V., Xiao, G., Zakharyaschev, M.: Ontology-based data access with a horn fragment of metric temporal logic. In: AAAI, pp. 1070–1076. AAAI Press (2017)
13. Brandt, S., Kalayci, E.G., Ryzhikov, V., Xiao, G., Zakharyaschev, M.: Querying log data with metric temporal logic. J. Artif. Intell. Res. **62**, 829–877 (2018)
14. Buschmann, F., Henney, K., Schmidt, D.C.: Pattern-Oriented Software Architecture, 4th edn. Wiley, Hoboken (2007)
15. Calì, A., Gottlob, G., Pieris, A.: New expressive languages for ontological query answering. In: Proceedings of AAAI, vol. 2011 (2011)
16. Ceri, S., Gottlob, G., Tanca, L.: What you always wanted to know about datalog (and never dared to ask). TKDE **1**(1), 146–166 (1989)
17. Chomicki, J., Imielinski, T.: Temporal deductive databases and infinite objects. In: PODS, pp. 61–73 (1988)
18. Clarke, E.M., Emerson, E.A.: Design and synthesis of synchronization skeletons using branching time temporal logic. In: Kozen, D. (ed.) Logic of Programs 1981. LNCS, vol. 131, pp. 52–71. Springer, Heidelberg (1982). https://doi.org/10.1007/BFb0025774
19. Dalgliesh, J.: How the Enterprise Knowledge Graph Connects Oil and Gas Data Silos. Maana Blog (2016). https://shorturl.at/rsxU2
20. Garcia-Molina, H., Ullman, J.D., Widom, J.: Database Systems - The Complete Book, 2nd edn. Pearson Education, London (2009)
21. Gottlob, G., Pieris, A.: Beyond SPARQL under OWL 2 QL entailment regime: rules to the rescue. In: IJCAI, pp. 2999–3007 (2015)
22. Graefe, G., McKenna, W.J.: The volcano optimizer generator: extensibility and efficient search. In: ICDE, pp. 209–218 (1993)
23. He, Q., Chen, B.C., Agarwal, D.: Building The LinkedIn Knowledge Graph. LinkedIn Blog (2016). https://shorturl.at/aouyW
24. Koymans, R.: Specifying real-time properties with metric temporal logic. Real-Time Syst. **2**(4), 255–299 (1990)
25. Leone, N., et al.: Enhancing DLV for large-scale reasoning. In: LPNMR, vol. 11481, pp. 312–325 (2019)
26. Leone, N., Manna, M., Terracina, G., Veltri, P.: Fast query answering over existential rules. ACM Trans. Comput. Log. **20**(2), 12:1–12:48 (2019)
27. Maier, D., Mendelzon, A.O., Sagiv, Y.: Testing implications of data dependencies. ACM Trans. Database Syst. **4**(4), 455–468 (1979)
28. Pnueli, A.: The temporal logic of programs. In: 18th Annual Symposium on Foundations of Computer Science (SFCS 1977), pp. 46–57 (1977)
29. Sciore, E.: Database Design and Implementation, 2nd edn. Springer, Cham (2020). https://doi.org/10.1007/978-3-030-33836-7
30. Tena Cucala, D.J., Walega, P.A., Cuenca Grau, B., Kostylev, E.V.: Stratified negation in datalog with metric temporal operators. In: AAAI, pp. 6488–6495 (2021)
31. Walega, P.A., Cuenca Grau, B., Kaminski, M., Kostylev, E.V.: Datalogmtl: computational complexity and expressive power. In: IJCAI, pp. 1886–1892 (2019)
32. Walega, P.A., Cuenca Grau, B., Kaminski, M., Kostylev, E.V.: Datalogmtl over the integer timeline. In: KR, pp. 768–777 (2020)
33. Walega, P.A., Cuenca Grau, B., Kaminski, M., Kostylev, E.V.: Tractable fragments of datalog with metric temporal operators. In: IJCAI, pp. 1919–1925 (2020)
34. Walega, P.A., Kaminski, M., Cuenca Grau, B.: Reasoning over streaming data in metric temporal datalog. In: AAAI, pp. 3092–3099 (2019)
35. Wang, D., Hu, P., Walega, P., Cuenca Grau, B.: Meteor: practical reasoning in datalog with metric temporal operators. In: Proceedings of AAAI-2022 (2022)

An Existential Rule Framework
for Computing Why-Provenance
On-Demand for Datalog

Ali Elhalawati⬤, Markus Krötzsch⬤, and Stephan Mennicke$^{(\boxtimes)}$⬤

Knowledge-Based Systems Group, TU Dresden, Dresden, Germany
{ali.elhalawati,markus.kroetzsch,stephan.mennicke}@tu-dresden.de

Abstract. Why-provenance—explaining why a query result is obtained—is an essential asset for reaching the goal of *Explainable AI*. For instance, recursive (Datalog) queries may show unexpected derivations due to complex entanglement of database atoms inside recursive rule applications. Provenance, and why-provenance in particular, helps debugging rule sets to eventually obtain the desired set of rules. There are three kinds of approaches to computing why-provenance for Datalog in the literature: (1) the complete ones, (2) the approximate ones, and (3) the theoretical ones. What all these approaches have in common is that they aim at computing provenance for all IDB atoms, while only a few atoms might be requested to be explained. We contribute an on-demand approach: After deriving all entailed facts of a Datalog program, we allow for querying for the provenance of particular IDB atoms and the structures involved in deriving provenance are computed only then. Our framework is based on terminating existential rules, recording the different rule applications. We present two implementations of the framework, one based on the semiring solver FPsolve, the other one based Datalog(S), a recent extension of Datalog by set terms. We perform experiments on benchmark rule sets using both implementations and discuss feasibility of provenance on-demand.

Keywords: Datalog provenance · Why-provenance · Datalog(S)

1 Introduction

Explainability and justification of data that stems from complex, even recursive, processes have attracted both, the community of knowledge representation as well as the database community. The reason is that recursive programs tend to get complicated, which makes it hard for users to debug, audit, establish trust in, or even query the data. Data provenance is one particular way of achieving these aspects and has a long-standing tradition in the field of relational databases and

© The Author(s), under exclusive license to Springer Nature Switzerland AG 2022
G. Governatori and A.-Y. Turhan (Eds.): RuleML+RR 2022, LNCS 13752, pp. 146–163, 2022.
https://doi.org/10.1007/978-3-031-21541-4_10

non-recursive queries [5,8]. For recursive queries, provenance for Datalog has been studied and found to be expressible with quite similar tools as the ones underlying provenance for non-recursive queries [10,13]. Provenance describes how annotations on database tuples or facts have been used to obtain a query result.

In this work, we explore the task of providing explainability for Datalog programs by *why-provenance* [5]. Why-provenance considers the witnesses of a derivation, which are sets of database atoms that can be used to achieve the derivation through reasoning. Previous works [3,12,14] contributed to computing why-provenance for databases, which are practical but restricted to non-recursive programs (e.g., SQL queries). Only a few works actually considered the implementation of why-provenance for Datalog. Most of it has been either on the theoretical side [9,10], bound to certain underapproximations of why-provenance [20], restricted to non-recursive Datalog programs [17], or require an expensive transformation of the instantiated rules in a Datalog program to a system of equations [11].

Since providing why-provenance for all the data derived from a database via a Datalog program is an expensive task (the set of all witnesses is generally exponential in the size of the database), we explore computing why-provenance for Datalog programs in a more practical framework. Instead of computing provenance for all atoms, we propose and implement an on-demand approach. Our contributions are summarized as follows:

- We introduce a novel on-demand approach to why-provenance computation restricting its computation to a given goal atom. This approach is a purely rule-based one (Sect. 3).
- Upon the structures we introduce for the on-demand approach, we show how to create a system of equations (on-demand) whose solutions, interpreted over the so-called why-semiring, are identical with the why-provenance of the goal atom (Sect. 4). This representation can be presented to a semiring solver, like FPsolve [11], in a serialized form.
- Based on the same structures used before, we provide a novel approach to computing why-provenance based on Datalog(S) rules (Sect. 5). Datalog(S) is a recent extension of Datalog having set terms as first-class citizens [7].
- We experimented with both of the aforementioned realizations and get a first insight on their runtime behavior (Sect. 6).

Beyond the main part of the paper (Sects. 3–6), we provide our basic notions in Sect. 2, related work in Sect. 7, and our conclusions and future work in Sect. 8.

2 Preliminaries

In this section, we introduce our notation for databases, Datalog, and provenance, in particular why-provenance. Therefore, we assume a fixed first-order vocabulary C of constants, V of variables ($C \cap V = \emptyset$), and P of predicate names. Each predicate name $p \in P$ has an arity $ar(p) \in \mathbb{N}$. A list of *terms* $t_1, \ldots, t_n$

$(t_i \in \mathbf{C} \cup \mathbf{V})$ is often abbreviated by $\vec{t}$ and has length $|\vec{t}| = n$. For convenience, we treat lists of terms $\vec{t}$ as sets when order is irrelevant. We call an expression $p(\vec{t})$ an *atom* if $p \in \mathbf{P}$, $\vec{t} \subseteq \mathbf{C} \cup \mathbf{V}$, and $|\vec{t}| = ar(p)$. An atom is *ground* if each of its terms is a constant and a finite set $\mathcal{D}$ of ground atoms is called a *database*.

A *Datalog rule* is a first-order formula of the form

$$\rho: \forall \vec{x}.p_1(\vec{t_1}) \wedge \ldots \wedge p_m(\vec{t_m}) \rightarrow q(\vec{u}), \tag{1}$$

where $p_1(\vec{t_1}), \ldots, p_m(\vec{t_m})$, and $q(\vec{u})$ are atoms using only variables in $\vec{x}$, such that each variable in $q(\vec{u})$ further occurs in some atom $p_i(\vec{t_i})$ *(safety)*. We call $q(\vec{u})$ the *head* of ρ (denoted $\mathsf{head}(\rho)$) and $p_1(\vec{t_1}) \wedge \ldots \wedge p_m(\vec{t_m})$ the *body* of ρ (denoted $\mathsf{body}(\rho)$). We may treat conjunctions as sets, e.g., to write $p_1(\vec{t_1}) \in \mathsf{body}(\rho)$, and tacitly omit the universal quantifiers for brevity. A variable-free rule is a *rule instance* (i.e., in which all atoms are ground atoms). A set of Datalog rules Σ is referred to as a *Datalog program*. A predicate p that occurs only in rule bodies of Σ is an *EDB predicate* (extensional database predicate); all other predicates are *IDB predicates* (intensional database predicates). Datalog programs Σ are evaluated over databases that use only EDB predicates of Σ. The distinction in EDB and IDB predicates is necessary for a construction in Sect. 3.

Datalog Semantics. The semantics of a Datalog program Σ over a database $\mathcal{D}$ can equivalently be defined via least models, least fixpoints of a consequence operator, or proof trees [1]. A *ground substitution* θ is a mapping from variables to constants. For a database $\mathcal{D}$ and a rule ρ, a *match* is a ground substitution θ with $\mathsf{body}(\rho)\theta \subseteq \mathcal{D}$. It is *satisfied* in $\mathcal{D}$ if $\mathsf{head}(\rho)\theta \subseteq \mathcal{D}$, and unsatisfied otherwise. A rule is satisfied if all of its matches are. Models and entailment (of ground facts) for Datalog is defined as usual. We will denote the *least model* of program Σ and database $\mathcal{D}$ as $\Sigma(\mathcal{D})$. An *immediate consequence operator* T_Σ can be defined on databases as $T_\Sigma(\mathcal{D}) = \{\mathsf{head}(\rho)\theta \mid \rho \in \Sigma, \theta \text{ is a match for } \rho \text{ on } \mathcal{D}\}$. The iterative application of T_Σ starting from the initial database converges to $\Sigma(\mathcal{D})$.

Example 1. Consider the database $\mathcal{D} = \{e(1, 2), e(2, 2), e(2, 3), e(4, 3)\}$ which may be interpreted as a directed graph $(\{1, 2, 3, 4\}, \{(1, 2), (2, 2), (2, 3), (4, 3)\})$. Furthermore, let $\Sigma = \{\rho_1, \rho_2\}$ with

$$\rho_1: \qquad e(x, y) \rightarrow t(x, y)$$
$$\rho_2: \ e(x, z) \wedge t(z, y) \rightarrow t(x, y)$$

Applying T_Σ iteratively to $\mathcal{D}$ yields additional t-atoms. As a result, $\Sigma(\mathcal{D}) = \mathcal{D} \cup \{t(1, 2), t(1, 3), t(2, 2), t(2, 3), t(4, 3)\}$. For instance, $t(1, 2)$ can be obtained by applying ρ_1 for $\theta_1 = \{x \mapsto 1, y \mapsto 2\}$. Another possibility to derive the same fact is by ρ_2 for match $\theta_2 = \{x \mapsto 1, y \mapsto 2, z \mapsto 2\}$. Of course, this application requires us to have also derived $t(2, 2)$, which can be done by ρ_1 and $\theta_3 = \{x \mapsto 2, y \mapsto 2\}$.

Graph of Rule Instances. One can describe the derivation steps of T_Σ in a suitable hypergraph. A *(vertex-labeled, directed) hypergraph* $\mathcal{H}$ has the form

$(\mathcal{V}, \mathcal{E}, \mathsf{tip}, \mathsf{tail}, \lambda)$, where $\mathcal{V}$ is a finite set of vertices, $\mathcal{E} \subseteq 2^{\mathcal{V}}$ is a set of hyper-edges, with each $e \in \mathcal{E}$ having $\mathsf{tip}(e) \in \mathcal{V}$ and $\mathsf{tail}(e) \subseteq \mathcal{V}$, and $\lambda : \mathcal{V} \to \mathcal{L}$ is a vertex labeling function for some set of labels $\mathcal{L}$. Note that we only allow a single tip per edge but many tails. $\mathcal{H}$ is a *hypertree* if the directed graph with edges $\{t \to \mathsf{tip}(e) \mid t \in \mathsf{tail}(e), e \in \mathcal{E}\}$ is a tree (with edges point-ing from children to parents); we write *leaves*$(\mathcal{H})$ for its leaves. The *graph of rule instances* for a Datalog program Σ and database $\mathcal{D}$ is the hypergraph $GRI(\Sigma, \mathcal{D}) := (\Sigma(\mathcal{D}), \mathcal{E}, \mathsf{tip}, \mathsf{tail}, \lambda)$, where $\mathcal{E} = \{(\rho, \theta) \mid \rho \in \Sigma, \theta \text{ } a \text{ } satisfied \text{ } match\ for \text{ } \rho \text{ } over \text{ } \Sigma(\mathcal{D})\}$ with $\mathsf{tip}(\rho, \theta) = \mathsf{head}(\rho)\theta$ and $\mathsf{tail}(\rho, \theta) = \mathsf{body}(\rho)\theta$. The labeling λ is simply the identity function (non-identity labelings will be needed below).

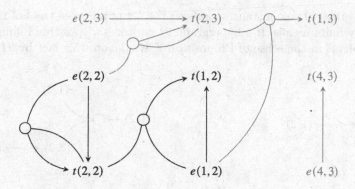

Fig. 1. The graph of rule instances of Σ and $\mathcal{D}$

Example 2. Reconsider Σ and $\mathcal{D}$ from Example 1. Each atom $A \in \Sigma(\mathcal{D})$ is a node in the graph of rule instances $GRI(\Sigma, \mathcal{D}) = (\Sigma(\mathcal{D}), \mathcal{E}, \mathsf{tip}, \mathsf{tail}, id_{\Sigma(\mathcal{D})})$. The hyperedges $(\mathcal{E})$ are determined by the rules and matches producing $\Sigma(\mathcal{D})$. For instance, $e = (\rho_1, \theta) \in \mathcal{E}$ with $\mathsf{tip}(e) = t(1,2)$ and $\mathsf{tail}(e) = \{e(1,2)\}$ for applying ρ_1 for match $\theta = \{x \mapsto 1, y \mapsto 2\}$. Figure 1 shows a depiction of the full graph, including all the edges. Arrow tips point to the result of applying function tip to the respective hyperedge. If an edge has a single tail-node, just like e above, we depict it as a simple directed edge. Edges having more than one tail-node use a small circle to join the tail-nodes via undirected edges. The distinction between the gray part and the rest of the graph will be explained in Sect. 3.

Proof Trees. An alternative approach to the semantics of Datalog is the proof-theoretic one, justifying inferred atoms $A \in \Sigma(\mathcal{D})$ in terms of so-called proof trees, a necessary prerequisite for provenance. A proof tree for A is a hypertree $T = (V, E, \mathsf{tip}, \mathsf{tail}, \lambda)$ with root node v such that $\lambda(v) = A$, $v \in$ *leaves*(T) implies $\lambda(v) \in \mathcal{D}$, and for each non-leaf node $v \in V \setminus$ *leaves*(T), there is exactly one edge $e \in E$ with $\mathsf{tip}(e) = v$ with a rule $\rho \in \Sigma$ and satisfied match θ in $\Sigma(\mathcal{D})$, such that $\lambda(\mathsf{tip}(e)) = \mathsf{head}(\rho)\theta$ and $\{B \mid B \in \mathsf{body}(\rho)\theta\} = \{\lambda(t) \mid t \in \mathsf{tail}(e)\}$. Such a proof tree explains one possible derivation of atom A, of which there may be infinitely many (due to recursion). Note that each atom $A \in \mathcal{D}$ has only a single proof tree, which has a single vertex and no edges. By $\mathbb{T}(A, \Sigma, \mathcal{D})$ (or just $\mathbb{T}(A)$ if Σ and $\mathcal{D}$ are clear from the context) we denote the set of all proof trees of $A \in \Sigma(\mathcal{D})$. There is a strong correspondence between $GRI(\Sigma, \mathcal{D})$ and the union of all the proof trees for all atoms $A \in \Sigma(\mathcal{D})$:

Proposition 1. *Let Σ be a Datalog program and $\mathcal{D}$ a database. Then*

$$GRI(\Sigma, \mathcal{D}) = (\Sigma(\mathcal{D}), \mathcal{E}, \text{tip}, \text{tail}, id_{\Sigma(\mathcal{D})}),$$

where for every $A \in \Sigma(\mathcal{D})$, proof tree $(V, E, \text{tip}_T, \text{tail}_T, \lambda) \in \mathbb{T}(A)$, and $e \in E$, there is an $e' \in \mathcal{E}$ such that $\lambda(\text{tip}_T(e)) = \text{tip}(e')$ and $\lambda(\text{tail}_T(e)) = \text{tail}(e')$.

Thus, the graph of rule instances *captures* the set of all proof trees of the atoms in $\Sigma(\mathcal{D})$ by finite means. If a hypergraph $\mathcal{H}$ captures a (possibly infinite) set of hypergraphs $\mathbb{H}$ in the sense of Proposition 1, we denote this fact by $\mathcal{H} > \mathbb{H}$.

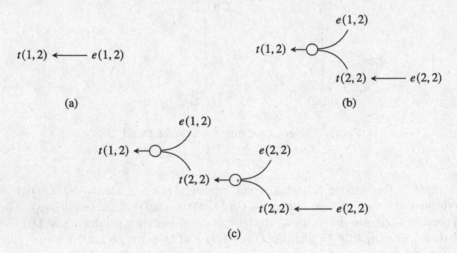

Fig. 2. A selection of proof trees for $t(1, 2)$

Example 3. In Fig. 2, we depict three different proof trees deriving $t(1, 2)$ from Σ and $\mathcal{D}$ (cf. Example 1). While tree (a) represents the derivation by rule ρ_1, as discussed earlier, trees (b) and (c) use one or two rule applications of ρ_2, prepended by a rule application of ρ_1. Note how in Fig. 2 (c), there are several nodes having the same label. Observe that the unfolding step performed between Fig. 2 (b) and (c) can be performed arbitrarily often, yielding an infinite set of proof trees for $t(1, 2)$.

Why-Provenance for Datalog. Provenance is about additional information, usually by means of annotations attached to the atoms of a database. Therefore, we assume a dedicated set K of annotations (e.g., sources, multiplicities, or costs) and provide for each atom $A \in \mathcal{D}$ an annotation $\alpha(A) \in K$. A *K-annotated database* is, thus, a pair $(\mathcal{D}, \alpha)$ such that $\mathcal{D}$ is a database and $\alpha : \mathcal{D} \to K$. To model tuples having no annotations we would assume special symbols like $\perp$ or $\emptyset$ to be part of K.

Let Σ be a Datalog program and $(\mathcal{D}, \alpha)$ a K-annotated database. Why-provenance takes the annotations of database atoms and provides a set of witnesses (sets of database annotations) from all those database atoms that can be used to infer a given atom $A \in \Sigma(\mathcal{D})$. In particular, the annotations of the leaf nodes of a single proof tree for $A \in \Sigma(\mathcal{D})$, as a set, form a witness in the why-provenance of A. For atom $A \in \Sigma(\mathcal{D})$ and a proof tree $T \in \mathbb{T}(A)$, we call the set $\{\alpha(\lambda(v)) \mid v \in leaves(T)\}$ a *witness for A*, denoted by $\alpha(T)$. *Why-provenance of A (w.r.t. Σ and $\mathcal{D}$)* $\mathbf{Why}(A, \Sigma, \mathcal{D})$ (or $\mathbf{Why}(A)$ for short) is the set of all witnesses for A, meaning $\mathbf{Why}(A, \Sigma, \mathcal{D}) := \{\alpha(T) \mid T \in \mathbb{T}(A)\}$. For every $A \in \Sigma(\mathcal{D})$, $\mathbf{Why}(A, \Sigma, \mathcal{D}) \subseteq 2^{2^{\mathcal{D}}}$ and since $\mathcal{D}$ is finite, the set of all witnesses for $A \in \Sigma(\mathcal{D})$ is also finite, despite the fact that $\mathbb{T}(A, \Sigma, \mathcal{D})$ may be infinite.

3 Rule-Based Provenance On-Demand

Throughout this section, we assume the fixed Datalog program Σ and database $\mathcal{D}$. We have seen that the graph of rule instances $GRI(\Sigma, \mathcal{D})$ captures all proof trees of all atoms $A \in \Sigma(\mathcal{D})$. However, this complete representation of the rule instances is exponential and, therefore, quite costly to always compute with the set $\Sigma(\mathcal{D})$, especially when we are considering a debugging scenario, in which the provenance of only a few atoms is ever queried. In this section, we present how we avoid the full construction of the GRI, but may still access the necessary parts of it, upon the query for why-provenance of a particular atom $A \in \Sigma(\mathcal{D})$. The key insight to our on-demand approach is that the *downward closure* of $A \in \Sigma(\mathcal{D})$ w.r.t. $GRI(\Sigma, \mathcal{D})$ captures all proof trees $T \in \mathbb{T}(A)$. For hypergraph $\mathcal{H} = (\mathcal{V}, \mathcal{E}, \mathrm{tip}, \mathrm{tail}, \lambda)$ and node $v \in \mathcal{V}$, we denote by $v^{\downarrow}$ the hypergraph $(\mathcal{W}, \mathcal{F}, \mathrm{tip}_{|\mathcal{F}}, \mathrm{tail}_{|\mathcal{F}}, \lambda_{|\mathcal{W}})$, such that $\mathcal{W}$ and $\mathcal{F}$ are the smallest sets satisfying (1) $v \in \mathcal{W}$ and (2) if $u \in \mathcal{W}$ and there is an edge $E \in \mathcal{E}$ with $\mathrm{tip}(E) = u$, then $E \in \mathcal{F}$ and $\mathrm{tail}(E) \subseteq \mathcal{V}$. Note, $\mathcal{W} \subseteq \mathcal{V}$ and $\mathcal{F} \subseteq \mathcal{E}$, justifying the domain restrictions $\mathrm{tip}_{|\mathcal{F}}$, $\mathrm{tail}_{|\mathcal{F}}$, and $\lambda_{|\mathcal{W}}$. Such downward closures are sufficiently representing proof trees in the sense of Proposition 1:

Proposition 2. *For $GRI(\Sigma, \mathcal{D}) = (\Sigma(\mathcal{D}), \mathcal{E}, \mathrm{tip}, \mathrm{tail}, \lambda)$ and $A \in \Sigma(\mathcal{D})$, we have $A^{\downarrow} > \mathbb{T}(A)$.*

Example 4. We stick with atom $t(1, 2) \in \Sigma(\mathcal{D})$ from Example 1, whose downward-closure is the black part of the GRI depicted in Fig. 1. Proof trees in Fig. 2 (a) and (b) directly embed into the relevant part of the GRI. Note that there is no proof tree of $t(1, 2)$ relating to the grayed-out parts of the GRI (cf. Fig. 1).

To achieve an *on-demand-driven* provenance computation we therefore perform two steps: First, we *record* the nodes of $GRI(\Sigma, \mathcal{D})$ (i.e., $\mathcal{V}$), during the derivation of $\Sigma(\mathcal{D})$. This is a necessary prerequisite to prepare for subsequent provenance computations. As we cannot use atoms as terms, we associate each atom $A \in \Sigma(\mathcal{D})$ with a term v_A that may be seen as an identifier for A. Second, when asked for the why-provenance of atom A, we only construct the downward closure $A^{\downarrow}$ by resorting to v_A. We subsequently show how we do both steps via rule-based reasoning using existential quantification in the head of Datalog rules only for the recording step.

For each predicate p occurring in Σ or $\mathcal{D}$, let p^+ be a fresh predicate name with $ar(p^+) = ar(p)+1$. For each atom $A = p(\vec{t})$, we introduce the aforementioned identifier v_A for A in the last component of its p^+-copy (i.e., $A = p(\vec{t})$ entails the atom $p^+(\vec{t}, v_A)$). We obtain such a copy by using the following rule for predicate p:

$$p(x_1, \ldots, x_{ar(p)}) \to \exists v. \ p^+(x_1, \ldots, x_{ar(p)}, v). \tag{2}$$

Existential quantification in rule heads leaves the realm of pure Datalog, but is here meant in a safe sense. State-of-the-art rule reasoners, like VLog [6], implement the standard chase which ensures that each atom is copied only once and, therefore, also associated to exactly one (new) identifier v_A. Any reasoner that guarantees this uniqueness constraint may be used to obtain the same results. For each predicate p occurring in Σ, we need to consider a respective rule (2). Let Σ^+ denote the set of all such rules. Note, Σ^+ does not depend on $\mathcal{D}$ because atoms with predicate names not occurring in Σ have no effect on the additional atoms derived in $\Sigma(\mathcal{D})$.

Upon the query for why-provenance of an atom $p(t_1, \ldots, t_n) \in \Sigma(\mathcal{D})$, we may now resort to $p^+(t_1, \ldots, t_n, v) \in (\Sigma \cup \Sigma^+)(\mathcal{D})$ as a starting point, where v indicates the base node from which the downward closure shall be computed. If we add the following rule to our overall rule set, we trigger the computation of the downward closure from v by the derived fact $G(v)$:

$$\forall x. \ p^+(t_1, \ldots, t_n, x) \to G(x) \tag{3}$$

We assume G to be a fresh predicate. For an atom A, let us denote its triggering rule (3) by $trig(A)$. For the construction of the downward closure, we match rule instances on atoms produced by rules in Σ^+ (e.g., p^+) and connect the associated nodes accordingly. To cope with the different numbers of atoms per rule, we use auxiliary fresh predicates $\mathcal{E}_1, \ldots, \mathcal{E}_k$, such that $ar(\mathcal{E}_i) = i$ $(1 \le i \le k)$. We pick a high enough $k \in \mathbb{N}$ (e.g., the maximum number of atoms in a rule of Σ). Then for each rule $\rho = p_1(\vec{t_1}) \wedge \ldots \wedge p_l(\vec{t_l}) \to q(\vec{u}) \in \Sigma$, we create the rule

$$G(v_0) \wedge q^+(\vec{u}, v_0) \wedge p_1^+(\vec{t_1}, v_1) \wedge \ldots \wedge p_l^+(\vec{t_l}, v_l) \to \mathcal{E}_{l+1}(v_0, v_1, \ldots, v_l) \wedge \bigwedge_{i=1}^{l} G(v_i), \tag{4}$$

where $v_0, v_1, \ldots, v_l$ is a list of variables distinct from those used in ρ. Note, having more than one head atom in a Datalog rule, as in (4), is just a shorthand for as many single-head rules as there are atoms in the head. Requiring the derivation of atoms $G(v_1), \ldots, G(v_l)$ makes sure that the downward closure is triggered recursively. Let Σ° be the set of rules like (4) for each $\rho \in \Sigma$. Additionally, add to Σ° one rule

$$q^+(\vec{t}, v) \to \mathcal{E}_1(v) \tag{5}$$

for each EDB predicate p of Σ. $\mathcal{E}_1$-atoms will later be used as the base case for provenance computation. For an atom $A \in \Sigma(\mathcal{D})$, adding $trig(A)$ to $\Sigma \cup \Sigma^+ \cup \Sigma^\circ$ suffices to fully describe the downward closure of A (via v_A) as follows:

Proposition 3. *Let $A \in \Sigma(\mathcal{D})$ and $\mathcal{M} = (\Sigma \cup \Sigma^+ \cup \Sigma^\circ \cup \{trig(A)\})(\mathcal{D})$, Then E with $tip(E) = v_{B0}$ and $tail(E) = \{v_{B1}, \ldots, v_{Bn}\}$ is an edge of $A^\downarrow$ if, and only if, there is a set $\{i_1, i_2, \ldots, i_n\} = tail(E)$, such that $\mathcal{E}_{n+1}(v_{B0}, v_{i_1}, \ldots, v_{i_n}) \in \mathcal{M}$.*

Throughout the next two sections, we incorporate these preliminary constructions in two solutions for obtaining why-provenance of atoms $A \in \Sigma(\mathcal{D})$. The first is based on a representation of why-provenance as the solutions to a system of equations [13] specific to $\Sigma(\mathcal{D})$. The second is a purely rule-based approach, incorporating the recent extension of Datalog by set primitives, called Datalog(S) [7].

4   Realization as Solutions to Systems of Equations

Green et al. [13] have shown that provenance for Datalog (over K-annotated databases) can be generalized to solutions of a *system of equations*, specific to the Datalog program Σ and the K-annotated database $(\mathcal{D}, \alpha)$, interpreted over certain semirings. In the equations we use a generalized join operator $\otimes$ (for combining the leaf nodes of a single proof tree) and $\oplus$ as the generalized union (for combining alternative proof trees). Furthermore, a system of equations uses variables from a set $\mathbb{V}$, such that for each atom $A \in \Sigma(\mathcal{D})$, $\mathbb{V}(A) \in \mathbb{V}$ and

$$\mathbb{V}(A) = \bigoplus_{T \in \mathbb{T}(A, \Sigma, \mathcal{D})} \left(\bigotimes_{B \in \alpha(T)} \mathbb{V}(B) \right) \qquad (6)$$

is the characteristic equation for A (w.r.t. Σ and $\mathcal{D}$). The system of equations for Σ and $\mathcal{D}$ is then the pair $(\mathbb{V}, \mathbb{E})$, such that $\mathbb{E}$ contains the characteristic equation (6) for each $A \in \Sigma(\mathcal{D})$. $(\mathbb{V}, \mathbb{E})$ is interpreted over semirings that provide different granularities of provenance information. For Datalog provenance, it is of utmost importance that the semiring at hand is ω-continuous, guaranteeing that infinite sums, like the ones introduced by (6) (recall that the set $\mathbb{T}(A, \Sigma, \mathcal{D})$ is generally infinite), have well-defined solutions. Fortunately, the semiring for why-provenance, $\mathbf{Why}(\mathbb{V}, K) = (2^{2^K}, \cup, \uplus, \emptyset, \{\emptyset\})$ enjoys this property. Note, for sets A and B of subsets of K, $A \uplus B := \{a \cup b \mid a \in A, b \in B\}$. An *assignment* over $\mathbf{Why}(\mathbb{V}, K)$ is a function $\beta : \mathbb{V} \to 2^{2^K}$. An assignment β is *valid for* $(\mathbb{V}, \mathbb{E})$ if, and only if, (a) $\beta(\mathbb{V}(A)) = \alpha(A)$ for each $A \in \mathcal{D}$, and (b) for each equation of the form (6),

$$\beta(\mathbb{V}(A)) = \bigcup_{T \in \mathbb{T}(A, \Sigma, \mathcal{D})} (\beta(\mathbb{V}(B_1)) \uplus \ldots \uplus \beta(\mathbb{V}(B_l))), \qquad (7)$$

where for each $T \in \mathbb{T}(A, \Sigma, \mathcal{D})$, $\alpha(T) = \{B_1, \ldots, B_l\}$ ($l \in \mathbb{N}$). Thus, operator $\oplus$ is evaluated via union ($\cup$) and $\otimes$ via cross-union ($\uplus$).

The general infinity of equations like (6) is impractical for providing actual tool support. Fortunately, an alternative system of equations makes use of the fixpoint approach to solving equations over semirings, encompassed by the finite representation of all proof trees, the graph of rule instances $GRI(\Sigma, \mathcal{D}) = (\Sigma(\mathcal{D}), \mathcal{E}, \text{tip}, \text{tail}, \lambda)$. For the finite system of equations, we use the set $\Sigma(\mathcal{D})$ as the set of variables. To make the distinction between $\Sigma(\mathcal{D})$ and its system of equation clear, we will denote the variable of $A \in \Sigma(\mathcal{D})$ by its identifier v_A (cf. Sect. 3). As set of equations $\mathbb{E}$, we have the following equation for each atom $A \in \Sigma(\mathcal{D})$:

$$v_A = \bigoplus_{E \in \mathcal{E}, \text{tip}(E) = v_A} \left(\bigotimes_{w \in \text{tail}(E)} w \right) \tag{8}$$

Green et al. [13] showed that systems of equations created from (6) are equivalent in their solutions with systems of equations using only finite equations of the form (8) (one for each $v_A \in \mathcal{V}$).

Based on (8), we can also obtain a system of equations on-demand for node v_A by pursuing the additional rules we added in the last section. Upon why-provenance query for $A \in \Sigma(\mathcal{D})$, let $\Sigma^\star = \Sigma \cup \Sigma^+ \cup \Sigma^\circ \cup \{trig(A)\}$ and $\mathcal{M} = \Sigma^\star(\mathcal{D})$. Then we derive the system of equations on-demand for A by querying for the atoms of relations $\mathcal{E}_1, \ldots, \mathcal{E}_k$. Of course, we will use the node identifiers as variables and define it by $V := \{v \mid p^+(\vec{i}, v) \in \mathcal{M}\}$ (due to Σ^+). For each variable $v \in V$, let $\mathcal{E}(v) := \{\{v_1, \ldots, v_l\} \mid 1 \leq l \leq k \wedge \mathcal{E}_{l+1}(v, v_1, \ldots, v_l) \in \mathcal{M}\}$. Both sets can be constructed by querying for the respective atoms in $\mathcal{M}$. The *system of equations for A on-demand* is $(V, \mathbb{E})$ where $\mathbb{E}$ is the set containing

$$v = \bigoplus_{E \in \mathcal{E}(v)} \left(\bigotimes_{w \in E} w \right) \tag{9}$$

for each $v \in V$. This is the system of equations we present a semiring solver like FPsolve [11]. Interpreted over the why-semiring, the valid assignments for v_A refer to the provenance of A.

5 Realization with Datalog(S)

Our second solution to why-provenance on-demand is a pure rule-based approach. Let us assume a Datalog program Σ, a database $\mathcal{D}$, an atom $A \in \Sigma(\mathcal{D})$ we want to know why-provenance for, and the rule set $\Sigma^\star$ containing Σ, Σ^+, Σ°, and $\{trig(A)\}$ (cf. Sect. 3). We now associate with each node identifier v (due to rules in Σ^+) sets of node identifiers that each represents a witness for the atom represented by A. Sets are not part of the terms in Datalog, but the recent extension of Datalog with sets [7] does include special set terms. The language facilitating basic set operations during reasoning is called Datalog(S) and will be briefly introduced in the first part of this section. Later on, we give a fixed set of Datalog(S) rules Σ^k_{Why} for Σ, capable of traversing the downward closure produced by $\Sigma^\star$ and collecting witnesses in the above-mentioned sense.

5.1   Datalog with Sets

Datalog(S) is a recent extension of Datalog that introduces a new term set, the set variables $\mathbf{V_S}$, which can be used in a Datalog(S) program. Furthermore, the set terms that can be used are defined inductively: (1a) $V \in \mathbf{V_S}$ is a set term, (1b) $\mathbf{0}$ is a set term representing the empty set in Datalog(S), (1c) for each term $t \in \mathbf{C} \cup \mathbf{V}$, $\{t\}$ is a set term, and (2) if T_1 and T_2 are set terms, then $(T_1 \bigcup T_2)$ is a set term. We often drop the parenthesis in unions. A Datalog(S) rule has the form

$$\forall \vec{x}, \vec{X}. \; \varphi[\vec{x}, \vec{X}] \to q(\vec{u}), \tag{10}$$

where $\vec{x} \subseteq \mathbf{V}$, $\vec{X} \subseteq \mathbf{V_S}$, $\varphi \cup \{q(\vec{u})\}$ is a set of atoms (potentially) with set terms, such that each variable in $\vec{u}$ is an element of $\vec{x} \cup \vec{X}$. Instances (and models) are variable-free sets of atoms or set atoms (i.e., atoms containing set terms). Since we use Datalog(S) only for the computation of provenance, we can assume databases to be set-atom-free ground instances. Substitutions must match set variables with set terms and variables in $\mathbf{V}$ with non-set terms, and matching rules are defined accordingly. The procedures evaluating a set of Datalog(S) rules, also called *Datalog(S) programs*, are similar to the ones for Datalog. Carral et al. provide a reasoning approach based on an encoding of Datalog(S) programs in existential rules [7]. We subsequently give a Datalog(S) program that traverse the downward-closure we constructed in Sect. 3.

5.2   Collecting Sets from Downward Closures

Let *prov* be a fresh binary predicate (i.e., it does not occur in $\Sigma^\star$). The rules collecting the witnesses as set terms produce *prov*-atoms with a node identifier in the first position and a set term (a witness) in the second. Recall that the model $\Sigma^\star(\mathcal{D})$ contains facts for the predicates $\mathcal{E}_1, \ldots, \mathcal{E}_k$ (for some $k \in \mathbb{N}$ determined by the rules in Σ). Furthermore, all database node identifiers v_A (with $A \in \mathcal{D}$) are represented by atoms $\mathcal{E}_1(v_A) \in \Sigma^\star(\mathcal{D})$. It is going to be these database node identifiers that will be carried along in the witnesses of atoms $B \in \Sigma(\mathcal{D})$. Therefore, we construct a set of Datalog(S) rules $\Sigma^k_{\mathbf{Why}}$ in which each rule introduces new *prov*-atoms as witness information. In the base case, rule

$$\mathcal{E}_1(x) \to prov(x, \{x\}) \tag{11}$$

belongs to $\Sigma^k_{\mathbf{Why}}$. Upon evaluation, the provenance of each database atom A is represented by the atom $prov(v_A, \{v_A\})$. For each $j \in \{1, \ldots, k-1\}$, the set $\Sigma^k_{\mathbf{Why}}$ contains the following rule:

$$\mathcal{E}_{j+1}(x_0, x_1, \ldots, x_j) \wedge \bigwedge_{i=1}^{j} prov(x_i, X_i) \to prov(x_0, X_1 \bigcup \cdots \bigcup X_j) \tag{12}$$

Since every edge of the downward closure effectively represents a rule instance, the union of all witnesses belonging to the body of rule instance is a witness for the head.

6   Implementation and Experimental Results

We implemented our on-demand approach (cf. Sect. 3) using VLog [6] and realized why-provenance computation with the approaches described in Sects. 4 and 5. We chose FPsolve [11] as the semiring solver since it offers a built-in implementation of the why-semiring. We emulated Datalog(S) by means of terminating existential rules, again using VLog, as described by Carral et al. [7]. For a given Datalog program Σ, we have run a script translating the program into $\Sigma^\star$ (cf. Sect. 3). VLog does not only perform the initial Datalog reasoning step, but is also crucial in the construction of the system of equations for FPsolve (Sect. 4) and for performing the necessary reasoning steps of our Datalog(S)-based process (Sect. 5).

As input, we used the DOCTORS scenario from the *Chasebench* [4] and a Datalog implementation of the EL ontology Galen[1] using the ELK reasoning calculus [15]. In particular, we rewrote the DOCTORS scenario into Datalog (originally, it contains existential rules), which we obtained by replacing all occurrences of existentially quantified variables uniformly by fresh constants. The DOCTORS scenario provides seven queries (q1–q7) alongside the dataset 100k, which we subsequently identify by the names of the queries. As for the EL ontology Galen, we queried for the rdfs:subClassOf-property. As input data for Galen we obtained 10%, 15%, 25%, 40%, and 50% random samples (subsequently referred to as g10, g15, ..., g50). We are well aware that such a random sampling may destroy a lot of the complicated reasoning in Galen. These initial experiments still allow for a glimpse on how the two on-demand provenance approaches handle increasing sizes of datasets, performance-wise.

Experimental Workflows. As input we get a Datalog program Σ and a database $\mathcal{D}$. Furthermore, why-provenance of (a randomly chosen) atom $A \in \Sigma(\mathcal{D})$ must be provided. We describe the tools and steps involved in the computation of $\mathbf{Why}(A)$.

Common Preparation: We have created the rule set $\Sigma^\star$ from Σ using python scripts. Then VLog reasoned for $\Sigma^\star(\mathcal{D})$ having created a node identifier v_B for each $B \in \Sigma(\mathcal{D})$ and the downward-closure $v_A^\downarrow$.

FPsolve Process: When we ask FPsolve for $\mathbf{Why}(A)$, we query $\Sigma^\star(\mathcal{D})$ as described in Sect. 4 and produce an input file f for FPsolve that represents a serialization of the downward-closure $v_A^\downarrow$. Then we call FPsolve on input f to produce the output of why-provenance (as a string). For this process, we could separate the times for (a) the common preparation step above, (b) the writing of f (which requires querying $\Sigma^\star(\mathcal{D})$), and (c) the time for FPsolve to solve the given system of equations.

Datalog(S) Process: VLog does not feature incremental reasoning, which means that we had to simulate the materialization for $\mathbf{Why}(A)$ in *one shot*: We measure the time taken by VLog to produce the materialization

---

[1] Galen is an ontologies found in the Oxford Library.

$(\Sigma^{\star} \cup \Sigma^{k}_{\mathbf{Why}})(\mathcal{D})$. The differences between the runtimes of the preparation step ($\Sigma^{\star}$ only) and the full materialization is inconclusive since different rule sets have unpredicatably different runtime behavior. Even if the one rule set is a superset of another, VLog may take less time for the materialization because additional rules may mean that there are shortcuts that were previously impossible.

As one why-provenance query appears insufficient – we could have just been lucky with the random choice of the atom $A \in \Sigma(\mathcal{D})$ – we have picked 50 atoms from $\Sigma(\mathcal{D})$ at random and repeated the processes for each of them separately. Therefore, we show aggregations of the runtime behavior. We have set a timeout of 200 s for each run. All experiments have been performed on a machine with an Intel(R) Xeon(R) CPU E5-2637 v4 @ 3.50 GHz processor, 378 GB of RAM, 1 TB of storage, and Debian GNU/Linux 9.13. Pointers to the datasets we have used in the experiments and the resulting runtimes we obtained are available on GitHub.

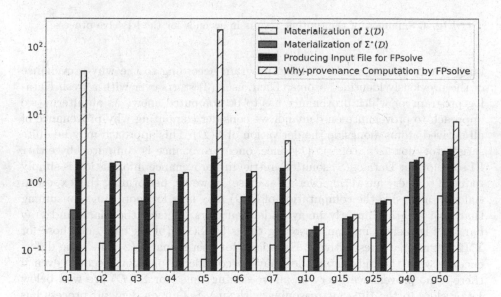

Fig. 3. Median runtimes of different phases of the FPsolve process

6.1   Feasibility of the On-Demand Approach to Why-Provenance

There are at least three user scenarios to consider for the question of feasibility of provenance on-demand: (1) the *provenance power user*, who constantly queries for the provenance of any atom that has been derived, (2) the *provenance non-user*, who never poses a query for provenance, and (3) the *Datalog debugger*, who looks at the materialization, finds a small number atoms (to be

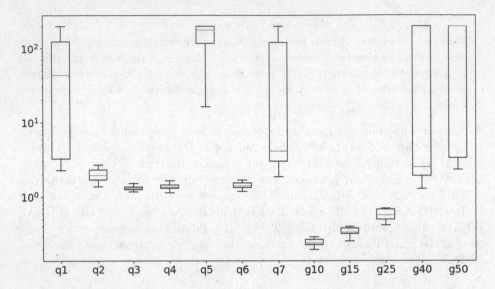

Fig. 4. Summary of the runtime results in seconds for the FPsolve process

buggy) and tries to fix the Datalog program according to the why-provenance of the previously identified atoms. Then, user (3) starts over with a fresh Datalog program for which provenance has to be computed anew. As an alternative approach to provenance on-demand, we consider computing why-provenance of all derived atoms alongside the derivation of $\Sigma(\mathcal{D})$. This approach may be quite satisfactory for user scenario (1) since, once provenance is computed by either FPsolve or our Datalog(S) solution, retrieving provenance information is simply reduced to query answering over a database. However, performing this exponential step alongside the computation of $\Sigma(\mathcal{D})$ may be a lot more time-consuming than just creating linearly many node identifiers. In fact, the blank and gray bars in Fig. 3 show median reasoning times for $\Sigma(\mathcal{D})$ (blank bar) and those for $\Sigma^{\star}(\mathcal{D})$ (gray bar), respectively. Especially for user scenario (2), the time difference between the different modes may be considered pleasant because even if there is no provenance query at all, reasoning times for $\Sigma^{\star}(\mathcal{D})$ are well below 1 s or close to the time for reasoning with just Σ. Our on-demand process has especially been designed for user scenario (3) and needs to be integrated with, for instance, Datalog synthesis processes like the one by Raghothaman et al. [18]. Here we can only tell from our experience with initial experiments with FPsolve: when trying to compute all provenance for all atoms, FPsolve took hours or even days to finish. By glimpsing on the runtime reports of the next subsection, we see that our Datalog(S) approach would work equally bad. A final evaluation comparing the on-demand approach with the "all provenance at once" approach is left for future work.

6.2   Performance of Why-Provenance Computation

For this experiment we report about the different time measurements we explained earlier for the two approaches. Note that the preparation times (common to both processes) have been reported in the previous subsection (cf. gray bars in Fig. 3).

The FPsolve Process. Additionally to the preprocessing step, producing the downward-closure, we can report on the median times for producing the input file for FPsolve (black bars in Fig. 3), which includes i/o operations to hard disk. As we can see, this part of the process takes some time but in most cases is superseded by FPsolve solving the system of equations (while solving also always includes reading the file we produced). In Fig. 4, we see a summary of the overall runtimes of the fifty runs for each query/scenario. The boxplots reflect on the ranges of runtimes (rectangles), the media runtime (orange line), and runtime deviations (whiskers). While most of the queries have somewhat stable runtime results, queries q1, q5, and q7 seem to have rather diverse ones. In our Galen experiments, we can see that from g40 (the 40% sample of Galen) on, we produce timeouts. At g50, almost all runs did not finish within the time bound. One reason may be that the file sizes (reflecting on the size of the system of equations) grows by orders of magnitude from one Galen sample to a bigger one.

Looking for reasons of why FPsolve sometimes has bad runtimes, we observed that the computed downward closures are significantly larger for queries q1, q5, q7 than for the other ones in DOCTORS (up to one order magnitude). The size of the downward closure correlates with the produced system of equations that is given as input to FPsolve. It appears as if reading (from disk) and solving bigger systems of equations is not the ideal use case for a tool like FPsolve. One way resolving the issue is to create a service pipeline that does not have the intermediate file representation that also has to be read from hard disk.

The Datalog(S) Process. Figure 5 reports on the overall runtime of our Datalog(S) process (interpretation is as for Fig. 4). On one hand, we observe more diversity in the smaller Galen samples than observed for FPsolve. On the other hand, we obtain even more stable runtimes for the queries in the DOCTORS scenario. By comparing Figs. 4 and 5, we see that FPsolve is faster than Datalog(S) in Galen experiments by fine margins. However, Datalog(S) was faster than FPsolve in the queries of the DOCTOR scenario, sometimes with significant differences as, for instance, in q1, q5 and q7. Our Datalog(S) solution has the advantage that we use a single tool, here VLog, that has been made for handling large amounts of data. Even the big structures produced for computing witnesses as sets can be handled in acceptable time. Especially the results in the DOCTORS scenario came as a surprise, given that the implementation of Datalog(S) we use is prone to introducing redundancy by means of having a single set represented several (but finitely many) times [7].

Whether it really pays off that we do not have to leave the reasoner for another (more specialized) tool is still an open question. A reasoner, particularly

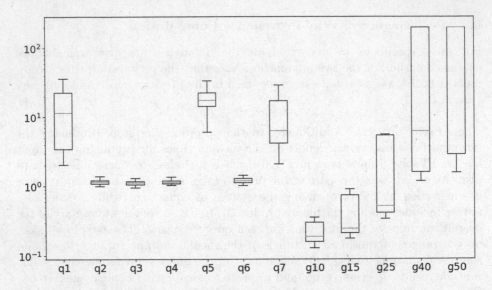

Fig. 5. Summary of runtime results in seconds for the Datalog(S) process

designed to evaluate Datalog(S) programs, may show a lot more improvement over the FPsolve process than we see with our implementation.

7   Related Work

We are not aware of any tool that computes why-provenance for Datalog programs besides FPsolve. However, several provenance notions as well as implementation ideas for Datalog provenance have been studied. GProM [3] and its extension PUG [17] provide why- and why-not-provenance for non-recursive Datalog programs with negations. These tools are also based on graph representations of the derivation process. Since they only consider non-recursive Datalog programs, they do not have to deal with cycles. Having only a graph depiction for a Datalog program with a huge database can be confusing and hard to trace, as edges and nodes in the graph can get overwhelming. In [20], Zhao et al. represent provenance in the form of *Proof Trees* that show the rule applications required to reach a particular derivation. The output of their provenance is the minimal proof tree, from which only a single witness can be derived. Similar ideas have been used as part of a synthesis process of Datalog programs [18]. However, presenting only a single witness does not cover the original notion of why-provenance, as we tackle it here. Deutch et al. [10] introduced provenance in the form of a finite circuit structure which is another representation of the proof trees view and the GRI. One result of this work has been the *absorptive semiring* for provenance, being incomparable to why-provenance. Köhler et al. [16] produce the graph of rule instances for Datalog programs using a rewriting with Skolem functions which is very similar to how we construct the downward closure by existential rules. They use this graph to provide the lineage of an atom A, being the union of all witnesses of A, an easier task than computing why-provenance which can completely be implemented in Datalog. Recently, an interesting approach has been investigated by Ramusat et al. [19] who view provenance computation as an operation of iterating over a graph to obtain a shortest path. They consider graph databases but we can imagine this work to also be generalizable to provenance for Datalog.

8   Conclusions

We presented an on-demand approach to why-provenance for recursive queries by means of Datalog programs. As a preprocessing step, we annotate each and every atom by a node identifier (linear in $\Sigma(\mathcal{D})$). We also showed how to compute the necessary information for computing (why-)provenance (a form of sub-hypergraph of the so-called graph of rule instances). These steps are purely rule-based and enable for subsequent why-provenance computation, given an atom A we want to know provenance of. We presented two realizations, one based on a semiring solver and one based on Datalog(S) reasoning. The latter solution builds on a recent extension of Datalog regarding set terms as first-class citizens. Our initial experiments show that there is room for improvement, for which more extensive experiments will be necessary. An interesting way to go is to exploit the recent characterization of certain provenances as (generalized) shortest paths [19]. Of course, this will leave the realm of a rule-based approach. We also believe that the graph of rule instances, as we compute it, can be used by Al-Rabbaa et al. [2] to give "good proofs" for Horn description logics with a translation into Datalog. The key task here will be to translate "good proofs" as obtained from traversing the GRI of the Datalog program into "good proofs" of the underlying description logics.

Acknowledgments. This work is partly supported by the German Research Foundation (DFG) in project number 389792660 (TRR 248, Center for Perspicuous Systems), by the Federal Ministry of Education and Research (BMBF) in project number 13GW0552B (KIMEDS, KI-assistierte Zertifizierung medizinischer Software) and in the Center for Scalable Data Analytics and Artificial Intelligence (ScaDS.AI), by BMBF and German Academic Exchange Service (DAAD) in project 57616814 (SECAI, School of Embedded Composite AI), as well as by the Center for Advancing Electronics Dresden (cfaed).

References

1. Abiteboul, S., Hull, R., Vianu, V.: Foundations of Databases. Addison Wesley, Boston (1994)
2. Al-Rabbaa, C., Borgwardt, S., Koopmann, P., Kovtunova, A.: Explaining ontology-mediated query answers using proofs over universal models. In: Governatori, G., Turhan, A.-Y. (eds.) RuleML+RR 2022. LNCS, vol. 13752, pp. 167–182. Springer, Cham (2022)
3. Arab, B.S., Feng, S., Glavic, B., Lee, S., Niu, X., Zeng, Q.: GProM - a swiss army knife for your provenance needs. Proc. IEEE Data Eng. Bull. **41**(1), 51–62 (2018)
4. Benedikt, M., et al.: Benchmarking the chase. In: Sallinger, E., Van den Bussche, J., Geerts, F. (eds.) Proceedings of 36th Symposium on Principles of Database Systems (PODS 2017), pp. 37–52. ACM (2017)
5. Buneman, P., Khanna, S., Wang-Chiew, T.: Why and where: a characterization of data provenance. In: Van den Bussche, J., Vianu, V. (eds.) ICDT 2001. LNCS, vol. 1973, pp. 316–330. Springer, Heidelberg (2001). https://doi.org/10.1007/3-540-44503-X_20
6. Carral, D., Dragoste, I., González, L., Jacobs, C., Krötzsch, M., Urbani, J.: VLog: a rule engine for knowledge graphs. In: Ghidini, C., et al. (eds.) ISWC 2019, Part II. LNCS, vol. 11779, pp. 19–35. Springer, Cham (2019). https://doi.org/10.1007/978-3-030-30796-7_2
7. Carral, D., Dragoste, I., Krötzsch, M., Lewe, C.: Chasing sets: how to use existential rules for expressive reasoning. In: Kraus, S. (ed.) Proceedings of 28th International Joint Conference on Artificial Intelligence (IJCAI 2019), pp. 1624–1631. ijcai.org (2019)
8. Cheney, J., Chiticariu, L., Tan, W.C.: Provenance in databases: why, how, and where. J. Found. Trends Databases **1**(4), 379–474 (2009)
9. Viegas Damásio, C., Analyti, A., Antoniou, G.: Justifications for logic programming. In: Cabalar, P., Son, T.C. (eds.) LPNMR 2013. LNCS (LNAI), vol. 8148, pp. 530–542. Springer, Heidelberg (2013). https://doi.org/10.1007/978-3-642-40564-8_53
10. Deutch, D., Milo, T., Roy, S., Tannen, V.: Circuits for datalog provenance. In: Schweikardt, N., Christophides, V., Leroy, V. (eds.) Proceedings of 17th International Conference on Database Theory (ICDT 2014), pp. 201–212. OpenProceedings.org (2014)
11. Esparza, J., Luttenberger, M., Schlund, M.: FPSOLVE: a generic solver for fixpoint equations over semirings. In: Holzer, M., Kutrib, M. (eds.) CIAA 2014. LNCS, vol. 8587, pp. 1–15. Springer, Cham (2014). https://doi.org/10.1007/978-3-319-08846-4_1
12. Glavic, B., Miller, R.J., Alonso, G.: Using SQL for efficient generation and querying of provenance information. In: Tannen, V., Wong, L., Libkin, L., Fan, W., Tan, W.-C., Fourman, M. (eds.) In Search of Elegance in the Theory and Practice of Computation. LNCS, vol. 8000, pp. 291–320. Springer, Heidelberg (2013). https://doi.org/10.1007/978-3-642-41660-6_16
13. Green, T.J., Karvounarakis, G., Tannen, V.: Provenance semirings. In: Proceedings of 26th Symposium on Principles of Database Systems (ACM SIGACT-SIGMOD-SIGART 2007), pp. 31–40 (2007)
14. Karvounarakis, G., Ives, Z.G., Tannen, V.: Querying data provenance. In: Elmagarmid, A.K., Agrawal, D. (eds.) Proceedings of International Conference on Management of Data (SIGMOD 2010), pp. 951–962. ACM (2010)

15. Kazakov, Y., Krötzsch, M., Simančík, F.: The incredible ELK: from polynomial procedures to efficient reasoning with $\mathcal{EL}$ ontologies. J. Autom. Reason. **53**, 1–61 (2013)

16. Köhler, S., Ludäscher, B., Smaragdakis, Y.: Declarative datalog debugging for mere mortals. In: Barceló, P., Pichler, R. (eds.) Datalog 2.0 2012. LNCS, vol. 7494, pp. 111–122. Springer, Heidelberg (2012). https://doi.org/10.1007/978-3-642-32925-8_12

17. Lee, S., Ludäscher, B., Glavic, B.: PUG: a framework and practical implementation for why and why-not provenance. Proc. VLDB **28**(1), 47–71 (2019)

18. Raghothaman, M., Mendelson, J., Zhao, D., Naik, M., Scholz, B.: Provenance-guided synthesis of datalog programs. Proc. ACM Program. Lang. 4(POPL), 62:1–62:27 (2020)

19. Ramusat, Y., Maniu, S., Senellart, P.: Provenance-based algorithms for rich queries over graph databases. In: Velegrakis, Y., Zeinalipour-Yazti, D., Chrysanthis, P.K., Guerra, F. (eds.) Proceedings of the 24th International Conference on Extending Database Technology (EDBT 2021), pp. 73–84. OpenProceedings.org (2021)

20. Zhao, D., Subotic, P., Scholz, B.: Debugging large-scale datalog: a scalable provenance evaluation strategy. Proc. ACM Trans. Program. Lang. Syst. **42**(2), 7:1–7:35 (2020)

Queries Over Ontologies

Explaining Ontology-Mediated Query Answers Using Proofs over Universal Models

Christian Alrabbaa⊚, Stefan Borgwardt⊚, Patrick Koopmann⊚,
and Alisa Kovtunova⁽✉⁾⊚

Institute of Theoretical Computer Science, Technische Universität Dresden,
Dresden, Germany
{christian.alrabbaa,stefan.borgwardt,patrick.koopmann,
alisa.kovtunova}@tu-dresden.de

Abstract. In ontology-mediated query answering, access to incomplete data sources is mediated by a conceptual layer constituted by an ontology, which can be formulated in a description logic (DL) or using existential rules. In the literature, there exists a multitude of complex techniques for incorporating ontological knowledge into queries. However, few of these approaches were designed for explainability of the query answers. We tackle this challenge by adapting an existing proof framework toward conjunctive query answering, based on the notion of universal models. We investigate the data and combined complexity of determining the existence of a proof below a given quality threshold, which can be measured in different ways. By distinguishing various parameters such as the shape of the query, we obtain an overview of the complexity of this problem for several Horn DLs.

1 Introduction

Description logics (DLs) are a family of knowledge representation formalisms that can be seen as decidable fragments of first-order logic using only unary and binary predicates [9]. This family contains very expressive DLs like $\mathcal{SROIQ}$, which underlies the standardized Web Ontology Language OWL 2,[1] as well as the light-weight DLs $DL\text{-}Lite_R$ and $\mathcal{EL}$, corresponding to the OWL 2 profiles QL and EL, respectively. We focus here on *Horn DLs* up to *Horn-$\mathcal{ALCHOI}$* [27,31], whose axioms can be expressed as *existential rules* (with equality) [14]. The complexity of standard reasoning problems such as entailment of axioms or facts (ground atoms) from an ontology (a finite set of axioms) has been studied for decades and is well-understood by now [9,30]. Another popular reasoning problem for DLs is that of *ontology-mediated query answering (OMQA)*, which generalizes query answering over databases by allowing to query implicit knowledge that is inferred by the ontology [15,31].

---

[1] https://www.w3.org/TR/owl2-overview/.

ⓒ The Author(s), under exclusive license to Springer Nature Switzerland AG 2022
G. Governatori and A.-Y. Turhan (Eds.): RuleML+RR 2022, LNCS 13752, pp. 167–182, 2022.
https://doi.org/10.1007/978-3-031-21541-4_11

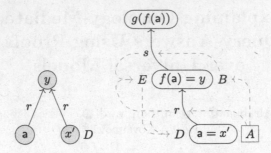

Fig. 1. The query (on the left) and the relevant part of the universal model (on the right) from Example 1.

Explaining DL reasoning has a long tradition, starting with the first works on *proofs* for standard DL entailments [12,29]. A popular and very effective method is to compute *justifications*, which simply point out the axioms from the ontology that are responsible for an entailment [10,22,32,35]. More recently, work has resumed on techniques to find proofs for explaining more complex logical consequences [3–5,23,24]. On the other hand, if a desired entailment does *not* hold, one needs different explanation techniques such as abduction [17,19,26] or counterinterpretations [8]. Explaining answers to conjunctive queries (CQs) has also been investigated before, in the form of abduction for missing answers over *DL-Lite* ontologies [17], provenance for positive answers in *DL-Lite* and $\mathcal{EL}$ [13,16], as proofs for *DL-Lite* query answering [11,20,36], as well as proofs and provenance for rule reasoning [21,33]. Inspired by the latter, we also investigate proofs for CQ answers, but consider more expressive DLs and want to find *good* proofs according to different quality measures. We focus on Horn DLs, for which every ontology has a *universal model* that captures exactly the query answers over the ontology [14]. While classically models are used for explaining missing entailments [8], this property allows us to use universal models also to explain positive query answers.

Example 1. Consider the fact $A(\mathsf{a})$, the existential rules (which can be expressed in Horn-$\mathcal{ALCHOI}$)

$$A(x) \to \exists y.\, r(x,y) \wedge B(y), \qquad s(x,y) \wedge r(z,x) \to E(x),$$
$$B(x) \to \exists z.\, s(x,z) \wedge A(z), \qquad E(x) \wedge r(y,x) \to D(y),$$

and the *conjunctive query* $\mathbf{q}(x) = \exists x',y.\, r(x,y) \wedge r(x',y) \wedge D(x')$. Individual a is an *answer* to $\mathbf{q}$ in this ontology. The query instantiated with this answer is depicted on the left in Fig. 1, using edges for binary predicates and node labels for unary predicates. To explain the answer, we show on the right of the figure the relevant part of the universal model of the ontology, where unary and binary predicates are represented similarly. The nodes represent objects in the model and are identified by *Skolem terms*, together with the assignments to the variables in the query. For example, $f(\mathsf{a})$ can be described as "the r-successor of a", which has to be present in any model of the ontology due to

Table 1. Summary of the combined complexity results for $\mathsf{OP}_{\mathsf{sk}}(\mathcal{L}, \mathsf{m})$.

Measure	DL-Lite		$\mathcal{EL}$		Horn-$\mathcal{ALCHOI}$
	tree-shaped	CQ	IQ	CQ	CQ
Domain size	NP-c [Theorem 9, 12]		in ExpTime [Theorem 9]		in NExpTime [Theorem 16]
Tree size	in P [Theorem 11]	NP-c [Theorem 9, 10]	P-c [Theorem 13]	NP-c [Theorem 13]	in PSpace [Theorem 16]
Proof size	NP-c [Theorem 9, 12]		in ExpTime [Theorem 17]		
Proof size bound	polynomial [Lemma 7]		exponential [Lemma 7]		double exponential [Lemma 14]

the first rule. The Skolem functions like f and g are created uniquely for each existentially quantified variable in the rules. In addition to explaining how the query is matched to the universal model, the dashed gray edges indicate a *proof* of $\mathsf{q}(\mathsf{a})$. For instance, $A(\mathsf{a})$, together with the first rule, implies the existence of the r-successor satisfying B, and $D(\mathsf{a})$ follows from $E(f(\mathsf{a}))$ and $r(\mathsf{a}, f(\mathsf{a}))$ through the last rule. To make this representation more accessible for larger proofs, in real applications we would show proof steps only on demand, whenever a user selects a fact to be explained in the model.

In previous work [3,5], we developed a formal framework for proofs in standard DL reasoning. We investigated the complexity of finding *small* proofs according to different proof measures: *(proof) size*, i.e. the number of distinct formulas in a proof, and *(proof) tree size*, i.e. the size when the proof is presented as tree, as it is done often in practice [2,24]. In this framework, proofs are generated by a so-called *deriver* that specifies which inferences are possible in a proof.

To be able to reuse results, the present work develops proofs for query answers within the same framework. In particular, in order to explain query answers using universal models, we introduce a special deriver that applies to a large family of Horn-DLs, and in which inferences in the proof directly correspond to the construction of the universal model. For such proofs, if we visualize them as in the example, another proof measure becomes relevant: the *domain size*, which is the number of elements from the universal model that are used in the proof. In the example, the domain size of the proof is 3. After introducing our deriver, we investigate the complexity of finding good proofs w.r.t. the different measures, as well as bounds on the size of the obtained proofs. An overview of our results is shown in Table 1. Because it introduces fresh objects, our deriver is only sound for a Skolemized version of the TBox, and not for the original TBox. At the end of the paper, we have a brief look at another deriver in which all inferences are sound w.r.t. the original TBox, and argue that, while the complexity of the resulting decision problem is often similar, this deriver is less helpful in explaining query answers to users. This paper extends initial results in this direction from a workshop paper [7]. Proof details can be found online [6].

2   Preliminaries

Logics. We assume basic knowledge about first-order logic and familiarity with terminology such as variables, terms, atoms, sentences, etc. Throughout the

Table 2. Sentences of *Horn-$\mathcal{ALCHOI}$*, where $A, B, C \in N_C$, $a \in N_I$, R, R_1, R_2 are *roles* of the form r or r^- *(inverse role)*, $r \in N_R$, and we identify $r^-(x,y)$ with $r(y,x)$.

(i)	$A \sqsubseteq B$	$A(x) \to B(x)$
(ii)	$A \sqcap B \sqsubseteq C$	$A(x) \wedge B(x) \to C(x)$
(iii)	$\exists R.A \sqsubseteq B$	$R(x,y) \wedge A(y) \to B(x)$
(iv)	$A \sqsubseteq \exists R.B$	$A(x) \to \exists y.\, R(x,y) \wedge B(y)$
(v)	$A \sqsubseteq \forall R.B$	$A(x) \wedge R(x,y) \to B(y)$
(vi)	$A \sqsubseteq \{a\}$	$A(x) \to x = a$
(vii)	$R_1 \sqsubseteq R_2$	$R_1(x,y) \to R_2(x,y)$

paper, we use $\mathcal{L}$ to refer to fragments of first-order logic. DLs are fragments of the two-variable fragment, for which we assume unary predicates to be taken from a countably infinite set N_C of *concept names*, binary predicates to be taken from a countably infinite set N_R of *role names*, and constants to be taken from a countably infinite set N_I of *individual names* [9]. Moreover, we use $\top$ and $\bot$ as special concept names that are always satisfied or always not satisfied, respectively. We focus on *Horn DLs* that can be represented using existential rules with equality [14]. An existential rule is a first-order sentence of the form $\forall \vec{y}, \vec{z}.\, \psi(\vec{y}, \vec{z}) \to \exists \vec{u}.\, \chi(\vec{z}, \vec{u})$, with the *body* $\psi(\vec{y}, \vec{z})$ and the *head* $\chi(\vec{z}, \vec{u})$ being conjunctions of atoms of the form $A(t_1)$, $R(t_1, t_2)$, or $t_1 = t_2$, where t_1 and t_2 are constants or variables from $\vec{z}$, $\vec{u}$ and $\vec{y}$. We usually omit the universal quantification.

For DLs, one usually uses a different, dedicated syntax. Table 2 shows the allowed rules in *Horn-$\mathcal{ALCHOI}$*, together with their representation in DL syntax, where, for simplicity, we assume the rules to be *normalized*. A set $\mathcal{T}$ of such rules is called *TBox* or *ontology*. In *Horn-$\mathcal{ALC}$*, only expressions of the forms (i)–(v) without inverse roles are allowed, $\mathcal{EL}$ further restricts *Horn-$\mathcal{ALC}$* by disallowing (v) and $\bot$, and *DL-Lite* only allows expressions $R_1 \sqsubseteq R_2$, $A \sqsubseteq C$, $C \sqsubseteq A$, and $A \sqcap B \sqsubseteq \bot$, where R_1, R_2 are (possibly inverse) roles, $A, B \in N_C$, and C is either a concept name or $\exists R.\top$, for a (possibly inverse) role R.

Query Answering. An *ABox* $\mathcal{A}$ is a set of ground atoms (called *facts*) of the form $A(a)$ or $r(a,b)$, which together with a TBox $\mathcal{T}$ forms a *knowledge base* (KB) $\mathcal{K} = \mathcal{T} \cup \mathcal{A}$. Its *signature* $\mathrm{sig}(\mathcal{K})$ is the set of all concept, role, and individual names $\mathrm{ind}(\mathcal{K})$ occurring in it. A *conjunctive query (CQ)* $\mathbf{q}(\vec{x})$ is an expression of the form $\exists \vec{y}.\, \phi(\vec{x}, \vec{y})$, where $\phi(\vec{x}, \vec{y})$ is a conjunction of atoms $A(t)$ or $r(s,t)$ and s, t are variables or constants. The variables in $\vec{x}$ are called *answer variables* and $\vec{y}$ are the *existentially quantified variables*. If $\mathbf{q}(\vec{x})$ contains only a single unary atom, it is called *instance query* (IQ). If $\vec{x}$ is empty, then $\mathbf{q}(\vec{x})$ is called *Boolean*. Note that ABox facts are a special case of Boolean CQs with only one atom and no variables. A tuple $\vec{a}$ of constants from $\mathcal{A}$ is a *certain answer* to $\mathbf{q}(\vec{x})$ over a KB $\mathcal{K}$, written $\mathcal{K} \models \mathbf{q}(\vec{a})$, if every model of $\mathcal{K}$ satisfies the sentence $\mathbf{q}(\vec{a})$. We may write $A(x) \in \mathbf{q}$ to indicate that $A(x)$ is an atom in ϕ. A *union of CQs*

(UCQ) is a disjunction of CQs sharing the same answer variables. A CQ $\mathbf{q}(\vec{x})$ is *UCQ-rewritable* over a TBox $\mathcal{T}$ if there exists a *UCQ* $\mathbf{q}_\mathcal{T}(\vec{x})$ such that, for every ABox $\mathcal{A}$ and tuple $\vec{a}$, $\mathcal{T} \cup \mathcal{A} \models \mathbf{q}(\vec{a})$ iff $\mathcal{A} \models \mathbf{q}_\mathcal{T}(\vec{a})$. This is the case, for example, for all CQs over *DL-Lite$_R$* TBoxes [15]. Since we consider proofs for a given, fixed answer $\vec{a}$, we consider only the Boolean CQ $\mathbf{q}(\vec{a})$, which we denote in the following simply as $\mathbf{q}$.

Proofs. Following the formal framework in [3–5], we view proofs in a logic $\mathcal{L}$ as finite directed hypergraphs (V, E, ℓ) where each vertex $v \in V$ is labeled by an $\mathcal{L}$-sentence $\ell(v)$, and every hyperedge is of the form $(S, d) \in E$ the finite set $S \subseteq V$ being the *premises* and $d \in V$ the *conclusion*, which we may depict as

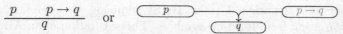

We call these edges also *inferences*. Proofs can be found by looking at derivation structures. Formally, a *derivation structure* over a KB $\mathcal{K}$ is a possibly infinite hypergraph as above in which each inference (S, d) is *sound*, that is, the labels of S logically entail the label of d, and every leaf (vertex without incoming edges) is labeled by an element of $\mathcal{K}$. A *proof* for an entailment $\mathcal{K} \models \eta$ is a finite derivation structure that (i) is acyclic, (ii) has exactly one sink (the conclusion), which is labeled by the goal sentence η, and (iii) in which each vertex v is the conclusion of at most one hyperedge (S, v). The *size* of a proof is the number of its vertices, and the *tree size* is the size of its tree unraveling, starting from the sink.

Proofs are usually generated based on a calculus or some reasoning system. This is formalized by the notion of a deriver, which, for a given entailment $\mathcal{K} \models \eta$, generates a derivation structure in which different possible proofs can be found. Formally, a *deriver* $\mathfrak{D}$ for a logic $\mathcal{L}$ is a function that takes as input an $\mathcal{L}$-theory $\mathcal{K}$ and an $\mathcal{L}$-sentence η, and returns a derivation structure $\mathfrak{D}(\mathcal{K}, \eta)$ over $\mathcal{K}$ that describes all inference steps that $\mathfrak{D}$ could perform in order to derive η from $\mathcal{K}$. This structure is not necessarily computed explicitly, but can be accessed through an oracle (in practice, this corresponds, for example, to checking whether an inference conforms to a calculus).

Remark 2. We argue that we can make some simplifying assumptions on the shape of *Horn-$\mathcal{ALCHOI}$* rules.

(a) To keep constructions easier, we assume TBoxes to be normalized as in [18,31]. Such a normalization can always be performed in polynomial time by introducing fresh names as abbreviations for complex formulas and applying standard transformations. We can transform a proof over a normalized TBox to a proof for the original non-normalized TBox by (i) replacing the new names with the original complex expressions, which may result in intermediate proof steps using atoms like $(\exists r.A)(x)$, and (ii) possibly introducing new inference steps corresponding to normalization steps. This increases the size of the proofs at most polynomially, which is why we believe our results are also relevant to non-normalized TBoxes.

(b) We assume KBs to be consistent. Since for Horn DLs, $\bot$ is only useful to create inconsistencies, we assume in the following that $\bot$ is never used.

3 A Deriver Using Universal Models

A distinguishing feature of Horn DLs is that every KB has a *universal model* which satisfies exactly the Boolean CQs that are entailed by the KB. In the literature on existential rules, the term *chase* refers to (different variants of) universal models [14]. Intuitively, a chase is constructed by applying rules to facts, where fresh objects are introduced for existential quantified variables. As we illustrate in the introduction, proofs connected to universal models can help to explain query answers. However, because we require inferences to be sound, our framework does not allow for an inference mechanism that introduces fresh objects. Our solution is to provide a deriver that is sound w.r.t. the *Skolemized* TBox, rather than the original TBox. By Skolemizing, we eliminate existential quantification using fresh function symbols. The saturation of an ABox using a Skolemized TBox produces the least Herbrand model, which in turn corresponds to the *Skolem chase* (a.k.a. semi-oblivious chase) [28] of the original TBox. In our case, existential quantification only occurs in rules of the form (iv) (see Table 2), which then get transformed into $A(x) \rightarrow r(x, f(x)) \wedge B(f(x))$ where f is unique for each existentially quantified variable. Given a TBox $\mathcal{T}$, we denote by $\mathcal{T}^s$ the result of Skolemizing all axioms in $\mathcal{T}$. A universal model of $\mathcal{T} \cup \mathcal{A}$ can then be obtained by "applying" the rules in $\mathcal{T}^s$ to $\mathcal{A}$ until a fixpoint is reached (which may result in an infinite set of atoms).

In the following, let $\mathcal{T} \cup \mathcal{A}$ be a KB in some DL $\mathcal{L}$ and $\mathbf{q}$ a Boolean CQ with $\mathcal{T} \cup \mathcal{A} \models \mathbf{q}$, which we want to explain. For this, we define an appropriate deriver over the extended logic $\mathcal{L}_{cq}$, which contains the results of Skolemizing the rules in Table 2 as well as all Boolean CQs. To provide good explanations, inferences should be simple, i.e. involve only small modifications of the premises. For TBox entailment, in [3–5], we considered derivers based on the inference schemas used by consequence-based reasoners. To obtain proofs for CQs, we present the deriver $\mathfrak{D}_{sk}$, which inspired by the approach from [11] and mainly operates on ground CQs that may use Skolem terms, but no existential quantification. Since ground atoms do not share variables, we mainly need to consider inferences on single atoms, which allows for fine-grained proofs (see Fig. 2). Only at the end we need to compose atoms to obtain the desired CQ $\mathbf{q}$.

The inference schemas of $\mathfrak{D}_{sk}$ are shown in Fig. 3. In (**MP**), $\alpha_i(\vec{t_i})$ and $\beta(\vec{s})$ are ground atoms, $\psi(\vec{y}, \vec{z}) \rightarrow \chi(\vec{z})$ is a Skolemized rule from $\mathcal{T}^s$, and there must be a substitution π such that $\pi(\psi(\vec{y}, \vec{z})) = \{\alpha_1(\vec{t_1}), \ldots, \alpha_n(\vec{t_n})\}$ and $\beta(\vec{s}) \in \pi(\chi(\vec{z}))$. (**E**) deals with equalities $t_1 = t_2$ by copying atoms $\alpha(\vec{t})$ that contain t_1 or t_2 (we consider =-atoms to be symmetric). We only apply (**E**) to replace top-level terms, not nested terms. Replacing also nested terms might be logically sound, but would not improve the readability of the proof, and is also not needed for completeness. To complete the proof, (**C**) combines several ground atoms into a conjunction, and (**G**) generalizes ground terms to variables in order to produce the final CQ (see Fig. 2). Note that the same atom can be used several times as a premise for (**MP**) or (**C**), which then however results in a *double connection* as in Fig. 2 for $r(\mathsf{a}, f(\mathsf{a}))$. Consequently, the premise (and the subproof above it) would be duplicated in the tree unraveling of the proof.

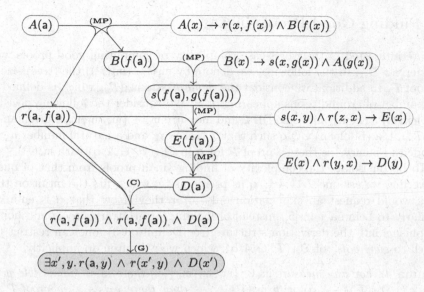

Fig. 2. A Skolemized proof for the example (colors are used for the ease of reading)

$$\frac{\alpha_1(\vec{t_1}) \quad \cdots \quad \alpha_n(\vec{t_n}) \quad \psi(\vec{y},\vec{z}) \to \chi(\vec{z})}{\beta(\vec{s})} \ \textbf{(MP)} \qquad \frac{\alpha(\vec{t}) \quad t_1 = t_2}{\alpha(\vec{t})[t_1 \mapsto t_2]} \ \textbf{(E)}$$

$$\frac{\alpha_1(\vec{t_1}) \quad \cdots \quad \alpha_n(\vec{t_n})}{\alpha_1(\vec{t_1}) \wedge \cdots \wedge \alpha_n(\vec{l_n})} \ \textbf{(C)} \qquad \frac{\phi(\vec{t})}{\exists \vec{x}. \phi(\vec{x})} \ \textbf{(G)}$$

Fig. 3. Inference schemas in $\mathfrak{D}_{sk}$ (modus ponens, equality, conjunction, generalization).

Definition 3. $\mathfrak{D}_{sk}(\mathcal{T}^s \cup \mathcal{A}, \mathbf{q})$ is an infinite derivation structure over $\mathcal{T}^s \cup \mathcal{A}$ with vertices for the axioms in $\mathcal{T}^s \cup \mathcal{A}$ and all Boolean CQs over $\mathrm{sig}(\mathcal{T}^s \cup \mathcal{A})$, and hyperedges for all possible instances of $(\mathbf{MP})$, $(\mathbf{E})$, $(\mathbf{C})$, and $(\mathbf{G})$ over these vertices.[2] An *(admissible) proof* in $\mathfrak{D}_{sk}(\mathcal{T}^s \cup \mathcal{A}, \mathbf{q})$ is a proof of $\mathcal{T}^s \cup \mathcal{A} \models \mathbf{q}$ that has a label-preserving homomorphism into this derivation structure.

It is easy to check that these inferences are sound. Moreover, they are also complete, i.e. if $\mathcal{T} \cup \mathcal{A} \models \mathbf{q}$ holds, then there exists a proof for it (w.r.t. $\mathcal{T}^s$). To see this, observe that we closely follow the (Skolem) chase construction for existential rules [14,28], where $(\mathbf{MP})$ corresponds to standard chase steps, and $(\mathbf{E})$ can be seen as merging domain elements in case of equalities ($(\mathbf{C})$ and $(\mathbf{G})$ are only relevant to obtain the final CQ). The resulting model M is universal, which means that $\mathcal{T} \cup \mathcal{A} \models \mathbf{q}$ implies $M \models \mathbf{q}$, which, in turn, shows that there must be a proof in $\mathfrak{D}_{sk}(\mathcal{T}^s \cup \mathcal{A}, \mathbf{q})$.

---

[2] This derivation structure is uniquely determined except for the names of the vertices, which are irrelevant for our purposes since we use only their labels.

4   Finding Good Proofs in $\mathfrak{D}_{sk}$

We are interested in the worst-case complexity of computing good proofs with our deriver $\mathfrak{D}_{sk}$. In the following, we denote by $\mathfrak{m}_s(\mathcal{P})$ $(\mathfrak{m}_t(\mathcal{P}))$ the (tree) size of a proof $\mathcal{P}$. In addition, we consider the *domain size* $\mathfrak{m}_d(\mathcal{P})$, which is defined as the number of ground terms appearing in $\mathcal{P}$. We consider the following decision problem $\mathsf{OP}_{sk}(\mathcal{L}, \mathfrak{m}_x)$ for some DL $\mathcal{L}$ and measure $\mathfrak{m}_x \in \{\mathfrak{m}_s, \mathfrak{m}_t, \mathfrak{m}_d\}$: given an $\mathcal{L}$-KB $\mathcal{T} \cup \mathcal{A}$, a (Boolean) CQ $\mathbf{q}$ such that $\mathcal{T} \cup \mathcal{A} \models \mathbf{q}$, and a natural number $n > 1$ encoded in binary,[3] is there a proof $\mathcal{P}$ for $\mathbf{q}$ in $\mathfrak{D}_{sk}(\mathcal{T}^s \cup \mathcal{A}, \mathbf{q})$ with $\mathfrak{m}_x(\mathcal{P}) \leq n$?

To better isolate the complexity of finding small proofs from that of query answering, we assume $\mathcal{T} \cup \mathcal{A} \models \mathbf{q}$ as prerequisite, which fits the intuition that users would request an explanation only after they know that $\mathbf{q}$ is entailed. Similarly to Lemma 7 in [5], instead of looking for arbitrary proofs and homomorphisms into the derivation structure (see Definition 3), one can restrict the search to *subproofs*[4] of $\mathfrak{D}_{sk}(\mathcal{T}^s \cup \mathcal{A}, \mathbf{q})$, which we will often do implicitly.

Lemma 4. *For any measure* $\mathfrak{m}_x \in \{\mathfrak{m}_s, \mathfrak{m}_t, \mathfrak{m}_d\}$, *if there is an admissible proof* $\mathcal{P}$ *w.r.t.* $\mathfrak{D}_{sk}(\mathcal{T}^s \cup \mathcal{A}, \mathbf{q})$ *with* $\mathfrak{m}_x(\mathcal{P}) \leq n$, *then there exists a subproof* $\mathcal{P}'$ *of* $\mathfrak{D}_{sk}(\mathcal{T}^s \cup \mathcal{A}, \mathbf{q})$ *for* $\mathcal{T}^s \cup \mathcal{A} \models \mathbf{q}$ *with* $\mathfrak{m}_x(\mathcal{P}') \leq n$.

Since domain size also satisfies the preconditions of Lemma 7 in [5], the statement of Lemma 4 can be shown similarly.

4.1   The Data Complexity of Finding Good Proofs

It is common in the context of OMQA to distinguish between *data complexity*, where only the data varies, and *combined complexity*, where also the influence of the other inputs is taken into account. This raises the question whether the bound n is seen as part of input for the data complexity or not. It turns out that fixing n trivializes the data complexity, because then n also fixes the set of relevant ABoxes modulo isomorphism, so that the problem can be reduced to UCQ entailment.

Theorem 5. *For a constant* n, *any* $\mathcal{L}$, *and any* $\mathfrak{m}_x \in \{\mathfrak{m}_s, \mathfrak{m}_t, \mathfrak{m}_d\}$, $\mathsf{OP}_{sk}(\mathcal{L}, \mathfrak{m}_x)$ *is in* AC^0 *in data complexity.*

One may argue that, since the size of the proof depends on $\mathcal{A}$, the bound n on the proof size should be considered part of the input as well. Under this assumption, our decision problem is not necessarily in AC^0 anymore. For example, consider the $\mathcal{EL}$ TBox $\{\exists r.A \sqsubseteq A\}$ and $q(x) \leftarrow A(x)$. For every n, there is an ABox $\mathcal{A}$ such that $A(a)$ is entailed by a sequence of n role atoms, and thus needs

---

[3] Unary encoding of n would make the problem much easier due to imposing a small (polynomial) upper bound on the (domain/tree) size of proofs. Hence, binary encoding puts more emphasis on the impact of the KB and the query on the decision problem.

[4] A subproof S of a hypergraph H is a subgraph of H that is a proof s.t. the leaves of S are a subset of the leaves of H.

a proof of size at least n. Deciding whether this query admits a bounded proof is thus as hard as deciding whether it admits an answer at all in $\mathcal{A}$, i.e. P-hard [34]. However, the problem stays in AC^0 for DLs over which CQs are UCQ-rewritable, e.g. $DL\text{-}Lite_R$ [15], because the number of (non-isomorphic) proofs that we need to consider is bounded by the size of the rewriting, which is constant in data complexity.

Theorem 6. *For any* $\mathfrak{m}_x \in \{\mathfrak{m}_s, \mathfrak{m}_t, \mathfrak{m}_d\}$ *and any* $\mathcal{L}$ *such that all CQs are UCQ-rewritable over* $\mathcal{L}$*-TBoxes,* $OP_{sk}(\mathcal{L}, \mathfrak{m}_x)$ *is in* AC^0 *in data complexity.*

4.2 Finding Good Proofs with Lightweight Ontologies

We now consider the combined complexity of our problems for $DL\text{-}Lite_R$ and $\mathcal{EL}$. In [3,5], we established general upper bounds for finding proofs of bounded size. These results depend only on the size of the derivation structure obtained for the given input. However, $\mathfrak{D}_{sk}$ does not produce finite derivation structures since there can be Skolem terms of arbitrary nesting depth. Nevertheless, proofs cannot be infinite, and therefore we first study how large proofs in $\mathfrak{D}_{sk}$ can get in the worst case. In particular, for $\mathcal{EL}$ one can enforce proofs that are binary trees of polynomial depth, and therefore of exponential size.

Lemma 7. *One can construct a TBox* $\mathcal{T}_{\mathcal{L},n}$ *in time polynomial in* n *such that* $\mathcal{T}_{\mathcal{L},n} \cup \{A(a)\} \models B(a)$*, but every proof of the entailment is of (domain/tree) size*

1. *polynomial in* n *for* $\mathcal{L} = DL\text{-}Lite_R$,
2. *exponential in* n *for* $\mathcal{L} = \mathcal{EL}$.

Moreover, there exists an $\mathcal{EL}$*-TBox* $\mathcal{T}$ *for which one can construct an ABox* $\mathcal{A}_n$ *in time polynomial in* n *such that* $\mathcal{T} \cup \mathcal{A}_n \models A(a)$*, but every proof of it is of a tree size exponential in* n.

To obtain matching upper bounds, we can bound the number of relevant Skolem terms in $\mathfrak{D}_{sk}$ by investigating which part of the universal model is necessary to satisfy the query $\mathbf{q}$.

Lemma 8. *For any CQ entailment* $\mathcal{T} \cup \mathcal{A} \models \mathbf{q}$*, there exists a proof of*

1. *(domain/tree) size polynomial in* $|\mathcal{T} \cup \mathcal{A}|$ *and* $|\mathbf{q}|$ *if* $\mathcal{L} = DL\text{-}Lite_R$,
2. *(domain) size exponential in* $|\mathcal{T}|$ *and* $|\mathbf{q}|$ *and polynomial in* $|\mathcal{A}|$ *if* $\mathcal{L} = \mathcal{EL}$,
3. *tree size exponential in* $|\mathcal{T} \cup \mathcal{A}|$ *and* $|\mathbf{q}|$ *if* $\mathcal{L} = \mathcal{EL}$.

This immediately allows us to show some generic upper bounds by guessing proofs up to the specified sizes.

Theorem 9. *For any* $\mathfrak{m}_x \in \{\mathfrak{m}_s, \mathfrak{m}_t, \mathfrak{m}_d\}$*,* $OP_{sk}(\mathcal{EL}, \mathfrak{m}_x)$ *is in* NExpTime *and* $OP_{sk}(DL\text{-}Lite_R, \mathfrak{m}_x)$ *is in* NP.

In some cases, we can show matching lower bounds via reductions from the Boolean query entailment problem. Using Lemma 8, we can find an upper bound n for any proof showing $\mathcal{K} \models q$ provided that it holds. To satisfy the prerequisites of OP_{sk}, we then extend $\mathcal{K}$ by a second KB $\mathcal{K}'$ in which $\mathcal{K}' \models q$, but only with a proof *larger* than n.

Theorem 10. *For* $m_x \in \{m_s, m_t\}$, $OP_{sk}(DL\text{-}Lite_R, m_x)$ *is* NP-*hard.*

To obtain tractability, we can restrict the shape of the query. The *Gaifman graph* of a query $\mathbf{q}$ is the undirected graph that uses the terms of $\mathbf{q}$ as nodes and has an edge between terms occurring together in an atom. A query is *tree-shaped* if its Gaifman graph is a tree. We can exploit this structure to deterministically explore in polynomial time all relevant proofs of minimal tree size over $DL\text{-}Lite_R$ KBs.

Theorem 11. *Given a* $DL\text{-}Lite_R$ *KB* $\mathcal{T} \cup \mathcal{A}$ *and a tree-shaped query* $\mathbf{q}$, *one can compute in polynomial time a proof of minimal tree size in* $\mathfrak{D}_{sk}(\mathcal{T}^s \cup \mathcal{A}, \mathbf{q})$.

The central property used in the proof of Theorem 11 is that for tree size the proof of each atom in $\mathbf{q}$ is counted separately, even if two atoms are proven in the same way. Since m_d and m_s do not exhibit this redundancy, we can show that the corresponding decision problems are already NP-hard for tree-shaped queries, and even *without a TBox*, via reductions from the propositional satisfiability problem.

Theorem 12. *Let* $\mathcal{L}$ *be an arbitrary DL and* $m_x \in \{m_s, m_d\}$. *For tree-shaped CQs,* $OP_{sk}(\mathcal{L}, m_x)$ *is* NP-*hard.*

For $\mathcal{EL}$, we can similarly show improved complexity bounds for the case of tree size, where the lower bounds are obtained using the same idea as for Theorem 10, however this time using the exponential bound on the tree size from Lemma 8.

Theorem 13. $OP_{sk}(\mathcal{EL}, m_t)$ *is* NP-*complete in combined, and in* P *in data complexity. For IQs, the problem is* P-*complete in combined complexity.*

4.3   Finding Good Proofs with Expressive Ontologies

We continue our journey towards more expressive DLs. First, we establish a more expressive counterpart of Lemma 7. This time, we can even enforce trees of exponential depth, by implementing a binary counter using concept names for the different bit values. To produce the entailment, the proof has to increment the counter all the way to the maximum value, and do so on every branch of a binary tree, which gives us the desired lower bound.

Lemma 14. *One can construct a* Horn-$\mathcal{ALC}$-*TBox* $\mathcal{T}_{\mathcal{L},n}$ *in time polynomial in* n *such that* $\mathcal{T}_{\mathcal{L},n} \cup \{A(a)\} \models B(a)$, *but every proof of the entailment is of (domain/tree) size doubly exponential in* n.

In the case of (domain) size, we can also find a matching upper bound. The general idea is using a kind of type construction. Intuitively, we identify the terms occurring the proof based on the predicates they occur in. Because there are at most exponentially many possibilities for this, we can bound the nesting depth of Skolem terms by an exponential, which gives a double exponential bound on domain size and size. For tree size, this is not so straightforward, and we leave the exact bounds for future work.

Lemma 15. *For any CQ entailment* $\mathcal{T} \cup \mathcal{A} \models \mathbf{q}$ *with* $\mathcal{T}$ *being a Horn-$\mathcal{ALCHOI}$-TBox, there exists a proof of (domain) size double-exponential in* $\mathcal{T}$ *and polynomial in* $\mathcal{A}$*.*

In contrast to Lemma 8 for *DL-Lite* and $\mathcal{EL}$, we cannot use Lemma 15 to reduce $\mathsf{OP}_{\mathsf{sk}}(\textit{Horn-}\mathcal{ALCHOI}, \mathsf{m})$ to query entailment in Horn-$\mathcal{ALCHOI}$ since a double exponential bound cannot be expressed using only polynomially many bits. On the positive side, the fact that the bound n is encoded in binary means that for $\mathsf{OP}_{\mathsf{sk}}(\textit{Horn-}\mathcal{ALCHOI}, \mathsf{m})$, we do not need to consider proofs of more than exponential size, which gives us a NExpTime upper bound for m_s; for m_d it holds as well since there are exponentially many facts over $\mathsf{sig}(\mathcal{T}^s \cup \mathcal{A})$ with a domain bounded by n. Using a technique from [5], we can even improve this to PSpace in the case of m_t.

Theorem 16. $\mathsf{OP}_{\mathsf{sk}}(\textit{Horn-}\mathcal{ALCHOI}, \mathsf{m}_\mathsf{x})$ *is in* NExpTime *for* $\mathsf{m}_\mathsf{x} \in \{\mathsf{m}_\mathsf{s}, \mathsf{m}_\mathsf{d}\}$, *and in* PSpace *for* $\mathsf{m}_\mathsf{x} = \mathsf{m}_\mathsf{t}$.

For m_s, we are able to improve this complexity even further using a more involved technique. The idea is to virtually construct the proof from *proof segments* which are represented using tuples of the form $\langle t, \textsc{In}, \textsc{Out}, \textsc{Size} \rangle$, where t is a term, In and Out are sets of atoms of restricted shape that may use a placeholder _ to represent *relative Skolem terms*, and Size is an integer. Intuitively, such a tuple tells us that it is possible to derive Out from In using a proof of size at most Size. t may optionally store what the placeholder _ stands for, provided that this is relevant for the query answer. We impose additional syntactic restrictions to ensure that there can be at most exponentially many such tuples. The decision procedure starts from a set of initial proof segments that correspond to proofs of polynomial size, and then step-wise aggregates proof segments to represent larger proofs, with the concise tuple representation making sure that there can be at most exponentially many such operations. We can thus prove the following theorem.

The main observation underlying this algorithm is that Horn-$\mathcal{ALCHOI}$ rules can only increase or decrease the nesting depth of a term by at most 1, while we can assume that (**E**) only replaces terms by constants. This introduces a kind of locality to proofs that allows us to decompose proofs in the way that is required by our method. Since for logics with number restrictions (such as Horn-$\mathcal{ALCHOIQ}$), this locality assumption failed, we did not consider such logics yet in our investigations.

Theorem 17. $\mathsf{OP}_{\mathsf{sk}}(\textit{Horn-}\mathcal{ALCHOI}, \mathsf{m}_\mathsf{s})$ *is in* ExpTime.

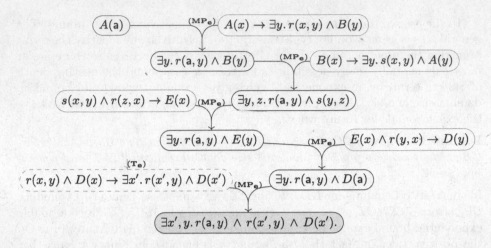

Fig. 4. A CQ proof for the example

5   Directly Deriving CQs

In addition to connecting proofs to the universal model, $\mathfrak{D}_{sk}$ has the advantage that we can work with single atoms, which makes it easy to see how the existential rules are applied. However, the resulting proofs are not sound w.r.t. the ontology $\mathcal{T}$, but only w.r.t. the Skolemized rules $\mathcal{T}^s$. In order to be sound w.r.t. $\mathcal{T}$, inspired by [20,36], we can work directly with Boolean CQs (see Fig. 4). Because these proofs do not work on universal models, and do not refer to introduced individuals directly, domain size is irrelevant in this setting, which is why we do not consider it here.

The corresponding inference schemas are shown in Fig. 5. Now, the basic inference ($\mathbf{MP_e}$) matches the left-hand side of a rule in $\mathcal{T}$ to part of a CQ and then replaces it by (part of) the right-hand side. Additionally, we allow to keep the replaced atoms from the original CQ. Again, ($\mathbf{MP_e}$) is admissible only if there exists a substitution π such that $\pi(\psi(\vec{y}, \vec{z})) \subseteq \phi(\vec{x})$, and then $\rho(\vec{w})$ is the result of replacing *any subset of* $\pi(\psi(\vec{y}, \vec{z}))$ in $\phi(\vec{x})$ by *any subset of* $\pi(\chi(\vec{z}, \vec{u}))$, where the variables $\vec{u}$ are renamed into new existentially quantified variables $\vec{u}'$ to ensure that they are disjoint with $\vec{x}$. To duplicate variables, we introduce tautological rules such as $P(x, z) \rightarrow \exists z'. P(x, z')$ via ($\mathbf{T_e}$), which yields $\exists z, z'. P(\mathsf{b}, z) \wedge P(\mathsf{b}, z')$ when combined with $\exists z. P(\mathsf{b}, z)$ using ($\mathbf{MP_e}$). The remaining inference schemas are similar to the ones in $\mathfrak{D}_{sk}$, but not restricted to ground atoms. For ($\mathbf{C_e}$), we rename the variables $\vec{y}$ to $\vec{u}$ to avoid overlap with $\vec{x}$.

Definition 18. [CQ Deriver] The derivation structure $\mathfrak{D}_{cq}(\mathcal{T} \cup \mathcal{A}, \mathbf{q})$ is defined similarly to $\mathfrak{D}_{sk}$, but using ($\mathbf{MP_e}$), ($\mathbf{T_e}$), ($\mathbf{E_e}$), ($\mathbf{C_e}$), and ($\mathbf{G_e}$). We also define $\mathsf{OP_{cq}}$ analogously to $\mathsf{OP_{sk}}$.

Proofs obtained through $\mathfrak{D}_{cq}$ are sound w.r.t. the original KB and do not depend on the notion of universal model. However, these proofs are more complex

$$\frac{\exists \vec{x}.\,\phi(\vec{x}) \qquad \psi(\vec{y},\vec{z}) \rightarrow \exists \vec{u}.\,\chi(\vec{z},\vec{u})}{\exists \vec{w}.\rho(\vec{w})} \; (\mathbf{MP_e}) \qquad \frac{}{\phi(\vec{x},\vec{y}) \rightarrow \exists \vec{x}.\,\phi(\vec{x},\vec{y})} \; (\mathbf{T_e})$$

$$\frac{\exists \vec{x}.\,\phi(\vec{x}) \wedge t_1 = t_2}{\exists \vec{x}.\,\phi(\vec{x})[t_1 \mapsto t_2]} \; (\mathbf{E_e}) \qquad \frac{\exists \vec{x}.\,\phi(\vec{x}) \qquad \exists \vec{y}.\,\psi(\vec{y})}{\exists \vec{x},\vec{u}.\phi(\vec{x}) \wedge \psi(\vec{u})} \; (\mathbf{C_e}) \qquad \frac{\exists \vec{x}.\,\phi(\vec{x},\vec{a})}{\exists \vec{x},\vec{y}.\,\phi(\vec{x},\vec{y})} \; (\mathbf{G_e})$$

Fig. 5. Inference schemas for $\mathfrak{D}_{cq}$.

since vertices are not labeled with single atoms anymore, making it harder to understand how a rule is applied in case of an ($\mathbf{MP_e}$) inference. Indeed, verifying individual ($\mathbf{MP_e}$) steps is even NP-hard, since it requires to match one set of atoms into another, which is equivalent to database query answering [1]. This could potentially be solved by also showing the substitutions corresponding to these inference steps to the user, but this would lead to even more information being included in a single inference step. In general, we believe that except for the advantage of soundness, proofs based on CQs are less helpful for explaining query answers to users. In case users still prefer an inference system that is sound w.r.t. the original TBox rather than just the Skolemized version, we observe that it is not hard to translate proofs based on $\mathfrak{D}_{sk}$ into proofs in $\mathfrak{D}_{cq}$ and vice versa.

Theorem 19. *Any proof $\mathcal{P}$ in $\mathfrak{D}_{cq}(\mathcal{T} \cup \mathcal{A}, \mathbf{q})$ can be transformed into a proof in $\mathfrak{D}_{sk}(\mathcal{T}^s \cup \mathcal{A}, \mathbf{q})$ in time polynomial in the sizes of $\mathcal{P}$ and $\mathcal{T}$, and conversely any proof $\mathcal{P}$ in $\mathfrak{D}_{sk}(\mathcal{T}^s \cup \mathcal{A}, \mathbf{q})$ can be transformed into a proof in $\mathfrak{D}_{cq}(\mathcal{T} \cup \mathcal{A}, \mathbf{q})$ in time polynomial in the sizes of $\mathcal{P}$ and $\mathcal{T}$. The latter also holds for tree proofs.*

This theorem also shows that this deriver is complete for query entailment since we already know that $\mathfrak{D}_{sk}$ is complete. However, it is not the case that *minimal* proofs are equivalent for these two derivers, i.e. a minimal proof may

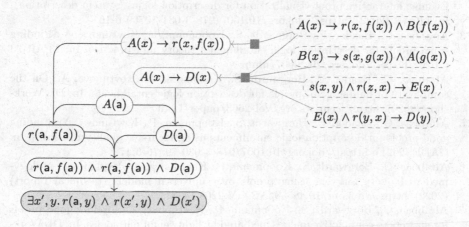

Fig. 6. A Skolemized proof for the example with hidden TBox inferences

become non-minimal after the transformation. Nevertheless, many of the results we have seen before also apply to $\mathfrak{D}_{cq}$ (see the extended version and [7] for details). However, due to duplication of atoms via $(\mathbf{T_e})$, some results can differ (cf. Theorem 12):

Theorem 20. *Let $\mathcal{L}$ be an arbitrary DL. For tree-shaped CQs, $\mathsf{OP}_{cq}(\mathcal{L}, \mathfrak{m_s})$ and $\mathsf{OP}_{cq}(\mathcal{L}, \mathfrak{m_t})$ are NP-hard.*

6   Conclusion

We have presented a general framework for generating proofs for answers to ontology-mediated queries. The central idea is to explain the reasoning steps that contributed to the answer by referring to a universal model. We have also shown some initial complexity results, and intend to obtain a more precise picture in the future. An interesting future direction is to investigate derivers that combine TBox and query entailment rules, e.g. $\mathfrak{D}_{sk}$ plus the rules of the ELK reasoner [25]. On one extreme end, one could completely hide all TBox reasoning steps, which could result in a proof like in Fig. 6, but it would be interesting to evaluate mixed proofs w.r.t. the comprehensibility of TBox- vs. query-based inferences. For explaining missing answers, we also want to investigate how to find (optimal) counter-interpretations or abduction results [26].

Acknowledgments. This work was supported by the DFG grant 389792660 as part of TRR 248 – CPEC (https://perspicuous-computing.science), and QuantLA, GRK 1763 (https://lat.inf.tu-dresden.de/quantla).

References

1. Abiteboul, S., Hull, R., Vianu, V.: Foundations of Databases (1995)
2. Alrabbaa, C., Baader, F., Borgwardt, S., Dachselt, R., Koopmann, P., Méndez, J.: Evonne: interactive proof visualization for description logics (system description). In: IJCAR (2022). https://doi.org/10.1007/978-3-031-10769-6_16
3. Alrabbaa, C., Baader, F., Borgwardt, S., Koopmann, P., Kovtunova, A.: Finding small proofs for description logic entailments: theory and practice. In: LPAR-23 (2020). https://doi.org/10.29007/nhpp
4. Alrabbaa, C., Baader, F., Borgwardt, S., Koopmann, P., Kovtunova, A.: On the complexity of finding good proofs for description logic entailments. In: DL Workshop (2020). http://ceur-ws.org/Vol-2663/paper-1.pdf
5. Alrabbaa, C., Baader, F., Borgwardt, S., Koopmann, P., Kovtunova, A.: Finding good proofs for description logic entailments using recursive quality measures. In: CADE (2021). https://doi.org/10.1007/978-3-030-79876-5_17
6. Alrabbaa, C., Borgwardt, S., Koopmann, P., Kovtunova, A.: Explaining ontology-mediated query answers using proofs over universal models (technical report) (2022). https://doi.org/10.48550/ARXIV.2208.14381
7. Alrabbaa, C., Borgwardt, S., Koopmann, P., Kovtunova, A.: Finding good proofs for answers to conjunctive queries mediated by lightweight ontologies. In: DL Workshop (2022). http://ceur-ws.org/Vol-3263/paper-3.pdf

8. Alrabbaa, C., Hieke, W., Turhan, A.: Counter model transformation for explaining non-subsumption in EL. In: Workshop on Formal and Cognitive Reasoning (2021). http://ceur-ws.org/Vol-2961/paper_2.pdf
9. Baader, F., Horrocks, I., Lutz, C., Sattler, U.: An Introduction to Description Logic (2017). https://doi.org/10.1017/9781139025355
10. Baader, F., Peñaloza, R., Suntisrivaraporn, B.: Pinpointing in the description logic $\mathcal{EL}^+$. In: Annual German Conference on AI (KI) (2007). https://doi.org/10.1007/978-3-540-74565-5_7
11. Borgida, A., Calvanese, D., Rodriguez-Muro, M.: Explanation in the DL-Lite family of description logics. In: On the Move to Meaningful Internet Systems: OTM (2008). https://doi.org/10.1007/978-3-540-88873-4_35
12. Borgida, A., Franconi, E., Horrocks, I.: Explaining $\mathcal{ALC}$ subsumption. In: ECAI (2000). http://www.frontiersinai.com/ecai/ecai2000/pdf/p0209.pdf
13. Bourgaux, C., Ozaki, A., Peñaloza, R., Predoiu, L.: Provenance for the description logic ELHr. In: IJCAI (2020). https://doi.org/10.24963/ijcai.2020/258
14. Calì, A., Gottlob, G., Lukasiewicz, T.: A general datalog-based framework for tractable query answering over ontologies. J. Web Semant. (2012). https://doi.org/10.1016/j.websem.2012.03.001
15. Calvanese, D., De Giacomo, G., Lembo, D., Lenzerini, M., Rosati, R.: Tractable reasoning and efficient query answering in description logics: the DL-Lite family. J. Autom. Reason. (2007). https://doi.org/10.1007/s10817-007-9078-x
16. Calvanese, D., Lanti, D., Ozaki, A., Peñaloza, R., Xiao, G.: Enriching ontology-based data access with provenance. In: IJCAI (2019). https://doi.org/10.24963/ijcai.2019/224
17. Calvanese, D., Ortiz, M., Simkus, M., Stefanoni, G.: The complexity of explaining negative query answers in DL-Lite. In: KR (2012). http://www.aaai.org/ocs/index.php/KR/KR12/paper/view/4537
18. Carral, D., Dragoste, I., Krötzsch, M.: The combined approach to query answering in Horn-$\mathcal{ALCHOIQ}$. In: KR (2018). https://aaai.org/ocs/index.php/KR/KR18/paper/view/18076
19. Ceylan, İ.İ., Lukasiewicz, T., Malizia, E., Molinaro, C., Vaicenavicius, A.: Explanations for negative query answers under existential rules. In: KR (2020). https://doi.org/10.24963/kr.2020/23
20. Croce, F., Lenzerini, M.: A framework for explaining query answers in *DL-Lite*. In: Faron Zucker, C., Ghidini, C., Napoli, A., Toussaint, Y. (eds.) EKAW 2018. LNCS (LNAI), vol. 11313, pp. 83–97. Springer, Cham (2018). https://doi.org/10.1007/978-3-030-03667-6_6
21. Elhalawati, A., Krötzsch, M., Mennicke, S.: An existential rule framework for computing why-provenance on-demand for datalog. In: Governatori, G., Turhan, A.-Y. (eds.) RuleML+RR 2022, LNCS, vol. 13752, pp. 146–163. Springer, Cham (2022). https://doi.org/10.1007/978-3-031-21541-4_10
22. Horridge, M.: Justification based explanation in ontologies. Ph.D. thesis, University of Manchester, UK (2011). https://www.research.manchester.ac.uk/portal/files/54511395/FULL_TEXT.PDF
23. Horridge, M., Parsia, B., Sattler, U.: Justification oriented proofs in OWL. In: ISWC (2010). https://doi.org/10.1007/978-3-642-17746-0_23
24. Kazakov, Y., Klinov, P., Stupnikov, A.: Towards reusable explanation services in protege. In: DL Workshop (2017). http://www.ceur-ws.org/Vol-1879/paper31.pdf
25. Kazakov, Y., Krötzsch, M., Simančík, F.: The Incredible ELK. J. Autom. Reason. **53**(1), 1–61 (2013). https://doi.org/10.1007/s10817-013-9296-3

182   C. Alrabbaa et al.

26. Koopmann, P.: Signature-based abduction with fresh individuals and complex concepts for description logics. In: IJCAI (2021). https://doi.org/10.24963/ijcai.2021/266

27. Krötzsch, M., Rudolph, S., Hitzler, P.: Complexities of horn description logics. ACM Trans. Comput. Logic (2013). https://doi.org/10.1145/2422085.2422087

28. Marnette, B.: Generalized schema-mappings: from termination to tractability. In: PODS (2009). https://doi.org/10.1145/1559795.1559799

29. McGuinness, D.L.: Explaining reasoning in description logics. Ph.D. thesis, Rutgers University, USA (1996). https://doi.org/10.7282/t3-q0c6-5305

30. Ortiz, M., Rudolph, S., Simkus, M.: Worst-case optimal reasoning for the Horn-DL fragments of OWL 1 and 2. In: KR (2010). http://aaai.org/ocs/index.php/KR/KR2010/paper/view/1296

31. Ortiz, M., Rudolph, S., Simkus, M.: Query answering in the Horn fragments of the description logics $\mathcal{SHOIQ}$ and $\mathcal{SROIQ}$. In: IJCAI (2011). https://doi.org/10.5591/978-1-57735-516-8/IJCAI11-178

32. Peñaloza, R.: Axiom-pinpointing in description logics and beyond. Ph.D. thesis, Technische Universität Dresden, Germany (2009). https://nbn-resolving.org/urn:nbn:de:bsz:14-qucosa-24743

33. Ramusat, Y., Maniu, S., Senellart, P.: Efficient provenance-aware querying of graph databases with datalog. In: GRADES-NDA ACM Workshop (2022). https://doi.org/10.1145/3534540.3534689

34. Rosati, R.: On conjunctive query answering in EL. In: DL Workshop (2007). http://ceur-ws.org/Vol-250/paper_83.pdf

35. Schlobach, S., Cornet, R.: Non-standard reasoning services for the debugging of description logic terminologies. In: IJCAI (2003). http://ijcai.org/Proceedings/03/Papers/053.pdf

36. Stefanoni, G.: Explaining query answers in lightweight ontologies. Diploma thesis, Technische Universität Wien, Austria (2011). http://www.cs.ox.ac.uk/files/7942/thesis.pdf

Seminaïve Materialisation in DatalogMTL

Dingmin Wang[✉], Przemysław Andrzej Wałęga, and Bernardo Cuenca Grau

Department of Computer Science, University of Oxford, Oxford, UK
{dingmin.wang,przemyslaw.walega,bernardo.cuenca.grau}@cs.ox.ac.uk

Abstract. DatalogMTL is an extension of Datalog with metric temporal operators that has found applications in temporal ontology-based data access and query answering, as well as in stream reasoning. Practical algorithms for DatalogMTL are reliant on materialisation-based reasoning, where temporal facts are derived in a forward chaining manner in successive rounds of rule applications. Current materialisation-based procedures are, however, based on a naïve evaluation strategy, where the main source of inefficiency stems from redundant computations. In this paper, we propose a materialisation-based procedure which, analogously to the classical seminaïve algorithm in Datalog, aims at minimising redundant computation by ensuring that each temporal rule instance is considered at most once during the execution of the algorithm. Our experiments show that our optimised seminaïve strategy for DatalogMTL is able to significantly reduce materialisation times.

Keywords: DatalogMTL · Temporal reasoning · Materialisation

1 Introduction

DatalogMTL is a temporal rule-based language that has found a growing number of applications in ontology-based data access [9–11] and stream reasoning [20], amongst others [13,16]. DatalogMTL extends Datalog [1,6] with operators from metric temporal logic [12] interpreted over the rational timeline. For example, the following rule states that travellers can enter the US if they had a negative test sometime in the last 2 days ($\diamondsuit_{[0,2]}$) and have held fully vaccinated status throughout the last 15 days ($\boxminus_{[0,15]}$):

$$Authorised(x) \leftarrow \diamondsuit_{[0,2]} NegativeLFT(x) \wedge \boxminus_{[0,15]} FullyVaccinated(x).$$

Datasets in this setting consist of temporal facts composed of a first-order fact annotated with a temporal interval, for example, $Authorised(John)@[13, 213.5]$.

DatalogMTL is a powerful KR language and standard reasoning tasks, such as consistency and fact entailment, are PSPACE-complete in data complexity [18]. This makes efficient implementation in data-intensive applications challenging.

The most common technique of choice in scalable Datalog reasoners is materialisation (a.k.a., forward chaining) [2,4,5,15]. Facts entailed by a program and

G. Governatori and A.-Y. Turhan (Eds.): RuleML+RR 2022, LNCS 13752, pp. 183–197, 2022.
https://doi.org/10.1007/978-3-031-21541-4_12

dataset are derived in successive rounds of rule applications until a fixpoint is reached; both this process and its output are often referred to as *materialisation*. The seminaïve algorithm forms the basis for efficient implementation by ensuring that each inference during rule application is only performed once, thus eliminating redundant computations. Once the materialisation has been computed, queries can be answered directly and rules are not further considered.

The use of metric temporal operators in rules, however, introduces a number of challenges for materialisation-based reasoning. First, interpretations over the rational timeline are intrinsically infinite, whereas partial materialisations computed during reasoning must be finitely represented. Second, in contrast to Datalog where materialisation naturally terminates, in DatalogMTL a fixpoint may only be reachable after infinitely many rounds of rule applications. As a matter of fact, reasoning techniques initially proposed for DatalogMTL were not materialisation-based. In particular, optimal decision procedures are automata-based [18], and reasoning is also feasible by reduction to satisfiability checking in linear temporal logic (LTL) [3]; finally, the Ontop system implements a query rewriting approach which is applicable only to non-recursive programs [9].

In our recent work [22], we proposed a materialisation-based procedure optimised for efficient application of DatalogMTL rules by means of suitable temporal indices, and where partial materialisations are succinctly represented as sets of temporal facts. We also identified a fragment of DatalogMTL [21] for which our materialisation-based procedure is guaranteed to terminate; this fragment imposes suitable restrictions which effectively disallow programs expressing 'recursion through time'. To ensure termination in the general case for consistency and fact entailment tasks, we proposed and implemented in the MeTeoR system [22] an algorithm combining materialisation with the construction of Büchi automata, so that the use of automata-based techniques is minimised in favour of materialisation; thus, the scalability of this approach in most practical cases is critically dependent on that of its materialisation component. The materialisation-based procedure in MeTeoR is, however, based on a *naïve* strategy where the main source of inefficiency stems from redundant computations.

In this paper, we propose a seminaïve materialisation-based procedure for DatalogMTL, which can be seamlessly applied in isolation to finitely materialisable fragments [21], or used in the general case in combination with automata-based techniques [22]. As in [22], our procedure iteratively performs *materialisation steps* which compute partial materialisations consisting of temporal facts; furthermore, each materialisation step performs a round of rule applications followed by a coalescing phase where temporal facts differing only in their (overlapping) intervals are merged together. However, in contrast to [22] and analogously to the classical seminaïve algorithm for Datalog [1], our procedure aims at minimising redundant computation by considering only rule instances that involve information newly derived in the previous materialisation step. Lifting the seminaïve strategy to DatalogMTL involves significant technical challenges. In particular, rule bodies now involve metric atoms, and derived temporal facts can be coalesced with existing facts in the previous partial materialisation. As a result, keeping track of new information and identifying the relevant rule instances to consider in each materialisation step becomes much more involved than in Datalog. We show that these difficulties can be overcome in an elegant and effective way, and propose additional optimisations aimed at further reducing redundancy for programs satisfying certain syntactic restrictions.

We have implemented our approach as an extension of MeTeoR and evaluated its performance. Our experiments show that our seminaïve strategy and the additional optimisations lead to significant reductions in materialisation times. A technical appendix containing full proofs of our technical results and the code for our implementation are available online.[1]

2   Preliminaries

We recapitulate the definition of DatalogMTL interpreted under the standard continuous semantics for the rational timeline [3].

A *relational atom* is a function-free first-order atom of the form $P(\mathbf{s})$, with P a predicate and $\mathbf{s}$ a tuple of terms. A *metric atom* is an expression given by the following grammar, where $P(\mathbf{s})$ is a relational atom, and $\diamondsuit, \blacklozenge, \boxminus, \boxplus, \mathcal{S}, \mathcal{U}$ are MTL operators indexed with intervals ϱ containing only non-negative rationals:

$$M := \top \mid \bot \mid P(\mathbf{s}) \mid \diamondsuit_\varrho M \mid \blacklozenge_\varrho M \mid \boxminus_\varrho M \mid \boxplus_\varrho M \mid M\mathcal{S}_\varrho M \mid M\mathcal{U}_\varrho M.$$

We call $\diamondsuit$, $\boxminus$, and $\mathcal{S}$ *past operators* and we call $\blacklozenge$, $\boxplus$, and $\mathcal{U}$ *future operators*. A *rule* is an expression of the form

$$M' \leftarrow M_1 \wedge \cdots \wedge M_n, \quad \text{for } n > 1, \tag{1}$$

with each M_i a metric atom, and M' is generated by the following grammar:[2]

$$M' ::= \top \mid P(\mathbf{s}) \mid \boxminus_\varrho M' \mid \boxplus_\varrho M'.$$

The conjunction $M_1 \wedge \cdots \wedge M_n$ in Expression (1) is the rule's *body* and M' is the rule's *head*. A rule is *forward-propagating* if it does not mention $\top$ or $\bot$, mentions only past operators in the body, and only future operators in the head. A rule is *backwards-propagating*, if it satisfies analogous conditions but with past operators replaced with future operators and vice versa. A rule is *safe* if each variable in its head also occurs in the body, and this occurrence is not in a left operand of $\mathcal{S}$ or $\mathcal{U}$. A *program* is a finite set of safe rules; it is forward- or backward-propagating if so are all its rules.

An expression is *ground* if it mentions no variables. A *fact* is an expression $M@\varrho$ with M a ground relational atom and ϱ an interval; a *dataset* is a finite set of facts. The *coalescing* of facts $M@\varrho_1$ and $M@\varrho_2$, where ϱ_1 and ϱ_2 are adjacent or have a non-empty intersection, is the fact $M@\varrho_3$ with ϱ_3 the union of ϱ_1 and ϱ_2. The *grounding* $\mathrm{ground}(\Pi, \mathcal{D})$ of program Π with respect to dataset $\mathcal{D}$ is the set of ground rules obtained by assigning constants in Π or $\mathcal{D}$ to variables in Π.

---

[1] https://github.com/wdimmy/MeTeoR/tree/main/experiments/RR2022.

[2] For presentation convenience, we disallow $\bot$ in rule heads, which ensures satisfiability and allows us to focus on the materialisation process itself.

Table 1. Semantics of ground metric atoms

$\Im, t \models \top$		for each t
$\Im, t \models \bot$		for no t
$\Im, t \models \diamondsuit_\varrho M$	iff	$\Im, t' \models M$ for some t' with $t - t' \in \varrho$
$\Im, t \models \diamondsuit_\varrho M$	iff	$\Im, t' \models M$ for some t' with $t' - t \in \varrho$
$\Im, t \models \boxminus_\varrho M$	iff	$\Im, t' \models M$ for all t' with $t - t' \in \varrho$
$\Im, t \models \boxplus_\varrho M$	iff	$\Im, t' \models M$ for all t' with $t' - t \in \varrho$
$\Im, t \models M_1 \mathcal{S}_\varrho M_2$	iff	$\Im, t' \models M_2$ for some t' with $t - t' \in \varrho$ and $\Im, t'' \models M_1$ for all $t'' \in (t', t)$
$\Im, t \models M_1 \mathcal{U}_\varrho M_2$	iff	$\Im, t' \models M_2$ for some t' with $t' - t \in \varrho$ and $\Im, t'' \models M_1$ for all $t'' \in (t, t')$

An *interpretation* $\Im$ specifies, for each ground relational atom M and each time point $t \in \mathbb{Q}$, whether M holds at t, in which case we write $\Im, t \models M$. This extends to atoms with metric operators as shown in Table 1. For an interpretation $\Im$ and an interval ϱ, we define the *projection* $\Im \mid_\varrho$ of $\Im$ over ϱ as the interpretation that coincides with $\Im$ on ϱ and makes all relational atoms false outside ϱ. An interpretation $\Im$ satisfies a fact $M@\varrho$ if $\Im, t \models M$ for all $t \in \varrho$. Interpretation $\Im$ satisfies a ground rule r if, whenever $\Im$ satisfies each body atom of r at a time point t, then $\Im$ also satisfies the head of r at t. Interpretation $\Im$ satisfies a (non-ground) rule r if it satisfies each ground instance of r. Interpretation $\Im$ is a *model* of a program Π if it satisfies each rule in Π, and it is a *model* of a dataset $\mathcal{D}$ if it satisfies each fact in $\mathcal{D}$. Program Π and dataset $\mathcal{D}$ are *consistent* if they have a model, and they *entail* a fact $M@\varrho$ if each model of both Π and $\mathcal{D}$ is a model of $M@\varrho$. Each dataset $\mathcal{D}$ has a unique least model $\Im_\mathcal{D}$, and we say that dataset $\mathcal{D}$ *represents* interpretation $\Im_\mathcal{D}$.

The *immediate consequence operator* T_Π for a program Π is a function mapping an interpretation $\Im$ to the least interpretation containing $\Im$ and satisfying the following property for each ground instance r of a rule in Π: whenever $\Im$ satisfies each body atom of r at time point t, then $T_\Pi(\Im)$ satisfies the head of r at t. The successive application of T_Π to $\Im_\mathcal{D}$ defines a transfinite sequence of interpretations $T_\Pi^\alpha(\Im_\mathcal{D})$ for ordinals α as follows: (i) $T_\Pi^0(\Im_\mathcal{D}) = \Im_\mathcal{D}$, (ii) $T_\Pi^{\alpha+1}(\Im_\mathcal{D}) = T_\Pi(T_\Pi^\alpha(\Im_\mathcal{D}))$ for α an ordinal, and (iii) $T_\Pi^\alpha(\Im_\mathcal{D}) = \bigcup_{\beta < \alpha} T_\Pi^\beta(\Im_\mathcal{D})$ for α a limit ordinal. The *canonical interpretation* $\mathfrak{C}_{\Pi,\mathcal{D}}$ of Π and $\mathcal{D}$ is the interpretation $T_\Pi^{\omega_1}(\Im_\mathcal{D})$, with ω_1 the first uncountable ordinal. If Π and $\mathcal{D}$ have a model, the canonical interpretation $\mathfrak{C}_{\Pi,\mathcal{D}}$ is the least model of Π and $\mathcal{D}$ [3].

3   Naïve Materialisation in DatalogMTL

In this section, we formulate the naïve materialisation procedure implicit in our theoretical results in [21] and implemented in the MeTeoR reasoner [22].

In order to illustrate the execution of the algorithm and discuss the inefficiencies involved, let us consider as a running example the dataset

$$\mathcal{D}_{\mathsf{ex}} = \{R_1(c_1, c_2)@[0, 1], R_2(c_1, c_2)@[1, 2], R_3(c_2, c_3)@[2, 3], R_5(c_2)@[0, 1]\}$$

and the program Π_{ex} consisting of the following rules:

$$R_1(x, y) \leftarrow \diamondsuit_{[1,1]} R_1(x, y), \qquad\qquad (r_1)$$
$$\boxplus_{[1,1]} R_5(y) \leftarrow R_2(x, y) \wedge \boxplus_{[1,2]} R_3(y, z), \qquad\qquad (r_2)$$
$$R_4(x) \leftarrow \diamondsuit_{[0,1]} R_5(x), \qquad\qquad (r_3)$$
$$R_6(y) \leftarrow R_5(y) \wedge \boxminus_{[0,2]} R_4(y) \wedge R_1(x, y). \qquad\qquad (r_4)$$

The naïve materialisation procedure applies a rule by first identifying the facts that can ground the rule body, and then determining the maximal intervals for which all the ground body atoms hold simultaneously. For instance, the procedure applies rule r_2 to $\mathcal{D}_{\mathsf{ex}}$ by first noticing that relational atoms $R_2(c_1, c_2)$ and $R_3(c_2, c_3)$ can be used to ground the rule body and then establishing that $[1, 1]$ is the maximal interval for which the metric atoms $R_2(c_1, c_2)$ and $\boxplus_{[1,2]} R_3(c_2, c_3)$ in the body of the relevant instance of r_2 are simultaneously true in $\mathcal{D}_{\mathsf{ex}}$; as a result, $\boxplus_{[1,1]} R_5(c_2)@[1, 1]$ can be derived, and so fact $R_5(c_2)@[2, 2]$ is added to the materialisation. In this way, the first round of rule application of the naïve materialisation procedure on Π_{ex} and $\mathcal{D}_{\mathsf{ex}}$ also derives fact $R_1(c_1, c_2)@[1, 2]$ using rule r_1 and fact $R_4(c_2)@[0, 2]$ using r_3. The following set of facts is thus derived as a result of a single step of application of the rules in Π_{ex} to $\mathcal{D}_{\mathsf{ex}}$:

$$\Pi_{\mathsf{ex}}[\mathcal{D}_{\mathsf{ex}}] = \{R_1(c_1, c_2)@[1, 2], \quad R_4(c_2)@[0, 2], \quad R_5(c_2)@[2, 2]\}.$$

The following definition formalises the notion of rule application.

Definition 1. *Let r be a rule of the form $M' \leftarrow M_1 \wedge \cdots \wedge M_n$, for some $n \geq 1$, and let $\mathcal{D}$ be a dataset. The set of* instances *for r and $\mathcal{D}$ is defined as follows:*

$$\mathsf{inst}_r[\mathcal{D}] = \big\{(M_1\sigma@\varrho_1, \ldots, M_n\sigma@\varrho_n) \mid \sigma \text{ is a substitution and, for each}$$
$$i \in \{1, \ldots, n\}, \varrho_i \text{ is a subset-maximal interval such that } \mathcal{D} \models M_i\sigma@\varrho_i\big\}.$$

The set $r[\mathcal{D}]$ of facts derived by r from $\mathcal{D}$ is defined as follows:

$$r[\mathcal{D}] = \{M\sigma@\varrho \mid \sigma \text{ is a substitution, } M \text{ is the single relational atom in } M'\sigma,$$
$$\text{and there exists } (M_1\sigma@\varrho_1, \ldots, M_n\sigma@\varrho_n) \in \mathsf{inst}_r[\mathcal{D}] \text{ such that } \varrho \text{ is the unique}$$
$$\text{subset-maximal interval satisfying } M'\sigma@(\varrho_1 \cap \ldots \cap \varrho_n) \models M\sigma@\varrho\}.$$
$$(2)$$

The set of facts derived from $\mathcal{D}$ by one-step application of Π is

$$\Pi[\mathcal{D}] = \bigcup_{r \in \Pi} r[\mathcal{D}]. \qquad\qquad (3)$$

Procedure 1: Naïve($\Pi,\mathcal{D}$)

Input: A program Π and a dataset $\mathcal{D}$
Output: A dataset representing the canonical interpretation $\mathfrak{C}_{\Pi,\mathcal{D}}$

1 Initialise $\mathcal{N}$ to $\emptyset$ and $\mathcal{D}'$ to $\mathcal{D}$;
2 **loop**
3     $\mathcal{N} := \Pi(\mathcal{D}')$;   `// derive new facts`
4     $\mathcal{C} := \mathcal{D}' \uplus \mathcal{N}$;   `// coalesce with the new facts`
5   **if** $\mathcal{C} = \mathcal{D}'$ **then return** $\mathcal{D}'$;
6     $\mathcal{D}' := \mathcal{C}$;

Once rule application has been completed and facts $\Pi_{\mathsf{ex}}[\mathcal{D}_{\mathsf{ex}}]$ have been derived, the partial materialisation $\mathcal{D}^1_{\mathsf{ex}}$ that will be passed on to the next materialisation step is obtained as $\mathcal{D}^1_{\mathsf{ex}} = \mathcal{D}_{\mathsf{ex}} \uplus \Pi_{\mathsf{ex}}[\mathcal{D}_{\mathsf{ex}}]$ by coalescing facts in $\mathcal{D}_{\mathsf{ex}}$ and $\Pi_{\mathsf{ex}}[\mathcal{D}_{\mathsf{ex}}]$, where the coalescing operator $\uplus$ is semantically defined next.

Definition 2. *For datasets $\mathcal{D}_1$ and $\mathcal{D}_2$, we define $\mathcal{D}_1 \uplus \mathcal{D}_2$ as the dataset consisting of all relational facts $M@\varrho$ such that $\mathcal{D}_1 \cup \mathcal{D}_2 \models M@\varrho$ and $\mathcal{D}_1 \cup \mathcal{D}_2 \not\models M@\varrho'$, for each ϱ' with $\varrho \subsetneq \varrho'$.*

The use of coalescing makes sure that intervals associated to facts are maximal. In our example, facts $R_1(c_1, c_2)@[0,1]$ in $\mathcal{D}_{\mathsf{ex}}$ and $R_1(c_1, c_2)@[1,2]$ are coalesced, so we have $R_1(c_1, c_2)@[0,2]$ in $\mathcal{D}_{\mathsf{ex}} \uplus \Pi_{\mathsf{ex}}[\mathcal{D}_{\mathsf{ex}}]$. Thus,

$$\mathcal{D}^1_{\mathsf{ex}} = \{R_1(c_1, c_2)@[0,2], R_2(c_1, c_2)@[1,2], R_3(c_2, c_3)@[2,3],$$
$$R_5(c_2)@[0,1], R_4(c_2)@[0,2], R_5(c_2)@[2,2]\}.$$

In the second round, rules are applied to $\mathcal{D}^1_{\mathsf{ex}}$. The application of r_1 derives fact $R_1(c_1, c_2)@[1,3]$ (from $R_1(c_1, c_2)@[0,2]$) and the application of r_2 rederives a redundant fact $R_5(c_2)@[2,2]$. In contrast to the previous step, rule r_4 can now be applied to derive the new fact $R_6(c_2)@[2,2]$. Finally, the application of r_3 derives the new fact $R_4(c_2)[2,3]$ and rederives the redundant fact $R_4(c_2)[0,2]$.

The procedure then coalesces fact $R_1(c_1, c_2)[1,3]$ with $R_1(c_1, c_2)[0,2]$ to obtain $R_1(c_1, c_2)[0,3]$; similarly, $R_4(c_2)[2,3]$ is coalesced with $R_4(c_2)[0,2]$ to obtain $R_4(c_2)[0,3]$. Thus, the second step yields the following partial materialisation:

$$\mathcal{D}^2_{\mathsf{ex}} = (\mathcal{D}_{\mathsf{ex}^1} \setminus \{R_4(c_2)[0,2], R_1(c_1, c_2)[0,2]\}) \cup$$
$$\{R_1(c_1, c_2)@[0,3], R_6(c_2)@[2,2], R_4(c_2)[0,3]\}.$$

In the third materialisation step, rules are applied to $\mathcal{D}^2_{\mathsf{ex}}$, and derive the new fact $R_1(c_1, c_2)@[1,4]$, as well as redundant facts such as $R_5(c_2)@[2,2]$, $R_4(c_2)@[0,2]$, $R_4(c_2)@[2,3]$, and $R_6(c_2)@[2,2]$. The procedure will then continue completing subsequent materialisation steps and stopping only if a fixpoint is reached.

Procedure 1 formalises this naïve materialisation strategy. As discussed, each iteration of the main loop captures a single materialisation step consisting of a round of rule application (c.f. Line 3) followed by the coalescing of relevant facts (c.f. Line 4). The resulting partial materialisation passed on to the following materialisation stem is stored as a dataset $\mathcal{D}'$ (c.f. Line 6). The procedure stops when a materialisation step does not derive any new facts, in which case a fixpoint has been reached (c.f. Line 5). In our example, materialisation will continue to recursively propagate the relational fact $R_1(c_1, c_2)$ throughout the infinite timeline, and the procedure will not terminate as a result. Furthermore, the number of redundant computations will increase in each subsequent materialisation step.

It is worth recalling that, even in cases where materialisation does not reach a fixpoint, it still constitutes a key component of terminating algorithms such as that implemented in MeTeoR [22]. Therefore, the performance challenges stemming from redundant computations remain a very significant issue in practice.

4   Seminaïve Evaluation

Seminaïve rule evaluation is the technique of choice for eliminating redundant computations in Datalog-based systems. The main idea is to keep track of newly derived facts in each materialisation step by storing them in a set Δ, and to make sure that rule applications in the following materialisation step involve at least one fact in Δ. In this way, the procedure considers each rule instance *at most once* throughout its entire execution and it is said to enjoy the *non-repetition* property. Note, however, that the same fact can still be derived multiple times by *different* rule instances; this type of redundancy is difficult to prevent and is not addressed by the standard seminaïve strategy.

Our aim in this section is to lift seminaïve rule evaluation to the setting of DatalogMTL. As discussed in Sect. 3 on our running example, a rule instance can be considered multiple times in our setting; for example, the instance $(R_2(c_1, c_2)@[1, 2], \boxplus_{[1,2]}R_3(c_2, c_3)@[1, 1])$ of r_2 is considered in both the first and second materialisation steps to derive $R_5(c_2)@[2, 2]$ twice since the naïve procedure cannot detect that facts $R_2(c_1, c_2)@[1, 2]$ and $R_3(c_2, c_3)@[2, 3]$ used to instantiate r_2 in the second step had previously been used to instantiate r_2. Preventing such redundant computations, however, involves certain challenges. First, by including in Δ just the newly derived facts as in Datalog, we could overlook relevant information obtained by coalescing newly derived facts with previously derived ones. Second, restricting application to relevant rule instances requires taking into account the semantics of metric operators in rule bodies.

Procedure 2 extends the seminaïve strategy to the setting of DatalogMTL while overcoming the aforementioned difficulties. Analogously to the naïve approach, each iteration of the main loop captures a single materialisation step consisting of a round of rule applications followed by the coalescing of relevant facts; as before, dataset $\mathcal{D}'$ stores the partial materialisation resulting from each iteration and is initialised as the input dataset, whereas dataset $\mathcal{N}$ stores the facts obtained as a result of rule application and is initialised as empty.

Following the rationale behind the seminaïve strategy for Datalog, newly derived information in each materialisation step is now stored as a dataset Δ,

---

Procedure 2: Seminaïve(Π,$\mathcal{D}$)

 Input: A program Π and a dataset $\mathcal{D}$
 Output: A dataset representing the canonical interpretation $\mathfrak{C}_{\Pi,\mathcal{D}}$
1 Initialise $\mathcal{N}$ to $\emptyset$, and both Δ and $\mathcal{D}'$ to $\mathcal{D}$;
2 **loop**
3    $\mathcal{N} := \Pi[\mathcal{D}' \mathbin{:} \Delta]$;
4    $\mathcal{C} := \mathcal{D}' \uplus \mathcal{N}$;
5    $\Delta := \{M@\varrho \in \mathcal{C} \mid M@\varrho \text{ entails some fact in } \mathcal{N} \setminus\!\!\setminus \mathcal{D}'\}$;
6   **if** $\Delta = \emptyset$ **then return** $\mathcal{D}'$;
7    $\mathcal{D}' := \mathcal{C}$;

---

which is initialised as the input dataset $\mathcal{D}$ and which is suitably maintained in each iteration; furthermore, Procedure 2 ensures in Line 3 that only rule instances, for which it is essential to involve facts from Δ (as formalised in the following definition) are taken into account during rule application.

Definition 3. *Let r be a rule of the form $M' \leftarrow M_1 \wedge \cdots \wedge M_n$, for some $n \geq 1$, and let $\mathcal{D}$ and Δ be datasets. The set of instances for r and $\mathcal{D}$ relative to Δ is defined as follows:*

$$\mathsf{inst}_r[\mathcal{D} \mathbin{:} \Delta] = \big\{ (M_1\sigma@\varrho_1, \ldots, M_n\sigma@\varrho_n) \in \mathsf{inst}_r[\mathcal{D}] \mid$$
$$\mathcal{D} \setminus \Delta \not\models M_i\sigma@\varrho_i, \text{ for some } i \in \{1,\ldots,n\}\big\}. \quad (4)$$

The set $r[\mathcal{D} \mathbin{:} \Delta]$ of facts derived by r from $\mathcal{D}$ relative to Δ is defined analogously to $r[\mathcal{D}]$ in Definition 1, with the exception that $\mathsf{inst}_r[\mathcal{D}]$ is replaced with $\mathsf{inst}_r[\mathcal{D} \mathbin{:} \Delta]$ in Expression (2). Finally, the set $\Pi[\mathcal{D} \mathbin{:} \Delta]$ of facts derived from $\mathcal{D}$ by one-step seminaïve application of Π is defined as $\Pi[\mathcal{D}]$ in Expression (3), by replacing $r[\mathcal{D}]$ with $r[\mathcal{D} \mathbin{:} \Delta]$.

In each materialisation step, Procedure 2 exploits Definition 3 to identify as relevant the subset of rule instances where some conjunct is 'new', in the sense that it cannot be entailed without the facts in Δ. The facts derived by such relevant rule instances in each iteration are stored in set $\mathcal{N}$ (c.f. Line 3).

As in the naïve approach, rule application is followed by a coalescing step where the partial materialisation is updated with the facts derived from rule application (c.f. Line 4). In contrast to the naïve approach, however, Procedure 2 needs to maintain set Δ to ensure that it captures only new facts. This is achieved in Line 5, where a fact in the updated partial materialisation is considered new if it entails a fact in $\mathcal{N}$ that was not already entailed by the previous partial materialisation. This is formalised with the following notion of 'semantic' difference between temporal datasets.

Definition 4. *Let $\mathcal{D}_1$ and $\mathcal{D}_2$ be datasets. We define $\mathcal{D}_1 \setminus\!\!\setminus \mathcal{D}_2$ as the dataset consisting of all relational facts $M@\varrho$ such that $M@\varrho \in \mathcal{D}_1$ and $\mathcal{D}_2 \not\models M@\varrho$.*

The procedure terminates in Line 6 if Δ is empty. Otherwise, the procedure carries over the updated partial materialisation and the set of newly derived facts to the next materialisation step.

We next illustrate the execution of the procedure on $\mathcal{D}_{ex}$ and Π_{ex}. In the first materialisation step, all input facts are considered as newly derived (i.e., $\Delta = \mathcal{D}$) and hence $\mathcal{N} = \Pi[\mathcal{D}' \vdots \Delta] = \Pi(\mathcal{D}')$ and the result of coalescing coincides with the partial materialisation computed by the naïve procedure (i.e., $\mathcal{C} = \mathcal{D}_{ex}^1$). Then, the procedure identifies as new all facts in $\mathcal{N}$ (i.e., $\Delta = \mathcal{N}$). In the second step, rule evaluation in Line 3 no longer considers the redundant instance of r_2 consisting of fact $R_2(c_1, c_2)@[1, 2]$ and metric atom $\boxminus_{[1,2]}R_3(c_2, c_3)@[1, 2]$ since they are respectively entailed by facts $R_2(c_1, c_2)[1, 2]$ and $R_3(c_2, c_3)[2, 3]$ in $\mathcal{D}' \setminus \Delta$. Finally, the procedure also disregards the redundant instance of r_3 re-deriving fact $R_4(c_2)[0, 2]$. In contrast, all non-redundant facts derived by the naïve strategy are also derived by the seminaïve procedure and after coalescing dataset $\mathcal{C} = \mathcal{D}_{ex}^2$. Set Δ is now updated as follows:

$$\Delta = \{R_1(c_2, c_2)@[0, 3], R_6(c_2)@[2, 2], R_4(c_2)@[0, 3]\}.$$

In particular, note that Δ contains the coalesced fact $R_4(c_2)@[0, 3]$ rather than fact $R_4(c_2)@[2, 3]$ derived from rule application. Datasets Δ and $\mathcal{D}' = \mathcal{D}_{ex}^2$ are passed on to the third materialisation step, where all redundant computations identified in Sect. 3 are avoided with the only exception of fact $R_6(c_2)@[2, 2]$, which is re-derived using the instance of r_4 consisting of facts $R_5(c_2)@[2, 2]$, $R_1(c_2, c_2)@[0, 3]$ and metric atom $\boxminus_{[0,2]}R_4(c_2)@[2, 3]$. Note that this is a new instance which was not used in previous iterations, and hence the non-repetition property remains true. Note also that, as with the naïve strategy, our seminaïve procedure does not terminate on our running example.

We conclude this section by establishing correctness of our procedure. To this end we next show that, upon completion of the k-th iteration of the main loop (for any k), the partial materialisation $\mathcal{D}'$ passed on to the next iteration represents the interpretation $T_\Pi^k(\mathfrak{I}_\mathcal{D})$ obtained by applying k times the immediate consequence operator T_Π for the input program Π to the interpretation $\mathfrak{I}_\mathcal{D}$ representing the input dataset $\mathcal{D}$. This provides a precise correspondence between the procedure's syntactic operations and the semantics of fixpoint computation.

Soundness relies on the observation that rule instances processed by seminaïve evaluation are also processed by the naïve evaluation; thus, $\mathsf{inst}_r[\mathcal{D} \vdots \Delta] \subseteq \mathsf{inst}_r[\mathcal{D}]$, for each r, $\mathcal{D}$, and Δ. As a result, each fact derived by the seminaïve evaluation is also derived by the naïve evaluation.

Theorem 1 (Soundness). *Consider Procedure 2 running on input Π and $\mathcal{D}$. Upon the completion of the kth (for some $k \in \mathbb{N}$) iteration of the loop of Procedure 2, it holds that $\mathfrak{I}_{\mathcal{D}'} \subseteq T_\Pi^k(\mathfrak{I}_\mathcal{D})$.*

Completeness is proved by induction on the number k of iterations of the main loop. In particular, we show that if $T_\Pi^k(\mathfrak{I}_\mathcal{D})$ satisfies a new fact $M@t$, then there must be a rule r and an instance in $\mathsf{inst}_r[\mathcal{D} \vdots \Delta]$ witnessing the derivation of $M@t$; otherwise, the fact would hold already in $T_\Pi^{k-1}(\mathfrak{I}_\mathcal{D})$. Hence, each fact satisfied by $T_\Pi^k(\mathfrak{I}_\mathcal{D})$ is derived in the kth iteration of our procedure.

Theorem 2 (Completeness). *Consider Procedure 2 running on input Π and $\mathcal{D}$. For each $k \in \mathbb{N}$, upon the completion of the kth iteration of the loop of Procedure 2, it holds that $T_{\Pi}^{k}(\mathfrak{I}_{\mathcal{D}}) \subseteq \mathfrak{I}_{\mathcal{D}'}$.*

5 Optimised Seminaïve Evaluation

Although the seminaïve procedure enjoys the non-repetition property, it can still re-derive facts that were already obtained in previous materialisation steps, thus incurring in a potentially large number of redundant computations. In particular, as discussed in Sect. 4, fact $R_6(c_2)@[2,2]$ is re-derived using rule r_4 in the third materialisation step of our running example, and it will also be re-derived in all subsequent materialisation steps (by different instances of rule r_4).

In this section, we present an optimised variant of our seminaïve procedure which further reduces the number of redundant computations performed during materialisation. The main idea is to disregard rules during the execution of the procedure as soon as we can be certain that their application will never derive new facts in subsequent materialisation steps. In our example, rule r_4 can be discarded after the second materialisation step as its application will only continue to re-derive fact $R_6(c_2)@[2,2]$ in each materialisation step.

To this end, we will exploit the distinction between recursive and non-recursive predicates in a program, as defined next.

Definition 5. *The* dependency graph *of program Π is the directed graph with a vertex v_P for each predicate P in Π and an edge (v_Q, v_R) whenever there is a rule in Π mentioning Q in the body and R in the head. Predicate P is* recursive *(in Π) if the dependency graph has a path containing a cycle and ending in v_P; otherwise P is* non-recursive. *A metric atom is* non-recursive *in Π if so are all its predicates; otherwise it is* recursive. *The* (non-)recursive fragment *of Π is the subset of rules in Π with (non-)recursive atoms in heads.*

In contrast to recursive predicates, for which new facts can be derived in each materialisation step, the materialisation of non-recursive predicates will be completed after linearly many materialisation steps; from then on, the rules will no longer derive any new facts involving these predicates.

This observation can be exploited to optimise seminaïve evaluation. Assume that the procedure has fully materialised all non-recursive predicates in the input program. At this point, we can safely discard all non-recursive rules; furthermore, we can also discard a recursive rule r with a non-recursive body atom M if the current partial materialisation does not entail any grounding of M (in this case, r cannot apply in further materialisation steps). An additional optimisation applies to forward-propagating programs, where rules cannot propagate information 'backwards' along the timeline; in this case, we can compute the maximal time points for which each non-recursive body atom in r may possibly hold, select the minimum t_r amongst such values, and discard r as soon as we can determine that the materialisation up to time point t_r has been fully completed.

Procedure 3: OptimisedSeminaïve($\Pi,\mathcal{D}$)

Input: A program Π and a dataset $\mathcal{D}$
Output: A dataset representing the canonical interpretation $\mathfrak{C}_{\Pi,\mathcal{D}}$

1 Initialise $\mathcal{N}$ to $\emptyset$, Δ and $\mathcal{D}'$ to $\mathcal{D}$, Π' to Π, $flag$ to 0, and S_r (for each $r \in \Pi$) to the set of body atoms in r that are non-recursive in Π;

2 **loop**

3 $\quad$ $\mathcal{N} := \Pi'[\mathcal{D}' \vdots \Delta]$;

4 $\quad$ $\mathcal{C} := \mathcal{D}' \uplus \mathcal{N}$;

5 $\quad$ $\Delta := \{M@\varrho \in \mathcal{C} \mid M@\varrho \text{ entails some fact in } \mathcal{N} \setminus\!\setminus \mathcal{D}'\}$;

6 $\quad$ **if** $\Delta = \emptyset$ **then return** $\mathcal{D}'$;

7 $\quad$ **if** $flag = 0$ & $\mathcal{D}'$ and $\mathcal{C}$ entail the same facts with non-recursive predicates **then**

8 $\quad\quad$ Set $flag$ to 1 and Π' to the recursive fragment of Π;

9 $\quad\quad$ **for** each $r \in \Pi'$ **do**

10 $\quad\quad\quad$ **if** there is $M \in S_r$ such that $\mathcal{D}' \not\models M\sigma@t$, for each substitution σ and time point t **then** $\Pi' := \Pi' \setminus \{r\}$;

11 $\quad$ **if** $flag = 1$ and Π' is forward propagating **then**

12 $\quad\quad$ **for** each $r \in \Pi'$ and each $M \in S_r$ **do**

13 $\quad\quad\quad$ $t_{max}^M :=$ maximum right endpoint amongst all intervals ϱ satisfying $\mathcal{D}' \models M\sigma@\varrho$, for some substitution σ;

14 $\quad\quad\quad$ $t_r :=$ minimum value in $\{t_{max}^M \mid M \in S_r\}$;

15 $\quad\quad\quad$ **if** $\mathcal{D}'$ and $\mathcal{C}$ coincide on all facts over intervals ϱ satisfying $\varrho^+ \leq t_r$ **then** $\Pi' := \Pi' \setminus \{r\}$;

16 $\quad$ $\mathcal{D}' := \mathcal{C}$;

The materialisation of the non-recursive predicates R_2, R_3, R_4, and R_5 of our running example is complete after two materialisation steps. Hence, at this point we can disregard rules r_2 and r_3 and focus on the recursive forward-propagating rules r_1 and r_4. Furthermore, the maximum time point at which R_4 and R_5 can hold is 3 and 2, respectively, and hence $t_{r_4} = 2$; thus, upon completion of the second materialisation step we can be certain that R_1 has been materialised up to t_r and we can also discard r_6. In subsequent materialisation steps we can apply only rule r_1, thus avoiding many redundant computations.

Procedure 3 implements these ideas by extending seminaïve materialisation. In each materialisation step, the procedure checks whether all non-recursive predicates have been fully materialised (c.f. Line 7), in which case it removes all non-recursive rules in the input program as well as all recursive rules with an unsatisfied non-recursive body atom (c.f. Lines 7–10). It also sets a flag to 1, which activates the additional optimisation for forward propagating programs, which is applied in Lines 11–15 whenever possible.

We conclude this section by establishing correctness of our procedure. We first observe that, as soon as the algorithm switches the flag to 1, we can be certain that all non-recursive predicates have been fully materialised.

Lemma 1. *Consider Procedure 3 running on input Π and $\mathcal{D}$ and let Π_{nr} be the non-recursive fragment of Π. If $flag = 1$, then $\mathfrak{C}_{\Pi_{nr},\mathcal{D}} \subseteq \mathfrak{I}_{\mathcal{D}'}$.*

Next, we show how we can detect if a forward-propagating program has completed materialisation of all facts (also with recursive predicates) up to a given time point. Namely it suffices to check that two consecutive partial materialisations satisfy the same facts up to a given time point. Note that our procedure checks this condition syntactically in Line 15.

Lemma 2. *If $\mathfrak{I}_{\mathcal{D}} \mid_{(-\infty,t]} = T_{\Pi}(\mathfrak{I}_{\mathcal{D}}) \mid_{(-\infty,t]}$, for a forward propagating program Π, dataset $\mathcal{D}$, and time point t, then $\mathfrak{I}_{\mathcal{D}} \mid_{(-\infty,t]} = \mathfrak{C}_{\Pi,\mathcal{D}} \mid_{(-\infty,t]}$.*

We can use this lemma to show that each rule discarded in Lines 10 and 15 can be safely ignored as it will have no effect in subsequent materialisation steps.

Lemma 3. *If in Procedure 3 a rule r is removed from Π' in Line 10 or in Line 15, then $\mathfrak{C}_{\Pi',\mathcal{D}' \uplus \mathcal{N}} = \mathfrak{C}_{\Pi' \setminus \{r\},\mathcal{D}' \uplus \mathcal{N}}$.*

Finally, using Lemmas 1 and 3 together with the soundness and completeness of our seminaïve evaluation (established in Theorems 2 and 1), we can show soundness and completeness of the optimised version of the procedure.

Theorem 3 (Soundness and Completeness). *Consider Procedure 3 running on input Π and $\mathcal{D}$. For each $k \in \mathbb{N}$, the partial materialisation $\mathcal{D}'$ obtained upon completion of the kth iteration of the main loop represents the interpretation $T_{\Pi}^k(\mathfrak{I}_{\mathcal{D}})$.*

We conclude by observing that our optimisation for forward-propagating programs in Lines 11–15 can be modified in a straightforward way to account also for backwards-propagating programs, as these two cases are symmetric.

6   Evaluation

We have implemented Procedures 2 and 3 as an extension of our open-source MeTeoR reasoner [22], which so-far implemented only the naïve strategy from Procedure 1 to perform materialisation.

For evaluation, we have considered the temporal extension of the Lehigh University Benchmark (LUBM) [8] used in previous evaluations of MeTeoR [22]. The benchmark provides a DatalogMTL program consisting of 56 Datalog rules obtained from the OWL 2 RL fragment of LUBM's ontology plus 29 temporal rules involving recursion and covering all metric operators of DatalogMTL. To make materialisation more challenging, we have included additional body atoms in some of the temporal rules. The benchmark also provides an extension of LUBM's data generator which randomly assigns intervals non-temporal facts. We used nine datasets $\mathcal{D}_1$–$\mathcal{D}_9$, each consisting of 10 million facts, but with an increasing number of constants occurring in these facts (and thus with a smaller number of intervals per relational fact), namely, these datasets contain 0.8, 1.0,

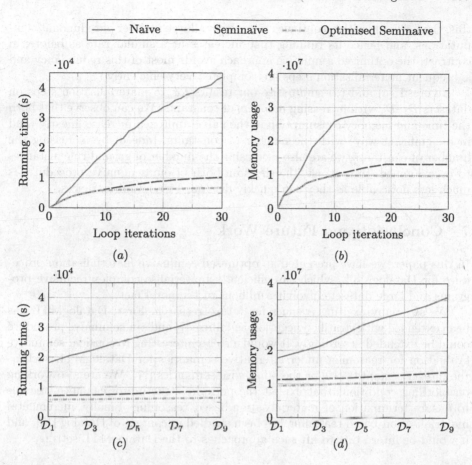

Fig. 1. Experimental results for dataset $\mathcal{D}_5$ in sub-figures (a) and (b), and for the first 15 iterations for datasets $\mathcal{D}_1$–$\mathcal{D}_9$ in sub-figures (c) and (d)

1.2, 1.3, 2.1, 2.5, 5.2, 10.1, and 15.8 million constants, respectively. We compared running time and memory requirements (maximal number of stored facts) of our procedures with that of the naïve approach as depicted in Fig. 1. Experiments were conducted on a Dell PowerEdge R730 server with 512 GB RAM and two Intel Xeon E5-2640 2.6 GHz processors running Fedora 33, kernel version 5.8.17.

Figures 1 (a) and (b) show time and memory usage on a single dataset $\mathcal{D}_5$ through the first 30 iterations of the procedures. As we can see, the seminaïve procedure significantly outperforms the naïve approach both in terms of running time and memory consumption, especially as materialisation progresses. In turn, the optimised seminaïve approach is able to start disregarding rules after 9 materialisation steps, and at that point it starts outperforming the basic seminaïve procedure. We can also observe that, at this point, many of the predicates have been materialised already and the number of new facts generated in each further step is very small (thus, memory consumption stops growing). Despite this, the naïve algorithm continues to perform a large number of redundant computations, and hence its running time increases at a similar rate as before; in contrast, the optimised seminaïve approach avoids most of this redundancy and subsequent materialisation steps are completed very efficiently.

Figures 1 (c) and (d) summarise our results for 15 materialisation steps on datasets $\mathcal{D}_1$–$\mathcal{D}_9$ with increasing numbers of constants. We can observe that both the time and memory consumption in the naïve approach increase linearly (and in a significant way) with the number of constants. Indeed, by increasing the number of constants, we are also increasing the number of ground rule instances to be examined. In contrast, the effect on both of our seminaïve procedures is much less noticeable as they can quickly disregard irrelevant instances.

7   Conclusion and Future Work

In this paper, we have presented an optimised seminaïve materialisation procedure for DatalogMTL, which can efficiently materialise complex recursive programs and large datasets involving millions of temporal facts.

We see many exciting avenues for future research. First, DatalogMTL has been extended with stratified negation-as-failure [7] and our seminaïve procedure could be extended accordingly. It would also be interesting to consider seminaïve evaluation for reasoning under alternative semantics for DatalogMTL such as the integer semantics [19] or the point-wise semantics [17]. We are also working on blocking conditions that exploit the periodic structure of canonical models to ensure termination of materialisation-based reasoning. Finally, incremental materialisation-based reasoning has been studied in context of Datalog [14], and it would be interesting to lift such approaches to the DatalogMTL setting.

Acknowledgments. This work was supported by the EPSRC project OASIS (EP/S032347/1), the EPSRC project UK FIRES (EP/S019111/1), and the SIRIUS Centre for Scalable Data Access, and Samsung Research UK.

References

1. Abiteboul, S., Hull, R., Vianu, V.: Foundations of Databases, vol. 8. Addison-Wesley, Reading (1995)
2. Bellomarini, L., Sallinger, E., Gottlob, G.: The vadalog system: Datalog-based reasoning for knowledge graphs. Proc. VLDB Endow. **11**(9), 975–987 (2018)
3. Brandt, S., Kalaycı, E.G., Ryzhikov, V., Xiao, G., Zakharyaschev, M.: Querying log data with metric temporal logic. J. Artif. Intell. Res. **62**, 829–877 (2018)
4. Bry, F., et al.: Foundations of rule-based query answering. In: Reasoning Web, pp. 1–153 (2007)
5. Carral, D., Dragoste, I., González, L., Jacobs, C.J.H., Krötzsch, M., Urbani, J.: Vlog: a rule engine for knowledge graphs. In: Proceedings of ISWC, pp. 19–35 (2019)
6. Ceri, S., Gottlob, G., Tanca, L.: What you always wanted to know about Datalog (and never dared to ask). IEEE TKDE **1**(1), 146–166 (1989)

7. Cucala, D.J.T., Wałęga, P.A., Cuenca Grau, B., Kostylev, E.V.: Stratified negation in Datalog with metric temporal operators. In: Proceedings of AAAI, pp. 6488–6495 (2021)

8. Guo, Y., Pan, Z., Heflin, J.: LUBM: a benchmark for OWL knowledge base systems. J. Web Semant. **3**(2–3), 158–182 (2005)

9. Kalaycı, E.G., Xiao, G., Ryzhikov, V., Kalayci, T.E., Calvanese, D.: Ontop-temporal: a tool for ontology-based query answering over temporal data. In: Proceedings of CIKM, pp. 1927–1930 (2018)

10. Kikot, S., Ryzhikov, V., Wałęga, P.A., Zakharyaschev, M.: On the data complexity of ontology-mediated queries with MTL operators over timed words. In: Proceedings of DL (2018)

11. Koopmann, P.: Ontology-based query answering for probabilistic temporal data. In: Proceedings of AAAI, pp. 2903–2910 (2019)

12. Koymans, R.: Specifying real-time properties with metric temporal logic. J. R Time Syst. **2**(4), 255–299 (1990)

13. Mori, M., Papotti, P., Bellomarini, L., Giudice, O.: Neural machine translation for fact-checking temporal claims. In: Proceedings of FEVER, p. 78 (2022)

14. Motik, B., Nenov, Y., Piro, R., Horrocks, I.: Maintenance of Datalog materialisations revisited. Artif. Intell. **269**, 76–136 (2019)

15. Motik, B., Nenov, Y., Piro, R., Horrocks, I., Olteanu, D.: Parallel materialisation of Datalog programs in centralised, main-memory RDF systems. In: Proceedings of AAAI (2014)

16. Nissl, M., Sallinger, E.: Modelling smart contracts with datalogmtl. In: Ramanath, M., Palpanas, T. (eds.) Proceedings of the Workshops of the EDBT/ICDT. CEUR, vol. 3135. CEUR-WS.org (2022)

17. Ryzhikov, V., Wałęga, P.A., Zakharyaschev, M.: Data complexity and rewritability of ontology-mediated queries in metric temporal logic under the event-based semantics. In: Proceedings of IJCAI, pp. 1851–1857 (2019)

18. Wałęga, P.A., Cuenca Grau, B., Kaminski, M., Kostylev, E.V.: DatalogMTL: computational complexity and expressive power. In: Proceedings of IJCAI, pp. 1886–1892 (2019)

19. Wałęga, P.A., Cuenca Grau, B., Kaminski, M., Kostylev, E.V.: DatalogMTL over the integer timeline. In: Proceedings of KR, pp. 768–777 (2020)

20. Wałęga, P.A., Kaminski, M., Cuenca Grau, B.: Reasoning over streaming data in metric temporal Datalog. In: Proceedings of AAAI, pp. 3092–3099 (2019)

21. Wałęga, P.A., Zawidzki, M., Cuenca Grau, B.: Finitely materialisable Datalog programs with metric temporal operators. In: Proceedings of KR (2021)

22. Wang, D., Hu, P., Wałęga, P.A., Grau, B.C.: MeTeoR: practical reasoning in Datalog with metric temporal operators. In: Proceedings of AAAI (2022)

Magic Sets in Interpolation-Based Rule Driven Query Optimization

Eva Feng[✉], David Toman, and Grant Weddell

University of Waterloo, Waterloo, Canada
{ehfeng,david,gweddell}@uwaterloo.ca

Abstract. Query reformulation under constraints is an essential part of modern query optimizers. This paper introduces an enhancement to an interpolation-based rule-driven query optimizer that extends the space of valid rewritings for a user query in order to find better execution plans otherwise not found. The enhancement is inspired by the so-called *magic set transformation* (MST). However, in contrast with the traditional use of MST, our approach uses MST-like transformation to derive *additional* formulae constituting a desirable extension to the space of query plans.

1 Introduction

Information systems rely critically on query optimizers to find efficient query plans for user queries over their underlying databases. More recent interpolation-based query optimizers [3,4,9,10] have proven to be more effective at finding such plans compared to earlier approaches. The input to an optimizer consists of a user query and a database schema composed of logical and physical constraints. The logical constraints, such as declarations of primary/foreign keys, are sentences over an alphabet of *logical atoms*, atoms that appear in user queries. The physical constraints are sentences over both the logical and the *physical atoms*, atoms that abstract data structures storing the actual data in the database system, such as B+trees. The goal of *query optimization* is to find performance-wise optimal query plan—a formula over the physical atoms that is logically equivalent to the user query under the database schema—among all query plans. The query optimization process is summarized in Fig. 1.

In this paper, we consider the interpolation-based optimizer presented in [10]. This optimizer is a two-phase system which (1) constructs a representation of a partial analytic tableau proof, called *conditional tableau*, and (2) performs query plan enumeration over physical atoms using results extracted from the conditional tableau. Since both database schemata and relational queries use a *range-restricted* subset of first-order logic [1], the first phase is implemented using forward chaining that applies rules on ground atoms. This yields an overall performance advantage in searching among many possible plans since one avoids the need for free variables, unification, etc., which are common in other tableau-based first-order theorem provers. Unfortunately, the forward chaining design also has a limitation which prevents the optimizer from fully utilizing the power

G. Governatori and A.-Y. Turhan (Eds.): RuleML+RR 2022, LNCS 13752, pp. 198–207, 2022.
https://doi.org/10.1007/978-3-031-21541-4_13

of interpolation-based optimizers, which we now illustrate with Examples 1 and 2. In presenting these examples, we introduce a view definition q to internalize a user query in the database schema.

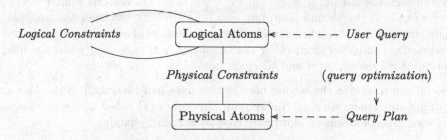

Fig. 1. Overview of query optimization

Example 1. Consider a query optimization problem for the user query $a(x) \wedge c(x)$ with respect to the database schema

Logical/Physical Constraints	View Definition		Rules
	$q(x) \leftrightarrow a(x) \wedge c(x)$	$\xrightarrow{\text{normalize}}$	$q(x) \rightarrow a(x)$
			$q(x) \rightarrow c(x)$
			$a(x) \wedge c(x) \rightarrow q(x)$
$c(x) \rightarrow \exists y. b(x,y)$	$\xrightarrow{\hspace{2em}\text{normalize}\hspace{2em}}$		$c(x) \rightarrow \exists y. b(x,y)$

presented as a set of rules and the set of physical atoms $\{a, b, c\}$. The system will generate the following two alternative query plans (among others):

$$a(x) \wedge c(x) \quad \text{and} \quad a(x) \wedge (\exists y. b(x,y)) \wedge c(x).$$

While the second plan seems redundant, it may still be more efficient than the first plan. This happens when a is large (has a large number of tuples), when checking the satisfaction of $\exists y. b(x,y)$ is relatively inexpensive compared to checking the satisfaction of $c(x)$, and when the intersection of x values in $a(x)$ and $b(x,y)$ is much smaller than the size of a.

Note that—intuitively—the atom $b(x,y)$ in the above example can be obtained from $c(x)$ by forward chaining the schema rules, and that $c(x)$ must be present in any query plan for $q(x)$; see Sect. 2 for details. Unfortunately, certain desirable query plans cannot be found due to the forward chaining nature of the system. A simple variation of the above example illustrates the issue:

Example 2. Consider the following modification of Example 1.

Logical/Constraints Constraints	View Definition		Rules
	$q(x) \leftrightarrow a(x) \wedge c(x)$	$\xrightarrow{\text{normalize}}$	same as Example 1
$c(x) \wedge b(x,y) \rightarrow \bot$	$\xrightarrow{\hspace{2em}\text{normalize}\hspace{2em}}$		$c(x) \wedge b(x,y) \rightarrow \bot$

The system will still generate the query plan $a(x) \land c(x)$, but not the plan

$$a(x) \land (\neg\exists y.b(x,y)) \land c(x),$$

even though the schema *implies* $c(x) \rightarrow \neg\exists y.b(x,y)$. For reasons similar to those for Example 1, the second plan may also be more efficient than the first plan, again, when a is large, when checking the satisfaction of $\neg\exists y.b(x,y)$ is relatively inexpensive compared to checking the satisfaction of $c(x)$, and when the intersection of x values in $a(x)$ and $b(x,y)$ is now close to the size of a.

The failure to derive the second plan in this case can be traced to the forward chaining implementation of the system: the rule $c(x) \land b(x,y) \rightarrow \bot$ is never executed since b atoms cannot be derived by forward chaining.

The Contribution: A straightforward way to rectify this problem is to extend the tableau construction by allowing negated atoms alongside the positive atoms. This, however, leads immediately to the need for handling free/universally quantified variables, unification, etc. In this paper, we propose an alternative solution inspired by the *magic set transformation* (MST) [2] that allows the conditional tableau construction to be based on efficient forward chaining of rules over ground atoms while providing a general solution to the problem illustrated by Example 2.

The remainder of the paper is organized as follows: Sect. 2 provides the necessary background and definitions for our proposed rewriting procedure. Due to space limitations, details which are not immediately relevant to our main contribution are omitted in Sect. 2 but can be found in [8,10]. Section 3 introduces the variant of MST used in this paper and illustrates both its necessity and efficacy. We conclude in Sect. 4 with directions of future research, which includes other applications of MST to query optimization, in particular with making the optimization algorithm(s) themselves more efficient.

2   Preliminaries and Definitions

Let Σ be the database schema and $q(\bar{y})$ be the view definition of the user query. Let the superscripts $.^L$ and $.^R$ denote a uniform renaming of symbols in a formula (or set of formulae) and the *physical* atoms p provide the alphabet of the interpolant, hereon called the query plan. Our approach is a variation on constructing an analytic tableau proof of the *entailment-style* formulation of the Beth definability condition [5],

$$\Sigma^L \cup \Sigma^R \cup \{\forall\bar{x}.p^L(\bar{x}) \leftrightarrow p(\bar{x}) \leftrightarrow p^R(\bar{x}) \mid p \text{ physical}\} \models \forall\bar{y}.q^L(\bar{y}) \rightarrow q^R(\bar{y}). \quad (*)$$

In contrast to the classical version of the Craig interpolation theorem [6,7], this modification allows our system to separate the theorem proving part of the problem, called the *conditional tableau*, from the plan enumeration phase based on *closing sets*, an abstraction of the conditional tableau constructed for a particular user query.

Conditional Tableau. As outlined in the introduction, our approach is a variation on the above and proceeds in two phases. In the first phase, we construct a *conditional tableau* consisting of two separate partial tableaux T^L and T^R that capture inferences in $\Sigma^L \cup \{q^L(\bar{c})\}$ and $\Sigma^R \cup \{q^R(\bar{c}) \to \bot\}$, respectively. Constructing these tableaux separately alleviates the need for renaming the formulae using superscripts in the rest of the paper. The main building blocks of a conditional tableau are so-called *conditional atoms*; both T^L and T^R are encoded as sets of such atoms:

Definition 1. *Let r be a ground atom (or $\bot$), $P = \{p_1, \ldots, p_n\}$ a set of ground physical atoms, and $B = \{i_1 : j_1, \ldots, i_m : j_m\}$ a set of pairs of numbers corresponding to a branch number and direction. We call $r[P]\langle B \rangle$ a conditional atom for r that depends on ground physical atoms in P (called dependencies) and that belongs to tableau branches described by the set B.*

The conditional tableau is constructed by applying the following rules on the initial conditional tableaux $T^L = \{q(\bar{c})[]\langle\rangle\}$ and $T^R = \{\}$ for a user query $q(\bar{x})$. In the table, we write $\mathbf{P}(a)$ and $\mathbf{B}(a)$ to refer to the dependencies and branches of a conditional atom $a(\bar{c})[P]\langle B \rangle$ substituted for an atom $a(x)$ in a rule, and where n is a fresh branch number whenever a new "or" is encountered.

Rules			$\mathbf{P}(b_1)[, \mathbf{P}(b_2)]$	$\mathbf{B}(b_1)[, \mathbf{B}(b_2)]$
$a_1(\bar{x}) \to b_1(\bar{y})$	$\bar{y} \subset \bar{x}$		$\mathbf{P}(a_1)$	$\mathbf{B}(a_1)$
$a_1(\bar{x}) \wedge a_2(\bar{y}) \to b_1(\bar{z})$	$\bar{z} \subseteq \bar{x} \cup \bar{y}$		$\mathbf{P}(a_1) \cup \mathbf{P}(a_2)$	$\mathbf{B}(a_1) \cup \mathbf{B}(a_2)$
$a_1(\bar{x}) \to \exists y. b_1(\bar{x}, y)$			$\mathbf{P}(a_1)$	$\mathbf{B}(a_1)$
$a_1(\bar{x}) \to b_1(\bar{x}) \vee b_2(\bar{x})$			$\mathbf{P}(a_1), \mathbf{P}(a_1)$	$\mathbf{B}(a_1) \cup \{n : 0\}, \mathbf{B}(a_1) \cup \{n : 1\}$

In addition, we use a *physical rule*, that adds a conditional atom $p[\{p\}]\langle\rangle$ to T^R (resp. T^L) when a physical atom $p[P]\langle B \rangle$ occurs in T^L (resp. T^R). We also use an additional rule $q(c) \to \bot$ in constructing T^R. Note that the use of the physical rule is always sound since it essentially adds a tautology $p \to p$; we use this observation again for the MST-based physical rule in Sect. 3.

Closing Sets and Query Plans. The second phase of our approach extracts so-called *closing sets* from T^L and T^R. These are minimal sets of physical literals that close every branch in T^L and T^R.

Definition 2 *(Closing Sets [10]).* We define closing sets constructively. A left (resp. right) closing set *is a minimal set of physical literals that close all open branches in T^L (resp. T^R). We write CS^L (resp. CS^R) to refer to the set of all closing sets for T^L (resp. T^R).*

The candidate closing sets for a tableau T are constructed as follows [10]:

1. Set $\mathsf{CS} := \{\{\neg r, p_1, \ldots, p_n\}\langle B \rangle \mid r[\{p_1, \ldots, p_n\}]\langle B \rangle \in T, r \text{ physical or } \bot\}$.

2. Repeat $\mathsf{CS} := \mathsf{CS} - \{S_1\langle B_1 \cup \{n.0\}\rangle, S_2\langle B_2 \cup \{n.1\}\rangle\} \cup \{S_1 \cup S_2\langle B_1 \cup B_2\rangle\}$ while $S_1\langle B_1 \cup \{n.0\}\rangle, S_2\langle B_2 \cup \{n.1\}\rangle \in \mathsf{CS}$ for some n.

This construction is applied both on T^L and T^R yielding CS^L and CS^R after discarding non-minimal candidate closing sets. Finally, to generate query plans, we can simply compute the sets L_P and R_P for a candidate formula using the table below and then compare these sets to the closing sets for T^L and T^R.

ψ :	ψ^L	ψ^R
$r(\bar{c})$:	$\{\{\neg r(\bar{c})\}\}$	$\{\{r(\bar{c})\}\}$
$\psi_1 \wedge \psi_2$:	$\psi_1^L \cup \psi_2^L$	$\{S_1 \cup S_2 \mid S_1 \in \psi_1^R, S_2 \in \psi_2^R\}$
$\psi_1 \vee \psi_2$:	$\{S_1 \cup S_2 \mid S_1 \in \psi_1^L, S_2 \in \psi_2^L\}$	$\psi_1^R \cup \psi_2^R$
$\neg\psi_1$:	ψ_1^R	ψ_1^L
$\exists x.\psi_1[x/a]$:	ψ_1^L	ψ_1^R

This construction relies on the remaining $\{\forall \bar{x}.p^L(\bar{x}) \leftrightarrow p(\bar{x}) \leftrightarrow p^R(\bar{x}) \mid p \text{ physical}\}$ formulae in $(*)$ above to complete the tableau proof of $(*)$. Overall, we have:

Proposition 1 ([8]). *Let Σ be a database schema, $q(\bar{x})$ a user query, and P a candidate plan. Then the following are equivalent:*

1. *For each $S \in \psi^X$ there is $S' \in \mathsf{CS}^X$ such that $S' \subseteq S$ for $X \in \{L, R\}$; and*
2. $\Sigma \models \forall \bar{x}.q(\bar{x}) \leftrightarrow \psi$.

The following example illustrates the conditional tableau construction and subsequent plan synthesis using the closing sets. We hereon only consider the normalized schema constraints.

Example 3. Consider a database schema $\Sigma = \{q(x) \rightarrow a(x), q(x) \wedge b(x,y) \rightarrow \bot, a(x) \rightarrow d(x) \vee q(x), d(x) \rightarrow \exists y.b(x,y)\}$ for a user query $q(x)$ and a set of physical atoms $\{a, b\}$. Let $\xrightarrow{\text{phys}}$ denote the application of a physical rule. The conditional tableau is then as follows:

T^L		T^R
$q(0)[]\{\}$		
$a(0)[]\{\}$	$\xrightarrow{\text{phys}}$	$a(0)[a(0)]\{\}$
		$d(0)[a(0)]\{0.0\}, \quad q(0)[a(0)]\{0.1\}$
$b(0,1)[b(0,1)]\{\}$	$\xleftarrow{\text{phys}}$	$b(0,1)[a(0)]\{0.0\}, \quad \bot[a(0)]\{0.0\}$
$\bot[b(0,1)]\{\}$		

The closing sets are $\mathsf{CS}^L = \{\{\neg a(0)\}, \{b(0,1)\}\}$ and $\mathsf{CS}^R = \{\{\neg b(0,1), a(0)\}\}$. Hence, since both $\psi^L = \{\{\neg a(0)\}, \{b(0,1)\}\}$ and $\psi^R = \{\{\neg b(0,1), a(0)\}\}$, $\psi = a(x) \wedge \neg\exists y.b(x,y)$ is a query plan for $q(x)$.

Applying the same approach to Examples 1 and 2 yields the results outlined in the introduction.

3   MST and Rule Rewriting

A Messy Guessing Game. Recall from the introduction that some negative atoms cannot be generated via forward chaining. We rectify this issue by guessing and generating tautologies $a(\overline{c}_a)[a(\overline{c}_a)]$ with appropriate arguments for the missing physical atoms. Let us illustrate this guessing game with Example 2.

Example 2 (Continued). Recall that $c(x) \wedge b(x,y) \rightarrow \bot$ is never executed because no conditional tableau rule contains $b(x,y)$ on the right hand side. Applying forward chaining, the left closing sets for Example 2 are $\{\neg a(0)\}$ and $\{\neg c(0)\}$, and the right closing set is $\{a(0), c(0)\}$. However, to generate the query plan '$a(x) \wedge (\neg \exists y.b(x,y)) \wedge c(x)$', we are missing the left closing set $\{b(0,1)\}$ because the system fails to generate its corresponding conditional atom $\bot[b(0,1)]$. To introduce b in the tableau, we mirror the physical rule and insert tautologies $b(c_1, c_2)[b(c_1, c_2)]$, where c_1, c_2 are Skolem constants. The task remains to *guess appropriate Skolem constants* for c_1, c_2 so that $\bot[b(0,1)]$ is generated. In this simple case, we obviously guess $c_1 = 0$ and $c_2 = 1$, where 1 is a new Skolem constant. However, in most cases, guessing appropriate arguments is a non-trivial task.

Example 2 shows how a simple guessing game can generate appropriate conditional atoms for missing plans. In the next example, we illustrate difficulties with chaining of negative atoms, which can make the guessing game messy. We also see how MST is used to solve the messy guessing game.

Example 4. Consider a database schema $\Sigma = \{q(x) \rightarrow d(x), q(x) \rightarrow a(x), d(x) \wedge a(x) \rightarrow q(x), a(x) \wedge b(x,y) \rightarrow \exists z.c(x,y,z), b_1(x,z) \wedge b_2(z,y) \rightarrow b(x,y)\}$ for a user query q and a set of physical atoms $\{a, b_1, b_2, c, d\}$.

This example contains both existential variables and chaining of negative atoms $b(x,y), b_1(x,z), b_2(z,y)$. The current system fails to produce conditional atoms for physical predicates b_1, b_2, c, resulting in missing plan '$d(x) \wedge \neg \exists y, z, t.((b_1(x,z) \wedge b_2(z,y)) \wedge \neg c(x,y,t)) \wedge a(x)$'.

To produce appropriate argument bindings in plans, we must make educated guesses for $c(x, y, t)$ depending on previous guesses for $b(x, y)$. Similarly, we guess $b(x, y)$ depending on previous guesses for $b_1(x, z)$ and $b_2(z, y)$. Hence, in the presence of chaining, the guessing game becomes messy since previously guessed arguments must be back propagated into new guesses. The key observation is that any solution that plays the messy guessing game correctly must perform back chaining on previously guessed arguments.

Since MST is a rule rewriting procedure designed to simulate back chaining using forward chaining evaluation, it precisely solves the messy guessing game for our forward chaining system. Ultimately, the goal is to guess as few conditional atoms as needed to extend the query plan space. Given the above considerations, MST-based rule rewriting provides a well-rounded solution given the positive and forward chaining nature of the system.

Magic Set Transformation for Conditional Tableau. As illustrated by Example 4, an MST-like rewriting procedure is necessary for argument back propagation. The idea is to create auxiliary magic atoms which serve as medium for back chaining needed to communicate argument bindings.

The rewriting procedure transforms conditional tableau rules R^o coupled with a set of physical predicate symbols into MST-enhanced rules $R^o \cup R^g \cup R^p$, where R^g are the rules that generate magic atoms, and R^p the rules that generate missing conditional atoms from magic atoms. The procedure consists of 3 stages: (a) a first stage that initializes the set of magic atoms P^m from rules with conjunction on their left-hand-sides; (b) a second stage that recursively computes magic atoms from right-hand-sides and uses P^s to record explored magic atoms; and (c) a final stage that computes the set of magic propagation rules R^p.

1. Initial Transformation. For each rule in R^o of the form

$$a(\overline{x}_a) \wedge b(\overline{x}_b) \rightarrow c(\overline{x}_c),$$

compute variable overlap $\overline{x}_{ab} = \overline{x}_a \cap \overline{x}_b$, and adornment string $A \in \{0,1\}^l$. Here, l is the number of arguments in $\overline{x}_b$, and $A_i = 1$ if the ith argument in $\overline{x}_b$ appears in $\overline{x}_{ab}$ ($A_i = 0$ otherwise). Create predicate $magic\_b^A(\overline{x}_{ab})$ for predicate b with respect to argument binding $\overline{x}_{ab}$. Add generation rule

$$a(\overline{x}_a) \rightarrow magic\_b^A(\overline{x}_{ab})$$

to R^g, and add new predicate $magic\_b^A$ to P^m. Note that conditional atoms $magic\_b^A(\overline{x}_{ab})[]\{\}$ always have empty conditions and branches. Repeat for rule $b(\overline{x}_b) \wedge a(\overline{x}_a) \rightarrow c(\overline{x}_c)$ where arguments are passed from b to a.

2. Chain Transformation. While P^m is non-empty, select $magic\_a^A \in P^m$, remove it from P^m, and add it to P^s. For each binary rule

$$b(\overline{x}_b) \wedge c(\overline{x}_c) \rightarrow a(\overline{x}_a)$$

with the right-hand-side matching $magic\_a^A$, compute the subset of arguments $\overline{x}_a^A$ from $\overline{x}_a$ indicated by A, and add magic generation rule

$$magic\_a^A(\overline{x}_a^A) \rightarrow magic\_b^{A'}(\overline{x}_{ab}^A)$$

to R^g, where $\overline{x}_{ab}^A = \overline{x}_a^A \cup \overline{x}_b$. Then, add one additional magic generation rule

$$magic\_a^A(\overline{x}_a^A) \wedge b(\overline{x}_b) \rightarrow magic\_c^{A'}(\overline{x}_{abc}^A)$$

to R^g, where arguments $\overline{x}_{abc}^A = (\overline{x}_a^A \cup \overline{x}_b) \cap \overline{x}_c$, and new adornment string A' computed from $\overline{x}_{abc}^A$ and $\overline{x}_c$. Repeat for the rule $c(\overline{x}_c) \wedge b(\overline{x}_b) \rightarrow a(\overline{x}_a)$ where arguments are passed from c to b. Transformations for all remaining rules are defined analogously. Add new predicates to P^m if not already in $P^m \cup P^s$.

3. Magic Propagation. For each predicate $magic\_a^A$ corresponding to some physical predicate a, add a special propagation rule (symmetric to physical rule) to R^p such that $magic\_a^A(\overline{x})$ generates conditional atom $a(\overline{x}_a)[a(\overline{x}_a)]$ on the same side of the tableau for its corresponding non-magic predicate, where the arguments indicated by A are copied from $\overline{x}$, and the rest of the arguments are fresh Skolem constants.

Soundness and Efficacy. Previous work on interpolation-based query optimizers show that conditional tableau rules are sound. Now we show that the MST-enhanced rules are sound and effectively generate appropriate negative conditions without using negative ground literals.

Theorem 1 *(Soundness of MST-enhanced Rules). Given original conditional tableau rules R^o, the MST-enhanced rewriting of R^o, denoted by R^m, is sound.*

Proof. Magic generation and magic propagation rules only insert tautologies which preserve soundness. Hence, since R^o is sound [8], R^m is sound.

In addition to soundness, the patterns seen in Example 2 and 4 generalize easily to complex input schemata containing arbitrarily many negative implications and long chains for which the missing physical atoms cannot be identified by inspection.

Theorem 2 *(Efficacy of MST-enhanced Rules). Let R^o be the set of original conditional tableau rules and R^m be its MST-enhanced rewriting. If a negative atom is logically implied on some branch of the conditional tableau, then it is generated with the correct dependencies and branches by forward chaining with respect to R^m.*

Proof. The base case is identical to Example 2. Efficacy generalizes to schemata with chaining by induction on the length of chains.

Example 2 (revisited). We now illustrate the MST-based rewriting procedure with Example 2. Performing the MST-based rewriting procedure on conditional tableau rules obtains the following MST-enhanced rules (some rules are redundant, but included for the sake of completeness):

$$R^o = \{q(x) \to a(x), q(x) \to c(x), a(x) \wedge c(x) \to q(x), c(x) \wedge b(x,y) \to \bot\};$$
$$R^g = \{c(x) \to magic\_b^{10}(x), b(x,y) \to magic\_c^1(x), a(x) \to magic\_c^1(x), c(x) \to$$
$$magic\_a^1(x), magic\_a^1(x) \to magic\_q^1(x), magic\_c^1(x) \to magic\_q^1(x),$$
$$magic\_q^1(x) \to magic\_a^1(x), magic\_q^1(x) \wedge a(x) \to magic\_c^1(x)\}; \text{ and}$$
$$R^p = \{magic\_b^{10}(x) \to \exists y.b(x,y), magic\_c^1(x) \to c(x), magic\_a^1(x) \to a(x)\}.$$

Executing the above MST-enhanced rules using forward chaining produces the following conditional tableau, where the missing atom $\perp[b(0,1)]$ is generated.

T^L		T^R
$q(0)[]\{\}$		
$a(0)[]\{\}$	$\xrightarrow{\text{phys}}$	$a(0)[a(0)]\{\}$
$c(0)[]\{\}$	$\xrightarrow{\text{phys}}$	$c(0)[c(0)]\{\}$
		$q(0)[a(0),c(0)]\{\}$
		$\perp[a(0),c(0)]\{\}$
$magic\_b^{10}(0)$		
$b(0,1)[b(0,1)]\{\}$		
$\perp[b(0,1)]\{\}$		

Hence, the MST rewriting procedure effectively generates the missing physical atoms without additional reasoning beyond rule transformation. Ultimately, this yields the sought-after plan $a(x) \wedge (\neg\exists y.b(x,y)) \wedge c(x)$. Similarly, applying the MST-based rule rewriting procedure to Example 4 yields MST-enhanced rules that generate the missing query plans even in the presence of chaining.

4   Conclusion

We present a novel rule rewriting procedure based on MST for a rule-based, forward chaining conditional tableau system, and show that our rule rewriting procedure can generate missing conditional atoms that usefully extend the space of query plans for a given query. With Examples 2 and 4 we have shown that certain patterns of negation generalize to complex schemata and queries. Moreover, if a chain of implications contains no physical predicates, one can easily preprocess the schema to inhibit magic transformation on such chains. This avoids redundant reasoning since logical predicates do not appear in closing sets or resulting plans.

Finally, observe that the usual magic guards used to prune the search space that are introduced by the standard algorithm for MST are unnecessary here. However, we plan on exploring the use of such guards for conditional tableau in future work to enable additional optimizations. It would also be constructive to compare the MST-based rewriting procedure with alternative solutions using different proof systems such as resolution.

References

1. Abiteboul, S., Hull, R., Vianu, V.: Foundations of Databases. Addison-Wesley, Boston (1995). http://webdam.inria.fr/Alice/
2. Bancilhon, F., Maier, D., Sagiv, Y., Ullman, J.D.: Magic sets and other strange ways to implement logic programs. In: ACM SIGACT-SIGMOD Symposium on Principles of Database Systems (PODS), pp. 1–15. ACM (1986)

3. Benedikt, M.: How can reasoners simplify database querying (and why haven't they done it yet)? In: ACM SIGMOD-SIGACT-SIGAI Symposium on Principles of Database Systems (PODS), pp. 1–15. ACM (2018)
4. Benedikt, M., Leblay, J., ten Cate, B., Tsamoura, E.: Generating plans from proofs: the interpolation-based approach to query reformulation. Synth. Lect. Data Manag. **8**(1), 1–205 (2016)
5. Beth, E.W.: On Padoa's method in the theory of definition. Indag. Math. **15**, 330–339 (1953)
6. Craig, W.: Three uses of the Herbrand-Gentzen theorem in relating model theory and proof theory. J. Symb. Logic **22**(3), 269–285 (1957)
7. Fitting, M.: First-Order Logic and Automated Theorem Proving. Texts in Computer Science, 2nd edn. Springer, New York (1996). https://doi.org/10.1007/978-1-4612-2360-3
8. Hudek, A., Toman, D., Weddell, G.: On enumerating query plans using analytic tableau. In: De Nivelle, H. (ed.) TABLEAUX 2015. LNCS (LNAI), vol. 9323, pp. 339–354. Springer, Cham (2015). https://doi.org/10.1007/978-3-319-24312-2_23
9. Toman, D., Weddell, G.: Fundamentals of Physical Design and Query Compilation. Synthesis Lectures on Data Management, Morgan & Claypool Publishers, San Rafael (2011)
10. Toman, D., Weddell, G.E.: An interpolation-based compiler and optimizer for relational queries (system design report). In: Eiter, T., Sands, D., Sutcliffe, G., Voronkov, A. (eds.) IWIL@LPAR 2017 Workshop and LPAR-21 Short Presentations. Kalpa Publications in Computing, vol. 1. EasyChair (2017)

Proofs, Error-Tolerance, and Rules

In the Head of the Beholder: Comparing Different Proof Representations

Christian Alrabbaa[1]([✉])[iD], Stefan Borgwardt[1][iD], Anke Hirsch[2],
Nina Knieriemen[2], Alisa Kovtunova[1][iD], Anna Milena Rothermel[2],
and Frederik Wiehr[2]

[1] Institute of Theoretical Computer Science, TU Dresden, Dresden, Germany
{christian.alrabbaa,stefan.borgwardt,alisa.kovtunova}@tu-dresden.de
[2] German Research Center for Artificial Intelligence (DFKI), Saarbrücken, Germany
{anke.hirsch,nina.knieriemen,anna_milena.rothermel,frederik.wiehr}@dfki.de

Abstract. Ontologies provide the logical underpinning for the Semantic Web, but their consequences can sometimes be surprising and must be explained to users. A promising kind of explanations are proofs generated via automated reasoning. We report about a series of studies with the purpose of exploring how to explain such formal logical proofs to humans. We compare different representations, such as tree- vs. text-based visualizations, but also vary other parameters such as length, interactivity, and the shape of formulas. We did not find evidence to support our main hypothesis that different user groups can understand different proof representations better. Nevertheless, when participants directly compared proof representations, their subjective rankings showed some tendencies such as that most people prefer short tree-shaped proofs. However, this did not impact the user's understanding of the proofs as measured by an objective performance measure.

1 Introduction

Explanations of automated decisions are currently an important topic of research. However, apart from the discussion about how explainable different AI methods are, the main task of explanations is *understanding*, i.e. that the information transmitted is actually received by the human user [32]. Even methods that are "explainable by design", such as logic-based ones, are not necessarily understandable by design when presenting them to laypersons.

In the area of Description Logics (DLs) [10], research on explanations first focused on proofs for explaining logical consequences [13,30], but it was quickly realized that often it is enough to point out a minimal set of responsible axioms from the ontology, i.e. so-called *justifications* [11,21,37]. While justifications are already very helpful for designing or debugging an ontology, depending on the complexity of the inference and the expertise of the user, more detailed proofs are needed to fully understand why the consequence follows from the axioms. Therefore, researchers have thought about providing (partial) proofs [23,26] and developed more user-friendly presentation formats, e.g. using natural language instead of logical formulas [33–35].

© The Author(s), under exclusive license to Springer Nature Switzerland AG 2022
G. Governatori and A.-Y. Turhan (Eds.): RuleML+RR 2022, LNCS 13752, pp. 211–226, 2022.
https://doi.org/10.1007/978-3-031-21541-4_14

Following a line of research on the understandability of description logic inferences and proofs [3–5,18,23,26,33,34], in this paper we compare the usefulness of different proof representations. In an effort to understand which approaches are most promising for improving explainability, we studied which representations of DL proofs are preferred by users (with and without prior experience in logic) and which of them actually lead to an increased performance when doing logic-related tasks. In this paper, we summarise the lessons learned after conducting four experiments. All studies use proofs in a traditional tree shape, e.g. based on consequence-based reasoning procedures [27,39], and linearized translations of these proofs into text, e.g. as done by various verbalization techniques [8,33,35]. These conditions are representative of the state-of-the-art in DL explanations. We hand-crafted all proofs for the studies, but tried to stay as close as possible to the actual output of these systems. The main goal throughout these studies was to find differences in user preferences between different user groups. Our *main hypothesis* was that users with a different level of experience with logic would work better with different proof representations, e.g. text- vs. tree-based ones. While this was not confirmed, we gained some insights about subjective preferences of proof presentations, e.g. that short, tree-shaped proofs are preferred in general.

Related Work. Several approaches for converting description logic axioms and proofs into textual representations have been developed and evaluated [1,8,29,34,35]. For example, generation of verbalized explanations for non-trivial derivations in a real world domain was tested on computer scientists in [35]. The authors distinguish short and long textual explanations, but the participants' opinions on conciseness turned out to be mixed and not too strong. In [29], it has been confirmed that statements in a controlled natural language are understood significantly better than the *Manchester OWL Syntax*, where DL axioms are expressed by sentences with words like "SubTypeOf", "DisjointWith", "HasDomain", etc. Moreover, the experiment [1] has shown that the Manchester syntax is not more effective than the formal DL syntax. Differently from previous studies [33–35], in most of our experiments we directly compared textual and tree proof formats. In [28], the authors look into various hybrid proof representations and evaluate them in terms of understanding. In contrast to our work, they focus on *defeasible logics*, they do not consider pure textual representations, and the user evaluation involved postgraduate students. The work described in [17] deals with explaining logical inconsistencies in a healthcare domain using natural language, but it does not consider graphical proof representations.

More details and printable versions of the surveys are available online.[1] Studies I–III have previously been presented in workshop papers [7,14].

2   Background

The proofs we use are loosely based on the DL $\mathcal{ALCQ}$ [10], but deep knowledge of this logic is not required here. We denote DL statements (called *axioms*) by α

---

[1] gitlab.perspicuous-computing.science/a.kovtunova/user-study-collection.

$$\frac{A \sqsubseteq \exists r.\top \qquad A \sqsubseteq \forall r.(B \sqcap C)}{\dfrac{A \sqsubseteq \exists r.(B \sqcap C)}{A \sqsubseteq \bot}} \qquad C \sqcap B \sqsubseteq \bot$$

$$\mathcal{O} = \{\, A \sqsubseteq \exists r.\top,$$
$$C \sqcap B \sqsubseteq \bot,$$
$$A \sqsubseteq \forall r.(B \sqcap C) \,\}$$

Fig. 1. A proof for the unsatisfiability of A w.r.t. $\mathcal{O}$, i.e. that $\mathcal{O} \models A \sqsubseteq \bot$.

Table 1. Different proof representations for our experiments.

Study	Text proofs	Length		Tree proofs		Domain		
		Long	Short	DL syntax	Arrows	Real	Nonsense	Letters
I	*	*	*	*		*		
II			*		*		*	
III	*		*		*		*	
IV	*		*		*			*

and *ontologies*, which are finite sets of axioms, by $\mathcal{O}$. Let $\mathcal{O}$ be an ontology and α be a consequence of $\mathcal{O}$ (written $\mathcal{O} \models \alpha$). The first step towards understanding why this consequence holds is to compute *justifications* [11,21,37], i.e. minimal subsets $\mathcal{J} \subseteq \mathcal{O}$ such that $\mathcal{J} \models \alpha$, which already point out the axioms from $\mathcal{O}$ that are responsible for α. However, actually understanding why α follows may require a more detailed proof. Informally, a *proof* is a tree consisting of inference steps $\frac{\alpha_1 \ldots \alpha_n}{\alpha}$, where each step is sound, i.e. $\{\alpha_1, \ldots \alpha_n\} \models \alpha$ holds (see Fig. 1). Often, such a proof is built from the *inference rules* of an appropriate calculus [9,39]. However, there also exist approaches to generate DL proofs that start with a justification, and extend it with intermediate axioms (*lemmas*) using heuristics [21,22], concept interpolation [36], or forgetting [3].

It is important that proofs are neither too detailed nor too short. In fact, a justification can itself be seen as a one-step proof of a consequence α, but if each element of the justifications seems reasonable to the user, then it can be hard to track down the precise interaction between these axioms that causes the problem. Axioms may not always behave as the user expects, e.g. "every A has only rs that are Bs" $(A \sqsubseteq \forall r.B)$ does not imply that "every A has an r that is a B" $(A \sqsubseteq \exists r.B)$. On the other hand, too many small proof steps can also be detrimental for understanding, because they are distracting. For example, it may happen that a reasoner includes the trivial step $\frac{C \sqcap B \sqsubseteq \bot}{B \sqcap C \sqsubseteq \bot}$ in Fig. 1 to make the two conjunctions match syntactically, which may not be necessary for understanding the essence of the proof. Apart from proof length, in our experiments we also use other ways of varying the proof representations (see Table 1). For example, in Studies II–IV we use a more flexible visualization of trees in which arrows are used instead of horizontal lines (see the supplementary PDF file in the repository (see footnote 1)).

A textual representation of a proof is necessarily a *linearization*, where the inference steps are explained in a sequence, for example in a top-down left-right order. A text corresponding to the tree proof in Fig. 1 could be the following:

Table 2. Overview of the experiments

Study	1-on-1 interview	Online[a] survey	# Participants			Avg. time (min)	Mean age (SD)	Pay
			Male	Female	Non-binary			
I	*		12	4	–	90	23.0 (1.71)	20 €
II		*	56	45	–	29	24.5 (6.8)	£ 5.20
III		*	102	71	–	51	24.8 (8.2)	£ 8.75
IV		*	41	66	1	44	25.9 (6.9)	£ 6.25

[a]The participants were recruited using Prolific (https://www.prolific.co/). No restrictions on participant background were imposed.

> Since every A has an r and every A has only rs that are Bs and Cs, every A has an r which is a B and a C. Since there is no object which is a C and a B at the same time, there is no object of type A.

Other aspects in which a text differs from a proof tree are that conjunctions (e.g. "since", "and") are used to illustrate proof steps and that statements may be repeated if they are reused later.

We use the formal DL syntax for tree proofs only in the first experiment over axioms expressing medical knowledge, e.g. the statement "there is no object which is both a compound and an atom at the same time" is presented as the expression $\mathsf{Atom} \sqcap \mathsf{Compound} \sqsubseteq \bot$. In the later experiments, we do not use real domains to avoid interference from prior knowledge about the domain. We also adopt the approach from [29,35] and avoid the formal syntax in order to include more participants. For example, in Study IV, $\mathsf{A} \sqsubseteq \exists \mathsf{r}.\top$ would be shown as "Every A has an r." In the remaining two experiments, we use nonsense names that vaguely look and sound English to enable more natural-sounding sentences, e.g. "Every woal is munted only with luxis that are kakes" instead of "Every A has only rs that are Bs and Cs" ($\mathsf{A} \sqsubseteq \forall \mathsf{r}.(\mathsf{B} \sqcap \mathsf{C})$); see also Table 1.

General Study Information. In Table 2 we summarize the demographic data for the experiments. All study participants were at least 18 years old. For the online surveys, we had to filter out participant answers of low quality. For this purpose, attention check questions, e.g. "In this statement, please choose "No"." were introduced. To compute all quantitative analyses, IBM SPSS Statistics (Version 26) for Windows [24] and the Macro PROCESS [20] was used. For all hypotheses, we used a p-value threshold of 0.05.

3   Study I – Are Short Proofs Preferred?

We started our investigation of participants' understanding of different proof representations by interviewing participants. Here, we used both textual proofs and classical tree proofs using DL syntax. To find out how detailed proofs should be, we used shortened versions for each of tree and text representations, in which some (easy) reasoning steps were omitted or merged. During the interviews, we observed whether participants' understanding differs between these four condition combinations. Moreover, we wanted to investigate if experience in logic influences the performance and preferences.

Conditions and Design. We used two different conditions with two levels each. One condition was the representational form of the proof, which was either text or tree. The other condition was the length of the proof, which was either short or long. Thus, there were the four following condition combinations: *Long Text*, *Short Text*, *Long Tree*, and *Short Tree*. We used a 2 × 2 within-subjects design, which means that each participant saw all four representations on four different proofs following a Latin square design (see footnote 1). The independent variable was the experience, while the dependent variable was the rating of the proofs.

Material. Proofs from the medical domain were chosen such that they represent unintuitive consequences, e.g. the unsatisfiability of a concept name, or that an amputation of a finger is also an amputation of the whole hand [12]. All four examples were chosen from the literature on DL explanations [12,25,31,38]. For each of them, four different proof representations were manually created, not automatically generated, to make them comparable in difficulty.

To make sure the participants really understood the proofs, a logic expert reviewed the video of each participant after each session. We used the think-aloud technique, so the expert was able to follow the participant's thoughts and rated the video based on the participant's understanding on a scale from 1 (no understanding) to 3 (complete understanding).

Further Information. To assess participants' experience, we asked them how they would rate their experience with propositional-, description-, and first-order logic on a scale from 1 (no knowledge) to 5 (expert). We evaluated how they rated the difficulty of each proof on a scale from 1 (very easy) to 5 (very difficult). To compare the proof representations, at the end of the experiment we asked the participants to rank the proofs based on their comprehensibility (first rank = very easy, fourth rank = very difficult). It was possible to give several proofs the same rank.

Participants (see Table 2). Our participants were recruited from undergraduate and graduate university students *with basic knowledge of logic*, which was required to understand the proofs. Screening criteria were familiarity with first-order logic (e.g. through a lecture), a stable Internet connection and the permission to record their handwriting and voice during the experiment. One participant was excluded since they did not understand the proofs but rated them as easy. The mean of the participant's experience with propositional logic was $M = 3.25$ ($SD = 1.0$), on a scale of 1 to 5. Furthermore, 37.5% of the participants seldomly worked with propositional logic, while 31.3% worked with it often.

Hypotheses. We stated three hypotheses concerning the participants' self-rating of the difficulty of the proofs and their self-rated experience with logic.

Hypothesis 1: It is easier to understand a short, concise explanation than a longer version (in the same representation format).

Hypothesis 2: Users with less experience in logic can understand the longer text better than a short tree proof. This will be shown by a lower difficulty rating of the long textual proof.

Hypothesis 3: Users with more experience in logic can understand a long tree proof better than a long text. This will be shown by a lower difficulty rating of the long tree proof.

Results. For *Hypothesis 1*, a multiple linear regression with contrast coding (K1, K2, K3) was conducted. K1 contrasted the textual representation against the tree. K2 contrasted the short vs. long proofs and K3 the interaction between the two general conditions. The three contrasts explained 14.2% of variance in the rating after each proof, $R^2 = .14$, $F(3, 60) = 3.30$, $p < .05$. Only K2 was found to be a significant predictor in the linear regression, $\beta = -.29$, $t(60) = -2.42$, $p < .05$. This means that the participants rated the shorter proofs as being easier than the longer ones, which was independent of the presentation format. Thus, *Hypothesis 1* could be supported by our data.

For *Hypotheses 2* and *3*, we computed moderator analyses with the two condition combinations as a predictor, the experience as a moderator variable and the rating after each proof as the criterion. However, neither *Hypothesis 2* nor *3* was supported by our data. Experience with logic did not make a difference on the understanding of the different proof representations.

Additionally to the three hypotheses, we used Friedman's test for comparing the comprehensibility ranking of the proof representations at the end of the experiment (first rank = very easy, fourth rank = very difficult). It revealed a significant difference in the ranking of the condition combinations, $\chi^2(3) = 15.29$, $p < .01$ with a moderate effect size (Kendall's $W = .32$). For the post-hoc pairwise comparisons, Bonferroni correction was used, which resulted in a p-threshold of 0.008, resulting in only two significant comparisons. The participants' ranking of condition combinations is shown in Fig. 2. The combination *Short Text* was preferred over *Long Text*, $Z = 1.53$, $p < .008$. The median ranking for *Short Text* and *Long Text* was 2 and 3.5, respectively. Additionally, *Short Tree* was preferred over *Long Text*, $Z = 1.50$, $p < .008$. *Short Tree* had the lowest median ranking with 1.5. Both comparisons showed moderate effect sizes with $r = 0.38$. The median ranking for *Long Tree* was 2.

4   Study II – Connecting Cognitive Abilities and Proof Understanding

Our first experiment revealed some weaknesses in our design choices. First, the direct interviews with each person meant that we were only able to include few participants. Therefore, in the following we designed our experiments using automated surveys. Second, the choice of proofs using real domains was not ideal, as sometimes participants immediately spotted axioms that were counterintuitive, without looking at the proof. This is why we started to use nonsense domains that could not interfere with participants' prior knowledge. Last but

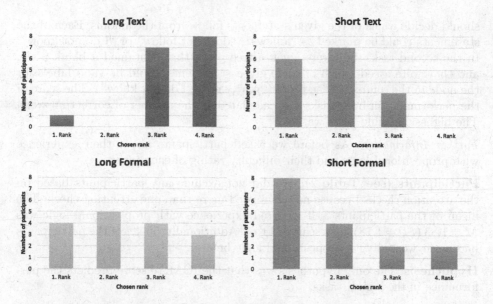

Fig. 2. The participants' ranking of conditions with 1 = very easy and 4 = very difficult

not least, the self-rating of experience in logic may be influenced by participants' confidence or a fear of negative evaluation. Thus, we wanted to replace the subjective experience rating by a more objective measure of an individual's ability to understand logical proofs. To evaluate the suitability of standardized tests for our purposes, we conducted the following experiment comparing the International Cognitive Ability Resource (ICAR16[2]) [16] questionnaire against the performance on tasks related to DL proofs.

Design. We used LimeSurvey[3] for hosting our online survey. Since we did not pre-screen our participants for experience with logic, we included an introduction explaining the structure of proof trees. In order to exclude the effect of tiredness, the order of the ICAR16 questions and the proof tasks was randomized.

Material. To assess the participants' cognitive abilities, the abbreviated form of ICAR16 was applied. It consists of 16 questions equally distributed over four types: matrix reasoning, letter and number series, verbal reasoning, and 3-dimensional rotation. In the end, a mean score was calculated by coding correct answers with 1 and incorrect answers with 0. Thus, the maximum score was 1, while the minimal score was 0. The internal consistency of ICAR16 is $\alpha = .81$ [16].

To test the performance with logical reasoning, participants had to solve two tasks. The first described a set of axioms (in natural language) and they

---

[2] https://icar-project.com/.
[3] https://www.limesurvey.org/.

should decide which of the given statements follow from the axioms. Each of the statements could be marked as "follows", "does not follow" or "I do not know". In the second task, they were given a tree proof that contained a blank node, and they were asked which of some given statements would be valid labels for the node in the context of the proof ("yes", "no", "I do not know"). The score of the performance in both tasks was calculated as the number of correct answers. The highest possible score was 24.

Further Information. As before we asked participants about their experience with propositional logic and their difficulty rating of each task.

Participants (see Table 2). We did not exclude any participants based on the attention checks because no one missed more than one attention check. The mean of the participants' self-reported experience with propositional logic was $M = 1.83$ ($SD = 1.18$), on a scale of 1 to 5. Additionally, 56.4% of the participants had never worked with propositional logic before.

Hypothesis. The only hypothesis was that the ICAR16 score predicts the performance in the logical tasks.

Descriptive Results. The mean of the ICAR16 scores was $M = 0.55$ ($SD = 0.24$) with the participants' performance being spread in a normal distribution. The maximal achieved score was 1, the minimum was 0. The mean of the score for both logical reasoning tasks was $M = 15.99$ ($SD = 3.3$), with the maximum score being 23 and the minimum 6. The performance in these tasks was also normally distributed across the participants.

Regression Analysis. A multiple regression analysis was carried out using the performance in the logical reasoning tasks as the dependent and the ICAR16 performance as the independent variable. The ICAR16 score significantly predicted the performance in the logical tasks ($F(1, 99) = 43.15$, $p < .001$). The ICAR16 explained 30% of the variation in the score of the logical tasks ($R^2 = .3$, $p < .001$), which can be interpreted as large effect size/high explained variance [15].

5   Study III – Logical Abilities and Proof Representation Preferences

We now return to our main research question of which proof representation is more preferred and results in a better performance in certain groups of participants. For this experiment we investigated interactive, static, tree and textual proof formats. Given that ICAR16 scores are highly correlated with performance on logical reasoning tasks, we used it in our next experiment to distinguish participants by their logical ability level. The goal was to find a difference in the (subjective) preferences and (objective) performance on each proof representation, depending on the user's level of logical reasoning ability.

Conditions and Design. We used two different conditions with two levels each. One condition was the proof representation; either tree-shaped or textual.

The other condition was the interactivity of the proof representation; either static or interactive. Thus, there were the four following condition combinations: (**ir**) interactive tree, (**sr**) static tree, (**ix**) interactive text, and (**sx**) static text. We again used a 2×2 within-subjects design with a Latin square design. The independent variable in the main study is the ICAR16 score. Objective performance (the number of correct answers) and subjective rating of proofs as well as proof rankings are dependent variables.

The survey was again implemented using LimeSurvey. As in the first experiment, the order of the ICAR16 and the proof question groups was randomized. Moreover, each participant was randomly assigned to one of the four groups according to the Latin square. Before the proof tasks, there was a short explanation and a small training example for both interactive formats (**ir**, **ix**).

Material. We again used ICAR16 to assess the participants' cognitive abilities.

We developed four artificial proofs of roughly the same difficulty level. The statements of each proof were given in textual form (also for (**ir**, **sr**)) using nonsense words. The (**ir**) version started with only the final conclusion visible, and participants could interact with each node to reveal or hide its predecessors in the tree. The (**ix**) worked in a different way. At the beginning, participants saw only the first sentence, i.e. the first assumption. The could then reveal the next sentences step-by-step, and also highlight the premises that were used to obtain a selected statement. Moreover, both interactive representations, (**ir**,**ix**), could be freely zoomed and panned. The interactive proofs were provided by a prototypical web application[4] for explaining DL entailments [2,6,19]. For this study, it was extended by a (linear) textual representation of proofs. The modes of interaction were kept relatively basic to avoid overwhelming participants who had little experience with logic and proofs.

For each proof, there were three questions. Each question had 6 answer options (plus "none of these" and "I don't know"). Questions were of the form "Which of the following would be a correct replacement for the deduction "XYZ" in the proof?" or "Which parts of the following summary/reformulation of the proof are incorrect?" In the end, a score was calculated based on the number of correct answers. Thus, the highest possible score was 12.

Further Information. We again asked participants about the experience with propositional logic and the difficulty rating of proofs, as well as a ranking of all four conditions they had seen according to their relative comprehensibility.

Participants (see Table 2). The mean of the participants' experience with propositional logic was $M = 1.76$ ($SD = 1$) on a scale between 1 and 5. Furthermore, 60.7% of the participants indicated that they had never worked with propositional logic. Due to technical errors, the proofs were not displayed for 3 participants, which were excluded. Four attention checks were implemented in the study. 13 participants with more than 2 incorrectly answered attention checks were excluded from the analysis.

---

[4] https://imld.de/evonne.

Hypotheses. We stated two hypotheses concerning the preferences and performance differences between the proof representations.

Hypothesis 1: It is easier to understand interactive proofs than static proofs. This will be shown by an increase in performance and by a higher comprehensibility rating for the interactive conditions.

Hypothesis 2: The relative level of comprehensibility of a tree-shaped vs. textual proof depends on the cognitive abilities. This will be shown by a difference in performance and difficulty rating between the condition combinations and in the final comprehensibility ranking, in dependence of the ICAR16 scores.

Results. After the assumptions were considered as tenable, a regression analysis was carried out, to confirm the results of Study II. Again, the predictive effect of the ICAR16 on the performance in the proofs was significant, $F(1, 171) = 24.8$, $p < .001$. With an $R^2 = .13$ (corrected $R^2 = .12$), the model shows a moderate explained variance (Cohen, 1988).

A median split ($mdn = .44$) was carried out to divide the participants into those who achieved high scores in the ICAR16 and thus presumably also have higher cognitive abilities and those who scored lower.

For ICAR16 the mean was $M = 0.46$, while it was $M = 2.36$ for the proof performance. The group containing those participants who scored low in the ICAR16 achieved $M = 1.9$ across all proofs. In contrast, the group of participants with high ICAR16 scores showed an overall proof performance of $M = 2.87$.

Performance and Comprehensibility Ratings. To compare the proof performance and the subjective comprehensibility ratings after each proof, we ran a multivariate analysis of variance (MANOVA). All the assumptions were considered as tenable. We found no significant overall difference between the conditions across the two ICAR groups, Pillai's Trace $= .01$, $F(6, 1376) = 1.41$, $p = .206$. Also when looking at the groups separately, we could not find any significant differences between the representations, neither in the low-ICAR group (Pillai's Trace $= .03$, $F(6, 712) = 1.90$, $p = .078$) nor in the group with high scores (Pillai's Trace $= .01$, $F(6, 656) = .53$, $p = .788$). Thus, we could not detect differences in the comprehensibility ratings as well as the performance between the various representations in each cognitive ability group and across the two groups.

Ranking. To evaluate the ranking of the four representations (1 = most comprehensible, 4 = least comprehensible), we ran a Friedman's test revealing a significant difference across both ICAR groups, $\chi^2(3) = 17.16$, $p = .001$, $n = 173$ (see Fig. 3, light bars). Post-hoc pairwise comparisons were Bonferroni-corrected and showed three significant comparisons. The (**ir**) was significantly more often ranked higher than the (**ix**) ($z = .40$, $p = .024$, Cohen's effect size $r = .03$) and also higher than static text ($z = -.50$, $p = .002$, Cohen's effect size $r = .04$). The (**sr**) representation was also ranked significantly higher than (**sx**), $z = .39$, $p = .032$, Cohen's effect size $r = .03$ (see Fig. 3).

A Friedman's test in the group with high ICAR performance showed a significant difference in the ranking of representations, $\chi^2(3) = 12.73$, $p = .005$,

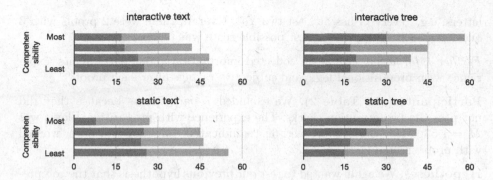

Fig. 3. Rankings of all 173 participants (light bars) and of the 83 participants with high ICAR scores (dark bars) for each condition combination.

$n = 83$ (see Fig. 3, dark bars). Bonferroni-corrected post-hoc pairwise comparisons revealed two significant comparisons. There is a significant difference between (**sr**) and (**sx**) ($z = .59$, $p = .019$, Cohen's effect size $r = .06$) with (**sr**) being ranked higher than (**sx**). The (**ir**) was also preferred before (**sx**), ($z = -.54$, $p = .041$, Cohen's effect size $r = .06$).

The low-ICAR-performers showed no significant difference in the ranking of representations, $\chi^2(3) = 6.70$, $p = .082$, $n = 90$.

6   Study IV – Final Experiment

The main shortcoming of the previous experiment was the difficulty of the proof tasks, which could be seen in the mean score of 2.36 out of 12. Therefore, we designed another experiment where the difficulty of the proof tasks was adjusted. We also did not include the interactive conditions to be able to focus more on the difference between the text vs. tree proofs. Furthermore, the number of proof tasks was reduced and the nonsense words were replaced by letters, to reduce the cognitive overload that some participants had reported in the previous study.

Conditions and Design. We only considered one condition with two levels, namely textual and tree-shaped proof representation. We also used a between-subjects design, which means that each participant saw either only text proofs or only tree proofs. Dependent variables were proof performance and subjective comprehensibility rating. The independent variable was the ICAR16 score.

We conducted the experiment via LimeSurvey. As before, the order of ICAR16 and the proof tasks was randomized. Each participant was randomly assigned to one of the two groups. We again included a short training example at the beginning of the proof tasks.

Material. We again used ICAR16 to assess the participants' cognitive abilities (see page 7). For the proof tasks, we used simplified versions of the proofs from the previous study, where additionally the nonsense words were replaced by letters, e.g. "every G has at least two Ys". Overall, there were 2 proofs with 3 questions each. Thus, the highest possible score was 6.

Further Information. We again collected information about participants' experience with propositional logic and subjective ratings after each proof.

Participants (see Table 2). We excluded 7 participants because they did not pass the two attention checks. The experience with propositional logic was $M = 1.53$ ($SD = 0.97$). Moreover, 69.4% indicated that they had never worked with propositional logic before.

Hypotheses. We again wanted to test our previous hypothesis that the comprehensibility of a tree-shaped vs. textual proof depends on the cognitive abilities. This would be shown by a difference in performance and difficulty rating between the conditions, in dependence of the ICAR16 scores.

Results. The mean of ICAR16 was $M = 0.36$ ($SD = 0.20$) while it was $M = 2.30$ ($SD = 1.25$) for the proof performance. We carried out a regression analysis to confirm the results of the previous two studies. These results should indicate that ICAR16 scores predict proof performance. This is a precondition for any following analyses, because we cannot split the sample based on the ICAR16 values if they are not sufficiently related to the proof values. The predictive effect of the ICAR16 on the proof performance was not significant, $F(1, 106) = 2.26$, $p = .135$, which is why we did not perform any further tests.

7   General Discussion

Our main hypotheses that experience with logic or logical ability influences the subjective rating or objective performance on different proof representations could not be confirmed (see Hypotheses 2 and 3 in Study I, Hypothesis 2 in Study III and the only hypothesis in Study IV). This may be partially due to the shortcomings of each of the experiments, which we discuss in more detail below. In addition, we could not find any advantage of specific representations when it comes to the performance on proof-related tasks, even when ignoring the ICAR16 scores (see Studies III and IV).

Nevertheless, our first experiment clearly showed a preference for shorter proofs based on the subjective difficulty ratings and relative rankings of the conditions by the participants. This shows that it is worthwhile to investigate techniques for automatically shortening proofs to remove easy or redundant steps that only distract the users. As a side result, in the second experiment we demonstrated that cognitive abilities as measured by the standardized ICAR16 questionnaire can be used as a predictor for the performance on logical reasoning tasks. The final ranking in third experiment showed a further subjective preference for the conditions with tree-shaped proofs over their textual counterparts, but this did not seem to impact the objective performance measure nor the subjective ratings the participants gave after each proof. These preferences were largely driven by the group with higher ICAR16 performance (cf. Fig. 3).

7.1 Limitations

A general shortcoming of our main hypothesis was perhaps that it was too specific. If there are any effects of proof representation between user groups, they were maybe too small to detect in our experiments. After the first study, we recruited more participants through the online platform Prolific, but this also came with a loss of quality in the responses that we could not completely control with the attention checks. Since everyone was paid the same amount of money, the goal of many participants was to complete the study as fast as possible. Several participants even finished the larger studies (including both ICAR16 and proof tasks) with successful attention checks in under 15 min, which hints at a loss of quality in the responses. A solution to this could be using open instead of multiple-choice questions. However, such answers must be evaluated manually by an expert according to a-priori fixed criteria.

Another limitation of the first study was also that it did not include an objective measure of performance; participants were simply asked to describe their process of understanding the proofs which was later rated by an expert. We therefore included objective proof tasks in Study III, which however were too hard for most of the participants. According to the aims of our study, we did not pre-select participants according to their experience with logic or field of studies. 55.5% of the participants had no experience with propositional logic and 60.7% had never worked with it. For many participants, even the ones with higher ICAR scores, the proof tasks were very challenging, resulting in a mean score of $M = 2.36$ out of a total of 12. 15 people commented about the high difficulty level in the end, and only 3 said the proofs were easy to understand. This resulted in many data points being clustered on the lower end of the scale and differences being more difficult to detect.

In general, a between-subjects design is better suited to show differences between proof representations because there is no interference between the conditions, but this requires even more participants. In the last study, we attempted to do this and also adjusted the difficulty of the proofs. Unfortunately, this study failed to exhibit even the strong connection between ICAR16 scores and proof performance that had been shown by the previous two studies. Possible reasons for this are that there were too few data points for the proof tasks (the maximal score was 6 since we did not want to overload the participants) and that the participants in general seemed to differ from previous studies. It seemed that participants showed higher ICAR16 scores in the second ($M = 0.55$, $SD = 0.24$) and third ($M = 0.46$, $SD = 0.24$) than in the fourth study ($M = 0.36$, $SD = 0.20$), and the self-reported experience with logic followed a similar pattern. This could be a reason why the ICAR16 scores did not predict the proof performance in Study IV.

7.2 Future Work

Although several of the experiments indicate a subjective preference of tree proofs over texts, we would like to study more formally whether this can also influence performance (independent of the membership to any particular user group such as logic experts or people with high cognitive abilities). In that context, it could also make a difference whether the individual statements in tree proofs are shown as natural language sentences or using logical syntax (as in our first study). Another question with a larger expected effect is whether showing proofs actually makes a difference when compared to only showing justifications, i.e. the premises/leafs of the tree proofs without intermediate inference steps.

Moreover, it would be promising to look at an ontology that is actively used in practice and to study domain experts performing specific relevant explanation tasks for this ontology. Ultimately, our studies are just a first step towards developing a user-centered interactive explanation tool for DL ontologies. Such a tool should also take into account individual differences, such as user preferences or the user's existing knowledge, e.g. in the form of a *background ontology* that the user is assumed to understand intuitively without needing an explanation.

Acknowledgements. This work was supported by the DFG grant 389792660 as part of TRR 248 – CPEC (https://perspicuous-computing.science), and QuantLA, GRK 1763 (https://lat.inf.tu-dresden.de/quantla).

References

1. Alharbi, E., Howse, J., Stapleton, G., Hamie, A., Touloumis, A.: The efficacy of OWL and DL on user understanding of axioms and their entailments. In: ISWC (2017). https://doi.org/10.1007/978-3-319-68288-4_2
2. Alrabbaa, C., Baader, F., Borgwardt, S., Dachselt, R., Koopmann, P., Méndez, J.: Evonne: interactive proof visualization for description logics (system description). In: IJCAR (2022). https://doi.org/10.1007/978-3-031-10769-6_16
3. Alrabbaa, C., Baader, F., Borgwardt, S., Koopmann, P., Kovtunova, A.: Finding small proofs for description logic entailments: theory and practice. In: LPAR-23 (2020). https://doi.org/10.29007/nhpp
4. Alrabbaa, C., Baader, F., Borgwardt, S., Koopmann, P., Kovtunova, A.: On the complexity of finding good proofs for description logic entailments. In: DL Workshop (2020). http://ceur-ws.org/Vol-2663/paper-1.pdf
5. Alrabbaa, C., Baader, F., Borgwardt, S., Koopmann, P., Kovtunova, A.: Finding good proofs for description logic entailments using recursive quality measures. In: CADE (2021). https://doi.org/10.1007/978-3-030-79876-5_17
6. Alrabbaa, C., Baader, F., Dachselt, R., Flemisch, T., Koopmann, P.: Visualising proofs and the modular structure of ontologies to support ontology repair. In: DL Workshop (2020). http://ceur-ws.org/Vol-2663/paper-2.pdf
7. Alrabbaa, C., Borgwardt, S., Knieriemen, N., Kovtunova, A., Rothermel, A.M., Wiehr, F.: In the hand of the beholder: comparing interactive proof visualizations. In: DL Workshop (2021). http://ceur-ws.org/Vol-2954/paper-2.pdf
8. Androutsopoulos, I., Lampouras, G., Galanis, D.: Generating natural language descriptions from OWL ontologies: the NaturalOWL system. JAIR **48**, 671–715 (2013). https://doi.org/10.1613/jair.4017
9. Baader, F., Brandt, S., Lutz, C.: Pushing the $\mathcal{EL}$ envelope. In: IJCAI (2005). http://ijcai.org/Proceedings/09/Papers/053.pdf

10. Baader, F., Horrocks, I., Lutz, C., Sattler, U.: An Introduction to Description Logic. Cambridge University Press, Cambridge (2017). https://doi.org/10.1017/9781139025355

11. Baader, F., Peñaloza, R., Suntisrivaraporn, B.: Pinpointing in the description logic $\mathcal{EL}^+$. In: KI (2007). https://doi.org/10.1007/978-3-540-74565-5_7

12. Baader, F., Suntisrivaraporn, B.: Debugging SNOMED CT using axiom pinpointing in the description logic $\mathcal{EL}^+$. In: KR-MED (2008). http://ceur-ws.org/Vol-410/Paper01.pdf

13. Borgida, A., Franconi, E., Horrocks, I.: Explaining $\mathcal{ALC}$ subsumption. In: ECAI (2000). http://www.frontiersinai.com/ecai/ecai2000/pdf/p0209.pdf

14. Borgwardt, S., Hirsch, A., Kovtunova, A., Wiehr, F.: In the eye of the beholder: which proofs are best? In: DL Workshop (2020). http://ceur-ws.org/Vol-2663/paper-6.pdf

15. Cohen, J.: Statistical Power Analysis for the Behavioral Sciences. Lawrence Erlbaum Associates (1988). https://doi.org/10.4324/9780203771587

16. Condon, D.M., Revelle, W.: The international cognitive ability resource: development and initial validation of a public-domain measure. Intelligence **43**, 52–64 (2014). https://doi.org/10.1016/j.intell.2014.01.004

17. Donadello, I., Dragoni, M., Eccher, C.: Explaining reasoning algorithms with persuasiveness: a case study for a behavioural change system. In: ACM Symposium on Applied Computing (2020). https://doi.org/10.1145/3341105.3373910

18. Engström, F., Nizamani, A.R., Strannegård, C.: Generating comprehensible explanations in description logic. In: DL Workshop (2014). http://ceur-ws.org/Vol-1193/paper_17.pdf

19. Flemisch, T., Langner, R., Alrabbaa, C., Dachselt, R.: Towards designing a tool for understanding proofs in ontologies through combined node-link diagrams. In: VOILA Workshop (2020). http://ceur-ws.org/Vol-2778/paper3.pdf

20. Hayes, A.F.: Introduction to Mediation, Moderation, and Conditional Process Analysis: A Regression-Based Approach. Guilford Publications, New York (2017). https://doi.org/10.1111/jedm.12050

21. Horridge, M.: Justification based explanation in ontologies. Ph.D. thesis, University of Manchester, UK (2011). https://www.research.manchester.ac.uk/portal/files/54511395/FULL_TEXT.PDF

22. Horridge, M., Bail, S., Parsia, B., Sattler, U.: Toward cognitive support for OWL justifications. Knowl.-Based Syst. **53**, 66–79 (2013). https://doi.org/10.1016/j.knosys.2013.08.021

23. Horridge, M., Parsia, B., Sattler, U.: Justification oriented proofs in OWL. In: ISWC (2010). https://doi.org/10.1007/978-3-642-17746-0_23

24. IBM: SPSS Statistics. https://www.ibm.com/products/spss-statistics

25. Kalyanpur, A.: Debugging and repair of OWL ontologies. Ph.D. thesis, University of Maryland, College Park, USA (2006). http://hdl.handle.net/1903/3820

26. Kazakov, Y., Klinov, P., Stupnikov, A.: Towards reusable explanation services in Protege. In: DL Workshop (2017). http://www.ceur-ws.org/Vol-1879/paper31.pdf

27. Kazakov, Y., Krötzsch, M., Simančík, F.: The incredible ELK. J. Autom. Reason. **53**(1), 1–61 (2013). https://doi.org/10.1007/s10817-013-9296-3

28. Kontopoulos, E., Bassiliades, N., Antoniou, G.: Visualizing semantic web proofs of defeasible logic in the DR-DEVICE system. Knowl. Based Syst. (2011). https://doi.org/10.1016/j.knosys.2010.12.001

29. Kuhn, T.: The understandability of OWL statements in controlled English. Semant. Web **4**, 101–115 (2013). https://doi.org/10.3233/SW-2012-0063

30. McGuinness, D.L.: Explaining reasoning in description logics. Ph.D. thesis, Rutgers University, NJ, USA (1996). https://doi.org/10.7282/t3-q0c6-5305
31. Meehan, T.F., et al.: Logical development of the cell ontology. BMC Bioinform. **12**, 1–12 (2011). https://doi.org/10.1186/1471-2105-12-6
32. Miller, T.: Explanation in artificial intelligence: insights from the social sciences. AI **267**, 1–38 (2019). https://doi.org/10.1016/j.artint.2018.07.007
33. Nguyen, T.A.T., Power, R., Piwek, P., Williams, S.: Predicting the understandability of OWL inferences. In: ESWC (2013). https://doi.org/10.1007/978-3-642-38288-8_8
34. Schiller, M.R.G., Glimm, B.: Towards explicative inference for OWL. In: DL Workshop (2013). http://ceur-ws.org/Vol-1014/paper_36.pdf
35. Schiller, M.R.G., Schiller, F., Glimm, B.: Testing the adequacy of automated explanations of EL subsumptions. In: DL Workshop (2017). http://ceur-ws.org/Vol-1879/paper43.pdf
36. Schlobach, S.: Explaining subsumption by optimal interpolation. In: JELIA (2004). https://doi.org/10.1007/978-3-540-30227-8_35
37. Schlobach, S., Cornet, R.: Non-standard reasoning services for the debugging of description logic terminologies. In: IJCAI (2003). http://ijcai.org/Proceedings/03/Papers/053.pdf
38. Schulz, S.: The role of foundational ontologies for preventing bad ontology design. In: BOG Workshop (2018). http://ceur-ws.org/Vol-2205/paper22_bog1.pdf
39. Simancik, F., Kazakov, Y., Horrocks, I.: Consequence-based reasoning beyond Horn ontologies. In: IJCAI (2011). https://doi.org/10.5591/978-1-57735-516-8/IJCAI11-187

Error-Tolerant Reasoning
in the Description Logic $\mathcal{EL}$
Based on Optimal Repairs

Franz Baader[ID], Francesco Kriegel[ID], and Adrian Nuradiansyah[✉][ID]

Theoretical Computer Science, Technische Universität Dresden, Dresden, Germany
{franz.baader,francesco.kriegel,adrian.nuradiansyah}@tu-dresden.de

Abstract. Ontologies based on Description Logic (DL) represent general background knowledge in a terminology (TBox) and the actual data in an ABox. Both human-made and machine-learned data sets may contain errors, which are usually detected when the DL reasoner returns unintuitive or obviously incorrect answers to queries. To eliminate such errors, classical repair approaches offer as repairs maximal subsets of the ABox not having the unwanted answers w.r.t. the TBox. It is, however, not always clear which of these classical repairs to use as the new, corrected data set. Error-tolerant semantics instead takes all repairs into account: cautious reasoning returns the answers that follow from all classical repairs whereas brave reasoning returns the answers that follow from some classical repair. It is inspired by inconsistency-tolerant reasoning and has been investigated for the DL $\mathcal{EL}$, but in a setting where the TBox rather than the ABox is repaired. In a series of papers, we have developed a repair approach for ABoxes that improves on classical repairs in that it preserves a maximal set of consequences (i.e., answers to queries) rather than a maximal set of ABox assertions. The repairs obtained by this approach are called optimal repairs. In the present paper, we investigate error-tolerant reasoning in the DL $\mathcal{EL}$, but we repair the ABox and use optimal repairs rather than classical repairs as the underlying set of repairs. To be more precise, we consider a static $\mathcal{EL}$ TBox (which is assumed to be correct), represent the data by a quantified ABox (where some individuals may be anonymous), and use $\mathcal{EL}$ concepts as queries (instance queries). We show that brave entailment of instance queries can be decided in polynomial time. Cautious entailment can be decided by a coNP procedure, but is still in P if the TBox is empty.

1 Introduction

Description Logics (DLs) [2] are a prominent family of logic-based knowledge representation formalisms, which offer a good compromise between expressiveness

Partially supported by the AI competence center ScaDS.AI Dresden/Leipzig and the German Research Foundation (DFG) in Project 430150274 and SFB/TRR 248.

G. Governatori and A.-Y. Turhan (Eds.): RuleML+RR 2022, LNCS 13752, pp. 227–243, 2022.
https://doi.org/10.1007/978-3-031-21541-4_15

and the complexity of reasoning and are the formal basis for the Web ontology language OWL.[1] Here we concentrate on the inexpressive and tractable DL $\mathcal{EL}$ [1], which is frequently used to represent ontologies in biology and medicine, such as the large medical ontology SNOMED CT.[2]

Like all large human-made digital artefacts, the ontologies employed in such applications may contain errors, and this problem gets even worse if parts of the ontology (usually the data) are automatically generated by inexact methods based on information retrieval or machine learning. Errors are often detected when reasoning finds an inconsistency or generates unintuitive consequences. To correct such a mistake, classical repair approaches propose to use maximal subsets of the ontology as repairs [9,17,19]. While these approaches preserve as many of the original axioms as possible, they may not be optimal w.r.t. preserving consequences. In a series of papers [3,7,8], we have investigated how to characterize and compute optimal repairs, which are defined to be ontologies entailed by the erroneous ontology whose consequence sets are maximal among all such ontologies. To illustrate the difference between classical and optimal repairs, assume that the (quantified) ABox consists of the assertions $owns(Ralf, x)$, $Red(x)$, and $Bike(x)$, where x is an anonymous individual, but that the consequence $\exists\, owns.(Red \sqcap Bike)(Ralf)$ is assumed to be incorrect. There are three classical repairs, obtained by respectively removing one of the assertions, but only one optimal repair, which consists of the assertions $owns(Ralf, y)$, $Red(y)$, $owns(Ralf, z)$, and $Bike(z)$. Clearly, this repair preserves more consequences (in the sense of instance relationships for $Ralf$) than each of the classical repairs.

In general, a given repair problem may have exponentially many repairs, both in the classical and the optimal sense, and it is often hard to decide which one to use. Error-tolerant reasoning does not commit to a single repair, but rather reasons w.r.t. all of them (within the classical or the optimal setting): cautious reasoning returns the answers that follow from all repairs whereas brave reasoning returns the answers that follow from some repair. For classical repairs of TBoxes in $\mathcal{EL}$, it was first investigated in [16,18], where it was shown that brave entailment is NP-complete and cautious entailment is coNP-complete. For more expressive DLs that can create inconsistencies, error-tolerant reasoning had been considered before, for the case where the error is an inconsistency, under the name of inconsistency-tolerant reasoning [10,11,15]. This latter work also uses the classical notion of repair.

In the present paper, we investigate error-tolerant reasoning in the DL $\mathcal{EL}$, using optimal repairs of ABoxes as the underlying set of repairs. To be more precise, we consider a static $\mathcal{EL}$ TBox (which is assumed to be correct, and thus cannot be changed), represent the data by a quantified ABox, and consider instance relationships between individuals and $\mathcal{EL}$ concepts as relevant consequences. In [3] it is shown that, in this setting, each repair is entailed by an

---

[1] https://www.w3.org/TR/owl2-overview/.

[2] https://www.snomed.org/.

optimal repair and that every optimal repair is equivalent to a so-called canonical repair, which is induced by a polynomially large repair seed function.[3]

For the case of brave reasoning, it is actually sufficient to know that every repair is entailed by an optimal one. From this, we obtain that a set of concept assertions is entailed by some optimal repair if, and only if, it is itself a repair. The latter property can be tested by performing a polynomial number of polynomial-time instance tests, which shows that brave reasoning is tractable.

Dealing with cautious reasoning is more complicated since we really need to check what is entailed by all optimal repairs. The first problem is then that, while seed functions are of polynomial size, the canonical repairs they induce may be of exponential size. The solution to this problem is that we work directly with the seed functions without computing the induced repairs. This is possible since we can show that entailment from the canonical repair induced by a given seed function can actually be decided in polynomial time in the size of the seed function, and not just in the size of the repair. The second problem is that, while the set of canonical repairs contains (up to equivalence) all optimal repairs, there may exist non-optimal canonical repairs. Thus, cautious reasoning cannot be done w.r.t. all canonical repairs. Nevertheless, for cautious entailment w.r.t. the empty TBox, we are able to provide a direct characterization, and can show that this condition can be checked in polynomial time. For cautious reasoning w.r.t. a non-empty TBox, we use the fact (shown in [6]) that the optimal repairs are induced by seed functions that are minimal w.r.t. an appropriate pre-order on such functions. Non-entailment can then be tested using a guess-and-check approach that guesses a seed function, checks whether it is minimal, and then checks non-entailment. To show that this yields an NP procedure for non-entailment, we must prove that minimality of a seed function can be tested in polynomial time. Overall, we obtain tractability of cautious reasoning w.r.t. the empty TBox, and a coNP upper bound for cautious reasoning w.r.t. a non-empty TBox. Whether this bound is tight remains an open problem.

2   Preliminaries

We start with recalling the DL $\mathcal{EL}$ as well as $\mathcal{EL}$ TBoxes and ABoxes, and then introduce quantified ABoxes and the entailment relation used in this paper to compare them. We assume that the reader is familiar with the basic notions of description and first-order logic and base our presentation on the one in [5].

The Description Logic $\mathcal{EL}$. Starting from a signature Σ, which is a disjoint union of a set Σ_I of *individual names*, a set Σ_C of *concept names*, and a set Σ_R of *role names*, $\mathcal{EL}$ concept descriptions are built using the grammar $C ::= \top \mid A \mid C \sqcap C \mid \exists r.C$, where A ranges over Σ_C and r over Σ_R. An $\mathcal{EL}$ *concept assertion* is of the form $C(a)$ where C is an $\mathcal{EL}$ concept description and $a \in \Sigma_I$, a *role*

---

[3] Since we are only interested in instance relationships, the appropriate entailment and equivalence relations between quantified ABoxes are IQ-entailment and IQ-equivalence [3].

assertion is of the form $r(a, b)$ where $r \in \Sigma_R$ and $a, b \in \Sigma_I$, and an *$\mathcal{EL}$ concept inclusion (CI)* is of the form $C \sqsubseteq D$ for concept descriptions C, D. An *$\mathcal{EL}$ ABox* $\mathcal{A}$ is a finite set of concept assertions and role assertions, and an *$\mathcal{EL}$ TBox* $\mathcal{T}$ is a finite set of concept inclusions. Since $\mathcal{EL}$ is the only DL considered in this paper, we will sometimes omit the prefix "$\mathcal{EL}$," and we will use "concept" as an abbreviation for "concept description."

The semantics of $\mathcal{EL}$ can be defined either directly in a model-theoretic way of by a translation into first-order logic (FO) [2]. In the translation, the elements of Σ_I, Σ_C, and Σ_R are respectively viewed as constant symbols, unary predicate symbols, and binary predicate symbols. $\mathcal{EL}$ concepts C are inductively translated into FO formulas $\phi_C(x)$ with one free variable x:

- concept A for $A \in \Sigma_C$ is translated into $A(x)$ and $\top$ into $A(x) \vee \neg A(x)$ for an arbitrary $A \in \Sigma_C$;
- if C, D are translated into $\phi_C(x)$ and $\phi_D(x)$, then $C \sqcap D$ is translated into $\phi_C(x) \wedge \phi_D(x)$ and $\exists r. C$ into $\exists y. (r(x, y) \wedge \phi_C(y))$, where $\phi_C(y)$ is obtained from $\phi_C(x)$ by replacing the free variable x by a different variable y.

CIs $C \sqsubseteq D$ are translated into sentences $\phi_{C \sqsubseteq D} := \forall x. (\phi_C(x) \rightarrow \phi_D(x))$ and TBoxes $\mathcal{T}$ into $\phi_{\mathcal{T}} := \bigwedge_{C \sqsubseteq D \in \mathcal{T}} \phi_{C \sqsubseteq D}$. Concept assertions $C(a)$ are translated into $\phi_C(a)$, role assertions $r(a, b)$ stay the same, and ABoxes $\mathcal{A}$ are translated into the conjunction $\phi_{\mathcal{A}}$ of the translations of their assertions.

Let α, β be ABoxes, concept inclusions, or concept assertions (possibly not both of the same kind), and $\mathcal{T}$ an $\mathcal{EL}$ TBox. Then we say that α *entails* β w.r.t. $\mathcal{T}$ (written $\alpha \models^{\mathcal{T}} \beta$) if the implication $(\phi_\alpha \wedge \phi_{\mathcal{T}}) \rightarrow \phi_\beta$ is valid according to the semantics of FO. Furthermore, α and β are *equivalent* w.r.t. $\mathcal{T}$ (written $\alpha \equiv^{\mathcal{T}} \beta$), if $\alpha \models^{\mathcal{T}} \beta$ and $\beta \models^{\mathcal{T}} \alpha$. In case $\mathcal{T} = \emptyset$, we will sometimes write $\models$ instead of $\models^{\emptyset}$. If $\emptyset \models^{\mathcal{T}} C \sqsubseteq D$, then we also write $C \sqsubseteq^{\mathcal{T}} D$ and say that C *is subsumed by D w.r.t. $\mathcal{T}$*; in case $\mathcal{T} = \emptyset$ we simply say that C is subsumed by D. The subsumption problem in $\mathcal{EL}$ is known to be decidable in polynomial time [1], and the same is true for all the entailment problems introduced above.

Quantified ABoxes. A *quantified ABox* (qABox) $\exists X. \mathcal{A}$ consists of a set X of *variables*, which is disjoint with Σ, and a *matrix* $\mathcal{A}$, which is a finite set of concept assertions $A(u)$ and role assertions $r(u, v)$, where $A \in \Sigma_C$, $r \in \Sigma_R$ and $u, v \in \Sigma_I \cup X$. The matrix is an ABox built over the extended signature $\Sigma \cup X$, but cannot contain complex concept descriptions. An *object* of $\exists X. \mathcal{A}$ is either an individual name in Σ_I or a variable in X.

Like $\mathcal{EL}$ ABoxes, quantified ABox $\exists X. \mathcal{A}$ can be translated into FO sentences, but where the elements of X are viewed as first-order variables rather than constants and are existentially quantified. Thus, entailment between two qABoxes (written $\exists X. \mathcal{A} \models^{\mathcal{T}} \exists Y. \mathcal{B}$) and between a qABox and a concept assertion (written $\exists X. \mathcal{A} \models^{\mathcal{T}} C(a)$) w.r.t. a TBox $\mathcal{T}$ can again be defined using the semantics of first-order logic.[4] If $\exists X. \mathcal{A} \models^{\mathcal{T}} C(a)$, then a is called an *instance* of C w.r.t. $\exists X. \mathcal{A}$ and $\mathcal{T}$.

---

[4] See [3,8] for more information on qABoxes.

Syntactically, not every $\mathcal{EL}$ ABox is a qABox, since $\mathcal{EL}$ ABoxes may contain concept assertions $C(a)$ for complex concepts C. However, every $\mathcal{EL}$ ABox can be translated into an equivalent qABox, by writing the FO translation of complex concepts C as a qABox. For example, if $C = \exists r.(A \sqcap B)$, then the $\mathcal{EL}$ ABox $\{C(a)\}$ is equivalent to the qABox $\exists\{x\}.\{r(a,x), A(x), B(x)\}$. Conversely, not every qABox can be expressed by an $\mathcal{EL}$ ABox since qABoxes may contain cyclic role relations between variables. For example, if $\mathcal{T}$ is empty, then the qABox $\exists\{x\}.\{r(a,x), r(x,x)\}$ is not equivalent to an $\mathcal{EL}$ ABox [5]. One might be tempted to think that one can just forget about the existential quantifier and use an individual b instead of the variable x. However, the ABox $\{r(a,b), r(b,b)\}$ is not equivalent to the above qABox since it entails non-trivial instance relationships for b, whereas $\exists\{x\}.\{r(a,x), r(x,x)\}$ does not. Also note that, while entailment between $\mathcal{EL}$ ABoxes and entailment of a concept assertion by a qABox can be decided in polynomial time, the entailment problem between qABoxes is NP-complete [3,8].

However, since in this paper we are only interested in the instance relationships that a given qABox entails, we can restrict our attention to IQ-entailment between qABoxes: the qABox $\exists X.\mathcal{A}$ IQ-*entails* the qABox $\exists Y.\mathcal{B}$ w.r.t. $\mathcal{T}$ (written $\exists X.\mathcal{A} \models_{IQ}^{\mathcal{T}} \exists Y.\mathcal{B}$) if $\exists Y.\mathcal{B} \models^{\mathcal{T}} C(a)$ implies $\exists X.\mathcal{A} \models^{\mathcal{T}} C(a)$ for each $\mathcal{EL}$ concept assertion $C(a)$. In contrast to the FO entailment introduced above, IQ-entailment between qABoxes can be decided in polynomial time. This is a consequence of the following result from [3]: given a qABox $\exists X.\mathcal{A}$ and an $\mathcal{EL}$ TBox $\mathcal{T}$, one can compute in polynomial time an IQ-*saturation* $\mathsf{sat}_{IQ}^{\mathcal{T}}(\exists X.\mathcal{A})$ such that the following statements are equivalent:

- $\exists X.\mathcal{A} \models_{IQ}^{\mathcal{T}} \exists Y.\mathcal{B}$
- $\mathsf{sat}_{IQ}^{\mathcal{T}}(\exists X.\mathcal{A}) \models_{IQ} \exists Y.\mathcal{B}$
- There is a simulation from $\exists Y.\mathcal{B}$ to $\mathsf{sat}_{IQ}^{\mathcal{T}}(\exists X.\mathcal{A})$.

The notion of simulation employed here is the usual one for labeled graphs, whose existence can be decided in polynomial time (see [3] for details).

3   Optimal and Canonical Repairs

We first introduce the notion of an optimal repair w.r.t. IQ-entailment and recall the approach for obtaining canonical IQ-repairs based on repair seed functions described in [3]. Then, we show that reasoning w.r.t. canonical repairs can be performed by considering the seed function rather than the induced canonical repair. Since the optimal repairs are exactly the canonical ones induced by minimal seed functions [3], we also investigate how minimality of a seed function can be decided. The reason for employing IQ-entailment is that we are only interested in the instance relationships entailed by a given qABox and TBox. We use repair requests to indicate which consequences are considered to be erroneous, and thus need to be removed. Formally, a *repair request* $\mathcal{R}$ is a finite set of concept assertions.

Definition 1. *Let $\mathcal{T}$ be an $\mathcal{EL}$ TBox, $\exists X.\mathcal{A}$ a qABox, and $\mathcal{R}$ a repair request.*

- *The qABox $\exists Y.\mathcal{B}$ is an IQ-repair of $\exists X.\mathcal{A}$ for $\mathcal{R}$ w.r.t. $\mathcal{T}$ if $\exists X.\mathcal{A} \models_{\mathsf{IQ}}^{\mathcal{T}} \exists Y.\mathcal{B}$ and $\exists Y.\mathcal{B} \not\models^{\mathcal{T}} C(a)$ for each $C(a) \in \mathcal{R}$.*
- *Such a repair $\exists Y.\mathcal{B}$ is optimal if there is no IQ-repair $\exists Z.\mathcal{C}$ such that $\exists Z.\mathcal{C} \models_{\mathsf{IQ}}^{\mathcal{T}} \exists Y.\mathcal{B}$, but $\exists Y.\mathcal{B} \not\models_{\mathsf{IQ}}^{\mathcal{T}} \exists Z.\mathcal{C}$.*

Not every repair request has a repair, but the ones that have can easily be identified. We call a repair request $\mathcal{R}$ *solvable* w.r.t. a TBox $\mathcal{T}$ if, for each quantified ABox $\exists X.\mathcal{A}$, there exists a repair of $\exists X.\mathcal{A}$ for $\mathcal{R}$ w.r.t. $\mathcal{T}$. As mentioned in [3], this is the case iff $\top \not\sqsubseteq^{\mathcal{T}} C$ for each $C(a) \in \mathcal{R}$.

In general, a given repair instance $\mathcal{T}, \exists X.\mathcal{A}, \mathcal{R}$ may have exponentially many non-equivalent optimal repairs. Repair seed functions can be used to define (a superset of) these repairs, by specifying, for each individual a in $\mathcal{A}$, which atoms should not hold for a in the repair. To take the TBox into account, one first constructs the IQ-saturation $\exists Y.\mathcal{B} := \mathsf{sat}_{\mathsf{IQ}}^{\mathcal{T}}(\exists X.\mathcal{A})$. We denote the set of all subconcepts of concepts occurring in $\mathcal{R}$ or $\mathcal{T}$ with $\mathsf{Sub}(\mathcal{R}, \mathcal{T})$. An *atom* is either a concept name or an existential restriction, and we denote the set of atoms in $\mathsf{Sub}(\mathcal{R}, \mathcal{T})$ with $\mathsf{Atoms}(\mathcal{R}, \mathcal{T})$.

Definition 2. *Let $\mathcal{T}$ be an $\mathcal{EL}$ TBox, $\exists X.\mathcal{A}$ a qABox, $\mathcal{R}$ a repair request, and $\exists Y.\mathcal{B}$ the IQ-saturation of $\exists X.\mathcal{A}$ w.r.t. $\mathcal{T}$. A repair type for an object u of $\exists Y.\mathcal{B}$ is a subset $\mathcal{K}$ of $\mathsf{Atoms}(\mathcal{R}, \mathcal{T})$ that satisfies the following three conditions:*

1. *$K \not\sqsubseteq^{\emptyset} K'$ for all distinct atoms $K, K' \in \mathcal{K}$.*
2. *$\mathcal{B} \models K(u)$ for every atom $K \in \mathcal{K}$.*
3. *$\mathcal{K}$ is premise-saturated, i.e., if $K \in \mathcal{K}$ and $C \in \mathsf{Sub}(\mathcal{R}, \mathcal{T})$ are such that $\mathcal{B} \models C(u)$ and $C \sqsubseteq^{\mathcal{T}} K$, then there is $K' \in \mathcal{K}$ with $C \sqsubseteq^{\emptyset} K'$.*[5]

A repair seed function (rsf) s assigns to each individual name $a \in \Sigma_{\mathsf{I}}$ a repair type $s(a)$ such that, for each unwanted consequence $C(a) \in \mathcal{R}$ with $\mathcal{B} \models C(a)$, there is an atom $K \in s(a)$ with $C \sqsubseteq^{\emptyset} K$.

As shown in [3], each rsf s induces a *canonical* IQ-repair, denoted as $\mathsf{rep}_{\mathsf{IQ}}^{\mathcal{T}}(\exists X.\mathcal{A}, s)$, and the set of canonical IQ-repairs covers all IQ-repairs in the sense that every repair is IQ-entailed by a canonical one. In particular, this implies that, up to IQ-equivalence, the set of canonical IQ-repairs contains all optimal IQ-repairs, and the set of optimal IQ-repairs also covers all IQ-repairs.

For the purposes of this paper, the exact definition of $\mathsf{rep}_{\mathsf{IQ}}^{\mathcal{T}}(\exists X.\mathcal{A}, s)$ is not relevant since we intend to work directly with the (polynomial-sized) rsf s rather than the (exponentially large) induced canonical repair. An important result that helps us to do this is the following lemma, which is an extension of Lemma XII in [4], whose proof is similar to the proof of Lemma VI in [14].

Lemma 3. *Let s be a repair seed function, b an individual in $\mathcal{A}$, and C an $\mathcal{EL}$ concept. Then $\mathsf{rep}_{\mathsf{IQ}}^{\mathcal{T}}(\exists X.\mathcal{A}, s) \models^{\mathcal{T}} C(b)$ iff $\exists X.\mathcal{A} \models^{\mathcal{T}} C(b)$ and $s(b)$ does not contain an atom that subsumes C w.r.t. $\mathcal{T}$.*

---

[5] A *repair pre-type* need only satisfy the first two conditions. If the TBox is empty, then this third condition is trivially true since one can take $K' = K$.

Since the right-hand side of this equivalence can obviously be checked in polynomial time (since $\exists X.\mathcal{A} \models^{\mathcal{T}} C(b)$ iff $\mathcal{A} \models^{\mathcal{T}} C(b)$) and $s(b)$ is of polynomial size, we obtain the following complexity result.

Proposition 4. *Given a qABox $\exists X.\mathcal{A}$, an $\mathcal{EL}$ TBox $\mathcal{T}$, a repair request $\mathcal{R}$, a repair seed function s, and an $\mathcal{EL}$ concept assertion $C(b)$, we can decide in polynomial time (in the size of $\exists X.\mathcal{A}$, $\mathcal{T}$, and $\mathcal{R}$) whether $C(b)$ is entailed w.r.t. $\mathcal{T}$ by the canonical IQ-repair induced by s.*

The set of canonical repairs may contain non-optimal repairs. A simple example is given by the empty TBox, the qABox $\exists\emptyset.\{A(a), B(a)\}$, and the repair request $\mathcal{R} = \{(A \sqcap B)(a)\}$. There are three seed functions s_1, s_2, s_3 with $s_1(a) = \{A\}, s_2(a) = \{B\}, s_3(a) = \{A, B\}$, which respectively induce the canonical repairs $\exists\emptyset.\{B(a)\}$, $\exists\emptyset.\{A(a)\}$, and $\exists\emptyset.\emptyset$. Whereas the first two are optimal repairs, the latter one is not optimal; in fact, it is strictly entailed by each of the former ones. Obviously, the reason for this is that $s_3(a)$ is contained both in $s_1(a)$ and in $s_2(a)$.

More generally, we can reflect entailment between canonical repairs by the following covering relation between seed functions. Given sets $\mathcal{K}$ and $\mathcal{L}$ of concept descriptions, we say that $\mathcal{K}$ is *covered* by $\mathcal{L}$ (written $\mathcal{K} \leq \mathcal{L}$) if, for each $K \in \mathcal{K}$, there is $L \in \mathcal{L}$ such that $K \sqsubseteq^{\emptyset} L$. Applying the covering relation argumentwise yields the following pre-order on seed functions: $s \leq t$ if $s(a) \leq t(a)$ for each $a \in \Sigma_{\mathsf{I}}$. The following result, which is an easy consequence of Lemma 3, was already mentioned in [6].

Lemma 5. $s \leq t$ iff $\mathsf{rep}_{\mathsf{IQ}}^{\mathcal{T}}(\exists X.\mathcal{A}, s) \models_{\mathsf{IQ}}^{\mathcal{T}} \mathsf{rep}_{\mathsf{IQ}}^{\mathcal{T}}(\exists X.\mathcal{A}, t)$.

Given any pre-order $\leq$, we write $\alpha < \beta$ if $\alpha \leq \beta$ and $\beta \not\leq \alpha$, and say that α is $\leq$-*minimal* ($\leq$-*maximal*) if there is no β such that $\beta < \alpha$ ($\alpha < \beta$). For repair seed functions s, t we have $s < t$ iff $s(a) \leq t(a)$ for all $a \in \Sigma_{\mathsf{I}}$ and there is $b \in \Sigma_{\mathsf{I}}$ with $s(b) < t(b)$. As an immediate consequence of Lemma 5, we obtain that the optimal repairs are induced by the minimal seed functions.

Proposition 6. *If s is a $\leq$-minimal rsf, then $\mathsf{rep}_{\mathsf{IQ}}^{\mathcal{T}}(\exists X.\mathcal{A}, s)$ is an optimal IQ-repair, and every optimal IQ-repair is IQ-equivalent to a canonical repair $\mathsf{rep}_{\mathsf{IQ}}^{\mathcal{T}}(\exists X.\mathcal{A}, s)$ for a $\leq$-minimal rsf s.*

In the rest of this section we show that $\leq$-minimality of seed functions can be decided in polynomial time. More precisely, we characterise non-minimality by showing how, for a given repair type, we can decide whether there exists a repair type that is strictly covered by it. As before, we denote by $\exists Y.\mathcal{B}$ the saturation $\mathsf{sat}_{\mathsf{IQ}}^{\mathcal{T}}(\exists X.\mathcal{A})$. We start by showing how, for a given repair type $\mathcal{K}$, a non-empty set $\mathcal{M}$ of atoms covered by it can be employed to construct a repair pre-type that is strictly covered by $\mathcal{K}$.

Definition 7. *Let $\mathcal{K}$ be a repair type for u and $\mathcal{M}$ be a non-empty subset of* Atoms$(\mathcal{R}, \mathcal{T})$ *such that $\mathcal{M} \leq \mathcal{K}$. We define the* lowering *of $\mathcal{K}$ w.r.t. $\mathcal{M}$ by*

$$
\mathsf{low}(\mathcal{K}, \mathcal{M}) := \mathsf{Max}_{\sqsubseteq^\emptyset} \left\{ E \left| \begin{array}{l} E \in \mathsf{Atoms}(\mathcal{R}, \mathcal{T}), \ \mathcal{B} \models E(u), \\ E \sqsubseteq^\emptyset K \text{ for some } K \in \mathcal{K}, \\ M \not\sqsubseteq^\emptyset E \text{ for each } M \in \mathcal{M} \end{array} \right. \right\}.
$$

Due to the $\mathsf{Max}_{\sqsubseteq^\emptyset}$ operator, which selects a representative for each equivalence class of $\sqsubseteq^\emptyset$-maximal elements, and the condition that each atom E in $\mathsf{low}(\mathcal{K}, \mathcal{M})$ must satisfy $\mathcal{B} \models E(u)$, we know that $\mathsf{low}(\mathcal{K}, \mathcal{M})$ is a repair pre-type for u. Next, we show that $\mathcal{K}$ strictly covers $\mathsf{low}(\mathcal{K}, \mathcal{M})$.

Lemma 8. $\mathsf{low}(\mathcal{K}, \mathcal{M}) < \mathcal{K}$

Proof. By definition, each atom in $\mathsf{low}(\mathcal{K}, \mathcal{M})$ is subsumed by some atom in $\mathcal{K}$, which means that $\mathsf{low}(\mathcal{K}, \mathcal{M}) \leq \mathcal{K}$.

To show that $\mathcal{K} \not\leq \mathsf{low}(\mathcal{K}, \mathcal{M})$, we consider an element $M \in \mathcal{M}$, which exists since we have assumed $\mathcal{M} \neq \emptyset$. Since $\mathcal{M} \leq \mathcal{K}$, there is an atom K in $\mathcal{K}$ such that $M \sqsubseteq^\emptyset K$. We show that K is not subsumed by any atom in $\mathsf{low}(\mathcal{K}, \mathcal{M})$.

Assume to the contrary that $K \sqsubseteq^\emptyset E$ for some atom $E \in \mathsf{low}(\mathcal{K}, \mathcal{M})$. Then $E \sqsubseteq^\emptyset K'$ for some $K' \in \mathcal{K}$, and thus $K \sqsubseteq^\emptyset K'$. Since the repair type $\mathcal{K}$ cannot contain distinct $\sqsubseteq^\emptyset$-comparable atoms, K and K' must be equal. We infer from $K \sqsubseteq^\emptyset E \sqsubseteq^\emptyset K'$ that E and K are equivalent, and thus $M \sqsubseteq^\emptyset K$ yield $M \sqsubseteq^\emptyset E$. This contradicts our assumption that $E \in \mathsf{low}(\mathcal{K}, \mathcal{M})$ $\square$

The lowering of $\mathcal{K}$ w.r.t. $\mathcal{M}$ need not be a repair type, but we can construct, for each atom $D \in \mathcal{K}$, a set $\mathcal{M}_D$ such that $\mathsf{low}(\mathcal{K}, \mathcal{M}_D)$ is a repair type.

Definition 9. *Let $\mathcal{K}$ be a repair type for u and $D \in \mathcal{K}$. We inductively define the following sets:*

$$
\mathcal{M}_D^0 := \{D\}
$$

$$
\mathcal{M}_D^{i+1} := \mathcal{M}_D^i \cup \left\{ F \left| \begin{array}{l} F \in \mathsf{low}(\mathcal{K}, \mathcal{M}_D^i) \text{ and there is } C \in \mathsf{Sub}(\mathcal{R}, \mathcal{T}) \\ \text{such that } \mathcal{B} \models C(u), \ C \sqsubseteq^\mathcal{T} F, \ \{C\} \not\leq \mathsf{low}(\mathcal{K}, \mathcal{M}_D^i) \end{array} \right. \right\}
$$

We further set $\mathcal{M}_D := \mathcal{M}_D^j$ where j is the minimal index such that $\mathcal{M}_D^{j+1} = \mathcal{M}_D^j$.

Since we can show by induction that $\mathcal{M}_D^i$ is non-empty and covered by $\mathcal{K}$ for all $i \geq 0$, $\mathcal{K}$ and $\mathcal{M}_D^i$ satisfy the conditions of Definition 7 on the arguments of low in the definition of $\mathcal{M}_D^{i+1}$.

Lemma 10. $\mathsf{low}(\mathcal{K}, \mathcal{M}_D)$ *is a repair type for u.*

Proof. We have already seen that $\text{low}(\mathcal{K}, \mathcal{M}_D)$ is a repair pre-type. It remains to prove that it is premise-saturated. Thus, let $F \in \text{low}(\mathcal{K}, \mathcal{M}_D)$ and $C \in \text{Sub}(\mathcal{R}, \mathcal{T})$ be such that $\mathcal{B} \models C(u)$ and $C \sqsubseteq^{\mathcal{T}} F$, and assume that C is not subsumed by any atom in $\text{low}(\mathcal{K}, \mathcal{M}_D) = \text{low}(\mathcal{K}, \mathcal{M}_D^j)$. Then $F \in \mathcal{M}_D^{j+1} = \mathcal{M}_D$, which yields a contradiction since $F \in \text{low}(\mathcal{K}, \mathcal{M}_D)$ requires that F does not subsume any atom in $\mathcal{M}_D$.   □

Next, we characterize the repair types that are strictly covered by a given repair type $\mathcal{K}$.

Lemma 11. *Let $\mathcal{K}$ and $\mathcal{L}$ be repair types for u. Then, $\mathcal{L} < \mathcal{K}$ iff there is some $D \in \mathcal{K}$ such that $\mathcal{L} \leq \text{low}(\mathcal{K}, \mathcal{M}_D)$.*

Proof. The if direction follows directly from Lemma 8. To show the only-if direction, assume that $\mathcal{L} < \mathcal{K}$, i.e., $\mathcal{L} \leq \mathcal{K}$ and $\mathcal{K} \not\leq \mathcal{L}$. The latter yields an atom $D \in \mathcal{K}$ that is not subsumed by any atom in $\mathcal{L}$. We show by induction that $\mathcal{L} \leq \text{low}(\mathcal{K}, \mathcal{M}_D^i)$ for all $i \geq 0$.

In the base case ($i = 0$), we have $\mathcal{M}_D^0 = \{D\}$. Consider an atom $L \in \mathcal{L}$. Since $\mathcal{L}$ is a repair type for u, it holds that $\mathcal{B} \models L(u)$. Since $\mathcal{L} \leq \mathcal{K}$, there is an atom $K \in \mathcal{K}$ such that $L \sqsubseteq^{\emptyset} K$. We distinguish two cases:

- Assume that $K = D$. Since D is not subsumed by an atom in $\mathcal{L}$, it holds that $D \not\sqsubseteq^{\emptyset} L$.
- Now let $K \neq D$. Since $\mathcal{K}$ is a repair type, it does not contain $\sqsubseteq^{\emptyset}$-comparable atoms, which specifically implies that $D \not\sqsubseteq^{\emptyset} K$. Thus $D \not\sqsubseteq^{\emptyset} L$ must hold as otherwise D would be subsumed by K.

In both cases we conclude that $\text{low}(\mathcal{K}, \mathcal{M}_D^0)$ contains either L itself or (if L is not maximal) an atom subsuming L, i.e., L is subsumed by an atom in $\text{low}(\mathcal{K}, \mathcal{M}_D^0)$.

We proceed with the induction step ($i \rightarrow i + 1$). Therefore let L be an atom in $\mathcal{L}$. Since $\mathcal{L}$ is a repair type for u, we have $\mathcal{B} \models L(u)$. Due to $\mathcal{L} \leq \mathcal{K}$ it further follows that L is subsumed by some atom K in $\mathcal{K}$. We show that $M \not\sqsubseteq^{\emptyset} L$ for each $M \in \mathcal{M}_D^{i+1}$. It then follows that $\text{low}(\mathcal{K}, \mathcal{M}_D^{i+1})$ contains either L itself or an atom subsuming L, and thus L is subsumed by an atom in $\text{low}(\mathcal{K}, \mathcal{M}_D^{i+1})$.

Assume to the contrary that there is an atom M in $\mathcal{M}_D^{i+1}$ such that $M \sqsubseteq^{\emptyset} L$. It cannot be the case that $M \in \mathcal{M}_D^i$ since this would lead to a contradiction with the induction hypothesis $\mathcal{L} \leq \text{low}(\mathcal{K}, \mathcal{M}_D^i)$. Thus, consider the case where $M \in \mathcal{M}_D^{i+1} \setminus \mathcal{M}_D^i$. According to Definition 9 it follows that $M \in \text{low}(\mathcal{K}, \mathcal{M}_D^i)$ and there is a subconcept $C \in \text{Sub}(\mathcal{R}, \mathcal{T})$ with $\mathcal{B} \models C(u)$, $C \sqsubseteq^{\mathcal{T}} M$, and $\{C\} \not\leq \text{low}(\mathcal{K}, \mathcal{M}_D^i)$. From $C \sqsubseteq^{\mathcal{T}} M$ and $M \sqsubseteq^{\emptyset} L$ it follows that $C \sqsubseteq^{\mathcal{T}} L$. Since $\mathcal{L}$ is a repair type for u, we infer that $\{C\} \leq \mathcal{L}$. Together with the induction hypothesis $\mathcal{L} \leq \text{low}(\mathcal{K}, \mathcal{M}_D^i)$, this yields $\{C\} \leq \text{low}(\mathcal{K}, \mathcal{M}_D^i)$, which is a contradiction.

Finally, recall that $\mathcal{M}_D$ is defined as $\mathcal{M}_D^j$ where j is the smallest index for which $\mathcal{M}_D^{j+1}$ equals $\mathcal{M}_D^j$. We thus obtain that $\mathcal{L} \leq \text{low}(\mathcal{K}, \mathcal{M}_D)$.   □

Using this lemma, we can now characterize non-minimality of an rsf.

Lemma 12. *A repair seed function on $\exists X.\mathcal{A}$ for $\mathcal{R}$ w.r.t. $\mathcal{T}$ is not $\leq$-minimal iff there exist an individual a and an atom $D \in s(a)$ such that $\{P\} \leq$ low$(s(a), \mathcal{M}_D)$ holds for each $P(a) \in \mathcal{R}$ with $\exists X.\mathcal{A} \models^{\mathcal{T}} P(a)$.*

Proof. If s is not $\leq$-minimal, then there is an rsf s' such that $s' < s$, i.e., there is $a \in \Sigma_{\mathsf{I}}$ such that $s'(a) < s(a)$. Since s' is an rsf, we have $\{P\} \leq s'(a)$ for all $P(a) \in \mathcal{R}$ with $\exists X.\mathcal{A} \models^{\mathcal{T}} P(a)$. By Lemma 11, $s'(a) < s(a)$ implies that there is $D \in s(a)$ such that $s'(a) \leq$ low$(s(a), \mathcal{M}_D)$. By transitivity, for each $P(a) \in \mathcal{R}$ with $\exists X.\mathcal{A} \models^{\mathcal{T}} P(a)$, we have $\{P\} \leq$ low$(s(a), \mathcal{M}_D)$.

To show the "if" direction, we construct a function $s' : \Sigma_{\mathsf{I}} \to \wp(\mathsf{Atoms}(\mathcal{R}, \mathcal{T}))$ such that $s'(b) := s(b)$ for each $b \in \Sigma_{\mathsf{I}} \setminus \{a\}$ and $s'(a) :=$ low$(s(a), \mathcal{M}_D)$. By Lemma 10, $s'(a)$ is a repair type for a. Since for each $P(a) \in \mathcal{R}$ with $\exists X.\mathcal{A} \models^{\mathcal{T}} P(a)$, we have $\{P\} \leq$ low$(s(a), \mathcal{M}_D)$, we infer that s' is an rsf on $\exists X.\mathcal{A}$ for $\mathcal{R}$ w.r.t. $\mathcal{T}$. Since $s'(b) = s(b)$ for each $b \in \Sigma_{\mathsf{I}} \setminus \{a\}$ and $s'(a) < s(a)$, by Lemma 8, we infer that s is not $\leq$-minimal. $\qquad\square$

Since there are linearly many atoms D in $s(a)$ and computing $\mathcal{M}_D$ and low$(s(a), \mathcal{M}_D)$ can be done in polynomial time, we obtain the following complexity result.

Proposition 13. $\leq$-*minimality of repair seed functions is in* P.

Let us illustrate the decision procedure for non-minimality suggested by Lemma 12 by a small example.

Example 14. Consider the TBox $\mathcal{T} := \{\exists r.A_1 \sqsubseteq \exists r.A_2\}$, the quantified ABox $\exists X.\mathcal{A} := \exists\{x\}.\{r(a, x), A_1(x), A_2(x), B_1(x), B_2(x)\}$, and the repair request $\mathcal{R} := \{\exists r.(A_1 \sqcap B_1)(a), \exists r.(A_2 \sqcap B_2)(a)\}$. If we define a function $s : \Sigma_{\mathsf{I}} \to \wp(\mathsf{Atoms}(\mathcal{R}, \mathcal{T}))$ such that $s(a) = \{\exists r.A_1, \exists r.A_2\}$, then $s(a)$ is a repair type for a and s is a repair seed function on $\exists X.\mathcal{A}$ for $\mathcal{R}$ w.r.t. $\mathcal{T}$.

We use Lemma 12 to show that s is not $\leq$-minimal. For this purpose, we consider the atom $\exists r.A_1$ in $s(a)$, and construct the set $\mathcal{M}^0_{\exists r.A_1} := \{\exists r.A_1\}$. By Definition 7, we have low$(s(a), \mathcal{M}^0_{\exists r.A_1}) = \{\exists r.(A_1 \sqcap B_1), \exists r.A_2\}$. However, this lowering set is not yet premise-saturated w.r.t. $\mathcal{T}$ since $\exists r.A_2$ is subsumed w.r.t. $\mathcal{T}$ by the subconcept $\exists r.A_1$, which is not subsumed w.r.t. $\emptyset$ by any atom from low$(s(a), \mathcal{M}^0_{\exists r.A_1})$. By Definition 9, we thus add $\exists r.A_2$ to $\mathcal{M}^0_{\exists r.A_1}$, which yields the set $\mathcal{M}^1_{\exists r.A_1} := \{\exists r.A_1, \exists r.A_2\}$. The corresponding lowering set is low$(s(a), \mathcal{M}^1_{\exists r.A_1}) = \{\exists r.(A_1 \sqcap B_1), \exists r.(A_2 \sqcap B_2)\}$. It is easy to see that this set is a repair repair type for a, which is strictly covered by $s(a)$. By looking at the repair request $\mathcal{R}$, we see that, for each concept assertion in $\mathcal{R}$, the respective concept is subsumed by some atom in low$(s(a), \mathcal{M}^1_{\exists r.A_1})$. Thus, the condition on the right-hand side of the equivalence in Lemma 12 is satisfied for low$(s(a), \mathcal{M}^1_{\exists r.A_1})$.

If we define $t(a) :=$ low$(s(a), \mathcal{M}^1_{\exists r.A_1})$, then t is an rsf such that $t < s$. By Lemma 5, $\mathsf{rep}^{\mathcal{T}}_{\mathsf{IQ}}(\exists X.\mathcal{A}, t)$ strictly IQ-entails $\mathsf{rep}^{\mathcal{T}}_{\mathsf{IQ}}(\exists X.\mathcal{A}, s)$. For example, the former repair entails $(\exists r.A_1)(a)$ whereas the latter does not. This can be seen using Lemma 3.

4   Error-Tolerant Reasoning w.r.t. Optimal Repairs

In error-tolerant reasoning, one does not commit to a single (classical or optimal) repair, but rather reasons w.r.t. all repairs. Brave entailment produces the consequences that are entailed by some repair whereas cautious entailment only produces consequences that are entailed by every repair. In the literature on inconsistency-tolerant and error-tolerant reasoning in the classical setting [10,11,15,16,18], IAR entailment (for "intersections of all repairs") is also considered, but in our setting of optimal repairs, where repairs are not necessarily subsets of the original ontology, it is not clear how to define this notion in an appropriate way.

If there is no repair, then everything is cautiously entailed and nothing is bravely entailed. We prevent this anomalous case by requiring that the repair request is solvable w.r.t. the given TBox.

Definition 15. *Let $\exists X.\mathcal{A}$ be a qABox, $\mathcal{T}$ an $\mathcal{EL}$ TBox, $\mathcal{R}$ a repair request that is solvable w.r.t. $\mathcal{T}$, and $\mathcal{Q}$ a finite set of $\mathcal{EL}$ concept assertions. Then $\mathcal{Q}$ is bravely entailed by $\exists X.\mathcal{A}$ w.r.t. $\mathcal{T}$ and $\mathcal{R}$ iff there is an optimal IQ-repair $\exists Z.\mathcal{C}$ of $\exists X.\mathcal{A}$ for $\mathcal{R}$ w.r.t. $\mathcal{T}$ such that $\exists Z.\mathcal{C} \models^{\mathcal{T}} C(a)$ for each $C(a) \in \mathcal{Q}$. It is* cautiously entailed *by $\exists X.\mathcal{A}$ w.r.t. $\mathcal{T}$ and $\mathcal{R}$ iff every optimal IQ-repair $\exists Z.\mathcal{C}$ of $\exists X.\mathcal{A}$ for $\mathcal{R}$ w.r.t. $\mathcal{T}$ satisfies $\exists Z.\mathcal{C} \models^{\mathcal{T}} C(a)$ for each $C(a) \in \mathcal{Q}$.*

In the following, we first show that brave entailment can be decided in polynomial time. For cautious entailment w.r.t. a TBox, the results proved in the previous section provide us with a coNP upper bound. Without a TBox, the complexity of cautious entailment drops to P.

4.1   Brave Entailment

The following lemma shows that brave entailment can be reduced to the instance problem in $\mathcal{EL}$.

Lemma 16. *The set of $\mathcal{EL}$ concept assertions $\mathcal{Q}$ is bravely entailed by $\exists X.\mathcal{A}$ for $\mathcal{R}$ w.r.t. $\mathcal{T}$ iff $\exists X.\mathcal{A} \models^{\mathcal{T}} \mathcal{Q}$ and no assertion in $\mathcal{P}$ is entailed by $\mathcal{Q}$ w.r.t. $\mathcal{T}$.*

Proof. If $\mathcal{Q}$ is bravely entailed, then there is an optimal IQ-repair $\exists Z.\mathcal{C}$ of $\exists X.\mathcal{A}$ for $\mathcal{P}$ w.r.t. $\mathcal{T}$ such that $\exists Z.\mathcal{C} \models^{\mathcal{T}} \mathcal{Q}$. Transitivity of entailment yields $\exists X.\mathcal{A} \models^{\mathcal{T}} \mathcal{Q}$. In addition, since $\exists Z.\mathcal{C}$ is a repair for $\mathcal{P}$, no assertion in $\mathcal{P}$ is entailed by $\exists Z.\mathcal{C}$ w.r.t. $\mathcal{T}$, and thus none can be entailed by $\mathcal{Q}$ w.r.t. $\mathcal{T}$.

Assume that $\exists X.\mathcal{A} \models^{\mathcal{T}} \mathcal{Q}$, and no assertion in $\mathcal{P}$ is entailed by $\mathcal{Q}$ w.r.t. $\mathcal{T}$. The set $\mathcal{Q}$ is an $\mathcal{EL}$ ABox, and thus there is a qABox $\exists Y.\mathcal{B}$ that is equivalent to $\mathcal{Q}$. Our assumptions on $\mathcal{Q}$ imply that $\exists Y.\mathcal{B}$ is an IQ-repair of $\exists X.\mathcal{A}$ for $\mathcal{R}$ w.r.t. $\mathcal{T}$. Since every repair is entailed by an optimal repair [3], there is an optimal IQ-repair $\exists Z.\mathcal{C}$ of $\exists X.\mathcal{A}$ for $\mathcal{P}$ w.r.t. $\mathcal{T}$ such that $\exists Z.\mathcal{C} \models^{\mathcal{T}} \exists Y.\mathcal{B}$, and thus $\exists Z.\mathcal{C} \models^{\mathcal{T}} \mathcal{Q}$. □

Since the instance problem in $\mathcal{EL}$ can be decided in polynomial time, this yields the following complexity result.

Theorem 17. *Brave entailment w.r.t. optimal* IQ*-repairs is in* P.

This approach for testing brave entailment can also be used to support computing a specific repair. In general, there may be exponentially many optimal repairs, but this set can be narrowed down by specifying not only consequences $\mathcal{R}$ to be removed, but also consequences $\mathcal{Q}$ that one wants to retain. Brave entailment can be used to check in polynomial time whether such a repair exists: in fact, Lemma 16 tells us that $\mathcal{Q}$ is bravely entailed by $\exists X.\mathcal{A}$ for $\mathcal{R}$ w.r.t. $\mathcal{T}$ iff the translation of $\mathcal{Q}$ into a qABox $\exists Y.\mathcal{B}$ is an IQ-repair of $\exists X.\mathcal{A}$ for $\mathcal{R}$ w.r.t. $\mathcal{T}$. In general, this repair will not be optimal. However, the next proposition shows that an rsf that induces an optimal repair entailing $\exists Y.\mathcal{B}$ (and thus also $\mathcal{Q}$) can be computed in polynomial time.

Proposition 18. *Let* $\exists Y.\mathcal{B}$ *be an* IQ*-repair of* $\exists X.\mathcal{A}$ *for* $\mathcal{R}$ *w.r.t.* $\mathcal{T}$. *Then we can compute in polynomial time a* $\leq$*-minimal rsf* t *such that* $\mathsf{rep}_{\mathsf{IQ}}^{\mathcal{T}}(\exists X.\mathcal{A}, t) \models_{\mathsf{IQ}}^{\mathcal{T}}$ $\exists Y.\mathcal{B}$. *Since* t *is* $\leq$*-minimal,* $\mathsf{rep}_{\mathsf{IQ}}^{\mathcal{T}}(\exists X.\mathcal{A}, t)$ *is optimal.*

Proof. We know that every repair is entailed by a canonical repair. The proof of this fact (see proof of Proposition 8 in [4]) actually shows how to compute in polynomial time an rsf that induces this canonical repair. Thus, in the setting of our proposition, we can compute in polynomial time an rsf s such that $\mathsf{rep}_{\mathsf{IQ}}^{\mathcal{T}}(\exists X.\mathcal{A}, s) \models_{\mathsf{IQ}}^{\mathcal{T}} \exists Y.\mathcal{B}$. If s is $\leq$-minimal, then we are done. Otherwise, the proof of Lemma 12 tells us how to find an rsf s' such that $s' < s$. The rsf s' differs from s in the image for one individual a, where $s'(a) = \mathsf{low}(s(a), \mathcal{M}_D) < s(a)$ for an atom $D \in s(a)$. If s' is $\leq$-minimal, then we are done. Otherwise, we can compute an rsf s'' such that $s'' < s'$, etc. Since the next lemma implies that the length of such a chain $s > s' > s'' > \ldots$ is polynomially bounded by the number of individual names in $\exists X.\mathcal{A}$ and the cardinality of $\mathsf{Atoms}(\mathcal{R}, \mathcal{T})$, we reach a $\leq$-minimal rsf t with $t < s$ after a polynomial number of steps. By Lemma 5, $\mathsf{rep}_{\mathsf{IQ}}^{\mathcal{T}}(\exists X.\mathcal{A}, t) \models_{\mathsf{IQ}}^{\mathcal{T}} \mathsf{rep}_{\mathsf{IQ}}^{\mathcal{T}}(\exists X.\mathcal{A}, s)$, and thus $\mathsf{rep}_{\mathsf{IQ}}^{\mathcal{T}}(\exists X.\mathcal{A}, t) \models_{\mathsf{IQ}}^{\mathcal{T}} \exists Y.\mathcal{B}$. □

Lemma 19. *Let* $\mathcal{S}$ *be a set of* $\mathcal{EL}$ *concepts of cardinality* m *and* $\mathcal{K}_0, \mathcal{K}_1, \ldots, \mathcal{K}_n$ *be subsets of* $\mathcal{S}$ *such that* $\mathcal{K}_0 > \mathcal{K}_1 > \ldots > \mathcal{K}_n$. *Then* $n \leq m$.

Proof. For subsets $\mathcal{K}$ of $\mathcal{S}$, we define

$$\downarrow \mathcal{K} := \{ C \mid C \in \mathcal{S} \text{ and } C \sqsubseteq^\emptyset K \text{ for some } K \in \mathcal{K} \}.$$

It is easy to see that $\mathcal{K} \leq \mathcal{L}$ iff $\downarrow \mathcal{K} \subseteq \downarrow \mathcal{L}$ holds for all subsets $\mathcal{K}, \mathcal{L}$ of $\mathcal{S}$. Thus $\mathcal{K}_0 > \mathcal{K}_1 > \ldots > \mathcal{K}_n$ implies $\downarrow \mathcal{K}_0 \supset \downarrow \mathcal{K}_1 \supset \ldots \supset \downarrow \mathcal{K}_n$. Since the cardinality of $\downarrow \mathcal{K}_0$ is bounded by the cardinality m of $\mathcal{S}$, this shows that $n \leq m$. □

Since, for solvable repair requests, the empty qABox $\exists \emptyset.\emptyset$ is a repair, Proposition 18 also yields the following result.

Corollary 20. *Let* $\mathcal{T}$ *be an* $\mathcal{EL}$ *TBox,* $\exists X.\mathcal{A}$ *a qABox, and* $\mathcal{R}$ *a repair request that is solvable w.r.t.* $\mathcal{T}$. *Then we can compute in polynomial time a* $\leq$*-minimal rsf* t, *which thus induces an optimal* IQ*-repair of* $\exists X.\mathcal{A}$ *for* $\mathcal{R}$ *w.r.t.* $\mathcal{T}$.

4.2   Cautious Entailment

Using the polynomiality results of Sect. 3, we can prove that cautious entailment is in coNP. For this, we show that non-entailment is in NP. To check whether Q is not cautiously entailed by $\exists X.\mathcal{A}$ w.r.t. $\mathcal{T}$ and $\mathcal{R}$, we guess a function $s : \Sigma_I \to \wp(\mathsf{Atoms}(\mathcal{R}, \mathcal{T}))$ and check whether (i) s is a repair seed function; (ii) s is $\leq$-minimal; and (iii) there is $Q(a) \in Q$ such that $\mathsf{rep}_{\mathsf{IQ}}^{\mathcal{T}}(\exists X.\mathcal{A}, s) \not\models^{\mathcal{T}} Q(a)$. Note that (i) can be decided in polynomial time by the definition of repair seed functions, (ii) by Proposition 13, and (iii) Proposition 4.

Theorem 21. *Cautious entailment w.r.t. optimal IQ-repairs is in coNP.*

Whether this upper bound is tight is still an open problem. If the TBox is empty, then we can show a polynomiality result.

The Case with an Empty TBox. We show the polynomial upper bound again for non-entailment, i.e., we try to find out whether there is an optimal repair that does not entail Q. First note that, if Q is not entailed by $\exists X.\mathcal{A}$, then it cannot be entailed by an optimal repair. Thus, it is sufficient to concentrate on the case where $\exists X.\mathcal{A}$ entails Q. For this case, the next lemma gives a characterization of non-entailment. While this characterization may look complicated, it is actually easy to see that its conditions can be checked in polynomial time. Intuitively, the reason why the case of the empty TBox is easier to handle is that then premise-saturatedness of repair types (see Definition 2) is trivially satisfied. More technically, this means that, in the characterization of non-minimality of a repair seed function in Lemma 12, the set $\mathcal{M}_D$ is equal to $\{D\}$, i.e., the iteration in Definition 9 terminates for $j = 0$. This gives us more control over how the sets $\mathsf{low}(s(a), \mathcal{M}_D)$ in Lemma 12 actually look like.

Lemma 22. *Let Q be a finite set of $\mathcal{EL}$ concept assertions such that $\exists X.\mathcal{A} \models Q$. Then Q is not cautiously entailed by $\exists X.\mathcal{A}$ w.r.t. $\mathcal{R}$ iff there exist $C(a) \in Q$, $D \in \mathsf{Atoms}(\mathcal{R})$, and $P(a) \in \mathcal{R}$ with $\mathcal{A} \models P(a)$ such that the following conditions are satisfied:*

1. *$P \sqsubseteq^{\emptyset} D$ and $C \sqsubseteq^{\emptyset} D$,*
2. *for each $D' \in \mathsf{Atoms}(\mathcal{R})$ with $D' \sqsubset^{\emptyset} D$ and $\mathcal{A} \models D'(a)$, we have $P \not\sqsubseteq^{\emptyset} D'$,*
3. *for each $P'(a) \in \mathcal{R} \setminus \{P(a)\}$ with $\mathcal{A} \models P'(a)$ and $P' \not\sqsubseteq^{\emptyset} D$, there is $E \in \mathsf{Atoms}(\mathcal{R})$ such that $P' \sqsubseteq^{\emptyset} E$ and $P \not\sqsubseteq^{\emptyset} E$.*

Proof. For the "only if" direction, if Q is not cautiously entailed by $\exists X.\mathcal{A}$ w.r.t. $\mathcal{R}$, then there exist $C(a) \in Q$ and a $\leq$-minimal rsf s on $\exists X.\mathcal{A}$ for $\mathcal{R}$ such that $\mathsf{rep}_{\mathsf{IQ}}(\exists X.\mathcal{A}, s) \not\models C(a)$. By Lemma 3, the latter implies that there is $D \in s(a)$ such that $C \sqsubseteq^{\emptyset} D$.

Next, we show that there is $P(a) \in \mathcal{R}$ such that $P \sqsubseteq^{\emptyset} D$ and $\mathcal{A} \models P(a)$. Since s is $\leq$-minimal (for the case of an empty TBox), Lemma 12 implies that, for each $a \in \Sigma_I$ and each $E \in s(a)$, there is $P_E(a) \in \mathcal{R}$ with $\mathcal{A} \models P_E(a)$ such that $\{P_E\} \not\leq \mathsf{low}(s(a), \{E\})$. However, $\{P_E\} \leq s(a)$ by the definition of repair seed functions. By Definition 7, the only atom from $s(a)$ that does not occur in $\mathsf{low}(s(a), \{E\})$ is E, which implies that $P_E \sqsubseteq^\emptyset E$. Consequently, there is $P(a) \in \mathcal{R}$ with $\mathcal{A} \models P(a)$ such that $P \sqsubseteq^\emptyset D$, which shows that Condition 1 of this lemma is satisfied by C, D, and P.

The construction of $\mathsf{low}(s(a), \{D\})$ removes D and replace it with those atoms $D' \in \mathsf{Atoms}(\mathcal{R})$ that are strictly subsumed by D such that $\mathcal{A} \models D'(a)$. However, $\{P\} \not\subseteq \mathsf{low}(s(a), \{D\})$ implies that, for each $D' \in \mathsf{Atoms}(\mathcal{R})$ with $D' \sqsubset^\emptyset D$ and $\mathcal{A} \models D'(a)$, we have $P \not\sqsubseteq^\emptyset D'$, i.e., Condition 2 is satisfied.

To show that Condition 3 is satisfied, we consider $P'(a) \in \mathcal{R} \setminus \{P(a)\}$ with $\mathcal{A} \models P'(a)$ and $P' \not\sqsubseteq^\emptyset D$. By the definition of an rsf, there must be $E \in s(a) \setminus \{D\}$ such that $P' \sqsubseteq^\emptyset E$. The fact that $\{P\} \not\subseteq \mathsf{low}(s(a), \{D\})$ implies that $P \not\sqsubseteq^\emptyset E$, which shows that Condition 3 of this lemma is indeed satisfied.

For the "if" direction, we assume that there exist $P(a) \in \mathcal{R}$ with $\mathcal{A} \models P(a)$ and $D \in \mathsf{Atoms}(\mathcal{R})$ such that all the three conditions of this lemma are satisfied. We construct the set

$$\mathcal{K} := \{D\} \cup \mathsf{Max}_{\sqsubseteq^\emptyset}(\{E \in \mathsf{Atoms}(\mathcal{R}) \mid \text{there is } P'(a) \in (\mathcal{R} \setminus \{P(a)\}), \mathcal{A} \models P'(a),$$
$$P' \not\sqsubseteq^\emptyset D, P' \sqsubseteq^\emptyset E, P \not\sqsubseteq^\emptyset E\}),$$

and show that it is a repair type. Since the TBox is empty, it suffices to consider only the first two properties of the definition of repair types (see Definition 2). The second property is immediately satisfied by the construction of $\mathcal{K}$. To show the first property, it is sufficient to prove that, for each $E \in \mathcal{K} \setminus \{D\}$, the atoms D and E are not $\sqsubseteq^\emptyset$-comparable. In fact, if $D \sqsubseteq^\emptyset E$, then $P \sqsubseteq^\emptyset E$, which contradicts our assumption that $E \in \mathcal{K} \setminus \{D\}$. If $E \sqsubseteq^\emptyset D$, then $P' \sqsubseteq^\emptyset D$ is a contradiction for some $P'(a) \in \mathcal{R} \setminus \{P(a)\}$, where $P' \sqsubseteq^\emptyset E$.

Using this set $\mathcal{K}$, we now define a function $s : \Sigma_\mathsf{I} \to \wp(\mathsf{Atoms}(\mathcal{R}))$ such that $s(a) := \mathcal{K}$ and $s(b) := \mathcal{M}_b$ for each individual $b \in \Sigma_\mathsf{I} \setminus \{a\}$, where $\mathcal{M}_b$ is a repair type for b and for each $R(b) \in \mathcal{R}$ with $\mathcal{A} \models R(b)$, there is $F \in \mathcal{M}_b$ such that $R \sqsubseteq^\emptyset F$. Such a repair type $\mathcal{M}_b$ exists for each $b \in \Sigma_\mathsf{I} \setminus \{a\}$ since $\mathcal{R}$ is solvable (see Proposition X in [4]).

We show that s is a repair seed function on $\exists X.\mathcal{A}$ for $\mathcal{R}$. For individuals $b \in \Sigma_\mathsf{I} \setminus \{a\}$, the condition on seed functions is satisfied, due to the way the sets $\mathcal{M}_b$ were chosen, i.e., such that $R(b) \in \mathcal{R}$ with $\mathcal{A} \models R(b)$ implies that there is an atom in $s(b)$ that subsumes R. We show that the corresponding condition also holds for $s(a)$. For $P(a)$, this is clear since is $D \in s(a)$ and $P \sqsubseteq^\emptyset D$. Furthermore, for each $P'(a) \in \mathcal{R} \setminus \{P(a)\}$, we distinguish two cases. If $P' \sqsubseteq^\emptyset D$, then we are done. Otherwise, by Condition 3, $P' \not\sqsubseteq^\emptyset D$ implies that there is $E \in \mathsf{Atoms}(\mathcal{R})$ such that $P' \sqsubseteq^\emptyset E$ and $P' \not\sqsubseteq^\emptyset E$. By the construction of $\mathcal{K}$, such an atom E occurs in $s(a) = \mathcal{K}$. This finally shows that s is an rsf on $\exists X.\mathcal{A}$ for $\mathcal{R}$.

Next, we show that, for each $\leq$-minimal rsf s' covered by s, the canonical repair induced by s' still does not entail $C(a)$. By Lemma 3, it is sufficient to show that $s'(a)$ contains an atom D' such that $D \sqsubseteq^\emptyset D'$. In fact, then $C \sqsubseteq^\emptyset D$ yields $C \sqsubseteq^\emptyset D'$ for $D' \in s'(a)$, and thus $C(a)$ is not entailed by the canonical repair induced by s', which is optimal since s' is minimal.

By contradiction, assume that there is a $\leq$-minimal rsf s' such that $s' \leq s$ and $D \not\sqsubseteq^\emptyset D'$ holds for all $D' \in s'(a)$. Thus, for each $D' \in s'(a)$, we have either

$D' \sqsubseteq^{\emptyset} D$ or $D' \not\sqsubseteq^{\emptyset} D$. Consider again the concept P. Since s' is an rsf, there is $D' \in s'(a)$ such that $P \sqsubseteq^{\emptyset} D'$. Suppose that $D' \sqsubseteq^{\emptyset} D$. However, this is a contradiction since Condition 2 of this lemma states that P is not subsumed by any concept that is strictly subsumed by D. Otherwise, $D' \not\sqsubseteq^{\emptyset} D$. Since $s' \leq s$, we have $D' \sqsubseteq^{\emptyset} E$, where $E \in s(a) \setminus \{D\}$. By the definition of $\mathcal{K}$, P is not subsumed by E. However, $P \sqsubseteq^{\emptyset} D'$ and $D' \sqsubseteq^{\emptyset} E$, which yields a contradiction. $\square$

This lemma reduces the non-entailment test to polynomially many subsumption and instance tests, each of which can be performed in polynomial time.

Theorem 23. *For an empty TBox, cautious entailment w.r.t. optimal IQ-repairs is in* P.

5   Conclusion

Inconsistency-tolerant and error-tolerant reasoning have been introduced in the DL literature [10,11,15,16,18] as a way to reason w.r.t. an inconsistent or erroneous ontology without having to commit to a specific repair. The usual entailment relations employed for this purpose are brave entailment (consequences entailed by some repair) and cautious entailment (consequences entailed by all repairs). In contrast to previous work, we use optimal repairs [3] instead of classical ones [9,17,19] when defining these relations. We investigated the complexity of the obtained entailment relations for the cases without and with a TBox, and could show a polynomial time upper bound for all cases except the one of cautious entailment with a TBox, for which we proved a coNP upper bound. The intuition underlying our use of optimal repairs is that a repair should not invent new consequences and should not have any of the unwanted consequences. A good repair should only remove consequences if this is required to achieve the other two goals.

Our approach for testing brave entailment can also be used to support computing a specific repair. In general, there may be exponentially many optimal repairs, but this set can be narrowed down by specifying not only consequences to be removed, but also ones that one wants to retain. We have shown that brave entailment can be used to check in polynomial time whether such a repair exists. In the positive case, we can compute in polynomial time a repair seed function that induces an optimal repair that entails all wanted consequences.

As pointed out in [16,18], cautious entailment can be used to reason w.r.t. an erroneous ontology while waiting for a corrected update to be published by the organization that maintains this ontology. If the application is not repair but privacy preservation, one can use cautious entailment to define a censor [12] that prevents revealing certain secrets. The reason is that, in contrast to brave entailment, the set of cautious consequences is closed under (classical) entailment.

As future work, we will investigate whether our coNP upper bound for cautious entailment with a TBox is tight, and whether a notion of IAR entailment that is appropriate for optimal repairs can be found. We also intend to add support for role assertions both in the repair request and in the query. Furthermore, it would be interesting to consider error-tolerant reasoning w.r.t. the optimal TBox repairs in [13].

References

1. Baader, F., Brandt, S., Lutz, C.: Pushing the $\mathcal{EL}$ envelope. In: IJCAI-05, Proceedings of the Nineteenth International Joint Conference on Artificial Intelligence. Professional Book Center (2005). https://www.ijcai.org/Proceedings/05/Papers/0372.pdf
2. Baader, F., Horrocks, I., Lutz, C., Sattler, U.: An Introduction to Description Logic. Cambridge University Press, Cambridge (2017)
3. Baader, F., Koopmann, P., Kriegel, F., Nuradiansyah, A.: Computing optimal repairs of quantified ABoxes w.r.t. static $\mathcal{EL}$ TBoxes. In: Platzer, A., Sutcliffe, G. (eds.) CADE 2021. LNCS (LNAI), vol. 12699, pp. 309–326. Springer, Cham (2021). https://doi.org/10.1007/978-3-030-79876-5_18
4. Baader, F., Koopmann, P., Kriegel, F., Nuradiansyah, A.: Computing optimal repairs of quantified ABoxes w.r.t. static $\mathcal{EL}$ TBoxes (extended version). LTCS-Report 21-01, Chair of Automata Theory, Institute of Theoretical Computer Science, Technische Universität Dresden, Dresden, Germany (2021). https://doi.org/10.25368/2022.64
5. Baader, F., Koopmann, P., Kriegel, F., Nuradiansyah, A.: Optimal ABox repair w.r.t. static $\mathcal{EL}$ TBoxes: from quantified ABoxes back to ABoxes. In: Groth, P., et al. (eds.) ESWC 2022. LNCS, vol. 13261, pp. 130–146. Springer, Cham (2022). https://doi.org/10.1007/978-3-031-06981-9_8
6. Baader, F., Koopmann, P., Kriegel, F., Nuradiansyah, A.: Optimal ABox repair w.r.t. static $\mathcal{EL}$ TBoxes: from quantified ABoxes back to ABoxes (extended version). LTCS-Report 22-01, Chair of Automata Theory, Institute of Theoretical Computer Science, Technische Universität Dresden, Dresden, Germany (2022). https://doi.org/10.25368/2022.65
7. Baader, F., Kriegel, F., Nuradiansyah, A.: Privacy-preserving ontology publishing for $\mathcal{EL}$ instance stores. In: Calimeri, F., Leone, N., Manna, M. (eds.) JELIA 2019. LNCS (LNAI), vol. 11468, pp. 323–338. Springer, Cham (2019). https://doi.org/10.1007/978-3-030-19570-0_21
8. Baader, F., Kriegel, F., Nuradiansyah, A., Peñaloza, R.: Computing compliant anonymisations of quantified ABoxes w.r.t. $\mathcal{EL}$ policies. In: Pan, J.Z., et al. (eds.) ISWC 2020. LNCS, vol. 12506, pp. 3–20. Springer, Cham (2020). https://doi.org/10.1007/978-3-030-62419-4_1
9. Baader, F., Suntisrivaraporn, B.: Debugging SNOMED CT using axiom pinpointing in the description logic $\mathcal{EL}^+$. In: Proceedings of the International Conference on Representing and Sharing Knowledge Using SNOMED (KR-MED 2008), Phoenix, Arizona (2008). http://ceur-ws.org/Vol-410/Paper01.pdf
10. Bienvenu, M., Rosati, R.: Tractable approximations of consistent query answering for robust ontology-based data access. In: IJCAI 2013, Proceedings of the 23rd International Joint Conference on Artificial Intelligence. IJCAI/AAAI (2013). https://www.ijcai.org/Proceedings/13/Papers/121.pdf

11. Calì, A., Lembo, D., Rosati, R.: On the decidability and complexity of query answering over inconsistent and incomplete databases. In: Proceedings of the Twenty-Second ACM SIGACT-SIGMOD-SIGART Symposium on Principles of Database Systems. ACM (2003). https://doi.org/10.1145/773153.773179

12. Cima, G., Lembo, D., Rosati, R., Savo, D.F.: Controlled query evaluation in description logics through instance indistinguishability. In: Proceedings of the Twenty-Ninth International Joint Conference on Artificial Intelligence, IJCAI 2020. ijcai.org (2020). https://doi.org/10.24963/ijcai.2020/248

13. Kriegel, F.: Optimal fixed-premise repairs of $\mathcal{EL}$ TBoxes. In: Bergmann, R., Malburg, L., Rodermund, S.C., Timm, I.J. (eds.) KI 2022. LNCS, vol. 13404, pp. 115–130. Springer, Cham (2022). https://doi.org/10.1007/978-3-031-15791-2_11

14. Kriegel, F.: Optimal fixed-premise repairs of $\mathcal{EL}$ TBoxes (extended version). LTCS-Report 22-04, Chair of Automata Theory, Institute of Theoretical Computer Science, Technische Universität Dresden, Dresden, Germany (2022). https://doi.org/10.25368/2022.321

15. Lembo, D., Lenzerini, M., Rosati, R., Ruzzi, M., Savo, D.F.: Inconsistency-tolerant query answering in ontology-based data access. J. Web Semant. **33**, 3–29 (2015). https://doi.org/10.1016/j.websem.2015.04.002

16. Ludwig, M., Peñaloza, R.: Error-tolerant reasoning in the description logic $\mathcal{EL}$. In: Fermé, E., Leite, J. (eds.) JELIA 2014. LNCS (LNAI), vol. 8761, pp. 107–121. Springer, Cham (2014). https://doi.org/10.1007/978-3-319-11558-0_8

17. Parsia, B., Sirin, E., Kalyanpur, A.: Debugging OWL ontologies. In: Proceedings of the 14th International Conference on World Wide Web (WWW 2005). ACM (2005). https://doi.org/10.1145/1060745.1060837

18. Peñaloza, R.: Error-tolerance and error management in lightweight description logics. Künstliche Intell. **34**(4), 491–500 (2020). https://doi.org/10.1007/s13218-020-00684-5

19. Schlobach, S., Huang, Z., Cornet, R., Harmelen, F.: Debugging incoherent terminologies. J. Autom. Reason. **39**(3), 317–349 (2007). https://doi.org/10.1007/s10817-007-9076-z

Bridging Between LegalRuleML and TPTP for Automated Normative Reasoning

Alexander Steen[1(✉)] and David Fuenmayor[2,3]

[1] University of Greifswald, Greifswald, Germany
`alexander.steen@uni-greifswald.de`
[2] University of Luxembourg, Esch-sur-Alzette, Luxembourg
`david.fuenmayor@uni.lu`
[3] University of Bamberg, Bamberg, Germany

Abstract. LegalRuleML is a comprehensive XML-based representation framework for modeling and exchanging normative rules. The TPTP input and output formats, on the other hand, are general-purpose standards for the interaction with automated reasoning systems. In this paper we provide a bridge between the two communities by (i) defining a logic-pluralistic normative reasoning language based on the TPTP format, (ii) providing a translation scheme between relevant fragments of LegalRuleML and this language, and (iii) proposing a flexible architecture for automated normative reasoning based on this translation. We exemplarily instantiate and demonstrate the approach with three different normative logics.

Keywords: Automated reasoning · LegalRuleML · Deontic logics

1 Introduction

Automated theorem proving (ATP) systems are computer programs that, given a set A of assumptions and a conjecture C as input, try to prove that C is a logical consequence of A, i.e., that it is impossible for C to be false whenever every formula from A holds. ATP systems conduct the whole reasoning process automatically, so that no user interaction is necessary during proof search.

In normative reasoning, logical formalisms are employed to represent and reason about different notions of norms, including obligations, permissions and prohibitions. In automated normative reasoning, the goal is hence to automate the reasoning process in the context of normative discourse by employing suitable logical systems. LegalRuleML [2,3] is a comprehensive XML-based representation framework for modeling and exchanging normative rules, e.g., legal norms originating from national laws of some particular country. The LegalRuleML

The second author acknowledges financial support from the Luxembourg National Research Fund (FNR) under grant CORE AuReLeE (C20/IS/14616644).

G. Governatori and A.-Y. Turhan (Eds.): RuleML+RR 2022, LNCS 13752, pp. 244–260, 2022.
https://doi.org/10.1007/978-3-031-21541-4_16

standard comes with fine-grained and expressive means for representing (possibly legal) norms in an *isomorphic* [4] fashion with respect to their original source(s). At the same time, LegalRuleML is *semantically underspecified*, in the sense that it deliberately does not prescribe a specific logic (or semantics) in which the represented norms are to be interpreted.

LegalRuleML has been employed by Robaldo et al. to provide an exhaustive formalization of the General Data Protection Regulation (GDPR) [24]. Palmirani and Governatori combine LegalRuleML with further technologies and approaches to present an integrated framework for compliance checking with legal rules, but also focusing on GDPR applications [22]. Still, there exist only comparably few systems that, in fact, automate reasoning processes based on normative knowledge. Notable examples are provided by Liu et al. who interpret legal norms in a defeasible deontic logic and provide automation for it [19], and the SPINdle prover [17] for propositional (modal) defeasible reasoning that has been used in multiple works in the normative application domain.

In contrast, there are many general-purpose ATP systems available for classical logics, e.g., for propositional logic, first-order predicate logic, and more recently for higher-order logic. These systems are being continuously improved and are increasingly becoming more effective, as witnessed by the results of the annual ATP system competition CASC [30]. The development of general-purpose ATP systems for normative reasoning is, on the other hand, complicated by the fact that there is no single logic acting as the de-facto standard formalism for normative reasoning. In general, the design and implementation of practically effective ATP systems is a non-trivial task and very laborious; and so it is easy to see that developing custom ATP systems for each distinct normative formalism is a quite unfeasible undertaking, in particular since, as witnessed in deontic logic (see Sect. 2.2), those formalisms behave as moving targets.

In this paper, we therefore propose to employ for this task general-purpose ATP systems for classical higher-order logic, and thus to reduce normative reasoning tasks to classical ATP problems in a general way. For this, we bridge between LegalRuleML and the TPTP language standard for ATP systems [31], so that any TPTP-compliant ATP system for higher-order logic can be reused as a reasoning backend for a wide range of normative logics.

The contributions of this paper are as follows:

- We define a logic-pluralistic domain specific language (DSL) for normative reasoning with TPTP-compliant ATP systems.
- We show how the DSL can be mechanically translated into ATP reasoning problems in different concrete normative logics.
- We describe a reasoning architecture that provides flexible means of automation for these normative logics.
- We present a prototypical implementation of the whole reasoning tool chain that is available as open-source code.

The remainder of this paper is structured as follows: In Sect. 2 we briefly survey the TPTP and the LegalRuleML standards, together with a very brief exposition of deontic logics as specific systems for normative reasoning. In Sect. 3, we discuss the role of logical pluralism in normative reasoning, which is one of the key motivations of this work. Subsequently, Sect. 4 presents the utilization of a TPTP format for normative rules. In Sect. 5 we then present a flexible and uniform approach for automating normative reasoning using general purpose ATP systems. Finally, Sect. 6 concludes and sketches further work.

An extended version of this paper is available on arXiv [27].

Related Work. Automation approaches by translation have been studied by Lam and Hashmi, where they translate LegalRuleML statements into a defeasible modal logic for which an automated reasoning tool exists [18]. Their approach is, however, fixed to one specific logic formalism as opposed to the logic-pluralistic view that we put forward in this work. Similarly, Boley et al. translate RuleML information to modal logic in TPTP format [9]. However, simple modal logics are not fully adequate for normative reasoning, see the brief discussion in Sect. 2.2. Our approach is in line with the LogiKEy methodology proposed by Benzmüller et al. [6], which makes use of expressive higher-order logics for flexibly encoding, reasoning, and experimenting with normative theories.

2   Preliminaries

2.1   The TPTP Infrastructure for ATP Systems

The *Thousands of Problems for Theorem Proving* (TPTP) library and infrastructure [31] is the core platform for contemporary ATP system development and evaluation. It provides (i) a comprehensive collection of benchmark problems for ATP systems; (ii) a set of utility tools for problem and solution inspection, pre- and post-processing, and verification; and (iii) a comprehensive syntax standard for ATP system input and output.

The TPTP specifies different ATP system languages varying in their expressivity [31]: The *first-order form* (FOF) represents unsorted first-order logic, the *typed first-order form* (TFF) represents many-sorted first-order logic, and *typed higher-order form* (THF) represents classical higher-order logic. An ATP problem generally consists of symbol declarations (if the language is typed), contextual definitions and premises of the reasoning task (usually referred to as *axioms*), and a conjecture that is to be proved or refuted in the given context. The core building block of the ATP problem files in TPTP languages are so-called *annotated formulas* of form . . .

$$language(name, role, formula[, source[, annotations]]) \, .$$

Here, *language* is a three-letter identifier for the intended language in which the annotated formula is expressed (`fof`, `tff` or `thf`). The *name* is a unique identifier for referencing to the annotated formula but has no other effect on the interpretation of it. The *role* field specifies whether the *formula* should be interpreted, among others, as an assumption (role `axiom`), a type declaration (role `type`), a definition (role `definition`) or as formula to be proved (role `conjecture`). The *formula* is an ASCII representation of the respective logical expression, where predicate and function symbols are denoted by strings that begin with a lower-case letter, variables are denoted by strings starting with an upper-case letter, the logical connectives ¬, ∧, ∨, →, ↔ are represented by ~, &, |, => and <=>, respectively. Quantifiers ∀ and ∃ are expressed by ! and ?, respectively, followed by a list of variables bound by it. The TPTP defines several interpreted constants starting with a $-sign, including $true and $false for truth and falsehood, respectively. In typed languages, such as TFF and THF, the type $i represents the type of individuals and $o is the type of Booleans. In TFF, explicit types of symbols may be dropped and default to n-ary function types ($i * ... * $i) > $i and n-ary predicate types ($i * ... * $i) > $o depending on their occurrence. Finally, the *source* and *annotations* are optional extra-logical information, e.g., about its origin, its relevance, or other properties. An example in TFF is as follows:

```
tff(union_def, axiom, ! [S, T, X]: (
                    member(X, union(S,T)) <=>
                    ( member(X, S) | member(X, T) ) ),
           source('definitions.ax'),
           [relevance(1.0)]).
```

In this example, a TFF annotated formula of name union_def is given that describes an axiom giving a fundamental property of set union and some auxiliary information about it. A complete description of the TPTP infrastructure and its input languages, including the syntax BNF, is provided by Sutcliffe [31] and the TPTP web page (tptp.org).

2.2 Deontic Logics and LegalRuleML

Deontic logics are logical systems intended to formally represent normative notions, such as obligations, permissions and prohibitions, their relationships, and their properties [14]. An early deontic logic, today still referred to as standard deontic logic (SDL), is based on simple modal logic **D**. In this context, the modal operators are usually denoted O (for obligation) and P (for permission), where $O\varphi \leftrightarrow \neg P\neg\varphi$ holds, and every instance of $O\varphi \rightarrow P\varphi$ is validated.

In normative reasoning contexts, usually other deontic logics are employed today. Dyadic deontic logics specifically address conditional norms of the form $O(\varphi|\psi)$ (read: *It ought to be φ given ψ*) [23], defeasible deontic logics address non-monotonic reasoning patterns with defeasible norms [15], and norm-based deontic logics model norms separately from factual expressions [20].

A prominent example illustrating the shortcomings of SDL related to conditional norms is Chisholm's paradox [13], paraphrased as follows:
Assume that your neighbors are in trouble (and you like them), then ...

(1) *You ought to go help your neighbors.*
(2) *If you go help your neighbors, you ought to tell them you are coming over.*
(3) *If you do not go help your neighbors, you ought not to tell them you are coming over.*

(4) *You do not go help your neighbors.*

The sentences (1) – (4) above appear to describe a plausible situation, and, intuitively, they also constitute a both logically consistent and independent set of sentences. Hence, arguably, an adequate formalization should respect these constraints. Chisholm's paradox here mainly serves as a running example that highlights the significant effects of interpreting normative information under different logical systems.

Table 1. Some possible formalizations of Chisholm's paradox.

Natural language	SDL-v1	SDL-v2	SDL-v3	DDL
You ought to go help your neighbors	$O\,h$	$O\,h$	$O\,h$	$O\,h$
If you go help your neighbors, you ought to tell them you are coming over	$O\,(h \to t)$	$O\,(h \to t)$	$h \to O\,t$	$O\,(t\|h)$
If you do not go help your neighbors, you ought not to tell them you are coming over	$\neg h \to O\,\neg t$	$O\,(\neg h \to \neg t)$	$\neg h \to O\,\neg t$	$O\,(\neg t\|\neg h)$
You do not go help your neighbors	$\neg h$	$\neg h$	$\neg h$	$\neg h$

Table 1 shows several different interpretations for Chisholm's scenario; three of them formalized using SDL, and the fourth formalized using a dyadic deontic logic (DDL) where h represents "helping your neighbors" and t represents "telling them you are coming over". As it happens, the set of formulas corresponding to the first SDL-formalization variant (SDL-v1) is inconsistent, thus allowing the derivation of every formula and, in particular, every obligation (e.g., $O\,k$ where k could represent "killing your neighbor"). In fact, the next two SDL-formalizations are not logically independent, and thus inadequate, see [16, §8.5] for a discussion. In dyadic deontic logics the conditional norms from above are represented using dyadic obligation operators as in $O(t|h)$ resp. $O(\neg t|\neg h)$ instead of material implications. These logic systems are specifically conceived in order to remedy shortcomings of SDL in addressing the so-called 'paradoxes' of deontic logic related to conditional obligations. Unsurprisingly, no logic formalism has yet been found which successfully addresses all of the many different deontic paradoxes and deficiencies, see [16, §8] for an exhaustive overview.

LegalRuleML. [2] is a comprehensive XML-based representation framework for modeling and exchanging normative rules. It extends the general RuleML standard [10] with specialized concepts and features for normative rules, legal contexts, interpretations, etc. In LegalRuleML, conditional deontic norms are represented using specialized rules called `PrescriptiveStatements` of the form ...

```
<lrml:PrescriptiveStatement>
  <ruleml:Rule closure="universal">
    <ruleml:if>  ... </ruleml:if>
```

```
    <ruleml:then> ... </ruleml:then>
  </ruleml:Rule>
</lrml:PrescriptiveStatement>
```

where both the if-node (the body) and the then-node (the head) may contain the LegalRuleML deontic operators Obligation, Permission and Prohibition, and combinations thereof using the usual connectives. The semantics of the deontic operators is left underspecified by LegalRuleML, so that any deontic logic may be assumed, e.g., via the appliesModality edge element, to interpret the represented norms. ConstitutiveStatements represent so-called *counts-as* norms, and they cannot have deontic operators in their head.

For a thorough introduction to LegalRuleML we refer to the literature [2,3].

2.3   Domain-Specific Languages

Domain-specific languages (DSLs) are formal languages (e.g. programming or logical languages) that have been designed for use in a particular domain. Their expressivity is deliberately restricted to allow for a higher degree of abstraction, and thus to better leverage specialized domain knowledge of their users.

DSLs can be divided into stand-alone and embedded. The former provide their own custom syntax and semantics, thus allowing for a maximal level of customization, but represent a significant implementation effort by requiring the provision of a complete compilation tool chain (parser, type-checker, etc.). The latter consist essentially in a collection of definitions encoded using a more expressive 'host' language; this way the existing infrastructure and tools of the host environment can be reused for the DSL. In this case we often speak of an object language (the DSL) that has been embedded into the host language.

In the context of embedded DSLs, one can further differentiate between two embedding techniques, termed *deep* and *shallow* embeddings. In a deep embedding, the terms of the object language are encoded as inductive data structures in the host language, i.e., as its abstract syntax tree (AST), and term interpretation functions (providing the semantics) can then be defined inductively, e.g. for evaluation/execution or optimization. In contrast, terms in shallow embeddings correspond to syntactic abbreviations of the host language, and thus directly encode the intended semantics of object-language expressions. Hence, evaluation in a shallow embedding corresponds to evaluation in its host language, bypassing the need for defining and inductively traversing an AST. In the context of (non-classical) logic a special technique, termed *shallow semantical embeddings* [5], has been developed to harness shallow embeddings to encode (quantified) non-classical logics into classical higher-order logic.

3   Logical Pluralism in Normative Reasoning

3.1   The Problem of Formalization

In computer science, the idea of mechanistically computing formal representations of natural language in a purely compositional way, made popular through the seminal work of Richard Montague [21], has been pursued with the help of automated reasoners during the last thirty or so years in the area known as *computational semantics* [7]. One of the main insights has been that the expressions in natural language are semantically underspecified in the sense that not enough information can be extracted from them to construct the sort of meaning representations Montague was dreaming of, that is, formulas in some formal logical language. Thus, interpreting ordinary sentences can lead to an unfeasible number of different meaning representations [11].

Among the main determinants behind this underspecification phenomenon, we find ambiguity (syntactic and semantic) and the lack of background knowledge. Among the proposed solutions to tackle the first issue, several kinds of *underspecified semantic representations* have been proposed. However, they have been seen as challenging the application of automated reasoning methods, since disambiguation often results in different formalizations licensing disparate sets of inferences [8]. This has been seen commonly as a problem according to the traditional conception that each natural-language statement shall be correlated with one most adequate ('correct') formalization.

On the other hand, the available (formalized) background knowledge is also a degree of freedom determining which inferences are to be drawn from a formalized set of sentences. This knowledge can be of a linguistic nature (e.g. lexica) or more domain-specific (e.g. ontologies and knowledge bases). In fact, the availability of adequate sources for background knowledge is a well-known bottleneck in the *computational semantics* endeavor. In this respect, RuleML and related knowledge representation and interchange standards, in particular LegalRuleML, play a fundamental role in enabling the interfacing with available normative knowledge sources and ontologies.

3.2   Formalizing Normative Discourse

The problem of formalization depicted above applies notably to the logical encoding of normative discourse. This has been experienced with particular intensity in the area of deontic logic. An example of the above is the Chisholm's paradox, as presented in Sect. 2.2, where we could appreciate how the task of adequately formalizing a set of simple natural-language sentences can give rise not only to different logical forms, but also to different ways of interpreting logical connectives, such as conditionals, (deontic) modalities, etc.

In this work, we aim at doing justice to the complex problem of formalizing normative discourse, and thus suggest to employ normative domain-specific languages (DSLs) as an intermediate representation format to encode normative knowledge in a *semantic underspecified* fashion, even reaching to the level of the logical connectives themselves, which thus require further specification for subsequent reasoning tasks. This introduces a component of *logical pluralism* into our approach, since (semantically underspecified) logical operators can (and will) be given concrete interpretations in different non-classical logics, see Sect. 5. Moreover, we aim at showing not only that such a DSL can (and should) be of a formal logical nature, but also that it can at the same time be fully machine-readable for subsequent consumption by automated reasoning tools. Hence we introduce an illustrative normative DSL *embedded* in a suitable TPTP language below.

4   Normative Knowledge Representation in the TPTP

TPTP traditionally focused on classical logic, e.g., standards and benchmark sets for classical propositional and (first- and higher-order) predicate logic formalisms. Only recently there have been some ongoing efforts on extending TPTP towards non-classical logics as well [29]. For this purpose, the TFF language has been extended with expressions of the form ...

   {*connective_name*} @ ($arg_1, \ldots, arg_n$)

where *connective_name* is either a TPTP-defined name (starting with a $ sign) or a user-defined name (starting with two $ signs) for a non-classical operator, and the arg_i are terms or formulas to which the operator is applied. TPTP-defined connectives have a fixed meaning and are documented by the TPTP; the interpretation of user-defined connectives is provided by third-party systems, environments, or documentation. Non-classical operators may optionally be parameterized with key-value arguments (see below for exemplary use). The so enriched TPTP language is denoted NXF (non-classical extended first-order form). An analogous extension of THF, called NHF (non-classical higher order form), has been introduced as well (not discussed here).

Non-classical logic languages often come with different logics (e.g., different semantics) associated with them. A prominent example are modal logic languages in which the properties of the box operator □ depend on the concrete modal logic at hand. For example, in modal logic **S5** all instances of $\Box\varphi \rightarrow \varphi$ are tautologies, while this is not the case in modal logic **K** – still both logics share the same vocabulary. In order to resolve these ambiguities and to specify the exact logic under consideration, non-classical TPTP adds *logic specifications* to the language [29]. They are annotated formulas of form (here: in NXF) ...

   tff(*name*, logic, *logic_name* == [*options*]).

where logic is the TPTP role, *logic_name* is a TPTP-defined or user-defined designator for a logical language and *options* are comma-separated key-value pairs that fix the specific logic based on that language. Of course, changing the *logic specification* may change the provability/validity of the underlying reasoning problem.

The NXF problem representing the formalization (SDL-v3) of Chisholm's paradox, as introduced in Sect. 2.2, in simple modal logic **D** is as follows (where {$box} represents the modal box operator, denoted O in SDL):

```
tff(spec, logic, $modal == [$modalities == $modal_system_D, ...]
tff(norm1, axiom, {$box} @ (help)).
tff(norm2, axiom, help => {$box} @ (tell)).
tff(norm3, axiom, ~help => {$box} @ (~tell)).
tff(fact1, axiom, ~help).
```

The first line specifies the modal logic to be used (here, modal logic **D**), while the remaining four lines encode the formulas from Sect. 2.2. For illustration purposes, not all of the logic parameters are shown in the *logic specification*. A list of logics supported by the TPTP so far, their parameters, and their representation is available in the literature [29].

4.1   NMF: A Normative DSL in TPTP

The non-classical TPTP formats introduced above allow for encoding non-classical logics for use with generic ATP systems. Nevertheless, each problem representation in that format needs to have a fixed underlying logic as specified by the logic specification. In the present work we want to allow for working with many different normative logics in a uniform way; for this sake we introduce an *embedded DSL* (Sect. 2.3) hosted on top of non-classical TPTP formats, and referred to as *Normative Meta Form* (NMF) in the remainder. This way, every file represented in NMF will be syntactically well-formed TPTP, and hence we can use standard TPTP tools, such as syntax checkers, for processing them. Also, available software packages for ATP systems, e.g. parsers, can be reused.

More specifically, NMF extends NXF from above as follows: The operator names `$$obligation`, `$$permission`, `$$prohibition`, and `$$constitutive` are introduced. They are binary operators, and interpreted as follows ...

- `{$$obligation} @ (body, head)` encodes "**head** is obligatory given **body**",
- `{$$permission} @ (body, head)` encodes "**head** is permitted given **body**",
- `{$$prohibition} @ (body, head)` encodes "**head** is prohibited given **body**",
- each of the three deontic operators may optionally be parameterized with the `bearer` option, e.g. `{$$obligation(bearer := x) @ (body, head)`, to denote a directed deontic statement towards entity `x`, and
- `{$$constitutive} @ (body, head)` encodes a constitutive norm (counts-as norm) that establishes the institutional fact that **body** counts as **head**.

Since NMF extends NXF, it does not come with a fixed logic and is thus semantically underspecified. We can choose a concrete interpretation of the underspecified deontic operators using the *logic specification* as follows ...

    tff(*name*, logic, $$normative == [$$logic == *target_logic*]).

where *target_logic* is some deontic logic identifier. We will describe the target logics currently supported in Sect. 5. For the time being, it is important to highlight that the description of the encoded norms will remain the same, regardless of which target logic we choose, and we only need to give a *logic specification* for the desired logic. Note that some deontic logics, such as SDL, do not come with built-in operators for conditional deontic expressions. Hence, our normative DSL (NMF) has been designed to abstract away the deontic operators of concrete logics, and we show in Sect. 5 how to translate from NMF to concrete deontic logics.

The running example of Chisholm's paradox can be encoded in NMF in a logically underspecified way (i.e. without a *logic specification*) as follows:

```
tff(norm1, axiom, {$$obligation} @ ($true, help)).
tff(norm2, axiom, {$$obligation} @ (help, tell)).
tff(norm3, axiom, {$$obligation} @ (~help, ~tell)).
tff(fact1, axiom, ~help).
```

Recall that NMF is defined on top of NXF and, as such, offers first-order quantification, predicate symbols and function symbols. An even more expressive, higher-order quantified, variant of NMF could be defined analogously on top of NHF (not discussed here).

4.2 Conversion from LegalRuleML to NMF

The top-level LegalRuleML statements are translated into NMF as presented in Table 2. Note that we are currently addressing only a small fragment of Legal-RuleML with this translation; many important metadata present in the Legal-RuleML documentation are not yet considered. In this initial stage we primarily target automation of normative codes as formalized using deontic logics. In particular, suborder lists are currently not supported, and also strengths/exception specifications of deontic statements are not yet captured.

The translation process recursively translates the prescriptive statements, constitutive statements and factual statements of LegalRuleML into formulas in NMF. For identification purposes, key references from LegalRuleML are kept as formula names in the TPTP representation, and additional (legal) references and associations, expressed via <lrml:LegalReferences> or <lrml:References> blocks, and assigned by <lrml:Associations> blocks, respectively, are kept during the translation as TPTP annotations (not shown in Table 2). If a deontic operator in LegalRuleML comes with a <lrml:Bearer> node, this is mirrored in NMF as sketched in Sect. 4.1.

The translation from LegalRuleML to the proposed logic-pluralistic TPTP-based DSL is prototypically implemented as part of the *tptp-utils* tool, available at GitHub[1]. *tptp-utils* will produce a NMF file according to the above translation scheme but without a *logic specification*. The latter can be added by the user in order to assume concrete interpretations of the normative statements, see Sect. 5. A *logic specification* could also be created automatically from the LegalRuleML document, deriving from respective appliesModality edges; this is an interesting venue for further work.

5 TPTP-Based Normative Reasoning Backends

The translation of LegalRuleML statements into a representation in the TPTP-based DSL introduced above does not yet allow the utilization of automated reasoning tools for automated normative reasoning. It does give, though, an abstract representation of the encoded information in a format that we can use to provide means for automation via the general TPTP automated reasoning

---

[1] See https://github.com/leoprover/tptp-utils and its README there.

Table 2. Translation scheme from a fragment of LegalRuleML to NMF. In each case except the last one the quantification closure of the formula is explicitly added to the TPTP translation; so that $\{V_1, \ldots, V_n\} = \mathrm{fv}(formula_1) \cup \mathrm{fv}(formula_2)$ and $Q =\ !$ if $cl = \texttt{universal}$ and $Q =\ ?$ if $cl = \texttt{existential}$. The explicit quantification is omitted if $n = 0$. $tr(.)$ is an adequate mapping from RuleML formulas to TPTP formulas.

LegalRuleML	NMF
```<lrml:PrescriptiveStatement key="id">` ` <ruleml:Rule closure="cl">` ` <ruleml:if> formula_1 </ruleml:if>` ` <ruleml:then>` ` <lrml:Obligation>` ` formula_2` ` </lrml:Obligation>` ` </ruleml:then>` ` </ruleml:Rule>` `</lrml:PrescriptiveStatement>```	`tff(id, axiom,` `    Q [V_1, ..., V_n] :` `    {$$obligation} @ (` `      tr(formula_1),` `      tr(formula_2) ) ).`
```<lrml:PrescriptiveStatement key="id">` ` <ruleml:Rule closure="cl">` ` <ruleml:if> formula_1 </ruleml:if>` ` <ruleml:then>` ` <lrml:Permission>` ` formula_2` ` </lrml:Permission>` ` </ruleml:then>` ` </ruleml:Rule>` `</lrml:PrescriptiveStatement>```	`tff(id, axiom,` `    Q [V_1, ..., V_n] :` `    {$$permission} @ (` `      tr(formula_1),` `      tr(formula_2) ) ).`
```<lrml:PrescriptiveStatement key="id">` ` <ruleml:Rule closure="cl">` ` <ruleml:if> formula_1 </ruleml:if>` ` <ruleml:then>` ` <lrml:Prohibition>` ` formula_2` ` </lrml:Prohibition>` ` </ruleml:then>` ` </ruleml:Rule>` `</lrml:PrescriptiveStatement>```	`tff(id, axiom,` `    Q [V_1, ..., V_n] :` `    {$$prohibition} @ (` `      tr(formula_1),` `      tr(formula_2) ) ).`
```<lrml:ConstitutiveStatement key="id">` ` <ruleml:Rule closure="cl">` ` <ruleml:if> formula_1 </ruleml:if>` ` <ruleml:then>` ` formula_2` ` </ruleml:then>` ` </ruleml:Rule>` `</lrml:ConstitutiveStatement>```	`tff(id, axiom,` `    Q [V_1, ..., V_n] :` `    {$$constitutive} @ (` `      tr(formula_1),` `      tr(formula_2) ) ).`
```<lrml:FactualStatement key="id">` ` formula_1` `</lrml:FactualStatement>```	`tff(id, axiom, tr(formula_1) ).`

infrastructure. To this end, two steps are necessary: (i) The transformation of the encoded norms into a concrete (deontic) logical formalism, and (ii) the provision of ATP systems that can reason within the respective logics.

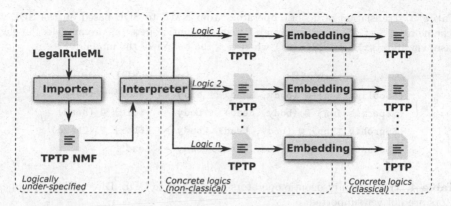

Fig. 1. Visualization of the transformation and automation process. One LegalRuleML file can be translated into multiple different TPTP reasoning problems which, in turn, can be reduced to classical reasoning problems in HOL for automation, if no special-purpose prover of the desired target logic is available.

The overall approach for logic-pluralistic automated reasoning presented in this paper is visualized in Fig. 1. The translation of LegalRuleML into NMF connects normative knowledge representation to the TPTP infrastructure, where both LegalRuleML and NMF are logically underspecified. Subsequently, the NMF representation is translated to multiple concrete logic problems formulated in (standard) non-classical TPTP. These problems are not logically underspecified anymore, as they have been encoded into specific deontic logics. Then, the resulting non-classical problems are automated using the *shallow semantical embeddings* approach [5,25], in which the problems are encoded into classical higher-order logic (HOL). This way, general purpose HOL ATP solvers can be employed for normative reasoning. Of course, also specialized ATP systems for the respective deontic logic could be employed. However, for many quantified non-classical logics there are no ATP systems available.

The NMF representation is interpreted with respect to a concrete logic by adding a *logic specification* to it. It is of form ...

    tff(*name*, logic, $$normative == [$$logic == *target_logic*]).

where *target_logic* is one of ...

- $$sdl, representing SDL as introduced above,
- $$aqvistE, representing Åqvist dyadic deontic logic **E** [1], and
- $$carmoJones, representing the dyadic deontic logic of Carmo and Jones [12].

Of course, this list can be extended with many more concrete logics for deontic reasoning. For the proof-of-concept presented in this paper, we restrict ourselves to these logics for the time being. An NMF problem with a *logic specification* can then be translated to a non-classical TPTP representation of the respectively chosen logic. The translation schemes for translating NMF into SDL and into DDL are presented in Tables 3 and 4.

Table 3. Translation of deontic operators from NMF to SDL based on the SDL-v3 scheme from Sect. 2.2 (narrow scope). Directed deontic operators are modeled, in each case, via `$box(#x)` resp. `$dia(#x)` where x is the bearer of the modality.

NMF	SDL
`{$$obligation} @ (body, head)`	`body => {$box} @ (head)`
`{$$permission} @ (body, head)`	`body => {$dia} @ (head)`
`{$$prohibition} @ (body, head)`	`body => {$box} @ (~head)`
`{$$constitutive} @ (body, head)`	`body => head`

Table 4. Translation of deontic operators from NMF to DDL. Directed deontic operators are not yet supported.

NMF	DDL
`{$$obligation} @ (body, head)`	`{$$obl} @ (head, body)`
`{$$permission} @ (body, head)`	`~{$$obl} @ (~head, body)`
`{$$prohibition} @ (body, head)`	`{$$obl} @ (~head, body) .`
`{$$constitutive} @ (body, head)`	`body => head`

In SDL the obligation operator is expressed using the modal logic $\Box$ operator; and the logic is specified to be modal logic **D** (as usual for SDL). Since SDL does not have any dyadic deontic operators, conditional norms are expressed via a material implication. DDL does provide a dyadic deontic operator that captures conditional norms, so the mapping is more natural here. Note that, for simplicity, the translation scheme currently follows the interpretation variant SDL-v3 (see Sect. 2.2) using a narrow-scope translation. It is planned to add further parameters to the translation so that the translation scheme can be chosen individually for each norm.

For the running example of Chisholm's paradox, as formalized in NMF in Sect. 4.1, the concrete output for SDL as reasoning target is as follows:

```
tff(target, logic, $modal == [$quantification == $constant,
                             $constants == $rigid,
                             $modalities == $modal_system_D]).
tff(norm1-sdl, axiom, {$box} @ (help)).
tff(norm2-sdl, axiom, help => {$box} @ (tell)).
tff(norm3-sdl, axiom, ~help => {$box} @ (~tell)).
tff(fact1-sdl, axiom, ~help).
```

In Åqvist system **E** the resulting representation is (note the different order of parameters in the dyadic deontic operator) ...

```
tff(target, logic, $$ddl == [$$system == $$aqvistE]).
tff(norm1-ddl, axiom, {$$obl} @ (help,$true)).
tff(norm2-ddl, axiom, {$$obl} @ (tell,help)).
```

```
tff(norm3-ddl, axiom, {$$obl} @ (~tell,~help)).
tff(fact1-ddl, axiom, ~help).
```

For the DDL of Carmo and Jones, the output is identical except that the *logic specification* gives $$carmoJones instead of $$aqvistE. For details on the non-classical logics supported by the TPTP and the deontic logics used above, we refer to the literature [25,29]. Note that in all three cases, the problems have a fixed semantics and can thus be processed by ATP systems. The presented translation process from NMF to the deontic logics is implemented in the **LET** tool for logic embeddings [25].

In a second step, the NXF problems are embedded into classical HOL problems, represented in the THF TPTP-format. This is also done via the **LET** tool. The automation of normative reasoning via shallow embedding into HOL, as illustrated by Benzmüller et al. via their LogiKEy methodology [6], has been successful for a broad range of applications [5].

In order to provide a seamless automation process, the **LET** tool has been included included into the higher-order ATP system Leo-III [26], so that the above problem statements in SDL and DDL can be given to Leo-III without the need for any external pre-processing via **LET** by the user. Unsurprisingly, Leo-III can automatically establish the unsatisfiability of the four SDL formulas norm1-sdl, norm2-sdl, norm3-sdl and fact1-sdl, thus proving their joint inconsistency; by contrast consistent conclusions can be drawn from the DDL representation.

6 Conclusion

In this paper we presented a flexible approach for using general-purpose (classical) ATP systems for normative reasoning. This is motivated, on the one hand, by the widespread availability of mature and practically effective ATP systems, and, on the other-hand, by practical challenges for providing ATP systems for the many different deontic logics employed in normative reasoning. Hence, we aim at bridging between the ATP systems community (users of the TPTP problem representation languages) and the normative knowledge representation and reasoning community (users of the LegalRuleML standard).

Our proposed approach consists in first translating a subset of LegalRuleML to a specifically crafted domain-specific language, denoted NMF, based on the TPTP standard for ATP systems. NMF is semantically underspecified and acts as an intermediate layer between natural-language representations and representations in specific logical formalisms. NMF is subsequently translated into different reasoning problems in concrete logics, represented in the recent non-classical TPTP standard. Finally, automation for non-classical TPTP is provided by *shallow semantical embeddings* into classical higher-order logic for which many different ATP systems exist. While from a purely conceptual knowledge representation perspective the intermediate NMF language might not be strictly necessary (i.e., LegalRuleML could be translated directly into concrete TPTP problem), we argue that the usage of a semantically underspecified TPTP-based representation language comes with several pragmatic advantages with respect to practical automation. The TPTP languages are the standard formats for automated reasoning and experimentation using ATP systems, hence lowering the engineering-related barriers of providing automation for different deontic logics, and at the same time providing an abstract language for experimentation with different logics and ATP systems. In particular, the standard TPTP problem library for ATP system evaluation collects abstract problems (so-called *generators*) from which concrete reasoning tasks can be generated. The NMF layer thus connects to these efforts by providing means for the logic-pluralistic representation of domain-specific reasoning benchmarks.

The different steps in this process have been implemented as open-source tools available at GitHub. By doing so, we provided a flexible reasoning infrastructure for logic-pluralistic normative reasoning that is in line with the LogiKEy methodology [6] for designing normative theories. In contrast to LogiKEy, our focus is on flexible reasoning via ATP systems instead of enabling the interactive use of proof assistants. Two examples, one of them being the discussed Chisholm's paradox, are available as supplemental dataset via Zenodo [28]. The dataset contains the initial LegalRuleML documents, their NMF representations and all translations to the three concrete logics.

Further Work. In this paper, we focused on three deontic logics as reasoning backends for NMF. We plan to extend the portfolio of supported deontic logics towards further relevant ones, including Input/Output logic [20]. It is planned to extend the translation tool to produce LegalRuleML output from deontic logic reasoning problems formulated in TPTP.

The DSL presented in this work is still prototypical. It does not yet capture many important aspects that are encoded in LegalRuleML documents. In particular, it is possible to extend our approach to a layered hierarchy of DSLs aiming for knowledge representation at different levels of abstraction (or domain-specificity), together with translation mechanisms for successively specifying their intended semantics. Furthermore, RuleML does allow to specify so-called *semantic profiles*. It seems a fruitful venue to closer connect these profiles to TPTP logic specifications in order to allow for a more principled approach to adjust the target logic in automation.

References

1. Åqvist, L.: Deontic logic. In: Gabbay, D., Guenthner, F. (eds.) Handbook of Philosophical Logic, pp. 605–714. Springer, Dordrecht (1984). https://doi.org/10.1007/978-94-009-6259-0_11
2. Athan, T., Boley, H., Governatori, G., Palmirani, M., Paschke, A., Wyner, A.Z.: OASIS LegalRuleML. In: ICAIL, pp. 3–12. ACM (2013)
3. Athan, T., Governatori, G., Palmirani, M., Paschke, A., Wyner, A.: LegalRuleML: design principles and foundations. In: Faber, W., Paschke, A. (eds.) Reasoning Web 2015. LNCS, vol. 9203, pp. 151–188. Springer, Cham (2015). https://doi.org/10.1007/978-3-319-21768-0_6

4. Bench-Capon, T.J., Coenen, F.P.: Isomorphism and legal knowledge based systems. Artif. Intell. Law **1**(1), 65–86 (1992)
5. Benzmüller, C.: Universal (meta-)logical reasoning: recent successes. Sci. Comput. Program. **172**, 48–62 (2019)
6. Benzmüller, C., Parent, X., van der Torre, L.W.N.: Designing normative theories for ethical and legal reasoning: LogiKEy framework, methodology, and tool support. Artif. Intell. **287**, 103348 (2020)
7. Blackburn, P., Bos, J.: Representation and Inference for Natural Language - a First Course in Computational Semantics. CSLI Publications, Stanford (2005)
8. Blackburn, P., Kohlhase, M.: Inference and computational semantics. J. Logic Lang. Inform. **13**(2), 117–120 (2004)
9. Boley, H., Benzmüller, C., Luan, M., Sha, Z.: Translating higher-order modal logic from RuleML to TPTP. In: RuleML (Supplement). CEUR Workshop Proceedings, vol. 1620. CEUR-WS.org (2016)
10. Boley, H., Paschke, A., Shafiq, O.: RuleML 1.0: the overarching specification of web rules. In: Dean, M., Hall, J., Rotolo, A., Tabet, S. (eds.) RuleML 2010. LNCS, vol. 6403, pp. 162–178. Springer, Heidelberg (2010). https://doi.org/10.1007/978-3-642-16289-3_15
11. Bunt, H., Muskens, R.: Computational semantics. In: Bunt, H., Muskens, R. (eds.) Computing Meaning, pp. 1–32. Springer, Dordrecht (1999). https://doi.org/10.1007/978-94-011-4231-1_1
12. Carmo, J., Jones, A.J.: Deontic logic and contrary-to-duties. In: Gabbay, D.M., Guenthner, F. (eds.) Handbook of Philosophical Logic, pp. 265–343. Springer, Dordrecht (2002). https://doi.org/10.1007/978-94-010-0387-2_4
13. Chisholm, R.M.: Contrary-to-duty imperatives and deontic logic. Analysis **24**(2), 33–36 (1963)
14. Gabbay, D., Horty, J., Parent, X., van der Meyden, R., van der Torre, L. (eds.): Handbook of Deontic Logic and Normative Systems. College Publications, Georgia (2013)
15. Governatori, G., Rotolo, A., Calardo, E.: Possible world semantics for defeasible deontic logic. In: Ågotnes, T., Broersen, J., Elgesem, D. (eds.) DEON 2012. LNCS (LNAI), vol. 7393, pp. 46–60. Springer, Heidelberg (2012). https://doi.org/10.1007/978-3-642-31570-1_4
16. Hilpinen, R., McNamara, P.: Deontic logic: a historical survey and introduction. In: Handbook of Deontic Logic and Normative Systems, vol. 1, pp. 3–136 (2013)
17. Lam, H.-P., Governatori, G.: The making of SPINdle. In: Governatori, G., Hall, J., Paschke, A. (eds.) RuleML 2009. LNCS, vol. 5858, pp. 315–322. Springer, Heidelberg (2009). https://doi.org/10.1007/978-3-642-04985-9_29
18. Lam, H., Hashmi, M.: Enabling reasoning with LegalRuleML. Theory Pract. Log. Program. **19**(1), 1–26 (2019)
19. Liu, Q., Islam, M.B., Governatori, G.: Towards an efficient rule-based framework for legal reasoning. Knowl. Based Syst. **224**, 107082 (2021)
20. Makinson, D., Van Der Torre, L.: Input/output logics. J. Philos. Logic **29**(4), 383–408 (2000)
21. Montague, R.: Universal grammar. Theoria **36**(3), 373–398 (1970)
22. Palmirani, M., Governatori, G.: Modelling legal knowledge for GDPR compliance checking. In: JURIX. FAIA, vol. 313, pp. 101–110. IOS Press (2018)
23. Prakken, H., Sergot, M.: Dyadic deontic logic and contrary-to-duty obligations. In: Nute, D. (ed.) Defeasible Deontic Logic, pp. 223–262. Springer, Dordrecht (1997). https://doi.org/10.1007/978-94-015-8851-5_10

24. Robaldo, L., Bartolini, C., Palmirani, M., Rossi, A., Martoni, M., Lenzini, G.: Formalizing GDPR provisions in reified I/O logic: the DAPRECO knowledge base. J. Log. Lang. Inf. **29**(4), 401–449 (2020)

25. Steen, A.: An extensible logic embedding tool for lightweight non-classical reasoning. In: PAAR@IJCAR. CEUR Workshop Proceedings, vol. 3201. CEUR-WS.org (2022)

26. Steen, A., Benzmüller, C.: Extensional higher-order paramodulation in Leo-III. J. Autom. Reason. **65**(6), 775–807 (2021). https://doi.org/10.1007/s10817-021-09588-x

27. Steen, A., Fuenmayor, D.: Bridging between LegalRuleML and TPTP for Automated Normative Reasoning (extended version) (2022). https://doi.org/10.48550/arxiv.2209.05090

28. Steen, A., Fuenmayor, D.: Supplemental data for the present article (2022). https://doi.org/10.5281/zenodo.6702576

29. Steen, A., Fuenmayor, D., Gleißner, T., Sutcliffe, G., Benzmüller, C.: Automated reasoning in non-classical logics in the TPTP world. In: PAAR@IJCAR. CEUR Workshop Proceedings, vol. 3201. CEUR-WS.org (2022)

30. Sutcliffe, G.: The CADE ATP system competition - CASC. AI Mag. **37**(2), 99–101 (2016)

31. Sutcliffe, G.: The TPTP problem library and associated infrastructure. From CNF to TH0, TPTP v6.4.0. J. Autom. Reason. **59**(4), 483–502 (2017)

Agents and Argumentation

A Rule-Based Behaviour Planner
for Autonomous Driving

Frédéric Bouchard$^{(\boxtimes)}$, Sean Sedwards , and Krzysztof Czarnecki

University of Waterloo, Waterloo, Canada
{frederic.bouchard,sean.sedwards,krzysztof.czarnecki}@uwaterloo.ca

Abstract. Autonomous vehicles require highly sophisticated decision-making to determine their motion. This paper describes how such functionality can be achieved with a practical *rule engine* learned from expert driving decisions. We propose an algorithm to create and maintain a rule-based behaviour planner, using a two-layer *rule-based theory*. The first layer determines a set of feasible parametrized behaviours, given the perceived state of the environment. From these, a resolution function chooses the most conservative high-level maneuver. The second layer then reconciles the parameters into a single behaviour. To demonstrate the practicality of our approach, we report results of its implementation in a level-3 autonomous vehicle and its field test in an urban environment.

Keywords: Autonomous driving · Behaviour planning · Rule learning · Rule engine · Structured rule base · Expert system · Explainable AI

1 Introduction

The motion planning problem in autonomous vehicles is computationally challenging [7] and is typically decomposed into three sub-problems [15]: (i) mission-planning; (ii) behaviour planning; and (iii) local planning. This structure is depicted on the right of Fig. 1. In our autonomous vehicle, the mission planner receives starting and target locations, and determines the sequence of lanes on which the autonomous vehicle must drive. This sequence is converted into intents (e.g. turning right at the next intersection) and is sent to the behaviour planner, along with the environment representation. The behaviour planner then generates a sequence of high-level parametrized driving maneuvers to navigate through the environment towards the specified goal. The local planner finds a smooth trajectory that meets the required behaviour and comfort. Finally, the trajectory is used by the vehicle controller to determine the steering, throttle, and braking commands.

Early approaches to behaviour planning used finite state machines [13,18]. Such systems are typically difficult to maintain because of the inherent complexity of the driving problem. Combinations of state machines, decomposing the problem into sub-problems, can mitigate this lack of maintainability [17]. The

G. Governatori and A.-Y. Turhan (Eds.): RuleML+RR 2022, LNCS 13752, pp. 263–279, 2022.
https://doi.org/10.1007/978-3-031-21541-4_17

Fig. 1. Motion planning architecture of our autonomous vehicle

resulting hierarchy of state machines often introduces the need of precedence tables [14], which is a concept that is also familiar to rule-based systems [5].

Recently, there has been a strong trend to use deep learning for autonomous driving tasks. End-to-end machine learning approaches have been shown to handle basic driving tasks [3], while imitation learning of behaviours [2] or trajectories [9] can produce highly nuanced behaviours in complex road environments. The success of deep learning is in part due to its ability to learn the structure of a problem at the same time as solving it [16]. Its main drawback is that the resulting policies lack transparency and explainability [12].

By contrast, rule-based systems have the advantage of structured knowledge, greatly aiding explainability, safety and trust. Early works proved the concept of sophisticated direct vehicle control using rules [14,25], while more recent work has tended to use rule-based systems indirectly, such as to validate, bound or improve driving policies [19,22]. Finding the structure of a problem remains an important challenge for rule-based systems [6,16], as is the maintenance and update of the rule base as the problem evolves. To mitigate these challenges, hybrid approaches distil rules from deep-leaned policies [4] or use pre-defined rules to constrain the action space of deep learning [10].

In this paper, we define a two-layered rule engine for behaviour planning and present an algorithm to create and maintain its rule-based theory. Rather than learn the structure, we decompose the problem into meaningful concepts, to maximize explainability. Our maintenance algorithm exploits this and allows a theory to be learned incrementally from a set of expert-provided examples that may be augmented over time. We have designed the layers to be modular, allowing us in future to add layers and construct "deep theories" when we extend the operational design domain (ODD) of our vehicle.

To demonstrate the success and practicality of our approach, we have used it to construct a prototype implementation that we have deployed in our autonomous vehicle (Fig. 1). We report the results of our vehicle's 110 km field test in a busy urban environment, during which our rule engine was able to make decisions at up to 300 Hz and achieve a similar level of autonomy (98%) to a highly-cited deep-learning approach [3]. While we acknowledge that this comparison is not rigorous, because the tasks and ODDs are not rigorously aligned, we nevertheless claim that our approach has the advantage of being able to immediately identify and potentially fix any logical errors of its decisions.

While there is much in the literature that may be considered related to our work, there appears to be very little that is directly comparable in terms of the levels of detail, implementation and practical achievement that we present. The following table summarizes our approach in the context of selected works that apply rule-based decision-making to autonomous driving.

Ref.	Explicit Layers	Unordered Rule Base	Learning Algorithm	Urban ODD	Realistic Perception	Validated in Reality
Ours	✓	✓	✓	✓	✓	✓
[19]	implicit	✓	✓			
[24]	implicit	✓		subset	✓	✓
[20]	implicit	✓			✓	
[8]	implicit			subset		
[25]	implicit			subset		
[14]	implicit					
[4]		✓		✓	✓	
[11]		✓		✓		
[21]		✓		subset		
[1]		unspecified		subset		
[10]				subset		

In Sect. 2 we describe the conceptual data structures, rules and functions of the layers that comprise our rule engine, explaining how a single behaviour is chosen from a set of feasible options. In Sect. 3 we define a backward-chaining coverage function and present an algorithm that uses it to learn and maintain the rule-based theory of the rule engine. We also outline a knowledge engineering cycle that makes use of our algorithm to incrementally build a set of rules. In Sect. 4 we present the practical results of using our prototype rule engine, emphasizing its successful deployment in an extended drive on public urban roads. We conclude in Sect. 5, highlighting challenges and ongoing work.

2   Rule Engine

In this section, we describe the two-layer rule-based theory that is the conceptual basis of our rule engine, noting that the syntactic sugar for expressing rules compactly, such as bounded quantifiers, and the many optimizations of our implementation are omitted to simplify our exposition.

Each layer of the theory uses a set of unordered "IF *antecedent* THEN *consequent*" rules that map a set of input properties to a set of parametrized output behaviours. The first layer, called the *maneuver layer*, takes properties of the external environment as input and outputs a candidate set of parametrized behaviours, which are then filtered according to their conservativeness. The resulting behaviours, which now share the same high-level maneuver, are then transformed to become the input of the second layer, called the *parameter layer*. The parameter layer resolves the different parameters and outputs a single high-level maneuver with its parameter.

2.1 Layers and Rules

Each layer of our rule-based theory is described by a tuple of finite sets $(\mathcal{O}, \mathcal{A}, \mathcal{V}, \mathcal{P}', \mathcal{C}, \mathcal{R})$. $\mathcal{O}$ is a set of objects recognized by the layer. $\mathcal{A}$ is a set of attributes that an object may have (colour, speed, etc.) $\mathcal{V}$ is a set of values that object attributes may take (green, 2.7, *True*, etc.) Triplets of type $(\mathcal{O}, \mathcal{A}, \mathcal{V})$ constitute *input properties*. For notational convenience, we write $\mathcal{O}_\mathcal{A}$ for $\mathcal{O} \times \mathcal{A}$ and express properties in the forms $(\mathcal{O}_\mathcal{A}, \mathcal{V})$ and $\mathcal{O}_\mathcal{A} := \mathcal{V}$. We call elements of $\mathcal{O}_\mathcal{A}$ *features*. We also include in $\mathcal{V}$ the special value *undefined* that may be assigned to any feature that is not defined. We say a property or feature is undefined if its value is *undefined*. $\mathcal{P}'$ is the set of *output properties*, defined analogously to input properties, but w.r.t. the objects and attributes of the subsequent layer. This allows the output of one layer to become the input of the next layer.

$\mathcal{C}$ is a set of logical constraints over features, which evaluate to either *True* or *False* and have the type $(\mathcal{O}_\mathcal{A}, \{=, \leq, \geq\}, \mathcal{V})$ or $(\mathcal{O}_\mathcal{A}, \{=, \leq, \geq\}, \mathcal{O}_\mathcal{A})$, with the obvious mathematical meaning. E.g., $Ego_{Approaching} = Intersection$, $Ego_{Speed} \geq LeadingVehicle_{Speed}$. We also include in $\mathcal{C}$ the trivial constraint *True* and note that the operators $\{\leq, \geq\}$ return *False* whenever they encounter an *undefined* property.

Each layer has an associated set of rules $\mathcal{R}$, in which a rule is a tuple of type $(\mathbb{P}(\mathcal{C}), \mathcal{B})$. The first element, referred to as the rule's *antecedent*, is a conjunction of constraints ($\mathbb{P}$ denotes the power set), and the second element, referred as the rule's *consequent*, is the behaviour induced when the antecedent evaluates to true. A behaviour $b \in \mathcal{B}$ has type $(\mathcal{H}, \mathbb{P}(\mathcal{P}'))$, in which $\mathcal{H} = \{Emergency\text{-}Stop, Stop, Yield, Decelerate\text{-}To\text{-}Halt, Pass\text{-}Obstacle, Follow\text{-}Leader, Track\text{-}Speed\}$ is the globally-defined set of high-level maneuvers we use in this work. We refer to the second element of the tuple as the behaviour's *parameter*. The syntax of rule antecedents is given by the following simple BNF grammar, in which a *constraint* is $c \in \mathcal{C}$:

$$\langle antecedent \rangle ::= \langle antecedent \rangle \text{ AND } \langle antecedent \rangle \mid constraint$$

The antecedent of a rule typically contains only a subset of available features, giving it only a partial view of the input, and thus capturing an abstract meaning.

We assume that the input to a layer is a complete set of properties that constitute a function $\mathcal{O}_\mathcal{A} \rightarrow \mathcal{V}$. We call this a *scene* and denote by $\mathcal{S}$ the set of all scenes. A scene for the first layer contains properties representing the road environment, whereas a scene for the second layer includes properties representing the candidate behaviours for the ego vehicle, generated by the first layer.

A rule r is then implicitly represented by a corresponding function $\mathcal{F}_r : \mathcal{S} \to \mathcal{B}$ that maps a scene $e \in \mathcal{S}$ to the behaviour $b \in \mathcal{B}$ that is r's consequent, or the empty set:

$$\mathcal{F}_r(e) := \begin{cases} b & \text{if the rule's antecedent evaluates to true} \\ \varnothing & \text{otherwise} \end{cases} \tag{1}$$

Given a rule-based theory $\mathcal{R}$ (a set of rules for a given layer), we lift (1) to a function $\mathcal{F}_\mathcal{R} : \mathcal{S} \to \mathbb{P}(\mathcal{B})$, where

$$\mathcal{F}_\mathcal{R}(e \in \mathcal{S}) := \{\mathcal{F}_r(e) \mid r \in \mathcal{R}\}. \tag{2}$$

2.2 Resolving a Single Behaviour

The maneuver layer outputs all the behaviours that are at least partially compatible with the perceived outside world, according to a set of rules denoted $\mathcal{R}_{man}$ and corresponding function $\mathcal{F}_{\mathcal{R}\,man}$ defined by (2). The following is an example of a rule in $\mathcal{R}_{man}$, where we expect the ego vehicle to stop at the stop line when it approaches an intersection regulated by a stop sign:

IF $Ego_{Approaching} = Intersection$ AND $Road_{HasStopLine} = True$
THEN $(Decelerate\text{-}To\text{-}Halt, \{Stop_{AtStopLine} := True\})$

The output of the maneuver layer will often contain behaviours with incompatible high-level maneuvers, i.e., with different elements of $\mathcal{H}$, as well as behaviours having the same high-level maneuver, but with different parameters. To eventually arrive at a single behaviour, we first narrow the range of behaviours seen in the output of the maneuver layer, using a relation $\succ$ that defines a total order over the conservativeness of high-level maneuvers. We can thus write $Emergency\text{-}Stop \succ Track\text{-}Speed$ to mean $Emergency\text{-}Stop$ is more conservative than $Track\text{-}Speed$. We then use the corresponding partial order relation $\succeq$ to define a resolution function

$$\lambda_{man}(\mathcal{F}_{\mathcal{R}\,man}(e \in \mathcal{S})) :=$$
$$\{(h, p) \in \mathcal{F}_{\mathcal{R}\,man}(e) \mid \forall (h', p') \in \mathcal{F}_{\mathcal{R}\,man}(e), h \succeq h'\}, \tag{3}$$

which returns the behaviours sharing the highest priority maneuver.

The output of λ_{man} is fed to the input of the parameter layer, following a transformation into a scene expected by the parameter layer, i.e., a function of type $(\mathcal{O}_\mathcal{A})_{par} \to \mathcal{V}_{par}$, where $(\mathcal{O}_\mathcal{A})_{par}$ and $\mathcal{V}_{par}$ are the features and values, respectively, of the parameter layer. We thus define a transformation function comprising the union of three sets:

$$\mathcal{T}_{par}(e \in \mathcal{S}) := \{p \mid (h,p) \in \lambda_{man}(\mathcal{F}_{\mathcal{R}\,man}(e))\}$$
$$\cup \{(Maneuver_h, True) \mid (h,p) \in \lambda_{man}(\mathcal{F}_{\mathcal{R}\,man}(e))\}$$
$$\cup \{(o_a, undefined) \mid o_a \in (\mathcal{O}_A)_{par} \backslash$$
$$\{(o_a)' \mid (h, ((o_a)', v)) \in \lambda_{man}(\mathcal{F}_{\mathcal{R}\,man}(e))\}\} \quad (4)$$

The first set contains all the parameters output by λ_{man}, now interpreted as input properties of the parameter layer. The second set is a singleton containing a property that encodes the chosen high-level maneuver. The third set contains properties that map all the undefined features to the *undefined* value.

The output of $\mathcal{T}_{par}$ corresponds to a single high-level maneuver with possibly ambiguous parameters. The purpose of the parameter layer is to resolve this ambiguity, using different properties and a different set of rules to the maneuver layer. We denote the parameter layer's rules and their corresponding function by $\mathcal{R}_{par}$ and $\mathcal{F}_{\mathcal{R}\,par}$, respectively. The following example parameter rule guarantees that whenever *Decelerate-To-Halt* does not target the stop-line, but instead targets the end of the lane, then this latter should be included in the final set of parameters:

IF $\quad\quad Maneuver_{Decelerate-To-Halt} = True$

AND $\quad StopAtStopLine = undefined$ AND $Stop_{AtEndOfLane} = True$

THEN $\quad\quad (Decelerate\text{-}To\text{-}Halt, \{Ego_{StopAt} := AtEndOfLane\})$

The output of the maneuver layer is a set of behaviours with the same high-level maneuver and parameters that are consistent with one another. The resolution function for the parameter layer returns a single behaviour with its parameter being the union of the parameters returned by the parameter layer:

$$\lambda_{par}\left(\mathcal{F}_{\mathcal{R}_{par}}(\cdot)\right) := \left(h \mid \exists (h,p) \in \mathcal{F}_{\mathcal{R}_{par}}(\cdot), \{p \mid (h,p) \in \mathcal{F}_{\mathcal{R}_{par}}(\cdot)\}\right) \quad (5)$$

The overall function of our rule engine is thus given by

$$RE(e \in \mathcal{S}) := \lambda_{par}\left(\mathcal{F}_{\mathcal{R}_{par}}(\mathcal{T}_{par}(e))\right),$$

which we also refer to as the driving policy. Figure 2 shows a diagrammatic representation of the rule engine: (i) sensors present a perceived state to the maneuver layer, which identifies a set of compatible, conservative behaviours using $\mathcal{R}_{man}$ and λ_{man}; (ii) $\mathcal{T}_{par}$ transforms and completes the resulting properties for input to the parameter layer; (iii) the parameter layer resolves a single behaviour using $\mathcal{R}_{par}$ and λ_{par}, which is sent to the local planner.

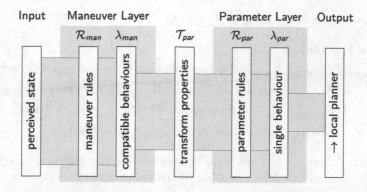

Fig. 2. Diagrammatic representation of two-layer rule engine

2.3 Inference Example

To give an intuition of how the rule engine makes a decision, we present a toy example based on the scene illustrated in Fig. 3: the autonomous (*Ego*) vehicle approaches an intersection regulated by a stop line, while a pedestrian concurrently negotiates the crosswalk. We exclude all elements of the rule engine not relevant to the scene, noting that this simple example is not intended to motivate the two-layered structure of the rule engine, which is required for the significantly greater complexity encountered in realistic applications.

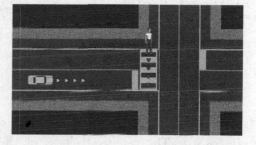

Fig. 3. Example scene: autonomous vehicle approaches intersection with crosswalk

The scene in Fig. 3, denoted s, is defined with a minimal set of features by

$$s := \{ Ego_{Approaching} := Intersection, \quad Ego_{Speed} := 35\,\mathrm{km/h},$$
$$Ego_{At} := undefined, \quad Road_{SpeedLimit} := 50\,\mathrm{km/h},$$
$$Crosswalk_{Obstructed} := True, \quad Road_{HasStopLine} := True \}.$$

We define a set of *Ego* behaviours relevant to s, having parameters specified w.r.t. the input features of the parameter layer:

$$b_1 := (Track\text{-}Speed, \{ Target_{Speed} := Road_{SpeedLimit} \})$$
$$b_2 := (Decelerate\text{-}To\text{-}Halt, \{ Stop_{AtEndOfLane} := True \})$$
$$b_3 := (Decelerate\text{-}To\text{-}Halt, \{ Stop_{AtStopLine} := True \})$$

We then define $\mathcal{R}_{man}$ using b_1, b_2 and b_3:

$$\mathcal{R}_{man} := \{(\{True\}, \qquad\qquad\qquad\qquad\qquad\qquad\qquad\qquad\qquad\qquad b_1)$$
$$(\{Ego_{Approaching} = Intersection, Crosswalk_{Obstructed} = True\}, \quad b_2)$$
$$(\{Ego_{At} = Intersection, Crosswalk_{Obstructed} = True\}, \qquad\quad b_2)$$
$$(\{Ego_{Approaching} = Intersection, Road_{HasStopLine} = True\}, \quad b_3)$$
$$(\{Ego_{At} = Intersection, Road_{HasStopLine} = True\}, \qquad\quad b_3)\}$$

We also define a set of relevant behaviours for the parameter layer, with parameters appropriate for the output of the rule engine:

$$b_4 := (\textit{Track-Speed}, \{Ego_{Speed} := Target_{Speed}\})$$
$$b_5 := (\textit{Decelerate-To-Halt}, \{Ego_{StopAt} := EndOfLane\})$$
$$b_6 := (\textit{Decelerate-To-Halt}, \{Ego_{StopAt} := StopLine\})$$

Using b_4, b_5 and b_6, we thus define $\mathcal{R}_{par}$:

$$\mathcal{R}_{par} := \{(\{Maneuver_{Track-Speed} = True\}, \qquad\qquad\qquad\qquad\qquad b_4)$$
$$(\{Maneuver_{Decelerate-To-Halt} = True, Stop_{AtEndOfLane} = True,$$
$$Stop_{AtStopLine} = undefined\}, \quad b_5)$$
$$(\{Maneuver_{Decelerate-To-Halt} = True, Stop_{AtStopLine} = True\}, \quad b_6)\}$$

Given the above definition of $\mathcal{R}_{man}$, it follows from (2) that $\mathcal{F}_{\mathcal{R}man}(s) = \{b_1, b_2, b_3\}$. The conservativeness of the high-level maneuvers is such that $\textit{Decelerate-To-Halt} \succ \textit{Track-Speed}$, hence $\lambda_{man}(\mathcal{F}_{\mathcal{R}man}(s))$ in (3) gives us:

$$\lambda_{man}(\cdot) = (\textit{Decelerate-To-Halt}, Stop_{AtEndOfLane} := True, Stop_{AtStopLine} := True)$$

This output is then transformed to the input format of the parameter layer using (4):

$$\mathcal{T}_{par}(s) := \{Maneuver_{Decelerate-To-Halt} := True, \quad Stop_{AtEndOfLane} := True,$$
$$Maneuver_{Track-Speed} := undefined, \quad Stop_{AtStopLine} := True,$$
$$Target_{Speed} := undefined\}$$

With our definition of $\mathcal{R}_{par}$ for the parameter layer, (2) determines the parameter of the selected high-level maneuver, giving us $\mathcal{F}_{\mathcal{R}par}(\mathcal{T}_{par}(s)) = \{b_6\}$. The final output of the rule engine is resolved by (5), giving $\lambda_{par}(\mathcal{F}_{\mathcal{R}par}(\mathcal{T}_{par}(s))) = b_6$.

3 Learning and Maintaining the Theory

To learn the theory, we assume an expert provides a finite set of training scenes $\mathcal{E} \subseteq \mathcal{S}$ and an associated labelling function $\mathcal{L} : \mathcal{E} \to \mathcal{B}$ that assigns a behaviour to every training scene. Given the characteristics of sets and functions, we know that every scene (a complete set of properties) is unique and is associated to exactly one behaviour. Since a property may be trivially converted to a constraint using equality, it follows that there always exists a set of rules that can correctly label every scene.

To facilitate learning, we define a backward-chaining *coverage function*

$$\Phi(r, \mathcal{R}, \lambda, \mathcal{T}, \mathcal{E}) := \{e \in \mathcal{E} \mid \mathcal{F}_r(\mathcal{T}(e)) \neq \varnothing, \mathcal{F}_r(\mathcal{T}(e)) \in \lambda(\mathcal{F}_\mathcal{R}(\mathcal{T}(e)))\},$$

which returns the subset of training scenes that *trigger* rule r, i.e., cause the rule to contribute to the resolved result of its theory $\mathcal{R}$, associated to a layer with the corresponding resolution function $\lambda \in \{\lambda_{man}, \lambda_{par}\}$ and property transformation function $\mathcal{T} \in \{\mathcal{T}_{man}, \mathcal{T}_{par}\}$. The use of the property transformation function allows the training of any layer to be performed with training scenes that are defined w.r.t. the input of the rule engine. $\mathcal{T}_{par}$ is given in (4). The maneuver layer requires no transformation, so $\mathcal{T}_{man}$ is simply the identity transformation,

$$\mathcal{T}_{man}(e \in \mathcal{S}) := e.$$

3.1 Rule Engine Update Algorithm

The main method of the Rule Engine Update algorithm (Algorithm 1) exploits the common structure of the two layers, calling the RuleUpdate subroutine (Algorithm 2) per layer. Since the rules of the parameter layer are dependent on those of the maneuver layer, Algorithm 2 is called on the maneuver layer first.

Algorithm 1: Rule Engine Update

input:	$\mathcal{E}$ training scenes	$\mathcal{R}_{man}$ base maneuver rules
	$\mathcal{L}$ labelling function	$\mathcal{R}_{par}$ base parameter rules

$\mathcal{R}_{man} \leftarrow \text{RuleUpdate}(\mathcal{E}, \mathcal{L}, \mathcal{R}_{man}, \lambda_{man}, \mathcal{T}_{man})$
$\mathcal{R}_{par} \leftarrow \text{RuleUpdate}(\mathcal{E}, \mathcal{L}, \mathcal{R}_{par}, \lambda_{par}, \mathcal{T}_{par})$
return $(\mathcal{R}_{man}, \mathcal{R}_{par})$

The rule engine works by filtering a set of candidate behaviours. The purpose of Algorithm 2 is to modify or create rules such that the set of behaviours output by a layer contains the correct behaviour for every training scene. Other than in unusual pathological cases (described below), the algorithm will find a theory that satisfies this requirement. The following description applies to either layer.

Algorithm 2 is given an existing theory $\mathcal{R}$ that may be empty—the algorithm will generate any new rules it needs. In line 1, the algorithm initializes an empty set of bad rules $\mathcal{R}_{Bad}$. This set is used to contain any rules that are discovered to have no coverage in the training scenes. Such rules may already exist in $\mathcal{R}$ or may be generated as candidates by the algorithm.

The outer loop of the algorithm is controlled by the existence of training scenes that are misclassified, i.e., when the set of output behaviours of the layer does not contain the specified label of the scene (line 2). If there are no misclassifications, the algorithm terminates correctly by returning the current theory in line 23. If there exist misclassified scenes, one is selected at random in line 3. We use random selection to avoid giving undue bias to any particular solution. If there is no rule whose consequent is the labelled behaviour with the chosen scene, the most general rule for this behaviour is added to $\mathcal{R}$ in lines 4 and 5. The main rule-generating section of the algorithm then follows.

A rule r that is triggered by the chosen misclassified scene is selected at random in line 8. Once again, random selection is used to avoid bias. line 9 generates the set of properties K, containing all the properties in the scenes that trigger r. line 10 then creates a set of feasible constraints C, given K and

---

Algorithm 2: Rule Update

input: $\mathcal{E}$ training scenes λ resolution function
       $\mathcal{L}$ labelling function $\mathcal{T}$ property transformation function
       $\mathcal{R}$ base rule set

1 $\mathcal{R}_{Bad} \leftarrow \varnothing$
2 **while** $(\varepsilon \leftarrow \{e \in \mathcal{E} \mid \mathcal{L}(e) \notin \lambda(\mathcal{F}_{\mathcal{R}}(\mathcal{T}(e)))\}) \neq \varnothing$ **do**
3 $\quad$ Select randomly $e \in \varepsilon$
4 $\quad$ **if** $\nexists r \in \mathcal{R} \mid \mathcal{F}_r(\mathcal{T}(e)) = \mathcal{L}(e)$ **then**
5 $\quad\quad$ $\lfloor$ $\mathcal{R} \leftarrow \mathcal{R} \cup \{(True, \mathcal{L}(e))\}$
6 $\quad$ **else**
7 $\quad\quad$ Select randomly $r := (antecedent, consequent) \in$
8 $\quad\quad\quad\quad\quad\quad\quad\quad\quad \{r \in \mathcal{R} \mid \mathcal{F}_r(\mathcal{T}(e)) \in \lambda(\mathcal{F}_{\mathcal{R}}(\mathcal{T}(e)))\}$
9 $\quad\quad$ $K \leftarrow \bigcup \Phi(r, \mathcal{R}, \lambda, \mathcal{T}, \mathcal{E})$
10 $\quad\quad$ $C \leftarrow GenerateConstraints(K, \{=, \leq, \geq\})$
11 $\quad\quad$ $\mathcal{R} \leftarrow \mathcal{R} \setminus \{r\}$
12 $\quad\quad$ **repeat**
13 $\quad\quad\quad$ **if** $C = \varnothing$ **then**
14 $\quad\quad\quad\quad$ $\lfloor$ **throw** $BadBaseRules$
15 $\quad\quad\quad$ $c \leftarrow GetConstraint(C, r, e, \mathcal{E}, \mathcal{L}, \mathcal{R}, \lambda, \mathcal{T})$
16 $\quad\quad\quad$ $C \leftarrow C \setminus \{c\}$
17 $\quad\quad\quad$ $r' \leftarrow (antecedent$ **AND** $c, consequent)$
18 $\quad\quad$ **until** $r' \notin \mathcal{R}_{Bad} \cup \mathcal{R}$;
19 $\quad\quad$ **if** $\nexists e \in \mathcal{E} \mid \mathcal{F}_{r'}(\mathcal{T}(e)) = consequent$ **then**
20 $\quad\quad\quad$ $\lfloor$ $\mathcal{R}_{Bad} \leftarrow \mathcal{R}_{Bad} \cup \{r'\}$
21 $\quad\quad$ **else**
22 $\quad\quad\quad$ $\lfloor$ $\mathcal{R} \leftarrow \mathcal{R} \cup \{r'\}$

23 **return** $\mathcal{R}$

the operators $\{=, \leq, \geq\}$. Each of these operators includes equality to ensure that every constraint covers the property observed in a training scene. The chosen rule r is then removed from the current theory $\mathcal{R}$ in line 11. This allows r to be updated and re-inserted or rejected if the update turns out to be bad, i.e., have no coverage in the training scenes.

The repeat loop in line 12–18 creates a novel candidate rule r' by adding a single constraint c to the antecedent of r in line 17. In line 15, function *GetConstraint* chooses c from C according to a heuristic criterion that aims to improve the chance that the misclassification will eventually be resolved, such as precision, coverage difference, rate difference, or Laplace estimate [5]. This implies that the new constraint will not conflict with the existing ones. A single additional constraint may not resolve the misclassification, but it is sufficient for the algorithm's correct termination that the candidate rule is novel w.r.t. the union of $\mathcal{R}_{Bad}$ and $\mathcal{R}$ (line). Informally, the existence of a novel candidate is ensured by the fact that every training scene is uniquely defined by its properties—which may be trivially converted into constraints—and that constraints may be added to a rule until it specifies a unique scene. A counterexample to this intuition is the unusual pathological case when a rule in the base rule set is triggered by a misclassified example and already contains all the constraints derivable from the training scenes. Under these circumstances, the repeat loop will exhaust all candidates and throw an exception (lines 13 and 14). In such a case, the aberrant rule must be removed from the base set.

On exiting the repeat loop, the candidate rule r' is guaranteed novel, but may not be good. If r' has no coverage in the training scenes, line 20 adds it to $\mathcal{R}_{Bad}$. If there is coverage, r' is added to $\mathcal{R}$, although this does not guarantee that it will immediately resolve the misclassification. This is achieved by the repeated checking and iteration provided by the outer loop, and by the non-zero chance that r' will be further refined, if this is necessary. The antecedents of rules thus increase monotonically, becoming more specific until the point at which they resolve a misclassification, or have no coverage and are rejected.

Algorithm 2 does not necessarily converge monotonically: adding a constraint to a rule makes it more specific, potentially increasing the number of misclassifications observed in line 2 before all necessary updates are completed. Removing bad candidate rules from $\mathcal{R}$ in line 20 leaves the theory temporarily incomplete and has the same effect. The number of bad rules in $\mathcal{R}_{Bad}$ does increase monotonically, thus ensuring eventual termination. In the worst case, the algorithm will suffer the exponential complexity of trying all rules, with all possible combinations of constraints. This does not happen in practice because function *GetConstraint* in line 15 avoids obvious conflicts and makes heuristically good choices.

3.2   Rule and Training Set Development

Our algorithms are sufficient to find a rule-based theory that perfectly agrees with a set of labelled training scenes; however, they do not guarantee the understandability of the theory's decisions. To bridge this gap between theory and practice, we give here an outline of a knowledge engineering cycle that allows an expert to incrementally build a set of discriminating training scenes and corresponding rules. The four steps of the cycle, illustrated in Fig. 4, are described below.

Discrepancy Identification. Rule set development is prompted by the existence of discrepancies between the actual and desired behaviour of the rule engine. These usually occur when the rule engine encounters a novel scene during deployment. Hence, the first step is to identify a scene that exemplifies the discrepancy, either from test suites, simulation testing, recordings of traffic flow, or open-road testing.

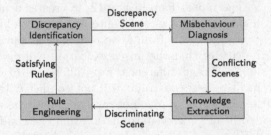

Fig. 4. Knowledge engineering cycle

Misbehaviour Diagnosis. A discrepancy is not necessarily a misbehaviour of the rule-based theory. To determine whether it is the fault of the theory or something external, such as perception noise, forward and backward chaining are used to identify the training scenes that also trigger the rules that misclassify the discrepancy scene. We call these scenes the conflicting scenes, since they are similar to the discrepancy scene but their behaviour label is different from the desired label for the discrepancy scene. This procedure is in line with how Algorithm 2 works. The comparison of the discrepancy and conflicting scenes helps understand the discrepancy. If the analysis reveals that the current decision for the discrepancy scene is reasonable as is, or that the problem is external to the rule-based theory, there is no need to proceed. Otherwise, the theory is deemed incomplete and the conflicting scenes, including the discrepancy scene, are passed to the next step.

Knowledge Extraction. The discrepancy scene along with its correct decision is an example of behaviour that must be incorporated in the theory; however, it may contain irrelevant properties that make it too specific to be used without modification, such as vehicles in the scene that are irrelevant to concluding the correct behaviour. Such properties increase the number of existing rules the new scene triggers, potentially causing Algorithm 2 to produce new rules that are unnecessarily complex and opaque. The purpose of this step is therefore to analyse the conflicting scenes and eliminate irrelevant properties from the discrepancy scene by setting them as undefined.

Rule Engineering. Once the discrepancy scene has been sanitized in the previous step, it is added to the existing set of training scenes. The rule-based theory is then updated using Algorithm 1, with input parameters $\mathcal{R}_{man}$ and $\mathcal{R}_{par}$ set to the existing theory. Assuming that this theory correctly classifies the previous training set (certainly true if it was produced by Algorithm 1), the outer loop of Algorithm 2 will necessarily select the discrepancy scene as the first misclassification to repair. The algorithm will then incrementally refine the rules, as previously described, until every training scene derives its expected behaviour.

Incorporating the sanitized discrepancy scene in the rule-based theory does not guarantee that the original misbehaviour will be cured, not even for the specific instance. The new theory is thus re-evaluated and the knowledge engineering cycle is repeated, until no further discrepancies are detected.

4   Experimental Results

Using the schema outlined in Sect. 2 as a guide, we developed a prototype rule engine in ECMAScript 2016–2017 [23] (standardized JavaScript), using polyfills to ensure consistent behaviour with different interpreters. Our prototype makes use of many optimizations not described in the text, including the use of quantifiers over constraints in the syntax of rule antecedents, and caching the results of rule antecedent evaluation (memoization). We executed the rule engine on Google's V8 interpreter[1] in all the experiments described below.

The software stack of our autonomous vehicle is based on the Robot Operating System (ROS), within which the behaviour planner is a ROS node written in C++. The behaviour planner node processes the autonomous vehicle's sensor data and communicates with the rule engine via JSON streams, using the RESTful application programming interface.

4.1   Driving Policy

To learn the sets of maneuver and parameter rules of our rule engine, we incrementally built a test suite consisting of 683 labelled scenes. Each scene was expertly curated following the method presented in Sect. 3.2. Using this test suite, we constructed a rule-based theory consisting of 330 maneuver rules and 16 parameter rules. The distributions of maneuver and parameter rules are shown in Figs. 5 and 6, respectively. From Fig. 5, we see that $111/330 \approx 33.6\%$ of the maneuver rules enforce an *Emergency-Stop*, delimiting the rule engine's operational design domain (ODD). However, we note that 63 of these rules are only required to ensure that the environment representation is well-formed and that its attributes are used coherently during software integration. These rules can therefore be removed once the integration is complete, and we may reasonably conclude that the autonomous vehicle can drive in an urban environment with only 267 maneuver rules. Figure 6 illustrates that the number of parameter rules for a given high-level maneuver reflects the number of different ways in which the maneuver is used.

---

[1] https://V8.dev.

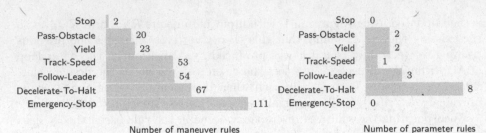

Fig. 5. Maneuver rule distribution   **Fig. 6.** Parameter rule distribution

4.2   Field Test

To demonstrate the viability of the rule-based theory within its ODD, the rule engine was deployed in the University of Waterloo autonomous vehicle (shown in Fig. 1) and tested by driving 110 km on public roads in full autonomy. During the public drive, the rule engine was able to serve queries at up to 300 Hz. Given that the typical rate of other components in our autonomous vehicle's software stack is 10 Hz, the rule-based theory was far from being the bottleneck.

The public drive was performed on a network of two-lane commercial roads constrained by four-way intersections and T-intersections, with precedence varying between the autonomous vehicle (AV) and other dynamic objects (DO). The route was planned to give the autonomous vehicle a non-trivial driving challenge. For instance, it had to effectively handle unprotected left-hand turns and avoid a myriad of parked vehicles. In this latter case, the rules were implemented to ensure that the autonomous vehicle could safely pass the parked vehicles by temporarily encroaching on the oncoming lane. The numbers of various road elements encountered and the numbers of different behaviours performed by our autonomous vehicle are as follows:

48	Four-way intersections, precedence for AV	120	Straight crossings
60	Four-way intersections, precedence for DO	36	Protected left turns
144	T-intersections, precedence for AV	84	Unprotected left turns
72	T-intersections, with precedence for DO	84	Right turns
24	Cul-de-sacs		

During the public drive, a safety driver had to intervene 58 times, with an average time between interventions of over 5 min and 30 s. This is comparable to the reported performance of the end-to-end deep-learning approach of [3]. Using metrics defined in that work, both approaches achieve ~98% autonomy, albeit with different ODDs. In our case, we believe that many of the interventions derive from limitations external to the rule engine and could be avoided.

Approximately 64% of the interventions were due to the driving scenario encountered being out of the ODD. Most of these scenarios involved interaction with dynamic objects that our prototype system was not programmed to detect, such as animals, bicycles, three-wheelers, and heavy vehicles. Approximately 36% of the interventions were due to the cautious design of the driving policy, resulting in deadlocks at some intersections when the dynamic object tracker was unable to determine whether a vehicle was parked or was slowly moving (and thus might have precedence to enter in the intersection).

5   Conclusion

We have defined a two-layer rule engine and provided an algorithm to create and maintain its rule-based theory. We have demonstrated the practicality of our approach by constructing a prototype that has been used to drive our level-3 autonomous vehicle more than 110 km in a busy urban environment. Our rule engine required few human interventions, achieving a similar degree of autonomy to that of a highly-cited state-of-the-art approach based on deep learning [3].

Our ongoing work is focused on extending the operational design domain (ODD) of our prototype rule engine, adding new high-level maneuvers and further stratifying its rule-based theory to handle more complex driving scenarios. Our current learning algorithm constructs a theory that perfectly agrees with the training scenes, or reports the inconsistency. To accommodate imperfect training data, which may contain unavoidable inconsistencies, we are also extending our algorithm to refine rules based on statistical performance. The resulting theory may then be more robust to inconsistencies encountered during deployment.

Although we encountered no problems of tractability in constructing our prototype, we realize that this might not be the case if there are significantly more rules or if the data structures are significantly enlarged. On the other hand, it is not clear that our rule-based approach will be less tractable than standard machine-learning approaches, which are known to be data inefficient. To investigate this, we have incorporated the two-layer rule engine into our reinforcement learning platform for autonomous driving [10]. This will allow us to make a direct comparison of tractability using the same ODD, and also to investigate how the rule engine performs when other vehicles drive unpredictably or adversarially.

Acknowledgment. This work was supported throughout its development by Fonds de Recherche du Québec – Nature et Technologies (FRQNT) and Natural Sciences and Engineering Research Council (NSERC) Discovery Grant. Author SS was supported by Japanese Science and Technology agency (JST) ERATO project JPMJER1603: HASUO Metamathematics for Systems Design.

References

1. Aksjonov, A., Kyrki, V.: Rule-based decision-making system for autonomous vehicles at intersections with mixed traffic environment. In: International Intelligent Transportation Systems Conference (ITSC), pp. 660–666. IEEE (2021)

2. Bansal, M., Krizhevsky, A., Ogale, A.S.: ChauffeurNet: learning to drive by imitating the best and synthesizing the worst. In: Robotics: Science and Systems XV. RSS Foundation (2019)

3. Bojarski, M., Del Testa, D., Dworakowski, D., Firner, B., Flepp, B., Goyal, P., et al.: End to end learning for self-driving cars. arXiv: 1604.07316 (2016)

4. Fu, Y., Li, C., Yu, F.R., Luan, T.H., Zhang, Y.: Hybrid autonomous driving guidance strategy combining deep reinforcement learning and expert system. Trans. Intell. Transp. Syst. (T-ITS) **23**(8), 11273–11286 (2022)

5. Fürnkranz, J., Gamberger, D., Lavrač, N.: Foundations of Rule Learning. Springer, Heidelberg (2012). https://doi.org/10.1007/978-3-540-75197-7

6. Fürnkranz, J., Hüllermeier, E., Mencía, E.L., Rapp, M.: Learning structured declarative rule sets - a challenge for deep discrete learning. arXiv: 2012.04377 (2020)

7. González, D., Pérez, J., Milanés, V., Nashashibi, F.: A review of motion planning techniques for automated vehicles. Trans. Intell. Transp. Syst. (T-ITS) **17**(4), 1135–1145 (2016)

8. Kapania, N.R., Govindarajan, V., Borrelli, F., Gerdes, J.C.: A hybrid control design for autonomous vehicles at uncontrolled crosswalks. In: Intelligent Vehicles Symposium (IV), pp. 1604–1611. IEEE (2019)

9. Kuderer, M., Gulati, S., Burgard, W.: Learning driving styles for autonomous vehicles from demonstration. In: International Conference on Robotics and Automation (ICRA), pp. 2641–2646. IEEE (2015)

10. Lee, J., Balakrishnan, A., Gaurav, A., Czarnecki, K., Sedwards, S.: WISEMOVE: a framework to investigate safe deep reinforcement learning for autonomous driving. In: Parker, D., Wolf, V. (eds.) QEST 2019. LNCS, vol. 11785, pp. 350–354. Springer, Cham (2019). https://doi.org/10.1007/978-3-030-30281-8_20

11. Likmeta, A., Metelli, A.M., Tirinzoni, A., Giol, R., Restelli, M., Romano, D.: Combining reinforcement learning with rule-based controllers for transparent and general decision-making in autonomous driving. Robot. Auton. Syst. **131**, 103568 (2020)

12. Lipton, Z.C.: The mythos of model interpretability. Queue **16**(3), 31–57 (2018)

13. Montemerlo, M., Becker, J., Bhat, S., Dahlkamp, H., et al.: Junior: the Stanford entry in the urban challenge. J. Field Robot. **25**(9), 569–597 (2008)

14. Niehaus, A., Stengel, R.F.: An expert system for automated highway driving. IEEE Control Syst. Mag. **11**(3), 53–61 (1991)

15. Paden, B., Čáp, M., Yong, S.Z., Yershov, D., Frazzoli, E.: A survey of motion planning and control techniques for self-driving urban vehicles. Trans. Intell. Veh. (T-IV) **1**(1), 33–55 (2016)

16. de Sainte Marie, C.: Learning decision rules or learning decision models? In: Moschoyiannis, S., Peñaloza, R., Vanthienen, J., Soylu, A., Roman, D. (eds.) RuleML+RR 2021. LNCS, vol. 12851, pp. 276–283. Springer, Cham (2021). https://doi.org/10.1007/978-3-030-91167-6_19

17. Shekhar, C., Moisan, S., Thonnat, M.: Use of a real-time perception program supervisor in a driving scenario. In: Intelligent Vehicles Symposium (IV), pp. 363–368. IEEE (1994)

18. Urmson, C., et al.: Autonomous driving in traffic: boss and the urban challenge. AI Mag. **30**(2), 17 (2009)

19. Vanderhaegen, F.: A rule-based support system for dissonance discovery and control applied to car driving. Expert Syst. Appl. **65**, 361–371 (2016)

20. Wang, Q., Ayalew, B., Weiskircher, T.: Predictive maneuver planning for an autonomous vehicle in public highway traffic. Trans. Intell. Transp. Syst. **20**(4), 1303–1315 (2019)

21. Xiao, W., et al.: Rule-based optimal control for autonomous driving. In: ACM/ IEEE 12th International Conference on Cyber-Physical Systems (ICCPS), pp. 143–154. ACM (2021)
22. Yay, E., Madrid, N.M., Ramírez, J.A.O.: Using an improved rule match algorithm in an expert system to detect broken driving rules for an energy-efficiency and safety relevant driving system. Procedia Comput. Sci. **35**, 127–136 (2014)
23. Zakas, N.C.: Understanding ECMAScript 6: The Definitive Guide for JavaScript Developers. No Starch Press, San Francisco (2016)
24. Zhao, L., Ichise, R., Sasaki, Y., Liu, Z., Yoshikawa, T.: Fast decision making using ontology-based knowledge base. In: Intelligent Vehicles Symposium (IV), pp. 173–178. IEEE (2016)
25. Zimmerman, N., Schlenoff, C., Balakirsky, S.: Implementing a rule-based system to represent decision criteria for on-road autonomous navigation. In: Spring Symposium on Knowledge Representation and Ontologies for Autonomous Systems. AAAI (2004)

Cooperation Among Groups of Agents in the Epistemic Logic L-DINF

Stefania Costantini[1,3] , Andrea Formisano[2,3(✉)] , and Valentina Pitoni[1]

[1] DISIM, Università di L'Aquila, via Vetoio-loc. Coppito, 67100 L'Aquila, Italy
{stefania.costantini,valentina.pitoni}@univaq.it
[2] DMIF, Università di Udine, via delle Scienze 206, 33100 Udine, Italy
andrea.formisano@uniud.it
[3] GNCS–INdAM, piazzale Aldo Moro 5, 00185 Rome, Italy

Abstract. The Logic of "Inferable" *L-DINF* has been recently proposed as a declarative framework to formally model via epistemic logic (aspects of) the group dynamics of cooperative agents. The framework permits to model groups of cooperative agents that can jointly perform actions. Various aspects of Multi-Agent Systems can be formalized in *L-DINF*, such as costs of actions, agents' preferences, and roles of agents within groups. In this paper we extend the framework by introducing the possibility of cooperation among different groups: if a group has not an agent with the right role for performing an action, the group can ask another group in order to have the action performed.

1 Introduction

The Logic of "Inferable" *L-DINF* [3,4,6] has been proposed to study the application of epistemic logics to the formalization of group dynamics involving Intelligent Agents participating to Multi-Agent Systems. The authors have developed *L-DINF* by taking into account various aspects that concern the interaction among agents within a group. The main aim consists in enabling modeling and reasoning about the development and execution of joint plans. In particular, the considered aspects include the possibility of modeling preferences about execution of actions, costs of actions and budget available to agents, mechanisms to share the cost within a group (where agents are thus able to support each other), actions that an agent is capable to perform (agents' "competences") and actions that an agent is allowed by the group to perform (agents' "role" in the group). The Logic of "Inferable" has been developed so as to enable the formalization of aspects of the "Theory of Mind" (ToM), which is an important social-cognitive skill that involves the ability to attribute mental states, including emotions, desires, beliefs, and knowledge both one's own and those of others,

Research partially supported by Action COST CA17124 "DigForASP" and by project INDAM GNCS-2022 InSANE (CUP_E55F22000270001).

G. Governatori and A.-Y. Turhan (Eds.): RuleML+RR 2022, LNCS 13752, pp. 280–295, 2022.
https://doi.org/10.1007/978-3-031-21541-4_18

and to reason about the practical consequences of such mental states. The framework supports the description of group dynamics, by modeling how an agent's set of beliefs evolves whenever the agent leaves a group or joins another group.

In this paper, we extend the framework so as to model situations in which different groups can support each other. In particular, this may happen when a group cannot perform an action because of insufficient competences (of its members). Consequently, to get the action executed, the group can "borrow" a competent agent from another group. The mechanism we introduce is in the direction of strengthening the cooperation between agents in a MAS, so that they may achieve their goals in a better and faster manner. In this way, a group, with the help of members of other groups, can fulfil objectives that would otherwise be unattainable. As we will see, in this approach the capabilities and roles of agents, as well as the conditions for lending an agent to another group, are defined at the semantic level. This is because the approach tries to combine the rigour of logic and attention to practical aspects: in this way, in fact, a designer will be able to specify these aspects in separate modules. In addition to ensuring modularity, this choice also contributes to keep the complexity of the logic reasonable enough to be practically manageable.

The paper is organized as follows. In Sect. 2 we introduce syntax and semantics of *L-DINF*, together with an axiomatization of the proposed logical system. In Sect. 3 we discuss an example of application of the new logic. In Sect. 4 we present our definition of canonical model of an *L-DINF* theory. Finally, in Sect. 5 we conclude. For an in-depth discussion on the relationship of logic *L-DINF* with related work, the reader may refer to [3] (we note here that our original inspiration is an existing logic by Lorini and Balbiani [2]).

2 Logical Framework

L-DINF is a logic composed of a static component and a dynamic component. The first, called *L-INF*, is a logic of explicit beliefs and background knowledge. The dynamic component, called *L-DINF*, extends the static one with dynamic operators. Such operators express the consequences of agents' inferential actions on their explicit beliefs.

2.1 Syntax

Let $Atm = \{p(t_1, t_2), q(t_3, t_4), \ldots, h(t_i, t_j), \ldots\}$ where p, q, h are predicate symbols and each $t_\ell \in \mathbb{N}$. Here an atomic proposition of the form $p(t_1, t_2)$ stands for "*p is true from the time instant t_1 to t_2*" with $t_1 \leqslant t_2$ (*Temporal Representation* of the external world). As a special case we can have propositions of the form $p(t_1, t_1)$, which stands for "*p is true in the time instant t_1*". Customarily, we also admit predicate symbols of higher arity, but in that case we assume that the first two arguments are those that identify the time duration of the belief (e.g., the atomic proposition $open(1, 3, door)$ means "*the agent knows that the door is open from time 1 to time 3*"). *Prop* denotes the set of all propositional formulas, that is, the set of all Boolean formulas built out of the set of atomic propositions Atm. The set Atm_A is the set of the physical actions that agents can perform, including "active sensing" actions (e.g., *"let's check whether it rains"*, *"let's measure the temperature"*, etc.). In what follows, I is a MTL "time-interval" [8] which is a closed finite interval $[t, l]$ or an infinite interval $[t, \infty)$, for any pair of expressions/values t, l such that $0 \leq t \leq l$. Let Agt be a set of agents and Grp be a set of groups of agents. As mentioned, agents can leave and join groups. Hence, given an element G of Grp and an interval I, we write G_I to emphasize the fact that the composition of G does not change during I. The language of *L-DINF*, denoted by $\mathcal{L}_{L\text{-}DINF}$, is defined by the following grammar:

$$
\begin{aligned}
\varphi, \psi ::=\ & p(t_1, t_2) \mid \neg\varphi \mid \varphi \wedge \psi \mid \mathbf{B}_i\varphi \mid \mathbf{K}_i\varphi \mid \Box_I\varphi \mid \\
& do_i(\phi_A, I) \mid can\_do_i(\phi_A, I) \mid do_{G_I}(\phi_A, I) \mid can\_do_{G_I}(\phi_A, I) \mid \\
& intend_i(\phi_A, I) \mid intend_{G_I}(\phi_A, I) \mid exec_i(\alpha) \mid exec_{G_I}(\alpha) \mid \\
& pref\_do_i(\phi_A, d, I) \mid pref\_do_{G_I}(i, \phi_A, I) \mid [G_I : \alpha]\varphi \mid \\
& lend(i, H_I, G_I, \phi_A) \\
\alpha \quad ::=\ & \vdash(\varphi, \psi) \mid \cap(\varphi, \psi) \mid \downarrow(\varphi, \psi) \mid \dashv(\varphi, \psi)
\end{aligned}
$$

where $p(t_1, t_2)$ ranges over Atm, $\phi_A \in Atm_A$, $i \in Agt$, $d \in \mathbb{N}$, I is a time interval, and $G_I, H_I \subseteq Agt$. (Other Boolean operators are defined from $\neg$ and $\wedge$ in the standard manner.)

The language of *inferential actions* of type α is denoted by $\mathcal{L}_{\mathsf{ACT}}$. The static part *L-INF* of *L-DINF*, includes only those formulas not having sub-formulas of the form $[G_I : \alpha]\varphi$.

Let us provide an intuitive semantics for the basic constructs of *L-DINF* (formal semantics will be introduced in Sect. 2.2).

The formula $intend_i(\phi_A, I)$ indicates the intention of agent i to perform the physical action ϕ_A in the interval I, in the sense of the BDI agent model [10]. Formulas of this form can be part of agent's knowledge base from the beginning or it can be derived later. In this paper we do not cope with the formalization of BDI, for which the reader may refer, e.g., to [7]. Hence, we will deal with intentions rather informally, also assuming that $intend_{G_I}(\phi_A, I)$ holds whenever all agents of group G_I intend to perform ϕ_A at a point in the time interval I.

The formula $do_i(\phi_A, I)$ indicates the *actual execution* of action ϕ_A by agent at a time point in I". Note that, we do not provide an axiomatization for do (and similarly do_{G_I}, that indicates the actual execution of ϕ_A by the group of agents G_I). In fact, we assume that in any concrete implementation of the logical framework, do_i and do_{G_I} are realized by means of a *semantic attachment* [11], that is, a procedure which connects an agent with its external environment in a way that is unknown at the logical level. The axiomatization only concerns the relationship between doing and being enabled to do.

The expressions $can\_do_i(\phi_A, I)$ and $pref\_do_i(\phi_A, d, I)$ are closely related to $do_i(\phi_A, I)$. In particular, $can\_do_i(\phi_A, I)$ must be seen as an enabling condition, indicating that the agent i is enabled to perform the action ϕ_A in the interval I, while instead $pref\_do_i(\phi_A, d, I)$ indicates the level d of preference/willingness of agent i to perform ϕ_A in the time interval I. The formula $pref\_do_{G_I}(i, \phi_A, I)$

indicates that agent i exhibits the *maximum level* of preference on performing action ϕ_A within all group members in the time interval I. Notice that, if a group of agents intends to perform an action ϕ_A, this will entail that the entire group intends to do ϕ_A, that will be enabled to be actually executed only if at least one agent $i \in G_I$ can do it, i.e., it can derive $can\_do_i(\phi_A, I)$.

Unlike explicit beliefs, i.e., facts and formulas acquired via perceptions during an agent's operation and kept in the *working memory*, an agent's background knowledge is assumed to satisfy *omniscience* principles, such as: closure under conjunction and known implication, closure under logical consequence, and introspection. In fact, $\mathbf{K}_i$ is actually the well-known S5 modal operator often used to model/represent knowledge. The fact that background knowledge is closed under logical consequence is justified because we conceive it as a kind of stable and reliable *knowledge base*, or *long-term memory*. We assume the background knowledge to include: facts/formulas known by the agent from the beginning, and facts the agent subsequently decided to store in its long-term memory (via a decision-making mechanism not covered here) after processing them in its working memory. We therefore assume that background knowledge is irrevocable, in the sense of being stable over time.

In the formula $\Box_I \phi$ the MTL interval "always" operator is applied to a formula, which means that ϕ is always true during the interval I. For simplicity, $\Box_{[0,\infty)}$ will sometimes simply be written as $\Box$.

The formula $lend(i, H_I, G_I, \phi_A)$, where H_I and G_I are two disjoint groups of agents and $i \in H_I$, states that, if none of the agents in G_I are authorized/enabled to perform ϕ_A, then the group H_I can lend agent i and i can perform ϕ_A, where of course i must be entitled to do so and authorized by its group.

A formula of the form $[G_I{:}\alpha]\,\varphi$, where α must be an inferential action, states that "φ holds after action α has been performed by at least one of the agents in G_I, and all agents in G_I have common knowledge about this fact".

Borrowing from [1,4,5], we distinguish four types of inferential actions α that allow us to capture some of the dynamic properties of explicit beliefs and background knowledge: $\downarrow(\varphi, \psi)$, $\cap(\varphi, \psi)$, $\dashv(\varphi, \psi)$, and $\vdash(\varphi, \psi)$. These actions characterize the basic operations of explicit belief formation through inference:

- $\downarrow(\varphi, \psi)$ is the inferential action which consists in inferring ψ from φ, where ψ is an atom, say $p(t_1, t_2)$: an agent, believing that φ is true and having in its long-term memory that φ implies ψ (in some suitable time interval including $[t_1, t_2]$), starts believing that $p(t_1, t_2)$ is true.
- $\cap(\varphi, \psi)$ is the inferential action which closes the explicit belief φ and the explicit belief ψ under conjunction. Namely, $\cap(\varphi, \psi)$ characterizes the inferential action of deducing $\varphi \wedge \psi$ from the beliefs φ and ψ.
- $\dashv(\varphi, \psi)$, where φ and ψ are atoms, is the inferential action that performs a simple form of "belief revision". That is, assuming φ and ψ are $p(t_1, t_2)$ and $q(t_3, t_4)$, respectively, an agent believing $p(t_1, t_2)$ and having in the long-term memory that $p(t_1, t_2)$ implies $\neg q(t_3, t_4)$, removes the timed belief $q(t_3, t_4)$ if the intervals match. Note that, should q be believed in a wider interval I such

that $[t_1, t_2] \subseteq I$, the belief $q(.,.)$ is removed concerning intervals $[t_1, t_2]$ and $[t_3, t_4]$, but it is left for the remaining sub-intervals, hence, it is "restructured".

– $\vdash(\varphi, \psi)$, where ψ is an atom, say $p(t_1, t_2)$; by means of this inferential action, an agent believing that φ is true (i.e., it is in the working memory) and that φ implies ψ in some suitable time interval including $[t_1, t_2]$, starts believing that $p(t_1, t_2)$ is true. This last action operates exclusively on the working memory without recovering anything from the background knowledge.

The formulas $exec_i(\alpha)$ and $exec_{G_I}(\alpha)$ express executability of inferential actions either by agent i, or by a group G_I (which is a consequence of the fact that any member of the group is able to perform the action). They have to be read as: "α is an inferential action that agent i (resp. an agent in G_I) can perform".

2.2 Semantics

Definition 1 introduces the notion of *L-INF model*, which is then used to define semantics of the static fragment of the logic. Let us begin by introducing a "time function" T that associates a time interval I with each formula:

– $T(p(t_1, t_2)) = [t_1, t_2]$; which, intuitively, should be read as "*p is true in the time interval $[t_1, t_2]$*". (By some abuse of notation, we have the special case $T(p(t_1, t_1)) = t_1$, which means "*p is true in the time instant t_1*");
– $T(\neg p(t_1, t_2)) = T(p(t_1, t_2))$; (in this case, the intended meaning is that "*p is not true in the time interval $[t_1, t_2]$*");
– $T(\varphi \text{ op } \psi) = T(\varphi) \uplus T(\psi)$ with $op \in \{\vee, \wedge, \rightarrow\}$, which is the unique smallest interval including both $T(\varphi)$ and $T(\psi)$;
– $T(\mathbf{B}_i\varphi) = T(\varphi)$;
– $T(\mathbf{K}_i\varphi) = T(\varphi)$;
– $T(\square_I\varphi) = I$;
– for formulas of the form $T([G_I : \alpha]\varphi)$ there are different cases depending on the inferential action α:[1]
  1. $T([G_I : \downarrow(\varphi, \psi)] \psi) = T(\psi)$;
  2. $T([G_I : \cap(\varphi, \psi)] (\varphi \wedge \psi)) = T(\varphi \wedge \psi)$;
  3. $T([G_I : \dashv(\varphi, \psi)] \psi) = J$, where J is the "restructured" interval in which ψ is believed after the belief update action (cf., page 4);
  4. $T([G_I : \vdash(\varphi, \psi)] \psi) = T(\psi)$;
– $T(do_i(\phi_A, I)) = T(do_{G_I}(\phi_A, I)) = I$;
– $T(can\_do_i(\phi_A, I)) = T(can\_do_{G_I}(\phi_A, I)) = I$;
– $T(intend_i(\phi_A, I)) = T(intend_{G_I}(\phi_A, I)) = I$;
– $T(pref\_do_i(\phi_A, d, I)) = T(pref\_do_{G_I}(i, \phi_A, I)) = I$;
– for formulas of the form $T(exec_{G_I}(\alpha))$ there are several cases depending on α:
  1. $T(exec_{G_I}(\downarrow(\varphi, \psi))) = T([G_I : \downarrow(\varphi, \psi)]\psi)$;
  2. $T(exec_{G_I}(\cap(\varphi, \psi))) = T([G_I : \cap(\varphi, \psi)](\varphi \wedge \psi))$;
  3. $T(exec_{G_I}(\dashv(\varphi, \psi))) = T([G_I : \dashv(\varphi, \psi)]\psi)$;

---

[1] Note that we are only defining $T([G_I : \alpha]\varphi)$ for the specific forms of α and φ that will come into play when defining the semantics of inferential actions (cf., Sect. 2.3).

4. $T(exec_{G_I}(\vdash(\varphi,\psi))) = T([G_I : \vdash(\varphi,\psi))]\psi)$;
- $T(exec_i(\alpha)) = T(exec_{\{i\}}(\alpha))$;
- $T(lend(i, H_I, G_I, \phi_A)) = I$.

Definition 1, below, depends on a given *set of worlds* W and on a *valuation function*, namely a mapping $V : W \longrightarrow 2^{Atm}$. For each world $w \in W$, let t_1 the minimum time instant of $T(p(t_1, t))$ where $p(t_1, t) \in V(w)$ and let t_2 be the supremum time instant (we can have $t_2 = \infty$) w.r.t. the atoms $p(t, t_2)$ in $V(w)$. When useful, we will make explicit these two time instants t_1 and t_2 by denoting w as w_I with $I = [t_1, t_2]$.

Note that many relevant aspects of an agent's behaviour are specified in the definition of *L-INF model*, including what mental and physical actions an agent can perform, what is the cost of an action and what is the budget that the agent has at its disposal, what is the degree of preference of the agent to perform each action. This choice has the advantage of keeping the complexity of the logic under control and making these aspects modularly modifiable.

As before, in what follows let *Agt* be the set of agents.

Definition 1. *A model is a tuple* $M = (W, N, \mathcal{R}, E, B, C, A, H, P, L, V, T)$ *where:*

- *W is a set of worlds (or situations);*
- $\mathcal{R} = \{R_i\}_{i \in Agt}$ *is a collection of equivalence relations on* W: $R_i \subseteq W \times W$ *for each* $i \in Agt$;
- $N : Agt \times W \longrightarrow 2^{2^W}$ *is a neighborhood function such that, for each* $i \in Agt$, *each* $w_I, v_I \in W$, *and each* $X \subseteq W$ *these conditions hold:*
  - **(C1)** *if* $X \in N(i, w_I)$ *then* $X \subseteq \{v_I \in W \mid w_I R_i v_I\}$,
  - **(C2)** *if* $w_I R_i v_I$ *then* $N(i, w_I) = N(i, v_I)$;
- $E : Agt \times W \longrightarrow 2^{\mathcal{L}_{ACT}}$ *is an executability function of mental actions such that, for each* $i \in Agt$ *and* $w_I, v_I \in W$, *it holds that:*
  - **(D1)** *if* $w_I R_i v_I$ *then* $E(i, w_I) = E(i, v_I)$;
- $B : Agt \times W \longrightarrow \mathbb{N}$ *is a budget function such that, for each* $i \in Agt$ *and* $w_I, v_I \in W$, *the following holds*
  - **(E1)** *if* $w_I R_i v_I$ *then* $B(i, w_I) = B(i, v_I)$;
- $C : Agt \times \mathcal{L}_{ACT} \times W \longrightarrow \mathbb{N}$ *is a cost function such that, for each* $i \in Agt$, $\alpha \in \mathcal{L}_{ACT}$, *and* $w_I, v_I \in W$, *it holds that:*
  - **(F1)** *if* $w_I R_i v_I$ *then* $C(i, \alpha, w_I) = C(i, \alpha, v_I)$;
- $A : Agt \times W \longrightarrow 2^{Atm_A}$ *is an executability function for physical actions such that, for each* $i \in Agt$ *and* $w_I, v_I \in W$, *it holds that:*
  - **(G1)** *if* $w_I R_i v_I$ *then* $A(i, w_I) = A(i, v_I)$;
- $H : Agt \times W \longrightarrow 2^{Atm_A}$ *is an enabling function for physical actions such that, for each* $i \in Agt$ *and* $w_I, v_I \in W$, *it holds that:*
  - **(G2)** *if* $w_I R_i v_I$ *then* $H(i, w_I) = H(i, v_I)$;
- $P : Agt \times W \times Atm_A \longrightarrow \mathbb{N}$ *is a preference function for physical actions* ϕ_A *such that, for each* $i \in Agt$ *and* $w_I, v_I \in W$, *it holds that:*
  - **(H1)** *if* $w_I R_i v_I$ *then* $P(i, w_I, \phi_A) = P(i, v_I, \phi_A)$;

- $L : Agt \times Grp \times Grp \times Atm_A \times W \longrightarrow \{$true, false$\}$ *is a lending function for agents. For each agent* i, *each* $G_I, H_I \in Grp$, *and action* ϕ_A, *the value of* $L(i, G_I, H_I, \phi_A, w_I) =$ true *iff w.r.t.* w_I *no agent in* G_I *can perform* ϕ_A *and* $i \in H_I$ *and* i *is enabled to perform* ϕ_A. *(Intuitively, in such case,* H_I *can lend* i *to* G_I *in order to get* ϕ_A *executed by* i). *Moreover, the following condition holds for all* $H_I, G_I \in Grp$, $i \in H_I$, *and* $w_I, v_I \in W$:

    (**M1**) *if* $w_I R_i v_I$ *then* $L(i, H_I, G_I, \phi_A, w_I) = L(i, H_I, G_I, \phi_A, v_I)$;
- $V : W \longrightarrow 2^{Atm}$ *is a valuation function;*
- T *is the "Time Function", defined before.*

To simplify the notation, let $R_i(w_I)$ denote the set $\{v_I \in W \mid w_I R_i v_I\}$, for $w \in W$. The set $R_i(w_I)$ identifies the situations that agent i considers possible at world w_I. It is the *epistemic state* of agent i at w_I. In cognitive terms, $R_i(w_I)$ can be conceived as the set of all situations that agent i *can retrieve* from its long-term memory and reason about. While $R_i(w_I)$ concerns background knowledge, $N(i, w_I)$ is the set of all facts that agent i explicitly believes at world w_I, a fact being identified with a set of worlds. Hence, if $X \in N(i, w_I)$ then, the agent i has the fact X under the focus of its attention and believes it. We say that $N(i, w_I)$ is the explicit *belief set* of agent i at world w_I.

Executability of inferential actions is determined by the function E. For an agent i, $E(i, w_I)$ is the set of inferential actions that i can execute at world w_I in time interval I. The value $B(i, w_I)$ is the budget the agent has available to perform inferential actions in time interval I. Similarly, the value $C(i, \alpha, w_I)$ is the cost to be paid by i to execute the inferential action α in the world w_I in time interval I. The executability of physical actions is determined by the function A. For an agent i, $A(i, w_I)$ is the set of physical actions that agent i can execute at world w_I in time interval I. $H(i, w_I)$ instead is the set of physical actions that agent i is enabled by its group to perform always in I. Which means, H defines the *role* of an agent in its group, via the actions that it is allowed to execute.

Agent's preference on execution of physical actions is determined by the function P. For an agent i, and a physical action ϕ_A, $P(i, w_I, \phi_A)$ is an integer value d indicating the degree of willingness of i to execute ϕ_A at world w_I.

Constraint (**C1**) imposes that agent i can have explicit in its mind only facts which are compatible with its current epistemic state. Moreover, according to constraint (**C2**), if a world v_I is compatible with the epistemic state of agent i at world w_I, then agent i should have the same explicit beliefs at w_I and v_I. In other words, if two situations are equivalent as concerns background knowledge, then they cannot be distinguished through the explicit belief set. This aspect of the semantics can be extended in future work to allow agents make plausible assumptions. Analogous properties are imposed by constraints (**D1**), (**E1**), and (**F1**). Namely, (**D1**) imposes that agent i always knows which inferential actions it can perform and those it cannot. (**E1**) states that agent i always knows the available budget in a world (potentially needed to perform actions). (**F1**) determines that agent i always knows how much it costs to perform an inferential action. (**G1**) and (**H1**) determine that an agent i always knows which physical actions it can perform and those it cannot, and with which degree of willingness, where (**G2**) specifies that an agent also knows whether its group gives it the permission to execute a certain action or not, i.e., if that action pertains to its *role* in the group. (**M1**) specifies that an agent also knows whether its group gives it the permission to be lent to an other group to perform an action.

Truth values of *L-DINF* formulas are inductively defined as follows.

Given a model $M = (W, N, \mathcal{R}, E, B, C, A, H, P, V, T)$, $i \in Agt$, $G \subseteq Agt$, $w_I \in W$, and a formula $\varphi \in \mathcal{L}_{L\text{-}INF}$, we introduce this shorthand notation:

$$\|\varphi\|_{i,w_I}^M = \{v_I \in W : w_I R_i v_I \text{ and } M, v_I \models \varphi\}$$

whenever $M, v_I \models \varphi$ is well-defined (see below). Then, we set:

(t1) $M, w_I \models p(t_1, t_2)$ iff $p(t_1, t_2) \in V(w_I)$ and $T(p(t_1, t_2)) \subseteq I$

(t2) $M, w_I \models exec_i(\alpha)$ iff $\alpha \in E(i, w_I)$ and $T(exec_i(\alpha)) \subseteq I$

(t3) $M, w_I \models exec_{G_I}(\alpha)$ iff $\exists i \in G_I$ with $\alpha \in E(i, w_I)$ and $T(exec_{G_I}(\alpha)) \subseteq I$

(t4) $M, w_I \models lend(i, H_I, G_I, \phi_A)$ if $L(i, H_I, G_I, \phi_A, w_I) = \text{true}$

(t5) $M, w_I \models can\_do_i(\phi_A, J)$ iff $\phi_A \in A(i, w_I) \cap H(i, w_I)$ and $J \subseteq I$

(t6) $M, w_I \models can\_do_{G_I}(\phi_A, J)$ iff $(\exists i \in G_I$ with $\phi_A \in A(i, w_I) \cap H(i, w_I)$ and $J \subseteq I) \vee (\exists\, H_I \in Grp \wedge \exists j \in H_I \wedge L(j, H_I, G_I, \psi_A, w_I) = \text{true with }$ $\phi_A \in A(j, w_I) \cap H(j, w_I)$ and $J \subseteq I \wedge pref\_do_{H_I}(j, \phi_A, J))$

(t7) $M, w_I \models pref\_do_i(\phi_A, d, J)$ iff $\phi_A \in A(i, w_I)$, $P(i, w_I, \phi_A) = d$ and $J \subseteq I$

(t8) $M, w_I \models pref\_do_{G_I}(i, \phi_A, J)$ iff $M, w \models pref\_do_i(\phi_A, d, J)$ for $d \in \mathbb{N}$ such that $d = \max\{P(j, w, \phi_A) \mid j \in G_I \wedge \phi_A \in A(j, w) \cap H(j, w)\}$ and $J \subseteq I$

(t9) $M, w_I \models \neg\varphi$ iff $M, w \not\models \varphi$ and $T(\neg\varphi) \subseteq I$

(t10) $M, w_I \models \varphi \wedge \psi$ iff $M, w \models \varphi$ and $M, w \models \psi$ with $T(\varphi), T(\psi) \subseteq I$

(t11) $M, w_I \models \mathbf{B}_i\varphi$ iff $\|\varphi\|_{i,w}^M \in N(i, w)$ with $T(\varphi) \subseteq I$

(t12) $M, w_I \models \mathbf{K}_i\varphi$ iff $M, v \models \varphi$ for all $v \in R_i(w)$ with $T(\varphi) \subseteq I$

(t13) $M, w_I \models \Box_J\varphi$ iff $T(\varphi) \subseteq J \subseteq I$ and for all $v_I \in R_i(w_I)$ it holds $M, w_I \models \varphi$.

As seen above, a physical action can be performed by a group of agents if at least one agent of the group can do it. In this case, the level of preference for performing this action is set to the maximum among those of the agents enabled to execute the action. Rule (t6) models the extension that we propose in this paper, stating that a group G_I can perform in a certain situation (world w_I) and time interval I an action ϕ_A (in time interval I) if it has the right competences and the right role internally (there exists agent $i \in G_I$ such that $\phi_A \in A(j, w_I) \cap H(j, w_I)$), or if there exists another group H_I including an agent j with the right features, and which is available to lend the agent to G (i.e., $L(j, H_I, G_I, \phi_A, w_I) = \text{true}$). Specifically, H_I will lend the agent who most prefers to perform the action in the time interval I.

For any inferential action α performed by any agent i, we set:

(t14) $M, w \models [G_I : \alpha]\varphi$ iff $M^{[G_I:\alpha]}, w \models \varphi$

where $M^{[G_I:\alpha]} = \langle W, N^{[G_I:\alpha]}, \mathcal{R}, E, B^{[G_I:\alpha]}, C, A, H, P, V, T \rangle$, is the model representing the fact that the execution of an inferential action α affects the sets of beliefs of agent i and modifies the available budget in a certain time interval I.

Such operation can add new beliefs by direct perception, by means of one inference step, or as a conjunction of previous beliefs. Hence, when introducing new beliefs (i.e., performing mental actions), the neighborhood must be extended accordingly.

The following condition characterizes the circumstances in which an action may be performed, and by which agent(s):

$$enabled_{w_I}(G_I, \alpha) : \quad \exists j \in G_I \left(\alpha \in E(j, w) \wedge \frac{C(j, \alpha, w_I)}{|G_I|} \leq \min_{h \in G_I} B(h, w_I)\right)$$

with $T([G_I{:}\alpha]\varphi) \subseteq I$. This condition states when an inferential action is enabled. In the above particular formulation (that is not fixed, but can be customized to the specific application domain) if at least an agent can perform it and if the "payment" due by each agent (obtained by dividing the action's cost equally among all agents of the group) is within each agent's available budget. In case more than one agent in G_I can execute an action, we implicitly assume the agent j performing the action to be the one corresponding to the lowest possible cost. Namely, j is such that $C(j, \alpha, w_I) = \min_{h \in G_I} C(h, \alpha, w_I)$. Other choices might be viable, so variations of this logic can be easily defined simply by devising some other enabling condition and, possibly, introducing differences in neighborhood update. Notice that the definition of the enabling function basically specifies the "concrete responsibility" that agents take while concurring with their own resources to actions' execution. Also, in case of specification of various resources, different corresponding enabling functions might be defined.

2.3   Belief Update

In this kind of logic, updating an agent's beliefs accounts to modify the neighborhood of the present world. The updated neighborhood $N^{[G_I{:}\alpha]}$ resulting from execution of a mental action α by a group G_I of agents is as follows.

$$N^{[G_I{:}\downarrow(\psi,\chi)]}(i, w_I) = \begin{cases} N(i, w_I) \cup \{||\chi||_{i,w_I}^M\} & \text{if } i \in G_I \text{ and } T([G_I : \downarrow(\psi,\chi)]\chi) \subseteq I \\ & \text{and } enabled_{w_I}(G_I, \downarrow(\psi,\chi)) \text{ and} \\ & M, w_I \models \mathbf{B}_i\psi \wedge \mathbf{K}_i(\psi \rightarrow \chi) \\ N(i, w_I) & \text{otherwise} \end{cases}$$

$$N^{[G_I{:}\cap(\psi,\chi)]}(i, w_I) = \begin{cases} N(i, w_I) \cup \{||\psi \wedge \chi||_{i,w_I}^M\} & \text{if } i \in G \text{ and} \\ & T([G : \cap(\psi,\chi)](\psi \wedge \chi)) \subseteq I \\ & \text{and } enabled_{w_I}(G_I, \cap(\psi,\chi)) \\ & \text{and } M, w_I \models \mathbf{B}_i\psi \wedge \mathbf{B}_i\chi \\ N(i, w_I) & \text{otherwise} \end{cases}$$

$$N^{[G_I{:}\vdash(\psi,\chi)]}(i, w_I) = \begin{cases} N(i, w_I) \cup \{||\chi||_{i,w_I}^M\} & \text{if } i \in G_I \text{ and } T([G_I :\dashv (\psi,\chi)]\chi) \subseteq I \\ & \text{and } enabled_{w_I}(G_I, \vdash(\psi,\chi)) \text{ and} \\ & M, w_I \models \mathbf{B}_i\psi \wedge \mathbf{B}_i(\psi \rightarrow \chi) \\ N(i, w_I) & \text{otherwise} \end{cases}$$

Notice that, after an inferential action α has been performed by an agent $j \in G_I$, all agents $i \in G_I$ see the same update in the neighborhood. Conversely, for any agent $h \notin G_I$ the neighborhood remains unchanged (i.e., $N^{[G_I:\alpha]}(h, w) = N(h, w_I)$). However, even for agents in G_I, the neighborhood remains unchanged if the required preconditions, on explicit beliefs, knowledge, and budget, do not hold (and hence the action is not executed). Notice also that we might devise variations of the logic by making different decisions about neighborhood update to implement, for instance, partial visibility within a group.

For formulas of the form $[G_I : \dashv(\psi, \chi)]\chi$, we take in account the following case: given $Q = q(j, k)$ such that $T(q(j, k)) = T(q(t_1, t_2)) \cap T(q(t_3, t_4))$ with $j, k \in \mathbb{N}$ and $P \equiv \big((M, w_I \models \mathbf{B}_i(p(t_1, t_2)) \wedge \mathbf{B}_i(q(t_3, t_4)) \wedge \mathbf{K}_i(p(t_1, t_2) \rightarrow \neg q(t_3, t_4)))$ and $(T([G_I :\dashv (p(t_1, t_2), q(t_3, t_4))]q(t_5, t_6)) \subseteq I)$ and there is no interval $J \supsetneq T(p(t_1, t_2))$ such that $\mathbf{B}_i(q(t_5, t_6))$ where $T(q(t_5, t_6))=J \big)$, we put:

$$N^{[G_I :\dashv(p(t_1,t_2),q(t_3,t_4))]}(i, w_I) = \begin{cases} N(i, w_I) \setminus \{\|Q\|_{i,w_I}^M\} & \text{if } P \text{ holds} \\ N(i, w_I) & \text{otherwise} \end{cases}$$

The following update of the budget function determines how each agent in G_I contributes to cover the costs of execution of an action, by consuming part of its available budget. We assume, however, that only inferential actions that add new beliefs have a cost. Hence, forming conjunctions and performing belief revision are actions with no cost. As before, for an action α, we require $enabled_{w_I}(G_I, \alpha)$ to hold and assume that $j \in G_I$ executes α. Then, depending on α, we have:

$$B^{[G_I:\downarrow(\psi,\chi)]}(i, w_I) = \begin{cases} B(i, w_I) - \frac{C(j, \downarrow(\psi,\chi), w_I)}{|G_I|} & \text{if } i \in G_I \text{ and } T([G_I : \downarrow(\psi,\chi)]\chi) \subseteq I \\ & \text{and } enabled_{w_I}(G_I, \downarrow(\psi,\chi)) \\ & \text{and } M, w_I \models \mathbf{B_{I}}_i\psi \wedge \mathbf{K}_i(\psi \rightarrow \chi) \\ B(i, w_I) & \text{otherwise} \end{cases}$$

$$B^{[G_I:\vdash(\psi,\chi)]}(i, w_I) = \begin{cases} B(i, w_I) - \frac{C(j, \vdash(\psi,\chi), w_I)}{|G_I|} & \text{if } i \in G_I \text{ and } T([G_I : \vdash(\psi,\chi)]\chi) \subseteq I \\ & \text{and } enabled_{w_I}(G_I, \vdash(\psi,\chi)) \\ & \text{and } M, w_I \models \mathbf{B}_i\psi \wedge \mathbf{B}_i(\psi \rightarrow \chi) \\ B(i, w_I) & \text{otherwise} \end{cases}$$

We write $\models_{L\text{-}DINF} \varphi$ to denote that $M, w_I \models \varphi$ holds for all worlds w_I of every model M.

We introduce below relevant consequences of our formalization, whose proof can be developed analogously to what done in previous work [3].

For any set of agents G_I and each $i \in G_I$, we have the following:

- $\models_{L\text{-}INF} (\mathbf{K}_i(\varphi \rightarrow \psi)) \wedge \mathbf{B}_i\varphi) \rightarrow [G_I : \downarrow(\varphi, \psi)] \mathbf{B}_i\psi$.
  Namely, if an agent has φ among beliefs and $\mathbf{K}_i(\varphi \rightarrow \psi)$ in its background knowledge, then as a consequence of the action $\downarrow(\varphi, \psi)$ the agent and any group G_I to which it belongs start believing ψ.

- $\models_{L\text{-}INF}$ $(\mathbf{K}(p(t_1,t_2) \rightarrow \neg q(t_3,t_4)) \wedge \mathbf{B}_i(p(t_1,t_2)) \wedge \mathbf{B}_i(q(t_3,t_4))) \rightarrow$ $[(G_I : \dashv(p(t_1,t_2),q(t_3,t_4)))](\mathbf{B}_i(q(t_5,t_6)))$ with $T(q(t_5,t_6)) = T(q(t_3,t_4)) \setminus T(q(t_1,t_2))$.

  Namely, if the agent i has $q(t_3,t_4)$ as one of its beliefs, q is not believed outside $T(q(t_3,t_4))$, the agent perceives $p(t_1,t_2)$ where $T(p(t_1,t_2)) \subseteq T(q(t_3,t_4))$, and has $\mathbf{K}_i(p(t_1,t_2) \rightarrow \neg q(t_3,t_4))$ in its background knowledge. Then, after the mental operation $\dashv(p(t_1,t_2),q(t_3,t_4))$, the agent starts believing $q(t_5,t_6)$ where $T(q(t_5,t_6)) = T(q(t_3,t_4)) \setminus T(q(t_1,t_2))$.

- $\models_{L\text{-}INF}$ $(\mathbf{B}_i\varphi \wedge \mathbf{B}_i\psi) \rightarrow [G_I : \cap(\varphi,\psi)]\mathbf{B}_i(\varphi \wedge \psi)$.

  Namely, if an agent has φ and ψ as beliefs, then as a consequence of the action $\cap(\varphi,\psi)$ the agent and any group G_I to which it belongs start believing $\varphi \wedge \psi$.

- $\models_{L\text{-}INF}$ $(\mathbf{B}_i(\varphi \rightarrow \psi)) \wedge \mathbf{B}_i\varphi) \rightarrow [G_I : \vdash(\varphi,\psi)]\mathbf{B}_i,\psi$.

  Namely, if an agent has φ among its beliefs and $\mathbf{B}_i(\varphi \rightarrow \psi)$ in its working memory, then as a consequence of the action $\vdash(\varphi,\psi)$ the agent and any group G to which it belongs start believing ψ.

2.4 Axiomatization

Below we introduce the axiomatization of our logic. The *L-INF* and *L-DINF* axioms and inference rules are the following:

1. $(\mathbf{K}_i\varphi \wedge \mathbf{K}_i(\varphi \rightarrow \psi)) \rightarrow \mathbf{K}_i\psi$;
2. $\mathbf{K}_i\varphi \rightarrow \varphi$;
3. $\neg\mathbf{K}_i(\varphi \wedge \neg\varphi)$;
4. $\mathbf{K}_i\varphi \rightarrow \mathbf{K}_i\mathbf{K}_i\varphi$;
5. $\neg\mathbf{K}_i\varphi \rightarrow \mathbf{K}_i\neg\mathbf{K}_i\varphi$;
6. $\mathbf{B}_i\varphi \wedge \mathbf{K}_i(\varphi \leftrightarrow \psi) \rightarrow \mathbf{B}_i\psi$;
7. $\mathbf{B}_i\varphi \rightarrow \mathbf{K}_i\mathbf{B}_i\varphi$;
8. $\Box_I\varphi \wedge \Box_I(\varphi \rightarrow \psi) \rightarrow \Box_I(\psi)$;
9. $\Box_I\varphi \rightarrow \Box_J\varphi$ with $J \subseteq I$;
10. $\dfrac{\varphi}{\mathbf{K}_i\varphi}$;
11. $[G_I : \alpha]p \leftrightarrow p$;
12. $[G_I : \alpha]\neg\varphi \leftrightarrow \neg[G_I : \alpha]\varphi$;
13. $exec'_{G_I}(\alpha) \rightarrow \mathbf{K}_i(exec_{G_I}(\alpha))$;
14. $lend(i, H_I, G_I, \phi_A) \rightarrow \mathbf{K}_i(lend(i, H_I, G_I, \phi_A))$;
15. $[G_I : \alpha](\varphi \wedge \psi) \leftrightarrow [G_I : \alpha]\varphi \wedge [G_I : \alpha]\psi$;
16. $[G_I : \alpha]\mathbf{K}_i\varphi \leftrightarrow \mathbf{K}_i([G_I : \alpha]\varphi)$;
17. $[G_I : \downarrow(\varphi,\psi)]\mathbf{B}_i\chi \leftrightarrow \mathbf{B}_i([G_I : \downarrow(\varphi,\psi)]\chi) \vee [G_I : \downarrow(\varphi,\psi)]\mathbf{B}_i\chi \leftrightarrow ((\mathbf{B}_i\varphi \wedge \mathbf{K}_i(\varphi \rightarrow \psi)) \wedge [G_I : \downarrow(\varphi,\psi)]\mathbf{B}_i\chi \leftrightarrow \mathbf{K}_i([G_I : \downarrow(\varphi,\psi)]\chi \leftrightarrow \psi))$;
18. $[G_I : \cap(\varphi,\psi)]\mathbf{B}_i\chi \leftrightarrow \mathbf{B}_i([G_I : \cap(\varphi,\psi)]\chi) \vee [G_I : \cap(\varphi,\psi)]\mathbf{B}_i\chi \leftrightarrow ((\mathbf{B}_i\varphi \wedge \mathbf{B}_i\psi) \wedge [G_I : \cap(\varphi,\psi)]\mathbf{B}_i\chi \leftrightarrow \mathbf{K}_i[G_I : \cap(\varphi,\psi)]\chi \leftrightarrow (\varphi \wedge \psi))$;
19. $[G_I : \vdash(\varphi,\psi)]\mathbf{B}_i\chi \leftrightarrow \mathbf{B}_i([G_I : \vdash(\varphi,\psi)]\chi) \vee [G_I : \vdash(\varphi,\psi)]\mathbf{B}_i\chi \leftrightarrow ((\mathbf{B}_i\varphi \wedge \mathbf{B}_i(\varphi \rightarrow \psi)) \wedge [G_I : \vdash(\varphi,\psi)]\mathbf{B}_i\chi \leftrightarrow \mathbf{K}_i([G : \vdash(\varphi,\psi)]\chi \leftrightarrow \psi))$;
20. $[G_I : \dashv(\varphi,\psi)]\neg\mathbf{B}_i\chi \leftrightarrow \mathbf{B}_i([G : \dashv(\varphi,\psi)]\chi) \vee [G_I : \dashv(\varphi,\psi)]\neg\mathbf{B}_i\chi \leftrightarrow ((\mathbf{B}_i\varphi \wedge \mathbf{K}_i(\varphi \rightarrow \neg\psi)) \wedge [G_I : \dashv(\varphi,\psi)]\neg\mathbf{B}_i\chi \leftrightarrow \mathbf{K}_i([G_I : \dashv(\varphi,\psi)]\chi \leftrightarrow \psi))$;

21. $intend_{G_I}(\phi_A, I) \leftrightarrow \forall i \in G_I intend_i(\phi_A; I)$;
22. $do_{G_I}(\phi_A, I) \rightarrow can\_do_{G_I}(\phi_A, I)$;
23. $do_i(\phi_A, I) \rightarrow can\_do_i(\phi_A, I) \wedge pref\_do_{G_I}(i, \phi_A, I)$;
24. $\dfrac{\psi \leftrightarrow \chi}{\varphi \leftrightarrow \varphi[\psi/\chi]}$.

We write $L\text{-}DINF \vdash \varphi$ to denote that φ is a theorem of $L\text{-}DINF$. It can be verified that the above axiomatization is sound for the class of $L\text{-}INF$ models, namely, all axioms are valid and inference rules preserve validity. In particular, soundness of axioms 17–20 follows from the semantics of $[G_I{:}\alpha]\varphi$, for each inferential action α, as previously defined. Notice that, by abuse of notation, we have axiomatized the special predicates concerning intention and action enabling. Axioms 21–23 concern, in fact, physical actions, stating that: what is intended by a group of agents is intended by all members of the group; and, neither an agent nor a group of agents can do what it is not enabled to do. Such axioms are not enforced by semantics, but should be guaranteed by the encoding of the behavior of agents done by the designer/programmer of the MAS at hand. In fact, axiom 21 requires the agents of a group to be cooperative. Axioms 22 and 23 ensure that agents will attempt to perform actions only if their preconditions are satisfied, that is, if they can perform such actions. We do not handle such properties in semantics as done, for example, in dynamic logic, because we want the definition of agents to be independent of the practical aspect, so we explicitly intend to introduce flexibility in the definition of such parts.

3   Problem Specification and Inference: An Example

In this section, we propose an example to explain the usefulness of this kind of logic. Consider a group G composed by three agents who collaborate to fix the road surface: the first agent a clears the road to fix, the second agent b prepares the asphalt and the third agent c drives the truck. The third is the only one who can drive the truck because he has the right license; the others are enabled to perform different tasks, such as, e.g., outline the works, put the road signs of the works, prepare the road surface, and so on.

In the same area there is a first-aid station (a second group H) where there are two other agents, d and e, who are there to handle emergencies.

The group G receives notification of a deadline for a road repair. Consequently, the members of G decide to organize to do it. The group will reason, and devise the intention/goal $\mathbf{K}_i(\square_I intend_{G_I}(road\_repaired(t_0, t_2), I))$. Here t_0 is the time instant when the group begins to organize to work on the road, whereas $I = [t_0, t_1]$, where t_1 is the deadline and t_2 is the time instant when they really finish repairing and $t_2 \leq t_1$.

Among the physical actions that agents of G can perform, we have:

prepare_road	*prepare_asphalt*	*place_road_signs*
drive_truck	*pave*	

Among the physical actions that agents of H can perform, we have:

$$provide\_first\_aid \qquad call\_ambulance\_if\_needed$$

The group G is now required to perform a planning activity. Assume that, as a result of the planning phase, the knowledge base of each agent i contains the following formula, that specifies how to reach the intended goal in terms of actions to perform and sub-goals to achieve:

$$\mathbf{K}_i\big(\Box_I intend_{G_I}(road\_repaired(t_0, t_2), I) \rightarrow$$
$$\Box_{I_1} intend_{G_I}(place\_road\_signs(t_0, t_3), I_1) \wedge$$
$$\Box_{I_2} intend_{G_I}(prepare\_asphalt(t_0, t_4), I_2) \wedge$$
$$\Box_I intend_{G_I}(drive\_truck(t_0, t_5), I)\big),$$

where $I_1, I_2 \subseteq I$, t_3 is the time when the agent placed the road sign and $t_3 \leq t_1$, t_4 is the time when the agent b actually finished preparing the asphalt ($t_4 \leq t_1$), and finally t_5 is the time instant when the other agent drove the truck with the asphalt in the right place. Thanks to axiom 21 (i.e., $intend_{G_I}(\phi_A, I) \leftrightarrow \forall i \in G_I\ intend_i(\phi_A, I)$), each agent has the specialized formula (for $i \leq 3$):

$$\mathbf{K}_i\big(\Box_I intend_i(road\_repaired(t_0, t_2), I) \rightarrow \Box_{I_1} intend_i(place\_road\_signs(t_0, t_3), I_1) \wedge$$
$$\Box_{I_2} intend_i(prepare\_asphalt(t_0, t_4), I_2) \wedge$$
$$\Box_I intend_i(drive\_truck(t_0, t_5), I)\big).$$

Therefore, the following formulas can be entailed by each agent:

$$\mathbf{K}_i\big(\Box_I intend_i(road\_repaired(t_0, t_2), I) \rightarrow \Box_{I_1} intend_i(place\_road\_signs(t_0, t_3), I_1)\big)$$
$$\mathbf{K}_i\big(\Box_I intend_i(road\_repaired(t_0, t_2), I) \rightarrow \Box_{I_2} intend_i(prepare\_asphalt(t_0, t_4), I_2)\big)$$
$$\mathbf{K}_i\big(\Box_I intend_i(road\_repaired(t_0, t_2), I) \rightarrow \Box_I intend_i(drive\_truck(t_0, t_5), I)\big).$$

Assume now that the knowledge base of each agent i contains also the following general formulas:

$$\mathbf{K}_i\big(\Box_{I_1}\big(intend_{G_I}(place\_road\_signs(t_0, t_3), I_1) \wedge can\_do_{G_I}(place\_road\_signs(t_0, t_3), I_1) \wedge$$
$$pref\_do_{G_I}(i, place\_road\_signs(t_0, t_3), I_1)\big) \rightarrow \Box_{I_1} do_{G_I}(place\_road\_signs(t_0, t_3), I_1)\big)$$
$$\mathbf{K}_i\big(\Box_{I_2}\big(intend_{G_I}(prepare\_asphalt(t_0, t_4), I_2) \wedge can\_do_{G_I}(prepare\_asphalt(t_0, t_4), I_2) \wedge$$
$$pref\_do_{G_I}(i, prepare\_asphalt(t_0, t_4), I_2)\big) \rightarrow \Box_{I_2} do_{G_I}(prepare\_asphalt(t_0, t_4), I_2)\big)$$
$$\mathbf{K}_i\big(\Box_I\big(intend_{G_I}(drive\_truck(t_0, t_5), I) \wedge can\_do_{G_I}(drive\_truck(t_0, t_5), I) \wedge$$
$$pref\_do_{G_I}(i, drive\_truck(t_0, t_5), I)\big) \rightarrow \Box_I do_{G_I}(drive\_truck(t_0, t_5), I)\big)$$

These formulas state that the group is available to perform each of the necessary actions. Which agent will perform each possible action ϕ_A? According to (t4) and (t7) defined in page 8, the agent is the one which best prefers to perform the action, among those that can do it. In the present situation, $pref\_do_{G_I}(i, \phi_A, I)$ identifies the agent i in the group with the highest degree of preference on performing ϕ_A. Moreover, $can\_do_{G_I}(\phi_A, I)$ is true if there is some agent i in the group which is able and allowed to perform ϕ_A, that is, it holds that $\phi_A \in A(i, w) \wedge \phi_A \in H(i, w)$. For each action ϕ_A required by the plan, there will be some agent i (let us assume for simplicity that it is unique), for which $do_i(\phi_A, I)$ can be concluded. In our case, agent a will conclude $do_a(place\_road\_signs(t_0, t_3), I_1)$; b will conclude $do_b(prepare\_asphalt(t_0, t_4), I_2)$ and c will conclude $do_c(drive\_truck(t_0, t_5), I)$. Assume now that the agent b during the preparation of asphalt has an accident. As a consequence an update of the goal must occur: the new goal is $\mathbf{K}_i(\Box_J intend_{G_J}(provide\_first\_aid(t_6, t_7), J))$. Here, t_6 is the time instant when the group begins to organize themselves for providing first aid, $J = [t_6, t_8]$ where t_8 is the maximum time instant within which first aid must be provided, t_7 is the time instant when they really complete administering first aid, and $t_7 \leq t_8$. Assume that the knowledge base of each agent i contains the following formula, that specifies how to reach the intended goal in terms of actions to perform and sub-goals to achieve:

$$\mathbf{K}_i(\Box_J intend_{G_J}(provide\_first\_aid(t_6, t_7), J) \rightarrow$$
$$\Box_{J_1} intend_{G_J}(provide\_first\_aid(t_6, t_9), J_1))$$

where $J_1 \subseteq J$, t_9 is the time instant when the agent have done the first aid and $t_9 \leq t_8$. Again, thanks to axiom 21, the following can be obtained by each agent (for each agent i):

$$\mathbf{K}_i(\Box_J intend_i(provide\_first\_aid(t_6, t_7), J) \rightarrow$$
$$\Box_{J_1} intend_i(provide\_first\_aid(t_6, t_9), J_1))$$

At this point a problem arises: none of the agents in the group G is allowed to perform the action $provide\_first\_aid$. A solution consists in borrowing another agent from group H, because both agents in H are enabled to perform such action. Hence, the action will be performed by agent $d \in H$, that we assume to be the one which best prefers to intervene. Thanks to the conditions expressing semantics of formulas (in particular, (t4)–(t7) in page 8), we can obtain that

$$\mathbf{K}_i(\Box_J intend_{H_J}(provide\_first\_aid(t_6, t_7), J) \rightarrow$$
$$\Box_{J_1} intend_{H_J}(provide\_first\_aid(t_6, t_9), J_1))$$

holds and that agent d can specialize such formula to obtain

$$\mathbf{K}_i(\Box_J intend_d(provide\_first\_aid(t_6, t_7), J) \rightarrow$$
$$\Box_{J_1} intend_d(provide\_first\_aid(t_6, t_9), J_1))$$

and, to finally enable the execution of the action $provide\_first\_aid$ by deriving the formula $do_d(provide\_first\_aid(t_6, t_9), J_1)$. Clearly, to reach this conclusion, further pieces of (background) knowledge enter into play, for instance, as happened for the planning developed by G, agent d might exploit formulas retrieved from its long-term memory, such as the following implication:

$$\mathbf{K}_i(\Box_{J_1}(intend_d(provide\_first\_aid(t_6, t_9), J_1) \wedge can\_do_d(provide\_first\_aid(t_6, t_9), J_1) \wedge$$
$$pref\_do_d(i, provide\_first\_aid(t_6, t_9), J_1)) \rightarrow \Box_{J_1} do_d(provide\_first\_aid(t_6, t_9), J_1)).$$

4   Canonical Model and Strong Completeness

Definition 2. *Let Agt be a set of agents. The* canonical L-INF *model is a tuple* $M_c = \langle W_c, N_c, \mathcal{R}_c, E_c, B_c, C_c, A_c, H_c, P_c, L_c, V_c, T_c \rangle$ *where:*

- W_c *is the set of all maximal consistent subsets of* $\mathcal{L}_{L\text{-}INF}$;
- $\mathcal{R}_c = \{R_{c,i}\}_{i \in Agt}$ *is a collection of equivalence relations on* W_c *such that, for every* $i \in Agt$ *and* $w_I, v_I \in W_c$, $w_I R_{c,i} v_I$ *if and only if (for all* φ, $\mathbf{K}_i \varphi \in w_I$ *implies* $\varphi \in v_I$);
- *For* $w \in W_c$, $\varphi \in \mathcal{L}_{L\text{-}INF}$ *let* $A_\varphi(i, w_I) = \{v \in R_{c,i}(w_I) \mid \varphi \in v\}$. *Then, we put* $N_c(i, w_I) = \{A_\varphi(i, w_I) \mid \mathbf{B}_i \varphi \in w_I\}$;
- $E_c : Agt \times W_c \longrightarrow 2^{\mathcal{L}_{ACT}}$ *is such that, for each* $i \in Agt$ *and* $w_I, v_I \in W_c$, *if* $w_I R_{c,i} v_I$ *then* $E_c(i, w_I) = E_c(i, v_I)$;
- $B_c : Agt \times W_c \longrightarrow \mathbb{N}$ *is such that, for each* $i \in Agt$ *and* $w_I, v_I \in W_c$, *if* $w_I R_{c,i} v_I$ *then* $B_c(i, w_I) = B_c(i, v_I)$;
- $C_c : Agt \times \mathcal{L}_{ACT} \times W_c \longrightarrow \mathbb{N}$ *is such that, for each* $i \in Agt$, $\alpha \in \mathcal{L}_{ACT}$, *and* $w_I, v_I \in W_c$, *if* $w_I R_{c,i} v_I$ *then* $C_c(i, \alpha, w_I) = C_c(i, \alpha, v_I)$;
- $A_c : Agt \times W_c \longrightarrow 2^{Atm_A}$ *is such that, for each* $i \in Agt$ *and* $w_I, v_I \in W_c$, *if* $w_I R_{c,i} v_I$ *then* $A_c(i, w_I) = A_c(i, v_I)$;
- $H_c : Agt \times W_c \longrightarrow 2^{Atm_A}$ *is such that, for each* $i \in Agt$ *and* $w_I, v_I \in W_c$, *if* $w_I R_{c,i} v_I$ *then* $H_c(i, w_I) = H_c(i, v_I)$;
- $P_c : Agt \times W_c \times Atm_A \longrightarrow \mathbb{N}$ *is such that, for each* $i \in Agt$ *and* $w_I, v_I \in W$, *if* $w_I R_{c,i} v_I$ *then* $P_c(i, w_I, \phi_A) = P_c(i, v_I, \phi_A)$;
- $L_c : Agt \times Grp \times Grp \times Atm_A \times W \longrightarrow \{\mathsf{true}, \mathsf{false}\}$ *is such that for all* $i \in Agt$ *and* $H_I, G_I \in Grp$ *and* $w_I, v_I \in W$, *if* $w_I R_{c,i} v_I$ *then* $L_c(i, H_I, G_I, \phi_A, w_I) = L_c(i, H_I, G_I, \phi_A, v_I)$;
- $V_c : W_c \longrightarrow 2^{Atm}$ *is such that* $V_c(w_I) = Atm \cap w_I$;
- T_c: *the time function defined as before (see Sect. 2.2).*

Let $R_{c,i}(w_I)$ denote the set $\{v_I \in W_c \mid w_I R_{c,i} v_I\}$, for each agent $i \in Agt$. M_c is an *L-INF* model as stated in Definition 1, since, it satisfies conditions (**C1**), (**C2**), (**D1**), (**E1**), (**F1**), (**G1**), (**G2**), (**H1**, (**M1**). Hence, it models the axioms and the inference rules 1–21 and 24 introduced before (while, as mentioned in Sect. 2.4, it is assumed that the axioms 21–23 are enforced by the specification of agent behaviour). Consequently, the following properties hold too. Let $w_I \in W_c$, then:

- given $\varphi \in \mathcal{L}_{L\text{-}INF}$, it holds that $\mathbf{K}_i \varphi \in w_I$ if and only if $\forall v_I \in W_c$ such that $w_I R_{c,i} v_I$ we have $\varphi \in v$;
- for $\varphi \in \mathcal{L}_{L\text{-}INF}$, if $\mathbf{B}_i \varphi \in w_I$ and $w_I R_{c,i} v$ then $\mathbf{B}_i \varphi \in v_I$;

Thus, $R_{c,i}$-related worlds have the same knowledge and N_c-related worlds have the same beliefs, i.e., there can be $R_{c,i}$-related worlds with different beliefs.

Proceeding in analogy to what was done in previous papers [3,6], we obtain the proof of strong completeness, which we omit for conciseness.

5   Conclusions

In this paper, we have extended the logic *L-DINF* to enable modeling and reasoning on cooperation between different groups of agents. Namely, we have introduced into the logic framework the possibility for a group to support another group that does not have among its members any agent with the right competences to carry out an action. For the new extended logic, that takes time into account, we revised the semantics previously appeared in [9] by proposing an enhanced treatment of formulas, together with a belief update mechanism. In future work, we intend to further extend the logic in the direction of formalizing more complex interactions and synergies among multiple groups of agents.

References

1. Balbiani, P., Duque, D.F., Lorini, E.: A logical theory of belief dynamics for resource-bounded agents. In: Proceedings of the 2016 International Conference on Autonomous Agents & Multiagent Systems, AAMAS 2016, pp. 644–652. ACM (2016)
2. Balbiani, P., Fernández-Duque, D., Lorini, E.: The dynamics of epistemic attitudes in resource-bounded agents. Stud. Logica **107**(3), 457–488 (2019)
3. Costantini, S., Formisano, A., Pitoni, V.: An epistemic logic for multi-agent systems with budget and costs. In: Faber, W., Friedrich, G., Gebser, M., Morak, M (eds.) JELIA 2021. LNCS (LNAI), vol. 12678, pp. 101–115. Springer, Cham (2021). https://doi.org/10.1007/978-3-030-75775-5_8
4. Costantini, S., Formisano, A., Pitoni, V.: An epistemic logic for modular development of multi-agent systems. In: Alechina, N., Baldoni, M., Logan, B. (eds.) EMAS 2021. LNCS, vol. 13190, pp. 72–91. Springer, Cham (2022). https://doi.org/10.1007/978-3-030-97457-2_5
5. Costantini, S., Formisano, A., Pitoni, V.: Temporalizing epistemic logic L-DINF. In: Calegari, R., Ciatto, G., Omicini, A. (eds.) Proceedings of CILC 2022, CEUR Workshop Proceedings. CEUR-WS.org (2022)
6. Costantini, S., Pitoni, V.: Towards a logic of "inferable" for self-aware transparent logical agents. In: Musto, C., Magazzeni, D., Ruggieri, S., Semeraro, G. (eds.) Proceedings of the Italian Workshop on Explainable Artificial Intelligence Co-located with 19th International Conference of the Italian Association for Artificial Intelligence, 2020. CEUR Workshop Proceedings, vol. 2742, pp. 68–79. CEUR-WS.org (2020)
7. Ditmarsch, H.V., Halpern, J.Y., Hoek, W.V.D., Kooi, B.: Handbook of Epistemic Logic. College Publications, Norcross (2015)
8. Koymans, R.: Specifying real-time properties with metric temporal logic. Real-Time Syst. **2**(4), 255–299 (1990)
9. Pitoni, V., Costantini, S.: A temporal module for logical frameworks. In: Bogaerts, B., et al. (eds.) Proceedings of ICLP 2019 (Tech. Comm.). EPTCS, vol. 306, pp. 340–346 (2019)
10. Rao, A.S., Georgeff, M.: Modeling rational agents within a BDI architecture. In: Proceedings of the Second International Conference on Principles of Knowledge Representation and Reasoning (KR 1991), pp. 473–484. Morgan Kaufmann (1991)
11. Weyhrauch, R.W.: Prolegomena to a theory of mechanized formal reasoning. Artif. Intell. **13**(1–2), 133–170 (1980)

Prudens: An Argumentation-Based Language for Cognitive Assistants

Vassilis Markos[1(✉)] and Loizos Michael[1,2]

[1] Open University of Cyprus, Nicosia, Cyprus
`vasileios.markos@st.ouc.ac.cy, loizos@ouc.ac.cy`
[2] CYENS Center of Excellence, Nicosia, Cyprus

Abstract. In this short system paper, we present our implementation of a prioritized rule-based language for representing actionable policies, in the context of developing cognitive assistants. The language is associated with a provably efficient deduction process, and owing it to its interpretation under an argumentative semantics it can naturally offer ante-hoc explanations on its drawn inferences. Relatedly, the language is associated with a knowledge acquisition process based on the paradigm of machine coaching, guaranteeing the probable approximate correctness of the acquired knowledge against a target policy. The paper focuses on demonstrating the implemented features of the representation language and its exposed APIs and libraries, and discusses some of its more advanced features that allow the calling of procedural code, and the computation of in-line operations when evaluating rules.

Keywords: Logical programming · Non-monotonic reasoning · Cognitive assistants

1 Introduction

The widespread adoption of Artificial Intelligence (AI) in everyday applications has led to an upsurging interest in the design of *cognitive assistants*, i.e., of systems "augmenting human intelligence", as put by Engelbart [2]. Naturally, such systems are required to be cognitively compatible with humans, in an effort to facilitate human-machine interaction, which makes, explainability and understandability natural prerequisites as well [3,12]. Considering the above desiderata, argumentation-based designs seem as a proper choice that can at the same time accommodate cognitive compatibility, while providing substantial potential for interpretability and explainability for such systems [6,10].

Having in mind the above, with this work we present a declarative programming language, Prudens, aiming to facilitate the design of cognitive assistants. Prudens is an argumentation-based language that can fully support efficient deduction as described in [11]. Moreover, Prudens is also compatible with machine coaching, a provably efficient human-in-the-loop machine learning methodology, under the Probably Approximately Correct (PAC) semantics

© The Author(s), under exclusive license to Springer Nature Switzerland AG 2022
G. Governatori and A.-Y. Turhan (Eds.): RuleML+RR 2022, LNCS 13752, pp. 296–304, 2022.
https://doi.org/10.1007/978-3-031-21541-4_19

[11,14]. Given its reliance on arguments, Prudens can also support the design of assistants that can explain their decisions, by providing the internal arguments that have led the system to draw a conclusion as an explanation.

The rest of this paper is structured as follows: (i) in Sect. 2 we present the basic syntax of Prudens; (ii) in Sect. 3 we present extended features of the language; (iii) in Sect. 4 we discuss currently ongoing and future works related to Prudens and; (iv) in Sect. 5 we conclude. All online resources regarding Prudens may be found at http://cognition.ouc.ac.cy/prudens/.

2   Basic Syntax and Semantics

First we discuss the basic syntax of Prudens, by describing the language's basic rule syntax and their prioritization as well as the underlying reasoning process.

2.1   Rule Syntax

The core ("vanilla") version of Prudens basically implements the knowledge representation language described in [11]. It provides *constants*, which correspond to entities of the universe of discourse, as well as *variables*, which serve as placeholders for constants. Moreover, first-order *predicates* (with variables and/or constants as arguments) as well as propositional ones are provided, encoding relations and conditions about the universe of discourse, respectively. *Literals* are either predicates themselves or negated, with negation being understood as classical negation within the scope of Prudens. Two literals corresponding to the same predicate but with opposite signs are *conflicting*. The language, building on the above, allows for if-then *rules*, which connect a set of premises, the rules' *body*, with a single literal, the rules' *head*. As with literals, two rules with conflicting heads are *conflicting* as well. Lastly, a list of rules alongside a priority relation defined over all pairs of conflicting rules comprise a *policy*. By default, priorities in a policy are determined by the rules' order of appearance. That is, the later a rule appears in the policy, the higher its priority is over conflicting ones. Also, a *context* is a set of *pairwise non-conflicting* literals, corresponding to a set of facts being known at the beginning of the reasoning process—see Sect. 2.2 for more. The language's "vanilla" constructs are shown in Table 1.

2.2   Reasoning

Reasoning in Prudens is performed utilizing prioritized forward-chaining semantics, by exhaustively inferring all possible facts through all policy rules, respecting priorities between them, given each time a set of currently known facts—initially, the *context*. For instance, consider the example policy shown in Fig. 1. In this case, a context containing isMonday and bobCalls would lead us infer atWork and -answerCall, as follows: (i) At first, knowing isMonday and bobCalls, R1 and R2 fire, allowing us to infer atWork and answerCall; (ii) Knowing atWork, rule R3 fires, leading to -answerCall, which conflicts with

Table 1. The syntax of Prudens.

Item	Syntax	Example
Constant	Any non empty string containing alphanumeric characters or underscores (a-zA-Z0-9_), starting with a lowercase latter (a-z)	`alice, office_2`
Variable	Any non empty string containing alphanumeric characters or underscores (a-zA-Z0-9_), starting with an uppercase latter (A-Z)	`User, Place_23`
Predicate	Any non empty string starting with a lowercase latter (a-z) and possibly followed by an arbitrary number of alphanumeric characters or underscores (a-zA-Z0-9_). In case of first-order predicates, a comma separated list of variables and/or constants should follow, enclosed in parentheses	`atHome, at(X, bob)`
Literal	A predicate, possibly preceded by a dash (-), indicating negation	`-atWork, friends(X, Y)`
Rule	A string starting with a non empty sequence of alphanumeric characters or underscores (a-zA-Z0-9_), followed by ::, followed by a comma-separated list of literals (body), followed by the keyword `implies`, followed by a single literal (head)	`R1 :: a, b implies z` `r2 :: f(X, 3) implies g(X)`

Policy	A semicolon-separated list of rules, preceded by the `@Knowledge` keyword	`@Knowledge`
		`R1 :: a implies z;`
		`R2 :: a, b implies -z;`

Context	A semicolon-separated list of pairwise non-conflicting literals.	`a; b; -at(work);`

`answerCall`, which is resolved by preferring `-answerCall` over `answerCall`, since the former was inferred by R3, which is of higher priority than R2. (iii) Having inferred `atWork` and `-answerCall`, nothing more may be inferred, so the process terminates. For more on Prudens's reasoning algorithm, see [11].

```
@Knowledge
R1 :: isMonday implies atWork;
R2 :: bobCalls implies answerCall;
R3 :: atWork implies -answerCall;
```

Fig. 1. A simple propositional policy regarding phone call management.

2.3 Custom Priorities and Dilemmas

Apart from order-induced implicit rule prioritization, one may define custom rule priorities in essentially two ways: programmatically, by providing a priority function as an optional argument to the Prudens's core reasoning function and; explicitly, by providing priorities within each rule's declaration. Regarding explicit priority manipulation, the language's "vanilla" rule syntax is extended to allow for priorities to be declared through integers following a rule's head, separated by a |, as in the policies shown in Fig. 2. There, numbers indicate priority, with negative values being allowed as well. So, given a context containing bobCalls; atWork;, the top policy in Fig. 2 would yield answerCall, since R1 is preferred over R2.

```
@Knowledge
R1 :: bobCalls implies answerCall | 1;
R2 :: atWork implies -answerCall | 0;

@Knowledge
R1 :: bobCalls implies answerCall | 1;
R2 :: atWork implies -answerCall | 1;
```

Fig. 2. Two policies with custom priorities.

Naturally, allowing for custom priorities, there might be cases where two rules are incomparable, either because no priority between them has been explicitly determined, or because they are of the same priority, as in Fig. 2 (bottom). Such cases are called *dilemmas*. Since there is no clear way to resolve a dilemma, the reasoning engine abstains from making a decision, ignoring both rules and proceeding with the reasoning process. Any dilemmas encountered throughout a reasoning cycle are noted and returned separately from the rest inferences.

3 Extended Syntax and Semantics

Apart from the language's core features presented in Sect. 2, there are several additional features that are offered by Prudens, as discussed below.

3.1 The Unification Predicate

Prudens comes with a built-in multipurpose binary predicate, denoted by ?=($\cdot$, $\cdot$). The unification predicate holds true provided that its two arguments are unifiable. So, for instance, given a rule like: R1 :: f(X), ?=(X, Y) implies g(Y); and a context containing f(2), we would get g(2) as an inference. In general, (function-free) unification is conceptualized as with most logical programming interfaces; so two constants unify if they are equal, a variable unifies with any constant and two (unassigned) variables always unify. We shall note at this point that the unification predicate might not be used as a head literal in any rule.

The very same predicate also allows for numerical operations within its arguments, provided that they do not invoke any variables that remain unassigned *once all other body predicates are grounded.* So, a rule like R1 :: f(X), ?=(Y, X+3) implies g(Y); with a context containing f(2) would infer g(5) but R2 :: f(X), ?=(Y-3, X) implies g(Y); with the same context would not, since there is no value assigned to Y by the time the predicate is evaluated. Any mathematical expressions within ?=(·,·) should adhere to ECMAScript 6 syntax.

```
@Knowledge
R1 :: calls(X), friend(X) implies answer(X);
R2 :: calls(X), time(H, M), ?lessThan(H, 17) implies -answer(X);

@Procedures
function lessThan(a, b) {
    return parseFloat(a) < parseFloat(b);
}
```

Fig. 3. A policy indicating that any calls before 17:00 should be rejected, with the help of a procedural predicate (lessThan), evaluating numerical comparisons.

3.2   On-the-Fly Math Operations

Prudens also allows for math operations to be executed within any predicate, given the restrictions mentioned above, about unassigned variables within the unification predicate. Also, similarly to the unification predicate, numerical operations may not be used in head literals. For instance, the following rule: R1 :: f(X, 2*X) implies double; given a context containing f(2,4) infers double. An equivalent rule, avoiding within-predicate operations, would be R2 :: f(X, Y), ?=(Y, 2*X) implies double;, which, however, introduces an additional variable, Y, and leads to slightly slower processing time. Thus, whenever possible, within-predicate math operations should be preferred against ?=(·,·).

3.3   Procedural Predicates

Prudens allows for users to determine their own procedural predicates through procedural code. Namely, one may provide general Boolean functions as a predicate's "definition". For instance, expanding our running call management example, let us consider the following scenario: we would like to answer all friends calls, on condition that it is past 17:00. Assuming that time(H,M) represents the time of the call, a policy that captures this functionality is shown in Fig. 3. There, the procedural binary predicate ?lessThan, which compares its two arguments and holds true whenever its first argument is less than its second, facilitates an efficient execution of numerical comparisons. So, a context containing calls(alice), friend(alice) and time(16,43) would result to -answer(alice) using the above policy. However, substituting time(16,43) with time(18,12) would result to answer(alice), as expected.

When working with procedural predicates there are several things one should keep in mind: (i) the @Knowledge keyword should *always* come before the

@Procedures keyword; (ii) predicate names, when referenced in a rule's body, should be preceded by a ?; (iii) procedural predicates are not allowed as rule heads; (iv) predicate declarations should adhere to ECMAScript 6 standards; (v) no function calls are allowed within a procedural predicate other than built-in functions of JavaScript; (vi) every argument of a procedural predicate is by default considered to be a string, so in case they are supposed to be treated as integers or floats, the built-in JavaScript parseInt and parseFloat functions should be used, respectively.

```
@Knowledge
R1 :: f(A), g(X) implies h(X,A);
```
```
@Knowledge
R1 :: f(A), g(X) implies h(X,A);
R2 :: h(X,b) implies z(X);
```

```
@Knowledge
R1 :: bobCalls implies answer;
R2 :: atWork implies reject;

C1 :: answer # reject;
```

Fig. 4. Two first-order policies (left) and one with a compatibility constraint (right).

3.4 Partially Grounded Contexts

Literals in a context, in contrast to what is demanded by the language's "vanilla" version, may be partially or even totally ungrounded. That is, a context may well contain literals like f(Y), even if Y is a free variable. In any such case, variables propagate throughout inferences, unifying with other variables whenever it makes sense. For instance, consider the policies shown left in Fig. 4. Using the top left one with a context containing f(Y); g(3); one infers h(3,Y). Using a context containing f(Y) with the policy shown bottom left in Fig. 4 this time, we infer z(3). Note here that fresh variables, not used elsewhere in the underlying policy, should be preferred in contexts.

3.5 Extended Conflict Semantics

In the vanilla version of the language, two literals are considered conflicting in case they stem from the same predicate but have opposite signs. Prudens, however, also allows for rules that determine broader conflicts between arbitrary predicates. Such rules are called *compatibility constraints* and adhere to the following syntax:

ruleName :: pred1 # pred2;

So, for instance, using the policy shown in Fig. 4 (right) and a context containing `bobCalls; atWork;`, one infers `reject`, since C1 declares `reject` and `answer` as conflicting literals. Note at this point that there are no assumed priorities between compatibility constraints, in contrast to what is the case with the rest rules in a policy.

4 Ongoing and Future Work

Below we briefly present some of the most prominent works in progress invoking Prudens as well as discuss possible future directions.

4.1 Deduction, Induction and Abduction

So far, Prudens has been utilized as the underlying deductive engine for machine coaching [11], an interactive human-in-the-loop methodology that allows a human coach to train a machine on a certain task by providing advice to it, echoing ideas from McCarthy's advice taking machines [9]. Furthermore, Prudens's semantics allow for abductive reasoning as well. Hence, a candidate domain of application is, among others, Neural-Symbolic Integration [4], where machine coaching could be used as an induction mechanism to train the symbolic module and Prudens could serve as the underlying knowledge representation language for both deduction as well as abduction, extending ideas found in [13].

4.2 Natural Language Interfaces

While cognitively easier than imperative programming, declarative programming still requires from the programmer to be accustomed to some sort of coding formalism. Consequently, interfaces that allow users to program using natural language provide a user-friendly and cognitively simple alternative to sheer coding. We are currently working towards two independent Natural Language Interfaces (NLIs). The first one relies on building a NL-to-Prudens translator utilizing machine coaching [5] to learn the underlying translation grammar. Here, Prudens itself is used at the meta-level as the interaction language between the human coach and the machine. The second one is the design of a Controlled NLI for Prudens, in the spirit of other works in the field of Logical Programming, like Logical English [7]. Apart from the aforementioned ongoing projects, Large Language Models are also under consideration as appropriate NL-to-Prudens translators, with the potential of also capturing Prudens's reasoning semantics [1].

4.3 Applications

At the time of writing this, there are two applications being developed utilizing Prudens in the background. The first one, a mobile call assistant, intends to use machine coaching so as to elicit a user's preferences regarding their calls and notifications management, with Prudens serving as the knowledge representation language in the background. Inspired by previous work on chess coaching [8], where again Prudens had been used in the background for deductive and inductive purposes, our second ongoing project is related to another strategy game: Minesweeper. There, users are asked to explain to an agent how to play Minesweeper successfully, again utilizing machine coaching as the learning methodology, with Prudens facilitating human-machine interaction.

5   Conclusions

We have presented Prudens, an argumentation-based language for the design of cognitive assistants. We have discussed its syntax as well as any additional features it provides. Moreover, we have presented several currently developed and future applications as well as extensions of Prudens, aiming to further facilitate the design of cognitive assistants by non-experts.

Apart from the aforementioned ongoing projects, we are also working on the direction of generating comprehensive visualizations about Prudens and its internal processes. Namely, effort is being put on visualizing the reasoning process of Prudens in a step-by-step manner, so as to facilitate user understanding and, consequently, build more trust with the end-user. At the same time, we are also working on knowledge-graph based explanation representations, again, as an attempt to make Prudens more accessible to a less expert audience. Ultimately, our goal is to build an easy to-use ecosystem for Machine Coaching, allowing for an efficient and thorough *in situ* assessment of Machine Coaching.

Acknowledgements. This work was supported by funding from the European Regional Development Fund and the Government of the Republic of Cyprus through the Research and Innovation Foundation under grant agreement no. INTE-GRATED/0918/0032, from the EU's Horizon 2020 Research and Innovation Programme under grant agreements no. 739578 and no. 823783, and from the Government of the Republic of Cyprus through the Deputy Ministry of Research, Innovation, and Digital Policy.

References

1. Chen, M., et al.: Evaluating large language models trained on code (2021). https://doi.org/10.48550/ARXIV.2107.03374, https://arxiv.org/abs/2107.03374
2. Engelbart, D.C.: Augmenting human intellect: a conceptual framework. In: SRI Summary Report AFOSR-3223 (1962)
3. de Graaf, M., Malle, B.F.: How people explain action (and autonomous intelligent systems should too). In: AAAI Fall Symposia (2017)
4. Hammer, B., Hitzler, P.: Perspectives of Neural-Symbolic Integration, vol. 77. Springer, Heidelberg (2007). https://doi.org/10.1007/978-3-540-73954-8
5. Ioannou, C., Michael, L.: Knowledge-based translation of natural language into symbolic form. In: Proceedings of the 7th Linguistic and Cognitive Approaches To Dialog Agents Workshop - LaCATODA 2021, pp. 24–32, Montreal, Canada (2021). http://ceur-ws.org/Vol-2935/#paper3

6. Kakas, A., Michael, L.: Cognitive systems: argument and cognition. IEEE Intell. Inform. Bull. **17**, 14–20 (2016)
7. Kowalski, R.: English as a logic programming language. New Gener. Comput. **8**(2), 91–93 (1990). https://doi.org/10.1007/BF03037468
8. Markos, V.: Application of the machine coaching paradigm on chess coaching. Master's thesis. School of Pure & Applied Sciences, Open University of Cyprus (2020)
9. McCarthy, J.: Programs with common sense. In: Proceedings of Teddington Conference on the Mechanization of Thought Processes (1958)
10. Mercier, H., Sperber, D.: Why do humans reason? Arguments for an argumentative theory. Behav. Brain Sci. **34**(2), 57–74 (2011). https://doi.org/10.1017/S0140525X10000968
11. Michael, L.: Machine coaching. In: IJCAI 2019 Workshop on Explainable Artificial Intelligence, pp. 80–86, Macau, China (2019). https://www.researchgate.net/publication/334989337_Machine_Coaching
12. Miller, T.: Explanation in artificial intelligence: insights from the social sciences. Artif. Intell. **267**, 1–38 (2019). https://doi.org/10.1016/j.artint.2018.07.007
13. Tsamoura, E., Hospedales, T., Michael, L.: Neural-symbolic integration: a compositional perspective. In: Proceedings of the AAAI Conference on Artificial Intelligence, vol. 35, no. 6, pp. 5051–5060 (2021). https://ojs.aaai.org/index.php/AAAI/article/view/16639
14. Valiant, L.G.: A theory of the learnable. In: STOC 1984: Symposium on Theory of Computing, pp. 1134–1142 (1984)

Author Index

Printed in the United States
by Baker & Taylor Publisher Services